Mark brings a fresh perspective to every issue with humorous, provocative and insightful thoughts. He's not your everyday preacher. Tom Murdough, Hudson, Ohio, Former Parishioner.

Mark's blogs conjure up the image of an open kitchen window. His writing makes me think of myself as his neighbor. I can picture myself outside watering my tomato plants or trimming the rose bushes. And through the open window of the blog, there is Mark sitting at the kitchen table with a cup of coffee, calling out a, "Howdy," spinning a yarn, sending forth a good laugh, or offering wisdom on faith or maybe fishing. Timothy Tutt, Austin Pastor, First Christian Church.

Why Mark's blogs are worth reading: He captivates the reader, sometimes through his fishing narratives, skillfully guiding the reader to a quiet place where phones don't ring, bosses don't demand, where life just slows down and simple "life" just needs to simply be rediscovered. He even hears the voice of a leaning tree. His stories lure you into his net of delicate, crystalline "hope".... He is a masterful fisherman of stories, people, and of sweet peace...Monica Schwabe Kahout, former parishioner, member of St. Pauls Church Confirmation Class, Chicago, 1968.

Mark's blogs give me inspiration, restore my faith and provide a wonderful, healthy perspective to my daily life. His writing gifts are a blessing. Tom Widlits, Schnell Family, Portland, Oregon.

Mark's stories allow me to slow down and take notice of the joys in everyday life and allow me to remember to say 'Thank You' to others. I guarantee your spirit will be refreshed with a daily dose. Jim Perillat, US Army Engineer, Redstone Arsenal, Alabama [Jim was member of Broadmoor Community Church, Colorado Springs, 1986-88]

Blogs are like appetizers - real food, but not the whole meal! The best ones are delicious, satisfying in their own way, but whetting the appetite for more. And, like all good finger food, they are consumed amid conversation, inviting engagement, reflection, challenge. Here, can I offer you an hors d'oeuvre? John Thomas, General Minister of United Church of Christ.

Blogs. Here and there and everywhere. Yet. Mark Miller's "Voice of my Heart," blogs he's written since October of 2010, are timeless. Yes, they are truths written on certain dates, but not in any instance or word contained or controlled by the calendar. He takes the common and brings new understanding, provocative thought and more than once in a while, a smile. But, down deep his reflections are neither shallow nor mirthful. Through this book Mark touches each of us with grace and encouragement. And when we least expect it, our souls are touched, hearts quickened and the new day more than abundant in hopeful expectancy. Mark prompts the possibilities of living more fully; it's our chance to birth it. A Clergy Friend.

Mark Miller's blogs always have something that surprises me. It may be a different take on a known topic, an unusual way with words, or a new way of looking at something old. But I finish reading one and say to myself, "Ah, how interesting!" Gail Crouch, Pastor, United Church of Christ, Seattle, Washington.

With humility, grace and a hefty portion of humor, Mark Miller reminds us to breathe and find the space to connect once again to our own hearts and to those of our fellow human beings. I am grateful for Mark's compassionate insight and ability to speak to my folly and my charm while honoring both simultaneously. Anna Bartkowski, Director, Hays County Dispute Resolution Center, San Marcos, Texas.

Voice of my Heart

Dr. Mark Henry Miller

authorHOUSE®

AuthorHouse™
1663 Liberty Drive
Bloomington, IN 47403
www.authorhouse.com
Phone: 1-800-839-8640

First published by AuthorHouse 10/12/2011

ISBN: 978-1-4670-3344-2 (e)
ISBN: 978-1-4670-3126-4 (sc)

Library of Congress Control Number: 2011916095

Printed in the United States of America

Any people depicted in stock imagery provided by Thinkstock are models,
and such images are being used for illustrative purposes only.
Certain stock imagery © Thinkstock.

This book is printed on acid-free paper.

Table of Contents

Tuesday, October 19, 2010

Posted on October 19, 2010 by Mark H Miller

Hello, Everyone–

This is the first step for my Blog. I will be sharing ideas as they develop. One of the purposes of the Blog is to share information that the book of pastoral epistles, "Hooked On Life," is about to be published by Whitefish Press. Their website has more information, www.whitefishpress.com

In addition, the 2nd book of epistles, "Cast Your Nets" is available at www.markhenrymiller.com [available from Authorhouse Publishing in Indianapolis or www.amazon.com]

Finally, within the next week or so we hope to have a new website constructed fully, www.drmarkhmiller.com

Grace and peace,

Mark.

Lessons that matter

Posted on October 26, 2010 by Mark H Miller

Someone inquired last week, "Now that you're 70, what are the most important lessons that have stuck?"

I'm sure there are more than many that didn't.

The first lesson occurred—not only important in ministry, but for each of us no matter our circumstance or vocation—came from a pastor-buddy in Elmhurst, Illinois, Ernie Huntzinger, "Mark, we each need to realize we are not someone else's opinion."

Ah, how sharp with clear focus. So often what others think of us does more than guide; it shapes. In ministry that had abundant truth, at times incapacitating. I recall how I forgot a church member's neighbor's surgery—had been told to be with him. I flat-forgot. Well, I never heard the end of it, because this family kept lists, mainly a gallery of what wasn't done correctly. [I never asked what grades they got in school!]

That mistake labeled my ministry—in their eyes.

A second lesson that is possible, but at times challenging: *May our willingness to understand be greater than our need to judge.* Actually related to the first, in terms of how we regard others.

Not sure, but it seems to me most people live life and regard others based upon their self-image. The ones who have high self-regard tend to look at life favorably.

A good way to learn this is to ask someone, "Please tell me the five most important events in your life." Almost without exception the *list* will be more a function of self-image in that moment than anything else.

A third lesson and I must admit I've used it with much energy and encouragement, especially with churches trying to not be insane: that is, doing the same thing over and over expecting different results, is this:

If we look more at our rear-view mirror than through our windshield, we'll probably have an accident.

You can put in the paragraph detailing that.

So it is on a Tuesday morning...Diane and I had the joy of watching Andrew's Schreiner Men's Basketball team in their first scrimmage last night at St. Mary's University in San Antonio. Goodness, Andrew's team did so well...especially for the first scrimmage. Their season begins in two weeks...we'll be there as often as we can to clap and cheer—but not yell so loud we end up with a technical foul! [That's a story for another day...the day in Copenhagen.]

So it is, hello Tuesday...you're looking promising through the windshield.

Thoughts about parenting

Posted on October 27, 2010 by Mark H Miller

He stood taller than the towering Douglas Fir Tree, just behind the fence off the right field line. I was 14, ready for my first pitch as a high school freshman. My father had parked his garbage truck at the corner of Alberta Park, 22nd and Ainsworth, interrupting his garbage hauling to watch his son, his left-handed almost clueless on what to pitch son.

Before I got the catcher's signal, I paused, *Oh Lord, may I do okay*, perhaps the briefest prayer ever, and then looked beyond the right field fence, behind first base. There my father, all six-feet-four of him, stood. Taller than the Douglas Fir against which he leaned.

I then looked beyond the left-field "fence," that was actually the west-edge-sidewalk to Alberta Park, and there, in their 1938 Oldsmobile, the one I inherited with the stick shift rising from the floorboard, a gear shift that didn't need a clutch, were my Miller grandparents, immigrants from Nordka, Russia along the Volga River. They knew little English and knew even less, if anything, about baseball.

It struck me. They were *right there as caring, as supporting, as giving more than anything that I give my best*…a great message about parenting…

How do each of us do at that? Parenting. Heard the phrase, think it means hovering, to be a helicopter parent, to have to know everything.

Not.

I don't want to know everything…tarnish and all is there for each of us.

I think of that this morning, shifting to my son, Andrew, and his basketball scrimmage on Monday night.

Brought me back to Copenhagen, Denmark, more than a few years ago, where Andrew was coaching a Danish semi-professional basketball team. I went there—was around Thanksgiving. Went to his game in a match-box gymnasium. No bleachers, just the bench for the players.

I sat at the end of the bench, clapping and cheering for Andrew's team.

Okay. Truth? Clapping and cheering for Andrew.

It was the end of the game, a one-point lead for Andrew's team. The referee made one of the worst calls imaginable—against Andrew's team—and as a parent, I considered it against Andrew. Hey, that happens…to each of us at one time or another.

I don't know if the referee spoke English, but he considered me more menace than supporter. I stood up and scowled at him and in less than smooth judgment offered, "That was a HORRIBLE call!"

He scowled back, went to the scorer's table, pointed at me and gave me the fated judgment: a technical foul.

Not a fun moment. Copenhagen, Denmark. A parent getting a technical foul.

Being a parent. Being a grandparent.

How does that go for you?

Do we know the difference between one who hovers and one who supports?

Back to the first pitch in 1954 for Jefferson High School.

One of the players for the other team, Ron Jee, [I will never forget his name] hit a home run that probably is still orbiting beyond the left field "fence" at Alberta Park. I looked at the ball as it went over a house and then noticed my Miller grandparents were clapping.

Clapping! For the guy who hit a home run off their grandson.

After the game I asked them about that, why they clapped. They responded in broken English but in whole meaning, "Oh, honey, we clapped because you made him look so good."

Got me.

Lessons That Matter [continued]

Posted on October 28, 2010 by Mark H Miller

Happened in early June, 1966, but it's clear as this morning; a lesson that came with lots of pain and regret.

For reasons I may never fathom–and that's okay not to have EVERYTHING figured out–upon the eve of my ordination on June 17, 1966, I was clear on the teacher who contributed the most to my life and understanding of a worthier manner of living: Miss Agnes Carter, 8th grade teacher at Vernon Grade School, Portland, Oregon, across from Alberta Park on Killingsworth Street.

The list of important and nurturing teachers was long…from each educational level of high school, university and seminary. The one, though who was number one forever and forever was Miss Carter.

Even this day I can rip off [we had *who can name them the quickest--I always lost to Judy Zeh and Dick Howells!*] the linking and being verbs and every preposition. But, even more we learned from Miss Carter her mantra, offered frequently, *Great minds run in the same channel…but still greater ones take a course of their own.*

Yes, we diagrammed sentences and knew how wrong someone was in answer, "How are you doing?" by responding, "I'm doing good." We were always tempted to comment, "And I hope you are doing it well."

It was like chalk screeching on a blackboard when someone would say, "He's better than me."

Anyway.

The truth reigned: I had never thanked Miss Carter for how she planted seeds of life and manner of living. She was the best–the very best.

I learned her address in north Portland. She had retired and lived alone. I knocked on the door, could hear her shuffle to the door. She opened the door, and looked with curiosity, squinting, her glasses perched on her white bunned hair, still a pencil sticking out over her ear.

"Yes, may I help you?"

I introduced myself and shared how she had graced and blessed me as an eighth grader and no less, was the best teacher ever.

She squinted, a puzzled look and said, "Well, is there anything else you want? If not, I need to excuse myself."

She closed the door.

I stood there, awash in regret, even sorrow and probably a touch of shame: **I had never thanked her for being the best until now...and she's absolutely clueless as to what was just shared.**

A tough moment birthed a resolution: if I can only focus upon the verity, I will make every effort to be more in gratitude than presumption. Never again, if I can only be on my game, will I not tell someone how they have brought good news. My goal is to make Thanksgiving more than a Thursday in November; make it a virtual way of life.

Now, fast forward to a month ago.

I answered the doorbell. It was a Fed Ex delivery man. It was a hot August afternoon [in Austin, Texas, that's always redundant]. I took the package and asked of the delivery man [certainly nudged by Miss Carter], "Sir, can I ask? Do people say thank you to you for bringing them important packages?"

He responded quickly, "Hardly ever. I'm just a token and they only want the package. The delivery man is for utility not benefit."

I had to offer, "Well, sir, please know that my wife and I are grateful... very much so...for your bringing this important package. We do not take you for granted. Know our gratitude is always greater than our presumption. You ARE appreciated. Have a good day."

He shook his head..once, then twice and looked sorrowful.

"Sir?"

He looked up and said, "Well, I guess I've got to do something when I get home tonight?"

"I'm sorry?"

"Yep. It's clear to me. I need to get home and thank my wife for all she does for me and our family. I haven't thanked her in a couple of years."

Lessons That Matter [cont'd.]

Posted on October 29, 2010 by Mark H Miller

I'm not sure it mattered. That's not a flush of "oh gosh," but probably a reality of the time and place.

Actually two lessons resulted.

My home church–Zion Congregational Church in Portland, Oregon–asked me to preach my first sermon. Was a week or two after my sixteenth birthday, summer of 1956. Think it was probably "safe," that is, a youth speaking on a low-attendance summer Sunday.

Obviously the sermon could not be based upon any theological wisdom, let alone education and experience. So, what to preach?

Preached what was important to me, guess that's what happened. My text–the "scripture" officially was Philippians 3:12-16, in which Paul urges focus upon giving a good effort in the moment. [Sounded pretty benign I would guess.]

But, what really was "the text," probably because the source sounded religious, was one of the "Ten Commandments of Baseball" by Billy Southworth. It went like this, *If what you've done yesterday looks big to you, then you haven't done much today.*

I believed that. Not sure much verbiage came out of the "pressing on to that which lies ahead" from the Apostle Paul. But, a WHOLE LOT measured making *this day, this moment, this possibility in this circumstance* as strong, viable and relevant as possible.

I'm sure I didn't use some of those multi-syllabic-words, but hey, at 16 the focus upon the day's effort seemed apt.

No less for today.

The other lesson I learned later.

Zion Congregational Church had two Sunday worship services then. Before the church atrophied and fled to the white suburbs. But, that's for another day.

On that June Sunday in 1966 my mother planned on their regular worship schedule—attend the second service.

But. My father had another game plan. He got up and started to put on his Sunday togs.

"Hank," my mother inquired, "What are you doing? It's too early to go to church. Mark has left and we can get there for the second service."

My father, who never made a short story long, responded, "Look at it this way, Es. If he were pitching both games of a doubleheader, we'd go to both, right?"

They were there. For both services. For both services. They were there.

Two indelibly relevant lessons for me to not forget: make the most of today and be present.

Moving Marble Water Tables…another lesson

Posted on November 1, 2010 by Mark H Miller

Not so much today, if at all, but in yester-decade I was an active [read that approaching full-time] movie devotee. In some parishes I served [never wanted to consider them perishes] we put together a film/discussion series, "Theology of the Movies."

Thought about that these past few weeks as Diane's second surgery for breast cancer gets scheduled [there were cancer cells remaining in the margin-tissue following her lumpectomy] and the new book of epistles, "Hooked On Life" made it from the print shop to the marketplace.

Been thinking: what impacted my life [now headed into my 7th decade], hopefully for the good? A lesson? An indelible imprint? Something that was riveting to the heart and energy for the life?

There have been a few of my "mind-heart-soul-sets" in recent blogs. Today, I look to one that kept coming at me the last few weeks: a scene from the great film based upon Ken Kesey's novel, *One Flew Over The Cuckoo's Nest*.

Maybe some of you are not familiar with one of my favorite characters of all time, Randle Patrick McMurphy, a central character in the 1975 film.

An introductory detail from Wikipedia: McMurphy is an Irish-American brawler found guilty of battery and gambling. He is a Korean War veteran who was a POW during the war. He is sentenced to a fairly short prison term, and decides to have himself declared insane in order to be transferred to a mental institution, where he expects to serve the rest of *his time in (comparative) comfort and luxury.* [Maybe its relevance is tied to the fact the insane asylum is in Salem, Oregon.]

McMurphy's ward in the mental institution is run by the tyrannical Nurse Ratched, who has cowed the patients — most of whom are there by choice — into dejected submission. The two hate each other on sight, and McMurphy goes on a crusade to flout Ratched's regime of rules and punishment, as well

12

as liberate the other patients from her grip. McMurphy becomes ensnared in a number of power-games with Nurse Ratched for the hearts and minds of the inmates.

The main reason this film is on my top-five list is that McMurphy [the initials, RPM were not accidental...measurement of a car's functioning and moving forward] is, at least for me and I pushed it during the church film seminars, a Christ-figure.

Christ figure? Yep. Someone who sets another free, guiding and empowering them to be who they are supposed to be. McMurphy was that. And, certainly metaphorically if not biblically, Ratched was the personification of a Pharisee, one who found the rules more important than dealing with the human condition. Important to realize that a ratchet wrench is a wrench that only turns one way.

The scene that lives with me and I encouraged it to be part of every clergy and church member's life, occurs when the inmates at the mental hospital place bets on whether or not McMurphy can move a gigantic marble hydrotherapy control panel in the washroom.

McMurphy tries. Personally, it's one of the greatest cinematic and life-shaping moments as the camera zooms to his throat..the carotid arteries bulge, almost bursting. The marble water table doesn't budge. But not because his effort lacked.

McMurphy stands, turns and says, "I tried. At least I did that."

It's one of the clearest lessons, at least for me. **To try. To give your fullest.**

Very much for me, to not give an effort is unacceptable. Yes, to be sharper, unconscionable.

It can be put in other ways: *do more than live up to your minimum. Don't establish mediocrity as a moral principle. Make sure others don't look and you and muse, "Gosh, you look at him— there's less than meets the eye.*

Shared this first day of November, a day when the Texas Rangers are on the edge of the abyss labeled defeat, a day before voting, a month that celebrates Thanksgiving and begins Advent.

Wow. It's all there.

And in the mix of it, who am I? Who are you? McMurphy? Nurse Ratched?

Keep trying.

Voting with your manner of living

Posted on November 2, 2010 by Mark H Miller

One-line statements have always been a joy. Seems they can be remembered more easily.

From two films these come to mind:

From "The Graduate," Benjamin is told the magic word for his future, "Plastics." Such a towering word, because in the 60's [that's 1960 and not 1860], the world of plastics did have futuring for those who needed to be solid financially. And yet, how unhelpful to have the focus of plastics. Because it refers, at least from this pen, as synthetic, surfacy, hard and inpenetrable. Hey, it's the preacher-voice happening there.

And from "Shawshank Redemption," Morgan Freeman, imprisoned it seems forever, with hope not even a spec in the horizon, comments to Tim Robbins, "Some people busy dying. Some people busy livin'. Better to be busy livin.'

I like that. A lot.

A partner to Freeman's sage perception, albeit a little syrupy, I remember from my childhood. A talk/music/story Portland radio station, think it was labeled Koin Clock, ended every program, "Today well lived makes every yesterday a dream of happiness and every tomorrow a vision of hope. Look well, therefore, to this day."

Or, from Mayo Angelo: *Yesterday is history. Tomorrow is mystery. Today is a gift…that's why it's called the Present.*

Four more, each of which chiseled its way into one of my novels, "Murder On Tillamook Bay," [will be published in January I hope—had to put in the promo here] the preacher in the novel, the one who gets murdered in the first chapter after catching a 30-plus pound fall Chinook salmon, offered them, all four of them:

Down deep he's shallow. In reference to a church member.

Better to die young....as late as possible

The wind found its voice.

The tears dropped from her chin.

Well, well. One-liners…and a couple of three-liners, or something of the sort.

Point being on Tuesday, November 2, 2010, a day of voting, the question is this: **how does each of us vote…in terms of how we will live today?**

A friend once defined being healthy as, *Standing up, breathing and still eating food through your mouth.*

Oh, for sure, that's got truth. But, the greater truth is to live this day with boldness and joy and hope. For remember, in Holy Week terms, Good Friday [the times of shadows and immeasurable pain and conflict], never wins. It doesn't.

16

Writing murder/mystery novels–a bumpy road

Posted on November 3, 2010 by Mark H Miller

For whatever reason not that there ALWAYS has to be one, I'm going to re-trace my "writing my first novel" and what happened to the hopes of publishing…not exactly dashed but certainly dimmed. May take a few days, but hey, time is a gift and I'll simply try to unwrap it.

Here goes.

There are significant moments when an "aha" happened that changed my life. Headed toward ministry was started at the age of 16 when a Jefferson High School classmate, Jeannette Butts, laughed at my question, "Jeannette, I don't know what I want to be?" [Again for a reason unknown I thought it a good thing to have vocation declared at the age of 16.]

She then paused, her smile still evident, "Mark, that's the dumbest question you could ask. Of course. You want to be a minister."

I went home that night, told my parents. My mother said, "That's wonderful." My father cleared his throat, "That's fine, son. Get a good night's sleep and we can talk about it in the morning."

Or the moment of discovery in the Denver Airport when I first met Diane, a year later we exchanged wedding vows and two days after that fished for steelhead on the Hoh River in Washington's Olympic Peninsula, deluged by 3 inches of rain. Now in our 10th year, we couldn't be happier.

Yes, Diane's breast cancer is a reality…and her 2nd surgery next Wednesday to capture the remaining cancer cells a hope it will be successful…but, down deep our relationship is anything but shallow. What a blessing the two pilots missed the originally scheduled flight and Diane and I, having never met, ended up standing by each other waiting to get a ticket on the remaining flight to Austin.

Back to the first paragraph, not sure of an "aha moment" where the interest in writing novels happened. Oh, I had done writing…the books of pastoral epistles are happily a printed product of same…but novels?

Someone, sometime, some place said, "Have you ever thought of writing a novel?"

To which end, I thought, cannot write a novel without learning how that should happen. To which second end, enrolled in a "First-time novel writing, how to begin" seminar, for five days at Ghost Ranch in northern New Mexico. First-time was hilariously misstated. There were 12 in the class: two housewives who hadn't written, yours truly who was a neophyte for sure, and 9 who ALREADY had novels published.

The teacher was a novelist from up-state New York, Mary Elsie Robertson, a Pulitzer-prize nominee.

We met from 9-12, Monday-Friday. The basics were clear: in writing fiction, make sure you know what you are talking about…for instance, don't write about playing bridge if you don't know the number-value of a King. And, as for the characters, each is someone I know embellished so they'd never figure it out. I start with actual people.

I took good notes.

Then, and I knew this would happen, our teacher said at the close of class on Thursday, "Tomorrow will be our last day. I want each of you to come with the first chapter—maximum of six pages, double-spaced, 12 Times New Roman font—of a new novel."

I loved it: when she got to the word "new," she paused and eye-balled the 9 veterans. The two housewives and I smirked to each other, ah, they cannot use what they've previously published.

But in less than a blink the smirk was erased and fear sped toward me.

The thoughts were clear and anything but rambling: I know I love to read murder-mysteries, but I'm no Lee Child or Lisa Scottoline

18

or James Patterson or Sue Grafton. [Didn't realize how one of them would play into my writing world later…that will come in a few days of blogging.]

A first chapter? I give cluelessness its quintessential meaning. Clueless.

So, I walked the surrounding desert of Ghost Ranch. Thinking and probing and wondering. Six pages…I'd rather write 20 pages on my realized eschatology or how the Parousia can be understood by church members. I'd rather write about how many ministers I worked with [I was Conference Minister in Austin at the time.] who honestly felt there were two kinds of leadership: those who were democratic and those who were effective.]

But no.

My first novel.

Then it hit me. A first-chapter-idea. I got it! I really did. Sort of.

Went back to my cabin, got out my trusty computer and hammered away. Read it through once to make sure verbs were conjugated [think Miss Carter would have been pleased with the grammar.] Printed it up…six pages exactly. And the required font style and size.

But, what about the content? Because I surmised the 9-noon on Friday would be each of us reading our six pages.

I was right.

And one after the other read their six-pages-first-chapter, including my neophyte-writing-housewife-buddies. Amazing stuff. Truly. The more they read the less confident I got.

Novel writing? Nah, a figment and not a declaration.

Eleven finished. I sat there, looked at my watch, the body-language of being out-a-time.

The teacher looked at her watch, read my mind and disagreed. "Mark, we've got plenty of time, you can still make your flight out of Albuquerque, let's hear your first chapter."

Think my gulp was audible.

But, hey, a guy's gotta do what a guy's gotta do, right? Someone needs to be on the first rung of the novel-writing ladder.

When I finished, the silence was very loud. Some would call it deafening. Certainly uncomfortable. Two of the students couldn't take it. They told me later. They got up, walked to the window-side of the room and looked out.

My teacher took a Kleenex and rubbed under her eyes.

Then, one of the students asked, "Mark, what in the world happens to him? Did he commit suicide…in the first chapter?"

I shook my head, "I have no idea. I have no idea where this is going. Just thought the dilemma was real and the minister honest with how fear clutches."

Left for Austin, still puzzled. About their reactions. And what I would do with the novel. What would the second chapter offer? I didn't know. Even thought of chucking the whole idea.

Two weeks later that changed. A hand-written letter from the teacher from her upstate New York writing studio, offered encouragement to keep writing, how the first chapter impacted her and volunteered to edit anything I wrote.

GULP.

There was no way I couldn't continue. To write a second chapter…and a third…and then….

Well, nothing goes totally well…and the writing was like a roller-coaster…as it continued.

More tomorrow.

Ten years ago it went like this: "Discouragement and hopelessness reigned. The pastor, still alone in his house, got up, noticed it was 3 a.m. Put on his pulpit robe over his pajamas, grabbed his keys and went to the garage. Turned the key, noticed the gas tank was full. Started the car. Looked up at the visor, saw the garage-door-opener, reached up, but only half-way. Put his hand down, then his head, and started to sob. The garage door remained closed."

Writing the novel–building the plane while flying

Posted on November 4, 2010 by Mark H Miller

Writing the first novel, in metaphorical terms at any rate, was building the plane while flying.

From what I know—and the learning curve is ever being climbed—each writer has a personal rhythm.

Some outline the entire book. Some write numerous novels at the same time [think Ellery Queen]. I started with one rhythm, and stuck with it, until the second novel. But, I'm ahead of myself. Too far.

Mine changed with each novel, for writing was not primary, not a full-time deal; being a pastor to clergy was. So, before I could figure out what happened to the minister in chapter one of "No One Is Innocent," there were places to go, people to see and lots of moderating. For truth be known, much of conference ministry is mediating local church conflicts. No one wants a call, "Mark, our pastor has not been responsible…" and then learn about myriad misconducts. But wanting and experiencing were often not on the same page, let alone the same book.

For me in the world of "No One Is Innocent," because I was single at the time living in a great home in Austin, most of the writing took place at the end of the day, no matter what the day held.

Oh, I did have a partner, my faithful and beautiful English Cocker Spaniel, Mercy. She was great, always "there," never doubting. How refreshing! In fact, I liked what a friend once offered, "Who am I? I am a person trying to become the person my dog thinks I am." I know. Not original. But effective.

Not sure, but when I'd be working on the novel, almost always late at night and often blasting away on the computer in the early morning hours, I would go into my home office [Mercy tagging along, of course], close the door and pull down the shades. The most frequent goal was one chapter…for that night.

How weird, right? But, somehow it felt like, that was okay, because , *it's novel time and one chapter got close to sufficiency.*

At one point, I was so engrossed in the developing chapter [remember, building an airplane in flight] the most favorite parishioner of all time had a heart attack. The pastor rushed to the hospital. It was a perilous situation…her life hung by a thread. As novelist, I liked her very much…one of those characters who made it clear she was an angel impersonating a human being.

As I'm fond of saying, *she was not one of those church members the minister would most like to trade.*

The pastor stayed in the ICU visitor room all night. At 6 a.m. the physician came, "I'm sorry, Reverend. Thelma didn't make it."

RIGHT THERE. She died. I hadn't planned it, but my fingers tapped away, well ahead of what I wanted.

She died.

I stopped and said to no one and yet everyone, "NO! I want her to live. She CAN'T die!"

But, it happened. Right there.

That was only the first blush of "No One Is Innocent."

The novel moved on.

Mary Elsie, my first novel-writing teacher and editor, went through some health issues so had to stop the editing, with profound regret [mine, too].

Which meant I was sad…but thanked her so much because she made sure the plane didn't crash en route… I then had to find a new editor. Because the minister was in trouble—lots of it—and I was only midway in figuring out how he could cope...and then, maybe the issue would be survival.

I couldn't write and edit within myself. I needed editing help.

Which brought into my life a new person and a horrible tragedy.

More tomorrow.

First Novel…troubles and discoveries toward publishing

Posted on November 5, 2010 by Mark H Miller

"Mark, do you know there's an Episcopal priest here in Austin who writes murder/mysteries? You should talk with him about his writing… and even more, learn if he has an editor, now that your teacher/editor cannot continue."

No, I didn't know who Charley Meyer is or anything about his writing. I did learn about his novels, read a couple [i.e. "Blessed are the Merciless" and "The Saints of God Murders"] contacted him for a breakfast.

He was great…cooperative, interested, supportive. Got some tips and then he offered the name of his editor ["Be aware she's not scholarship-fee-based."] and said he'd like to meet again.

We never met again, because the news two weeks later in the Austin headlines told the horrible story that Charley Meyer and his wife were killed in a head-on accident on Highway #290 as they headed for Houston. They were headed to M.D. Anderson Cancer Hospital so his wife could get breast cancer treatment. Someone came across the highway and didn't correct the error. How tragic.

The Lubbock, Texas editor said she'd help. Sent her the first 80 pages of "No One Is Innocent," and she was kind, "Thanks for your first material. Here are some suggestions." Enclosed with her note were 85 pages of corrections. Guess there were miles and miles to travel on my computer. Her sage advice was helpful and we continued to the end.

Two notable *who would have guessed this?*

Wanting to finish the book I went to Frisco, Colorado on a 3-month sabbatical leave from my Austin conference ministry position to stay in friends' condo/townhome. Before I left, Diane suggested, "Mark, you might consider a homicide or two in your novel."

The first draft was about the challenges [read that *formidable obstacles*] for the minister. But no murders.

En route to Frisco, I spent a week one night in a New Mexico motel, very nondescript, except in the bathroom were the initials *B&C*. The motel was so old I called Diane that night, "Diane, guess what? I'm in a motel where Bonnie and Clyde stayed!"

Hey, remember I write fiction.

Inserted one homicide…a parishioner who was found on a dark and stormy night [not original, but neophyte-writing it was ten years ago] strangled to death, propped up in the front pew of the church. The minister, of course, was charged with homicide because the strangling rope was the belt from his pulpit robe.

As I wrote and then finished "No One Is Innocent," two "never figured but how blessed I am" events happened.

First, I love to write, but am not a marathon writer. Set up a pattern of writing in the morning 'til early afternoon. Took a nap, then headed for a river to fly-fish. Then wrote in the evening.

A nice rhythm.

But, I only knew one river and a small stretch of it. So, without any referencing I called Mountain Angler in Breckenridge and asked for a guide. The question was asked, "Sir, can you tell me a little about yourself? That way I can be a good matchmaker."

I thought at first, *Geesh, I've not contacted Harmony.com have I?*

The next morning I showed up at Mountain Angler..my guide was late. He arrived, "Hi, Mark? My name's Matt Krane."

That was a blessing beyond blessing. We spent the day on private ranch water, Muddy Creek west of Kremmling. The day was perfect, my first cast resulted in about a 20" rainbow that snapped my leader after a 10-minute fracas.

I would cast a while, then a tap on my shoulder. Matt pointed to the sky, "Mark, look at those clouds…they are great."

He then pointed up a canyon, "Ah, look, a red hawk. See it?"

It was like my own national geographic adviser. Fabulous. We discussed politics, religion and the dreaded whirling disease for Rainbow trout. I learned he is a man of considerable gifts: fishing guide, photographer, sky-patrol for Breckenridge Ski area and folk singer. I doubt there's a Jerry Garcia song he cannot sing.

And, all you have to do is mention a movie and he has a memorable line from it.

Amazing. He has become like a brother and is my Rabbi Guide. The picture on the cover of "Hooked On Life" Matt took and there's an epistle about him in the book. All because I didn't want to write all day.

I got home to Austin with the book finished. Ah, my first novel. A night later, a murder/mystery author came to Austin for a book-signing: Sue Grafton. She's the "alphabet-murder" novelist.

A crazy idea hit me. Sat down and wrote her a letter, showed up at the Barnes & Noble and listened to her share about getting started in writing a novel. Think she had written 15 novels before one got printed.

It was then time for book-signing. I also noted I was there with maybe two other men and about 250 women. No problem.

I walked up to her table, thanked her for her sharing and put an envelope on the table, the letter inside on some words about "No One Is Innocent" and a query about how to get an agent…or get published.

The next morning my phone rang, "Dr. Miller? This is Sue Grafton calling. I'm at the Austin Airport, but I wanted you to know that I've read the first two chapters of your novel and your synopsis. Thanks for sharing them with me. I'd like you to send me 50 more pages…here's an address. You have a fine novel, it appears. Let me read more and I'll see how I can help you."

ARE YOU KIDDING ME? SUE GRAFTON WANTS TO SEE PART OF "NO ONE IS INNOCENT???"

I'm pretty sure I got to the post office before her plane left Austin.

Hopes dashed…for a while

Posted on November 8, 2010 by Mark H Miller

When something unexpected happens, something more than pleasant and hopeful, the mind refuses to quiet.

After Sue Grafton asked for 50 pages of "No One Is Innocent," I saw it…clear as a mind would provide and promise beckon, *She'll love the novel, have one of her associates ask for the full manuscript…and then decide to hand me over to her agent who will contact…oh, it doesn't matter, someone known well to all bookstores in publishing. Oh boy, this is THE break…and the novel is still ink that needs to dry. So to speak.*

Could even become a movie—Hollywood, or maybe an indie film maker would grab it, because the preacher in "No One Is Innocent" is anything but conservative. He'd only thought of himself as liberal with a large L. In fact, he mused, "If you would consider me an airplane politically or theologically, I wouldn't have a right wing." He loved that one-liner and saved it for when the listener would grimace if not scowl. So, publishing, cinema…all because of Sue Grafton's phone call.

Months passed.

And then the envelope.

I wondered if Funk and Wagnalls had reviewed it—just like with the Academy Awards.

I sat by myself and am sure the eyes glistened. Reminded me of receiving the letters of acceptance to the university and then to the seminary. Reminded me of my first call to ministry from Fred Trost and Herb Davis.

My eyes didn't stay glistened. In fact they blinked more than once. I looked at the envelope…was it addressed to me?

Yep.

Had to be the shortest letter I've ever received and the longest fall I've ever experienced: *Dr. Miller—good luck with your writing. Regards, Sue Grafton.*

I then remembered what she said at the Austin bookstore, "I wrote 15 novels before getting one published."

NO!

Did that mean I had to write 14 more?

Really?

Well, Mark Henry Miller, welcome to reality. Look at it this way, *At least the first letter sparked an interest. Maybe with some editing and re-considering what happens to my preacher, the spark can lead to a fire... maybe???*

The next ten years ended up receiving over 80 letters of "I'm sorry," from literary agents, publishers and even friends of friends of friends.

Let's face it...as I plunged into novels 2,3 and 4, perhaps on my way to 15...this is a tough market...murder/mystery and thrillers are the virtual dime/dozen.

Then...

...yes, then it happened. I learned about a press that preferred book material that had to do with fishing and/or hunting. Well, I'd never shot Bambi and had no nudge to do so. But, the second novel, "Murder On Tillamook Bay" is all about fishing and ministry and murder. In fact, the first chapter includes it all.

This publisher said, "Send your whole book...we have another fisherman who's written a novel—he lives in Maine...so after the first of the year we can publish them together. We're looking to expand our publishing options. It looks to us that a novel with fishing and murder and ministry...a new step we'd like to take."

Well, truth is this: the communiqué from the publisher is better than "Good luck with your writing."

And, should this happen…and I do believe it will…I will send the first copy to Sue Grafton and thank her…for her challenge.

Why? Because, "Good luck with your writing" could have been a death knell. But it also could have been a great challenge. And it was. So, I will thank her for her taking the time to read fifty pages of "No One Is Innocent," even if it didn't match her criteria for competent writing from a novelist wannabe.

More than forty years later...

Posted on November 9, 2010 by Mark H Miller

Sunday was a treat. Got to preach at St. Paul's E&R-United Church of Christ in Dallas. My wonderful friend, Jim Blume, hosted me. He was on the Search/Call Committee that selected me to become the Conference Minister—back in 1997—to come to Austin, serving as Conference Minister for the South Central Conference. Then it was about 100 churches to work with—throughout Texas and Louisiana and the mission project, Back Bay Mission in Biloxi, Mississippi.

Jim was/is the legal counsel for the conference [and, now for the Christian Church Disciples of Christ of the Southwest] so he helps more than 500 churches when they have legal talons clutching at their world. In addition to being one of the best friends in the world, Jim had the same surgery as Diane, so is great in helping her through some of the post-surgical potholes [this was not the cancer surgery].

And another addition, Jim has been the best legal counsel in the world for us in fending off a real estate law suit, filed by a guy who subsequently filed for bankruptcy. The lawsuit, if it weren't so personal, is really pointless, a real sham. But, it's got the HOLD button pressed to it while the plaintiff, who made it clear he was way more arrogant than intelligent, gets his act together.

What was really special about Sunday, in addition to thoroughly enjoying worship and the very receptive and attentive congregation [I told them how much I enjoy that particular Sunday—no one falls asleep because they each had an hour more of it—with the fall-back time change] and their post-worship fellowship time, was a special breakfast.

A short explanation that will lead to some wonderful connectors.

About a month earlier I got a surface-mail letter [how rare are those, right?] from a woman who was in my FIRST [emphasis for importance here] confirmation class, circa April of 1967, at St. Pauls Church in Chicago, my first parish. [Which is better than my first perish.]

Pam Becker. I remembered her name, remembered when she babysat my son, Matthew, who was born in October of 1969 and remembered all the youth activities.

Of all things Pam had been attending St. Paul's Church in Dallas and learned I was preaching this past Sunday. She wrote to say hello and wondered if we could have breakfast.

How delightful it was. And, for sure, we recognized each other. Certainly not the same hair and for double-sure not the same weight. Still, how special. To remember when.

Besides, Pam tracked down some contact e-mails and Facebook [I'm not really quick with that, but perhaps should be....some day] with her other confirmation classmates.

Most of all, we had a chance to reflect upon more than 40 years since we had seen each other. Wow.

And now, a chance to touch base with unsuspecting souls...all part of the class of '67, Confirmation, St. Pauls Church, Chicago, Illinois.

Could end up being some fascinating and also curious Cold Cases. Love it.

Surgery today…

Posted on November 10, 2010 by Mark H Miller

Surgery today…in a bit. Diane's lumpectomy, a couple of weeks ago, didn't remove all the cancer cells. This morning the surgeon, who is competent-plus, will go after the remaining cells. The good news from the lumpectomy is the cancer cells hadn't reached the sentinel lymph node. Now we hope today will be a full cancer cell removal day!

Diane's attitude on a 1-10 as for being positive and energy on the resolute scale, for both is somewhere around a 14.

How, though, are we, down deep? I do believe as well as we can be. We know cancer happens. It happened to Diane's identical twin sister, Cheryl, four years ago, the same cancer. Cheryl's doing well now.

What we don't believe—and for sure, I never have because of my parents who never believed cancer was a judgment "from above." Never. Rather, cancer is part of the human condition…and for some, it aggresses itself beyond control.

Now, that's not to say in some circumstances we don't bring cancer on… because of lousy dieting, smoking or being around cancer-conditioned environment. For instance, it's hard to work in a coal mine and stay cancer-free.

But, when talking with my doctor today, who removed some cysts, no matter how hard it gets, no matter how rugged tomorrow's terrain looks, Good Friday never wins. It doesn't. Period.

One attitude about life's circumstance Diane shared from one of her seminary courses. In an introduction to the Book of Matthew in the New Testament, it offered, *Matthew tells the story in such a way that not only is everything previous to us completed in Jesus; we are completed in Jesus. Every day we wake up in the middle of something that is already going on, that has been going on for a long time: genealogy and geology, history and culture, the cosmos—God. We are neither accidental nor incidental to the story. We get orientation, briefing, background, reassurance.*

I find that more than instructive. Each of us, cancer or not, seminary student or not, retired minister or not, is neither accidental nor incidental. Great stuff.

Coupled with a quote I read recently from Dorothy Day, especially when the talons of despair scratch at us. She maintained, *No one has the right to sit down and feel hopeless; there is too much work to do.*

Okay, a little preachy. But look at it this way...I'm not preaching next Sunday, so the Blog gets some hints of what I might say if I were preaching.

Now, to the hospital...and Diane's surgery. We pray with hope and give thanks for your caring. We are the better for it.

Veteran's Day–Two Images

Posted on November 11, 2010 by Mark H Miller

Thursday morning, Veteran's Day, a time to be grateful [more than a nod and one "put your hands together" moment] for those who keep freedom to be more than a good idea.

For us, with more than a nod of affirmation and respect for our armed services, it's the day after Diane's second breast cancer surgery. Time and again it's true—surely not simply for us but for countless friends and parishioners and colleagues—the 24-plus hours after surgery are horrible. The pain pushes and pulls and keeps sleep minimal.

But, in about 8 hours it will be the 25th post-surgery hour, so hopefully the pain will subside and finally leave Diane.

Two images on this day in the mix of what appears to be successful surgery—the surgeon for whom we have the highest regard was born in Lebanon and when 7 a terrorist bomb exploded near him, ripping into his stomach, after which he almost bled to death. He didn't.

Now a top-flight Austin surgeon. He said to us, "I look at every day as a miracle for I am alive, have a beautiful family and can help people, especially those with cancer." Goodness, what a beautiful person who happens to be a surgeon. He indicates the test will let us know if all the cancer cells were removed. That we'll learn next week during our next appointment. He's very optimistic—and we pick up on that—big-time.

The two images, one good and the other simply horrific.

In that order.

About a week ago Diane needed a bone-density test. The technician [not sure of title] administering the test gave "Nurse Ratched" its best impersonation. Tough, stern, almost angry. Certainly rigid and demanding. Unpleasant and negative to the core. Once into the test—

more than a few minutes—Diane commented to the effect, *Thank you for helping me; hopefully this test will give us important information.*

Diane said once a word of gratitude [genuine from Diane to the core, because that's her persona] was shared, "Nurse Ratched" left and "Florence Nightingale" arrived...like turning a switch to being cooperative, caring, kind.

Gosh, one word of gratitude, to say *Thank You.*

It made a difference.

Second image today.

For some people, their anger and wrath and ability to find something wrong is unmatchable.

This happened after worship.

It was one of the most offensive moments in my ministry...ever, ever, ever.

A church member whom I had not met and who hadn't been in worship since I arrived and as you can appreciate not since that Sunday I wish I could forget, came out.

I reached to shake his hand to let him know I was pleased to have met him. He refused my hand, took a step back from me, stood as rigid as he could, clicked his heels together, stiffed his arm at my face, "Seig Heil!"

Are you kidding me?

Hello, Anger and Wrath and Contempt, right?

Turns out [and as I recalled it was a Sunday about 2 months since one of our members was killed in the Middle East] I hadn't mentioned our troops in the pastoral prayer. An innocent and unintended omission.

This saluting person could not have been more offended.

My efforts to contact him were thwarted by his other family members.

So, on Veteran's Day, two images—a word of gratitude to a medical technician and a word of contempt from an irate parishioner.

I need to embrace the former and throw away the latter.

Hard to not recall when someone spits in your face. But, I'm gonna try. I'm gonna try.

More than a phone call

Posted on November 12, 2010 by Mark H Miller

It was not the reaction I anticipated. Certainly not what was needed.

The call was to schedule an appointment for Diane…not for the cancer-situation, but as a follow-up to a different surgery she had last April. The scheduling conversation was fine, the conversation ordinary. Until the call was referred to the physician's nurse whom we wanted to inform about Diane's lumpectomy and 2nd surgery.

Simply a *heads-up*.

No sooner had this been said, "We wanted you to know about Diane and what she's dealing with…" than "HOW COULD YOU DO THAT? WHY DIDN'T YOU HAVE OUR DOCTOR PERFORM THOSE SURGERIES? WHY? IS THERE SOMETHING WRONG WITH HIM?"

Ever get close to hanging up? Ever get close to shouting back? Ever get close to, "….what about Diane in this conversation? This is about her not about you or your doctor. Get a clue, woman!"

Rather I explained our choice of surgeon had not rejected HER boss. We simply went with our family physician's recommendation of a surgeon whose specialty is breast surgery.

It strikes me this morning, less than 24 hours later from this less than appreciated exchange, the reaction of the nurse, only if it were ordinary was anything but and in the common flow of exchanges was actually common.

Sad but true.

It strikes me people think of themselves first. People function more from "what's in this for me?" than a focus upon what they are told and whom it affects.

I'm sure none of us, including myself, is innocent here, all the time.

I'm also sure in the important admonition *to love your neighbor as yourself*, the key, the hardly ever by-passed key is the "love of the self." My perception is EVERYTHING pivots around the reality of self-love, self-cognition, self-understanding.

When that's weak, when that's lame, when either self-worth has eroded or an overriding hubris is in play, caring for another, figuring out this conversation focused on Diane and not our choice of surgeon, rarely occurs.

But, hey, it's Friday, two days after surgery. Diane feels better, the pain is less. That's more important, waaaaaay more important than a nurse's irritating response. Right?

Today…glowing or glowering?

Posted on November 15, 2010 by Mark H Miller

Monday morning. The calendar's listing important events for the week. Many doctor appointments…for Diane and me…with the most important on Wednesday when we meet with the surgeon to learn the test results from her second surgery. Then we meet with the oncologist to map out next-steps to get well.

Next steps to get well.

Seems to me that is the rhythm of everyone's life, except for those whose arrogance exceeds their intelligence.

Ever met those people? For whatever reason, and in most cases it's because of a shaken self-image [cite last week's reflections], they are in constant denial that what happens is not always someone else's fault. If they cannot complain they cannot function. They are incapable of spelling whine without an h. And, for the even greater reason it's frustrating, because to visit with them and understand lowers everyone's IQ on the maturity and responsibility and mutuality scales.

But I don't want to go there.

Next steps to get well.

I live with the belief, more than assumption for it's based upon six decades of walking, climbing, falling, getting up, climbing again, these realities prevail:

…none of us is perfect.

…each of us can learn that God doesn't keep a record of wrongs.

…the finest goal is to realize we are God's opinion and not someone else's ultimately.

41

...each day can live on its own and does not need dependence upon what has just happened.

Although.

Sometimes what just happened can make the new day glowing or glowering.

Today it's glowing.

Why?

Because my son Andrew's Schreiner University's Men's Basketball team starts their season tonight, a new season, a chance to make this season a time for excellence.

Because friends are looking at the glass as half-full.

And, yes I admit without pause or compromise, because the Broncos won yesterday, handily.

Okay.

It's Monday.

Time to get with it.

You, too?

A Meal to remember…and more

Posted on November 16, 2010 by Mark H Miller

It was a memorable moment. Not sure of the year, but either 1967 or 1968, maybe even 1969 but I doubt it.

Confirmation was big-time for St. Pauls Church in Chicago…and for all the right reasons. I've always believed that time of learning helps construct good values and a viable relationship with the church. One of the most caring and competent confirmands was Monica Schwabe. Her parents had migrated from Germany. Her father, I believe, owned and managed apartment buildings. Think they lived in a lovely first floor of a walk-up on Arlington or Wrightwood, very close to our 3rd floor walk-up on Fullerton, so walkable.

After a powerful confirmation service–all three pastors, Trost, Davis and Miller [sounds like a law firm, doesn't it?] participated–Gary, Monica's father, in a casual manner offered, "Mark, why don't you and your wife come over to our home this afternoon, about 4 pm? We're having *a little something* to celebrate Monica joining the church."

I focused upon the *little something*.

At 3 p.m. my wife fixed what amounted to a large brunch, the whole enchilada [I can use Mexican metaphors now living in Austin,Texas]: sausage/bacon/omelet, waffles, toast, blackberry jam. I remember the jam because that was a *must* having been born in Portland, Oregon. To say the least, it was a large–make that huge–meal that never thought for a moment about calories, cholesterol or what would happen at 4 p.m. with Gary and Eleanor and their daughter Monica.

We walked–make that waddled–to their lovely home.

I came close to fainting when the door opened and learned in a heartbeat that Gary Schwabe was the master of understatements. Not even close to *little something*. Extended family filled the living room and the table, with cloth napkins, and lots of place settings, awaited us.

Cannot say exactly, but it was at least six courses of *little somethings*. *Shrimp appetizers, salad, soup, vegetables, potatoes, prime rib, and lots of cake for dessert, followed by some sherbet. And bread, lots and lots of bread that Monica's mother and grandmother had made…from scratch.*

Fortunately we made it through the meal…barely…and double-waddled home. So, if anyone asks me, "Can you remember a meal in your life?", that perhaps tops the list. Fortunately, no one gave a speech on world hunger…but they should have. And guilt would have abounded. To fast the next week was not a problem; it was a relief!

Crazy reflection on a Tuesday morning, November 16, 2010, as I'm about to write Monica, whom I have not seen or been in contact with since December, 1969, when I left beloved St. Pauls Church in Chicago in order to serve the First Congregational Church in Eugene, Oregon.

Not sure what triggers this—oh yeah I do—one of those confirmands, Pam Becker, contacted me a month ago and that began the dominoe progression—getting back in touch with the youth in my first ministry. And to think, that was 44 years ago, which makes them close to retirement. Goodness.

But it's worth it…very much so.

I wonder. Will she remember her confirmation *little something* meal?

Couldn't drink the first cup of coffee

Posted on November 17, 2010 by Mark H Miller

Sipping coffee this morning floods me with memories. Memories that begin with my first cup of coffee that I wasn't allowed to drink.

Cannot tell you the age, but maybe five, or at least pushing it.

Do know it was summer and a treat was when I got to ride with my father and grandfather in the garbage truck to the dump.

I know, psychology friends have a feast...*the dump*?

Yes. What it meant most of all was to sit in the cab between my father and grandfather.

But, I'm off track. Back to the coffee.

My mother would take me to my grandparent Miller's house...at the corner of N.E. 9th and Failing, 1034 N.E. Failing I recall. [Can you recall the address of grandparents? I can even remember the first phone number of our own Portland home, GA 9040. With a party line. Wait a turn and not fuss that SOMEONE could always listen in.]

My Grandmother Miller, an immigrant from Nordka, Russia along the Volga River, spoke little English. That didn't matter, because I know I mattered.

It was the welcoming drill...once a week...in the summers...in Portland, Oregon.

Mom would drop me off, my Grandmother Miller stood at the back door, drooped shoulders but a smile that could scare any pain away. I'd get the world's biggest hug. I used to take a deep breath to make sure I would still be breathing when it was over. My Grandmother Miller was the master of the squeeze-big-time-hug.

She'd then sit me down at the off-balanced kitchen table. I was too young to know I could get a couple sugar packets and put them under what appeared to be the short leg. But hey, maybe they didn't have sugar packets in 1945?

She'd then bring the coffee.

Recipe as follows: coffee so strong I didn't think it needed a cup. She'd fill the cup to the half-way mark, then top it off with sugar and cream, stir and place in front of me.

But. Rule #1: DON'T DRINK THE COFFEE. Why? Its purpose was not for drinking; it was for dunking.

For next to the cup was a plate laden with toasted German rye bread that my Grandmother Miller fixed…from scratch. The bread was soaked with melted butter and strawberry jam. I'd take the toast, dunk it, portionally at a time, of course, and savor my first cup of coffee via toasted rye bread.

Ah, heaven on earth. At least to a 5-year old.

That memory comes to me as I sip this morning's coffee. But, also for two other reasons.

One, on my new Kindle. What a treat, gifted from Diane when I had indicated I didn't think it was worth it. That early "oh, don't bother" was one of my more imprudent statements. I love the Kindle. Am doing much more reading and enjoying not paying hefty prices.

I'm mid-way through one of the most fascinating and frightening— both at the same time—novels, Room, A Novel by Emma Donoghue, a fictional story of a 5-year-old boy and his mother, living every day of his life in a small room, spending the full 24-hours only with each other. Other than most late-nights when their captor comes in to be with his mother and the child hovers in a wardrobe closet, his bedroom. It's been a long time since I've read a novel that's so captivating and creative and dangerous.

Triggers more thoughts about what happens to Tricia Gleason, my protagonist, in the murder/mystery novel, the venue Frisco, Colorado and the lame summer she spends as an intern minister after her first seminary year. The novel is still marinating in my mind…but the novel I'm now reading, its compelling nature, has me getting stoked.

But, there's more going on right now, this Wednesday morning, November 17, 2010, than a novel and a first cup of coffee.

Many days in the past months have been looking back, remembering incidents, events, turning points in my life's journey. The most joyful part of it has been to re-connect with important people. To share with them anecdotally where we intersected along the way and how I'm the better for it. And, who knows, maybe they are too.

That doesn't mean every day is spent with a rear-view mirror larger than my windshield. But it helps to keep a focus on these 70 years… and hopefully many more to come.

All of that comes now as I sip the coffee, open up my Kindle and see what happens to the 5-year-old and his mother and then this early afternoon as Diane and I visit the surgeon to learn the lab-test results of her second surgery for breast cancer, hope upon hope the cells are no longer in residence.

Thanksgiving...more than a day

Posted on November 18, 2010 by Mark H Miller

So much. So very much. Even when days are cloudy, rain splatters plans and the wind finds its voice.

So much. So very much. For which to be grateful.

In fact, the more I ponder, the more I believe, and have held this close to my heart for more than two weeks, THANKSGIVING is not so much a day in November [coming a week from today, for sure] but a way of life, for double-sure.

This Thursday morning, the gratitude is for the surgeon's report yesterday that the lab tests from Diane's second surgery show no cancer cells in the margin-tissue surrounding the tumor. What was there has been excised. As I've learned, that doesn't mean Diane's "cancer-free," because evidently for every one of us, that's not the case. But it does mean cancer is not rampaging, the lymph nodes are unaffected. As a surgeon friend explained to me last night, "In my 35 years of dealing with breast cancer, for the lymph nodes to be free and the size of the tumor, 1 centimeter, the news is most encouraging. Radiation will be helpful as will continual examinations. Know, though, it is a great report." I agree!

This Thursday morning, the gratitude is for my son, Andrew, whose Schreiner University basketball team won their first game of the season, defeating Trinity University in San Antonio. According to the SU news article the last time SU beat Trinity was in 1992. Are you kidding me? And for those who have a tendency to wag on such information, no, 1992 was not the last time they played each other! It's a tremendous first step for the players and Andrew. Tremendous. Because for years and years, make that decades, Schreiner has not won more than 6 games any season. This season? Could be different. Coach Miller knows what he's doing...excellent recruitment...good team work...lots of enthusiasm and energy and encouragement [the three E's].

This Thursday morning, the gratitude is for my family, especially the grandchildren. The newest of God's gifts to us, Taylor, has begun to smile and coos without pause. How good is that? And her brother, now 2, beams in pointing to his sister. We'll have Thanksgiving Day with them and Jennifer's parents, visiting from Seattle. A good time to say words of gratitude.

This Thursday morning, the gratitude is for God, who puts up with me, who doesn't rant when I screw up, who claps and cheers when verbs get conjugated and who blesses life and who doesn't keep a record of rights and wrongs. Rather, knows you and me, remembers you and me and when we limp, reaches out a healing hand, when our hubris overflows slows it down and when we are not sure value and caring have a place, when we think life isn't worth it, brings goodness to us and tells us, "I am with you, no matter what; I am with you, without compromise; keep on keeping on."

May it always be…no matter our place, no matter our time, no matter our circumstance. May it always be that Thanksgiving is MUCH MORE than the designated November Thursday. May it be that Thanks-giving is a veritable way of life, no matter what.

To be so much better

Posted on November 19, 2010 by Mark H Miller

A world of extremes gets headlines, but a world of connecting conveys and manifests value.

A man in Wisconsin, in hearing that Bristol Palin is still in the television Dancing with the Stars contest, got out his shotgun and blew away his television. A SWAT team was called.

Following last Sunday's Cleveland Browns/New York Jets game in Cleveland, which the Jets won in overtime, a father and his son wearing Jets shirts were pelted with food as they left the stadium and then in the parking lot a rabid and I'm gonna guess not model of sobriety Cleveland fan ran and tackled the boy, slamming him to the asphalt. The boy was 8 years old.

On that incident, Colin Cowherd, a morning ESPN talk show host, whom I find the most should be listened to sports guy, because he is incapable of blabbing, is most always stimulating and provoking and for sure, never, ever says, He's better than me, went ballistics yesterday on the dastardly act of the Cleveland fan, offering to buy anyone who identifies the twerp a season's ticket to the Browns games next season. The Jets and the Browns have apologized to the offended family and have offered to host them for a future game, no expenses to them. The family has declined the offers.

And then into that world, I read an interview in the current ESPN THE MAGAZINE in which Kenny Mayne interviews the current starting quarterback for the Buffalo Bills, Ryan Fitzpatrick, a Harvard graduate with a degree in economics. The interview was refreshing:

KM: Ever set your wife and kids up in the living room and run plays with them to get extra reps?
RF: I do, but it's frustrating with the young ones, because they jump offside and I have to send them to their room. Then we don't have enough people anymore.

50

KM: Do they understand the significance of their dad playing in one of the biggest leagues in the world?

RF: No. My 3 year-old, Brady, sees me on TV, and I think he thinks everyone's dad is on TV. But he'll tell me, "Hey, Dad, tomorrow I'm going to tackle all the other dads, because all the other dads tackle you."

Occurs to me that's all part of life…dealing with it. And most of the time, especially with anger/rage manifest, the issue is not the issue. I'll bet you with the irate Wisconsin man—oh sure, he thinks Sarah Pain is a Palin—but a deep search would discover that's really displacement. The issue may be a recent unemployment or a quagmired family or something in the realm of whatever. So, he popped his television set.

Or the Browns fan—maybe he's still trying to get over the Drive by John Elway when the Broncos took the heart out of the Browns, going 98 yards with practically no time left and then winning in overtime—or maybe he lost a ton of money because Cleveland had been playing well and really should have beaten the Jets.

Where does this go? It's not to suggest to not be a fan. Wow, when the Broncos won their first Super Bowl defeating the Packers, my sons called each other [we are really unrepentant and uncompromising Bronco fans—who could tell, right?] and said, "Okay, now we can die."

But that—indicating an extreme—is SO MUCH BETTER—than grabbing a shotgun or tackling an 8-year old, slamming him down. Just like the comment from Ryan Fitzgerald brought a laugh—because a father using his family for football in the living room is SO MUCH BETTER than never getting your family together for anything.

As I started, considering this Friday and subsequently this weekend, a world of extremes gets headlines, but a world of connecting conveys and manifests value.

Connect. That's key. But the manner of connecting is just as significant. For sure.

Monday of Thanksgiving week–start of holidays…

Posted on November 22, 2010 by Mark H Miller

Monday morning…let the holidays begin, right? Diane has XM on her car radio. I like one of the "Oldies" music stations. Obviously no surprise there. I don't know the "newies."

[Reminds me of a time when Andrew was coming to Austin to visit— think he was in Copenhagen at the time coaching basketball. I was having a pretty difficult day—driving 40,000 miles annually to work with churches can do that—was in my conference ministry days.

He started the conversation, "Pop, wide spread panic."

I said, "Andrew, how did you know?"

"Nah, Dad, not a condition. It's a rock group—they'll be in Austin… can you get us a couple of tickets?"]

Back to the oldie music. I was listening last week and EVERY SINGLE SONG WAS CHRISTMAS. Not a turn-on, for sure. So I switched back to ESPN and mused about sports.

Andrew's game last night was a heart stopper. They were 2-0 starting the season, probably the first time in Schreiner University history that has happened. On Saturday night they beat the #15 ranked Division III team in the country and tops in their league…at THEIR gym.

Last night, the first home game for Schreiner, with 2 seconds to go Andrew's best shooter made a 3-point shot to tie the game. The gym was packed…first home game…Andrew's "New Team" was doing their best…ended up losing 104-103 in double-overtime. Exhausting, exhilarating, frustrating. I'm proud of Andrew and his players. They should have a very strong season.

Am all over the map this morning…wondering if I should get back into an interim ministry. Certainly love being home, but the "want to preach and do pastoral care" bug is nipping. We'll see if an interim becomes available. Yes, I love the writing…and it's been heartening how many friends and churches are interested in "Hooked On Life." That feels good. Had the book-signing in Dallas recently and two more scheduled—one in Austin on December 4 and one in San Marcos on December 19. A new experience, this book-signing business. No one can read my signed name…but it's printed clearly on the book, so no problem, right?

But, to preach on Sunday…ah, that's something I miss.

Diane and I look forward to spending Thanksgiving with Andrew and his family in Boerne. Diane has been requested to be the Pumpkin Pie Lady—she makes the best pumpkin pie in the world. So, Wednesday's a cooking day.

She's starting to feel better after the second surgery. It will be helpful to start the radiation schedule…and get beyond that. She continues attending seminary and really loves it. I'm so proud of her. She wrote a paper recently that is the best statement I've ever read about the necessity of "Forgiveness," on the "Forgive seven times seventy" passage. I'm hoping she'll let me share it with clergy colleagues. It's really a great reflective piece. My goodness, can she write.

We also learned yesterday that one of my most favorite cousins will visit us a few days immediately after Christmas. That's a good thing.

Broncos play tonight in San Diego. They win and they have a chance to make the play-offs. They lose and it's "turn out the lights" for any chance at that. But I'm sure Matthew and Andrew and I will cheer like crazy for our beloved Broncos. Yes, indeed.

And just thought of this in closing: November 22. A dreaded day in history. Dallas. President Kennedy. November 22, 1963. What's that, 47 years ago? In many ways it seems like yesterday. I bet every one of us, if alive and cognitive by then [where did THAT come from?] can remember exactly where we were and what we were doing when we got that news.

I was walking across the campus of Yale Divinity School and someone shared the news. I remember attending Yale's worship service that Sunday morning and William Sloane Coffin preached…focused upon the difficulty and necessity of believing in God during such times.

The assassination. Not a good moment. And, if I wanted to, which I don't, could list numbers of not-good-political-moments. But not now.

It's Monday morning and I will pause in reflection. Offer prayers.

And then, as Andrew's college coach, Bill Brown, used to tell him and the players at Kenyon College in Ohio, "Keep on keeping on."

That's good stuff.

On to that this day.

Thoughts on Ministry…and the rarity of change

Posted on November 23, 2010 by Mark H Miller

It is clear—no fog on this window—when looking at the ministry, that is, serving a church as an ordained minister—there are some dynamics that should not occur and some statements that should remain muted.

Collected over the years:

A minister in the United Church of Christ blasted Southern Baptists, "I never would want one—they are too right-winged for me."

The counter statement came from a former Southern Baptist who became ordained in the United Church of Christ, in edited language [he never worried about profanity since with it he never lacked profundity], "You are full of nuts. I LOVE taking in Southern Baptists, because when they grow up they join the UCC…and they never forget to tithe."

Another.

A dynamic often eschewed by ministers: pastoral care, especially in the hospital or in the nursing homes. I knew one minister who did whatever he could to not get to the hospital. To the relief of his congregation and himself, he left church ministry. I know another minister who had a parishioner's mother in the hospital for 4 months and this minister only called on the mother the day before she was released, considering that adequate pastoral care.

Here's the truth…in ministry at any rate. A person [choose the gender] can be dull in preaching, sloppy in administration, faulty in planning, even might fall asleep in the pulpit on Saturday night going over the sermon, and can state the thought the Tea Party should have stayed in Boston's Harbor. ALL of that will never be held against the minister if the minister [again, choose the gender] gets to the hospital, takes Holy Communion at least quarterly to the homebound. That minister will even be more loved and affirmed if that minister sits down when hospital visiting [on a chair and not on the bed!] so it's not a hello, goodbye and one-sentence prayer. And even more, that minister will be appreciated by not staying in the hospital room more than ten minutes.

Hey, everyone's got their own timer...ten minutes was/is mine.

And now to what will not be pabulum comment. And I realize this will not, along with the pabulum, be ingested smoothly.

Seat belts. Here it comes.

In ministry there's always hope for change, for a person to turn his/her life around, to make a new/fresh start in getting out of the quagmire of difficult circumstances. And yes, hope.

However, and this perhaps smashes the teeth of the mouth of ministry and church and the transforming Presence of the Holy Spirit.

It has been my experience, time and again and more, that people don't change. They don't. I can roster legions who are the same today as they were decades ago. Certainly that's not good pastoral texting. But, for the overwhelming most part, the idiosyncratic ways of people pop up...in what seems to be forever or ad infinitum, whichever takes longer.

I've had that experience recently in touching base with parishioners/friends/colleagues with whom in many cases there's been at least a 30 years gap. What they communicate and the manner by which they convey their ideas/beliefs/persuasions...wow, nothing has changed. In other words, those who impersonate angels as human beings continue to do so.

And those who are genuinely irritating continue the pattern of masters of being irksome, even feckless.

I know...it's important to believe this isn't the case. And maybe someday I'll be surprised.

But I doubt it.

If it can be remembered, doubt is not denial; doubt is suspension of judgment.

Living the day before...

Posted on November 24, 2010 by Mark H Miller

165 days. 165 days until the Royal Wedding. In a way, that's refreshing... to have something to look forward to, as this will be, for many.

And *for many*, whose days are one long suicide, who wonder when they reach up if they'll ever touch bottom, who just know they have not even lived up to their minimum, who realize people talk more about their age than their wisdom, a Royal Wedding can be a dose of happiness, or at least a smile, a sigh that love IS in the air for Prince William and Kate Middleton. And when that happens, the smirk is abandoned.

I think about this today...the day before Thanksgiving...for that is *our time*...to gather tomorrow, hopefully with family as in years gone-by. No we won't pay attention to the national calorie average for Thanksgiving Dinner—for those curious or even cynical it's 3,400—and maybe for just a moment, we'll put to the side the negative, the untoward, the meanness of life.

But, on this day, for reasons I cannot identify but know...in a sense every day we live, it is the *day before*.

And down deep I realize this: when I am loved, which is the case from my family and my God and many, many friends who have reached out with such power in support of Diane and me through the medical hoops, the *day before* is more than not, every day, a good day. Because today well lived, as the old Portland, Oregon radio station offered, makes every yesterday a dream of happiness and every tomorrow a vision of hope.

Even more, today is the first day of the rest of my life. I don't mire as I enter my 7th decade, I don't bog down that there's no steelhead fishing in Texas, I don't slog along knowing radiation is in our future. Rather, I rejoice, I really do. For today is God's gift which is why it's called the present. And all I have is today, in terms of my breathing, my walking, my living.

57

May it be…a good day, not because of what happens, but because I am loved…and that, for sure, pushing certainty to center stage, is the best cause, and when necessary the only cause that keeps me going.

In my understanding of how others live…there are those, to put it theologically, who in every day, at least in terms of their consciousness, want to LEAP from Palm Sunday to Easter Sunday, in denial the Good Fridays of life ever happen.

And there are those who believe that Good Friday is a permanent place beyond which nothing meaningful or helpful happens.

Not.

Life is the full enchilada…Palm Sunday, Maundy Thursday, Good Friday and Easter. And in my day, today and every day I live, I know, Good Friday doesn't win. Easter wins.

So, today, good morning. Let's make the most of it.

Thanksgiving…work ethic…pumpkin pies…twinged drinks and more…much, much more: wonderful

Posted on November 25, 2010 by Mark H Miller

I'm not sure why—given more than history—it is called the *Protestant Work Ethic*.

Because it's been the case that I've known multiple Jewish Work Ethics, Catholic Work Ethics, yes even Republican and Democratic Work Ethics. Haven't reached the Tea Party Work Ethics yet, but certainly there's one or two out there.

Pushing the thought this morning came from last night. Diane gives Work Ethic a clear and vivid definition. Yes, she's got more than an armada of challenge with the health issues, not to say three major papers due after Thanksgiving for her seminary classes—although that's a good thing, for the papers preempt any tests. Sweet. Still, last night was special.

My son, Andrew, made it clear, "Dee [his moniker], PLEASE make your special pumpkin pie." And she did. Not one, or two or three. But six! So all family members will benefit…Andrew and his family and Jennifer's parents as we celebrate this day together. Then her sister… followed, I anticipate, her son and family. Of course, at least one for our own enjoyment.

She worked hours and hours, then made dinner. This was all special given how much strength is compromised by the six surgeries this year. Goodness. She is really remarkable.

Thanksgiving. Not only the joy of sharing it with Diane and extended families. This day, perhaps like no other, triggers memories of so many others who never would be found sloughing—not only the job, but a veritable manner of life.

I think primarily of my parents…Hank and Es…they worked more than anyone I know. My mother would get up early to fix breakfast for my father, do a load or two of wash, some ironing of shirts or pants, get my sister and me up for piano lessons [one of life's less valued chores, for me at least], make us breakfast, lunch for school, then work 8 hours as a secretary for Northwestern Mutual Life, get home and have dinner ready. I cannot remember having any dinner at 6238 N.E. 25th Avenue in Portland when the 4 of us weren't there.

My father never slacked. He would haul garbage five days a week, starting at 5 a.m....and at times on Saturday when a customer had brush or had cleaned their house and boxes stacked high by their garage. And, he NEVER missed a game that I pitched in high school...

In those days garbage hauling was not having the truck load it at the curb...no sirreee. Rather my father would walk to the back of his customers' houses, empty their trash into his barrel, climb stairs on the side of the truck and empty his barrel. Then, when the garbage about spilled over the side of the truck, he would stomp it down. Automation of garbage hauling was still to come.

Work ethic. This morning I think of it...along with Thanksgiving as a child and youth...our family with Uncle Peter and Aunt Pauline and cousins Philip and Molly Beth. At their Gladstone home...sitting around the table...and it was my mother who brought the pumpkin pie. Wow, just thought of that.

It became "our secret," my Uncle Peter and me. Think it started when I was 14. My first drink, something we hushed rather faithfully. I asked for 7-up, but the soda was never clear; rather it had a brown twinge to it. Later as I walked into their kitchen did I see what caused that first "twinged drink on Thanksgiving." I saw the Wild Turkey Bourbon bottle standing on the counter. Aha, I thought it had a rather sweet and yet a new taste. Go figure, right?

But, today is today. And today we'll bring the pumpkin pie. How's that go? *What goes around.....*

And tomorrow, God willing and creeks that don't load over their banks [my version] we'll get to getting to...the projects, the energy.

Because God makes it clear: we are blessed by grace and are asked to not take grace too seriously. Give energy, give effort, make a difference.

Truth? It's a whole lot better than sloth or inertia or letting someone else do what we know is ours to get done.

And, all this, wondering what the dentist saw on my inside cheek and why this wheezing persists. The doctor said I needed an asthmatic inhaler…sign of something new?

THAT we'll see about. But, for today, it's off to Boerne and Andrew and extended family.

A postscript from yesterday that I don't want to forget.

Boerne, Texas, Andrew and family's home, is northwest of San Antonio.

Yesterday at the post office [I get there often to send books off to friends], Guy, one of the really good guys—we have developed more than a "How are you?" exchange, asked, "Where will you spend Thanksgiving?"

Figuring I needed to be his personal Mapquest, I explained where Boerne is.

He smiled, nodded, "Yep, know it well. That's where I was raised. My father built every road and dug every septic system in the county."

Whoa. What a treat to know that. Now, it's getting ready to go to Boerne, Guy's home….and Andrew's.

Crazy world…it shrinks every day.

Favorite Television Show?

Posted on November 26, 2010 by Mark H Miller

I wonder if everyone's got a favorite television program.

No less, did there used to be a cannot miss program and now, it's different?

My own answer goes like this…

As a child, when we were the only player on the block with a television [Portland had no television, but that didn't stop my father. He put up a 30-ft antenna attached to our chimney—it pointed to Seattle and on our BRAND NEW Philco television set we could get snowy pictures only from KING-TV, Channel 5. I loved to watch NBA basketball weekly summary on Sunday afternoons, right after "Victory At Sea." And then, in October I would rush home from Vernon Grade School during lunch break to catch glimpses of the World Series—always on NBC—and try to find the baseball in the snowy screen. Actually scooting home at lunch meant I could have my mother's incredibly tasty toasted cheese and ham sandwiches. Oh, yes, indeed].

Then when Portland got television a popular time was the "Ed Sullivan Show." I always wondered how someone who slurred words excessively could be so popular.

In seminary it was "The Fugitive." Maybe that's where the novel-writing seed got planted—who knows?—when it took so long to find the real killer, one arm and all.

Fast forward, with a surprise.

Pretty much I'm a 206 guy. That's the Direct TV ESPN channel. Or I get to Spurs games or Cubs games…and for sure, even though they're an embarrassment this season, Broncos' games.

Have never focused upon Reality Shows or Survival Shows—not sure why, but maybe it's because they come across as artificial and phony.

Then the surprise. Diane and I are now in our tenth year of marriage. [That's NOT the surprise!!!] There are programs she really loves, each of which I wouldn't pay a minute's attention to, were you to ask me before I met Diane.

Some particular ones are What Not to Wear, HGTV, World's Greatest Loser, Iron Chef.

It struck me this morning, because we had talked about it, how much I value those programs.

For reasons that are both, at least to me, telling and compelling.

What Not To Wear: How life can be transforming...how a person who dresses like an unmade bed or a wedding cake left out in the rain [love those images] and thinks of themselves as being an insult to others, can find meaning in looking more alive and attractive. At the end of the show when the person featured is received home, a powerful moment.

HGTV, programs on buying homes or apartments or renovations: How important it is for the couple to work together, to give and take, to define and be resolute about their values in how much money to spend, where to live and the importance of a house becoming a home.

World's Greatest Loser: The incredible value of realizing, I need to do something about my life and my obesity, and the fact it takes others to help it happen. STAY FOCUSED comes across as a theme for me. For it's much more than losing weight [this winces the day after Thanksgiving, for sure!]; it has to do with living longer and better and enhancing a self-image that bounces on bottom.

Iron Chef: How important, how vital, how absolutely necessary, in whatever you do, to believe it's the most important thing you can do in your life and the necessary ingredient: PASSION. These chefs are the real deal...as they create new dishes, combine ingredients and then get judged. The judgment part, at least for me, is less important than the effort. Oh boy, do they engage the preparation, making sure it works.

Passion—without it is like watching that old Philco and the snowy picture...yep, the program's there, but it lacks focus and purpose.

So, the day after Thanksgiving...nudged by what you like to watch... and now, for me, I'm much more than a 206 guy. That's a good thing. How about you?

The shadow lurks in the hearts of....

Posted on November 27, 2010 by Mark H Miller

Shadow?

My valued friend, Mike Murray, Presbyterian Minister and consultant of the first-rank, shared at breakfast, when we discussed how the untoward sometimes picks our number, "Mark, we really need to realize we all, each of us, has a shadow."

Think I heard that upon more than one occasion, stemming if memory has some benefit, from Karl Jung, the Swiss Psychiatrist.

To this, enter a personal shadow millions witnessed, summarized briefly in Yahoo.com's commentary—ah, if the facts would only be so short-lived:

A game that the Broncos seemingly had in hand slipped away when normally efficient kicker Kyle Brotzman missed a 26-yard field goal with 2 seconds left in regulation and another from 29 yards in overtime.

Background is Boise State, marching like a steamroller through their football season, ranked #4 in the nation, played in Reno against the University of Nevada, ranked #19. At stake was the highest bowl games, BCS focused. Great honor, highest recognition, and to the participating school, financial bonanza, something like $1 million above expenses.

In only their first game against Virginia Tech, was Boise State challenged. Every other game was "over" no later than midway in each third quarter.

Last night they were well ahead of Nevada going into the 3rd quarter.

Then the game turned. And Boise State's status was "brinking." With 9 seconds left in a tied game, Boise State had one final play. Inexplicably to Nevada fans, not to say their coach, Boise State's stellar quarterback completed a sensational pass ending up on Nevada's 9 yard line with 2 seconds remaining.

Enter Brotzman, college football's leading scorer, to kick a game-winning field goal, to at least secure his team's #4 ranking and a possible BCS championship game date in January.

But. No.

The kick was wide right.

Overtime.

A second chance for Brotzman in overtime, but a field goal went wide left.

Nevada then had their chance for a score and took advantage of the overtime with their field goal kicker winning the game.

Personally I wasn't bothered by Nevada's victory, because it could mean a BCS bowl bid to Stanford, should they beat Oregon State today. [Yes, a son of Oregon is okay to root against Oregon State today.]

But deeper, what a horrible experience for Kyle Brotzman.

Devastating.

In reflecting upon this, partnered with my morning breakfast with Mike Murray, it IS the case we each have a shadow, at least one moment we'd love to erase, delete, make "un-happen."

However, let's be honest. It's probably the case, when we remember a person, the FIRST THING that comes to mind is the dramatic moment...think Simpson and a white Bronco speeding on a LA freeway...think Woods driving into a tree on Thanksgiving evening... think Buckner "erroring" the Mets grounder to lose the game for the Red Sox.

Well, what of it? What do we do with a Buckner moment? With the shadow?

Truth reigning, I'm not sure.

Truth reigning, people are going to remember what they remember. We cannot do anything with it, not really.

Truth reigning, stuff happens to everyone...often beyond delusion which we often author.

It happens.

And, we can get guiltier than is reasonable. Much guiltier.

Just have two responses this 2nd day after Thanksgiving...actually three.

First, guilt at its deepest level is our judgment of ourselves. It really is. WE can keep a shadowed moment a ruling force.

Second, I try to not get frozen in time, but do what can be done to live, excuse the phrase, beyond any "shadow of doubt." Maybe that's why my horrible sense of guilt in missing a panel discussion with Dr. Martin Luther King, Jr. in August of 1958, was lessened considerably when the first steps I took as an ordained minister in July of 1966 was to walk close to Dr. King up State Street in Chicago in support of Civil Rights. Didn't serve as an erasure, but helped remove the mantel of failure from my head.

And third, not let any moment define our lives. Rather, life is the fullness of living every day. To know that down deep, especially when we miss a field goal, makes life not so bad after all. The inner shadows are there, but that should never mean our lives, how they are lived, are without light...for ourselves and through our living, for others.

Impact for the good? We may never know.

Posted on November 28, 2010 by Mark H Miller

Here's my guess. My guess is we don't realize, and a good chance we'll never know, how we impact others for the good. But it does happen upon occasion, rare as it is, we learn of a favorable moment.

I have a clergy friend who preached an Advent sermon. She learned the sermon transformed a couple that Sunday. They were depressed beyond words because their only son, their day-brightening son, was serving in Vietnam. Every day was dark and windy and worse than chilling. They had decided to not purchase a Christmas tree that December…didn't have the spirited heart for same.

After the sermon, the minister learned years later, the couple sat in the car and said to each other, "We can have hope—the sermon explained it—yes she preached a wonderful sermon today." They then drove to a cut-your-own-Christmas-tree-farm and purchased a tree.

Impact for the good.

Another clergy friend met a former parishioner at a clergy conference. He hadn't seen her for 20 years and was surprised to see the parishioner at a clergy event. He then was told, "You probably don't know this, because I haven't shared it before, but you preached a sermon twenty years ago that changed my life. I had been wrestling with the question of God's will in my life and your sermon told me—heard it as God's voice—that I should attend seminary. So I did and now I'm in ministry for 15 years. Thanks for that sermon."

Humorous part of this, the clergy friend shared, neither of them could remember anything specific about the sermon.

Still another clergy friend [I realize it does appear that my only friends beyond extended family are clergy or fishing guides!] shared that he saved a former parishioner's life without knowing it. My friend had been on a long trip with family. When he returned home the phone rang. He answered it and it was this long-time-ago parishioner. The clergy friend was hassled with other things and indicated he couldn't talk now. Actually he shared he was rude and didn't move beyond the "How are you?, Fine, thanks" social greeting and hung up.

What he learned months later the former parishioner planned to commit suicide that very day and simply wanted to call her former pastor to say good-bye. She was so infuriated by the rude reception, anger took over and she stalled the suicide. It is still stalled according to my friend.

It occurs to me this day, November 28, the first Sunday of Advent, that there's much in our life and through our living, where we impact for the good.

The key is not to think of ourselves as people of impact, though. The key is to simply live as fully and well as we can…hoping people will be impacted, even if we hang up abruptly. Truth is much we'll never know.

That's just fine.

What's not just fine is to hold back because we don't think we matter.

And.

When someone's blessed us, when someone's offered a soft/kind word of caring/hope, it wouldn't hurt to let them know. Because at times to let them know is more than appreciated.

Blaming God

Posted on November 29, 2010 by Mark H Miller

I PRAISE YOU 24/7!!!...AND THIS HOW YOU DO ME!!!YOU EXPECT ME TO LEARN FROM THIS??? I'LL NEVER LEARN FROM THIS!!!HOW???I'LL NEVER FORGET THIS!!!ILL NEVER FORGET THIS. THX THO... Steve Johnson Twitter on November 28, 2010

The sportswriter's commentary: *Players always thank God after a victory, so it's sort of refreshing to see one blame Him after a loss. Not that I think the Almighty is overly concerned with sporting events or played any role in Johnson taking his eyes off the ball, but I'm glad Steve Johnson does. It must be nice to live a consequence-free environment where all errors can be blamed on a supreme being. I'm trying that next time I get pulled over for speeding.* Chris Chase, Shutdown Corner Sports Blog

Ah, November 29, 2010 is the date on the calendar. The above two quotes were taken from Yahoo.com's NFL report page. I course it every day on my way to the Denver Post summary [now considered an obituary] of the Broncos' latest debacle.

The back story is Steve Johnson's a wide receiver for the Buffalo Bills, a team that is better than the Broncos, which doesn't say much quite honestly. At any rate, though, they played the Pittsburgh Steelers yesterday...it was overtime which means the first team to score wins. The Buffalo quarterback threw a perfect pass to Johnson, who flat-out dropped it in the end zone —no defender close enough to matter. Catch it and "all praise to God" I imagine.

But now. To blame God? As Chris Chase offers in his commentary, that is a new approach.

The narrative, though, shallows out. To not let that happen is to ask, *What is God's role in our living?*

I was asked that once by a very good friend, Sam Smith, then the Chicago Bulls' basketball writer for the *Chicago Tribune*, on the place of

God in sports. Question pondered, "Does God help the winning team more than the losing team?"

My own bloggish answer is this: God is with us, God cares about how we are. BUT. [I like to believe the deeper notion always follows the conjunctive "but."] God is not going to intervene in a game's dynamics, no more than God forces the results.

That doesn't mean God doesn't care or isn't involved. Not at all.

That doesn't mean God isn't impacting the Korea's this morning. I am grateful South Korea has cancelled their artillery show on the blighted island. For sure.

I've never seen God as favoring one side. God favors each person, that each person lives in a full manner, as I like to offer, a worthier manner of life [thanks to the Apostle Paul], and for me personally, a manner that reflects the spirit and life-world of Jesus.

To consider that it's God's fault is lame. Very lame.

Whenever I played baseball, before I warmed up in a game, I went by myself and prayed, "God, thank you for gifting me as a baseball pitcher. I will do my best. May I know you are with me."

Pray for victory? Never.

Blame God for losing. Double-never.

Thank God for life. Always. No matter how each day unfolds.

I wonder. Steve Johnson wears number 13. Wonder if he'll blame the number the next time. Rather, than deal with the truth. He dropped the pass. God's hand didn't intervene.

Postscript:

Goodness. All this on November 29, 2010. A day very special to me. Not because of a ranting professional football player. But, because on this day in 1934, seventy-six years ago by my simple mathematics, Henry Miller and Esther Schnell entered into the covenant of marriage… and six years later, June 17, 1940, their son was born. Baptised him *Mark Henry Miller* and on that day, Mark's father broke all precedent and didn't let the godparents, two aunts, carry him forward to the baptismal font. "Nope," offered Hank Miller, "he's my son and I'm holding him."

Turns out that was the first Sunday Hank Miller started to attend church every Sunday.

And I bet. I double-bet. Whenever Hank Miller's son was clobbered, sent to the bench because of bad pitches, Hank Miller never pointed a finger at God, "It's YOUR fault!"

Nah, no way.

But what Hank Miller did is ask, "What can we learn from this?" He asked that as we stood in the family driveway, he with the catcher's mitt and I with the pitcher's glove. He held the glove where the fast ball was to be targeted and then the curve ball. If Hank's son missed, the garage door felt the tennis ball, *smack.* The trick was to have as few *smacks* as possible.

But, never, ever, ever to blame God.

Not just another day…never is

Posted on November 30, 2010 by Mark H Miller

Ever had a day…or a sequence of thoughts…when it's like your world is swirling and you don't know why?

Which leads to unsequentialed but not inconsequential thoughts.

Today we see the radiologist, learning the specifics for Diane's radiation. The oncologist mentioned it would be seven weeks at 5x/week, but we'll see. What strikes me in this is not the radiation. Not the cancer. Not the uncertainty. Not the, now make it seven surgical procedures Diane's had this year, the last three taking on the breast cancer. What strikes me is her character, her tenacity, her absolute refusal to whine and moan. She, unlike many parishioners and clergy with whom I have worked over the years—make that decades—never has begged an answer, "Why me? God, what have I done wrong?"

Fortunately her theology doesn't paint God as a scorekeeper with a whistle lanyarded around God's neck. That doesn't mean she's repressed in feelings or inexpressive of thoughts and hope and concerns. But, she deals with reality with more reality than musing on what might be. She's focused, clear on her faith and her future. *In a word, she may not know what the future holds, but she knows who holds that future.* And it isn't she or I.

That's good stuff.

Another tact.

I just heard a commentary from the most provoking and profound sports commentator, Colin Cowherd, who pointed out, *we live in results-oriented society.* His example is Lebron James, people saying now that the well-publicized Miami Heat are barely above .500 this season, about James, "He's a loser!" Well, my take is their team has losses, but that doesn't mean he's a loser. Cowherd pointed out how can he be a loser when he won the NBA's Most Valuable Player twice and the Cavaliers won the most league games two years running?

My companion reflection would be on the Denver Broncos. They are dreadful with a 3-8 record. But, that doesn't mean that Kyle Orton the quarterback or the players are losers.

Further reminds me the first year I played high school baseball. Our team was miserable, winning one game. That summer [circa 1950 something or other] we lost one game in American Legion play.

How come? The win/loss record indicates whether or not you are a loser? I don't believe that.

My consideration is losing and winning have to do with the journey and not the destination. The question is, far more for me, *Do you give a damn? Do you have passion? Are you the best you can be? Have you given a real/full effort?*

Of course, winning is more fun and more recognized. But, just because the game is lost, does that mean entitlement to "loser"?

Not on my watch.

So, bring on the radiation. Cheer for effort.

And life, the rest of today, all of tomorrow and all the tomorrows that are be? Look out, baby, because here we come. You bet.

What prompts this is not sports or cancer. What prompts this is my God…who's never worn a referee's shirt and doesn't own a whistle. And who says, "I know your name. I will not forget it. I am with you…no matter what."

That's worth celebrating…living in the *no matter what*.

Open Letter to Senator John McCain

Posted on December 1, 2010 by Mark H Miller

December 1, 2010

Dear Senator McCain:

For many reasons I respect you—as a serviceman who gave fully of himself so our country could maintain freedom and justice—as an imprisoned soldier who gave tenacity and courage their clearest definition—as a Senator serving our country with energy and intelligence. There is no doubt in my mind that your thoughts and your votes are neither shallow nor reactionary.

In all this, although I respect you, my support is not without exception.

I urge you to reconsider your stated position in opposition to repealing the ***don't ask don't tell*** policy of our United States Military. It is more than the strong survey results of more than 40,000 military personnel serving our country, the majority of whom urge repeal. It is more than our U.S. House of Representatives who voted to repeal the policy.

The real issue is primarily about the sexual orientation of homosexuality. For it is my persuasion, admittedly a perception and not documented person by person, MOST of those against the repeal are really against homosexuality, maintaining homosexuality is wrong—wrong biblically and immoral sexually.

As a point of reference I am not homosexual. I am, though, an ordained minister in the United Church of Christ, a denomination who maintains, and has since 1972 when Bill Johnson, an openly gay seminarian, was ordained, that ordination doesn't pivot on sexual orientation, but upon a call from God, and that for anyone seeking ordination the issue of sexuality in a covenantal relationship requires fidelity and integrity.

More to the point, a biblical cause championed against homosexuality is particularized. It stems from the book of Leviticus that also mandates it is corrupting to eat shrimp and wear "mixed cloth," which gives polyester no chance.

Specifically most people condemning homosexuality based upon scripture are selective literalists—that is, they take their persuasion [read that bias] to the biblical narrative and not the reverse. In addition, in no manner or content does Jesus Himself speak against homosexuality. Rather, His declaration for a worthier manner of life emphasizes caring for the other as God cares for each of us, God's beloved sons or daughters.

My own position is firm: *one's sexual orientation is not a decision; it is a discovery.* I do not believe, haven't ever in fact, that homosexuality is a sin. Rather whether heterosexual or homosexual is who a person is…created by God…and encouraged in a monogamous relationship to be faithful.

Not for a moment do I believe the survey is wrong. Nor do I believe any man or woman wanting to serve our country through military commitment, who is resolved to defend our liberty as a serviceman or servicewoman, should be kept from doing so because of sexual orientation.

I encourage you to reconsider your opposition to the repeal.

With respect and regards, I remain cordially yours,

Dr. Mark Henry Miller

What's important? Knowing why…maybe yes and maybe no

Posted on December 1, 2010 by Mark H Miller

There are times…probably more than musing or "only occasionally"—when I wonder why something is important.

Certainly the obvious is not puzzling: wanting Diane to move past the radiation and find 2011 to lack health-issue-barraging. Really. Seven surgical procedures in one year? Unrelenting. Nothing more important than to have that only viewed in the rear-view mirror.

Other health issues will certainly not remain hidden, but the cancer-reality is crucial to manage.

What we have found is EVERY doctor and most nurses [one had an overbearing-ness but I was hesitant to ask her if she ever heard of Nurse Ratched] are better than competent and caring. They bring a human presence along with their medical expertise. And, that's important.

They care, their heart is not hidden and their focus—to bring health—is never blurred. I am impressed—very much so—at what a difference it makes to have a doctor who knows what the medical needs for healing are and with it, no compromise in being a caring presence. In fact, I told one physician that I "sense you have a pastor's heart." His pause and blinking eyes reflected his appreciation and not his *do you know what you're talking about?*

Although in the medical terrain, probably shifting from humor to truth, I shared with Diane that coursing through 2010 we've become acquainted with almost every medical department at Austin Diagnostic Clinic. And the follow-up: for myself, if this is what happens at 70, becoming 80 can take its own sweet time.

I don't wonder why it's important to have a book published, why it's important that I am considering re-entry into interim ministry and looking forward to my next fishing junket, to be spent with one of my most favorite guides.

In all these realities, there is one accomplishment that speaks volumes to me of the importance of 2010. And, for the life of me, I am not clear why. Maybe one reading this can muse and respond definitively the "why-ness" of it.

I feel really good—and Diane and I spoke to it because it's good for her, too—that in 2010 we cleaned our garage.

That doesn't mean we are sloppy people, that we relish the disorganized. To think that of me is to be virtually clueless. Even though my thoughts may dash and dart like a water-bug zagging across a pond, I am well organized.

It feels good to come home and find, at least in the garage, everything's in its place. That means when I need a Phillip's screwdriver [I was probably a teenager before I learned the Phillip's screwdriver wasn't a special drink] I can find it. When I need to get the Christmas decorations, I can find them.

The garage is no longer this and that hiding in some stuffed corner.

Why is that important? Not sure. But I know it is.

And then it's important the red ants don't have a chance. And, it's important to know our beloved dog Gracie should never have turkey. We'll remember that. But, that's for another day.

How about you? What makes your "important in 2010" list?

More than a flash of light...much more

Posted on December 2, 2010 by Mark H Miller

Last night's headline brought back a memory, fresh as yesterday but distant in time by 42 years.

Chicago shutters infamous public housing project.

It went on to say that two families remained and refused to vacate—but would be forced out quickly.

The housing project, Cabrini-Green, was home for thousands of families when I arrived in Chicago for my first ministry, circa 1966. As you might surmise, "housing project" was somewhat euphemistic for "Negroes only." Shed all euphemisms...it was the northside ghetto.

Cabrini-Green on the northside of Chicago's Loop [downtown] was south of North Avenue.

North Avenue, running from the lake west through the Chicago suburbs was more than a mile wide when it came to housing. If you were white you lived north and if not? Well, you know what that meant.

The memory that comes back was an evening when racial tensions were more than evident. Chicago was a breath or two from exploding.

On the remembered night we had a youth meeting at our St. Pauls Church located on Fullerton Parkway, about a mile north of North Avenue. Two of our high school youth, Leo and George Blevins, hard workers in our summer day camp program, great for the group spirit, lived with their mother in Cabrini-Green.

Because racial tensions were on overload I offered to have them stay in our apartment that night, rather than be in danger by going home. Their mother was home with other family surrounding her.

She was insistent...and I understood completely, "Pastor Miller, please bring my babies home."

I drove them to the curb of Cabrini-Green, offered to walk with them to their building's entrance. I'm pretty sure I wore a clergy collar, because it was important to us clergy to be identifiable. They said they'd be fine. I noticed two police cars parked just ahead, their lights dimmed, the exhaust evident.

I stayed in the car...watched until Leo and George went into the building...a high building as I recall of at least ten floors, maybe higher.

Because it was cold I had my heater on full blast and windows closed. Just before they entered their building I saw two flashes of light, not knowing what that was all about.

After I returned home Leo called, "Mark, did you see what happened?"

Not sure his reference, I asked for more.

A frozen moment for me when he continued, "Mark, there were two rifle shots that smashed windows above our building's entrance when we walked in. We are afraid, but other family is with us, so we'll be okay."

Now, to this day...triggered by the announcement today that Cabrini-Green is no longer and the two remaining families will be forced out in the next day or so...I remember that night.

I cannot say who fired the shots. Leo and George had their theory. You can guess their belief. I couldn't verify, but I knew that racial tensions caused horrible, horrible conflict.

Not a good memory. And, I cannot say I have any idea where and how Leo and George are this day as the life/world/realities of Cabrini-Green end. I know that George wanted to be a Chicago policeman and I did what I could to encourage that. However, after that night, his hopes for wearing a police badge lessened. And I knew why.

Dumbing down...not always helpful

Posted on December 3, 2010 by Mark H Miller

William Sloane Coffin, the one whom I quote the most frequently, once said, so Coffinesque—laced with humor and girded with truth, "Think how many great things have been done in life by people not smart enough to know they weren't logical or even possible."

That preaches. At times dumbing-down is not imprudent.

The other side of that, an inquiry by a friend as we exchanged perceptions on how ministry can happen, "What are the dumbest things you've done in ministry?"

Triggered a whole mess of thoughts.

This would be in the "If I had to do it over" world.

First a qualifier. To answer another question, "Would you want to start over again, say at age five?", my answer would be an escalating and bold NO! Because that would mean most likely there would be no current friends. Even more, no Diane or Matthew or Andrew. Nope, it is what it was, what it is and what it will be.

But, to do over. Yep, if only I hadn't dumbed down.

First, was to go to a church where I was promised, even entitled, "Senior Minister Designate" [within 2 years when the current minister would retire] and it never happened. Wasn't ever going to happen. And, of all things, I discovered that in less than two weeks after my arrival when the schedule of rotating Sundays for preaching got tossed out the window. Could have been an entry in the Guinness Book of World Records for shortest tenured ministry.

But it wasn't.

The good part of that is it fueled me to explore other "manner of ministry as pastor of the congregation," which meant a television talk show [No, Johnny Carson wasn't threatened, but still, 30 minutes each week with guests who knew a lot of about the ill effects of war, poverty, racism, homophobia was valued, a fine personal learning experience.], establishing a shelter for battered women so exile to the streets wasn't needed, a youth hostel, a committee to grant scholarships to parents on welfare so they could attend the local community college and membership on the city's Human Rights Commission. No time for self-pity. None.

The blockage led to an expansion of ministry, led to a partnering with kindred social justice-advocates. The rejection changed my understanding of how ministry might be relevant…and goodness, even liberating. Sometimes when you don't get what you want and end up with what you need—that's a good thing.

One other [of the many, many others] "do it over, please," was really stupid.

It was my first ministry in Chicago. One of my prime responsibilities was to be Director of a Children's Summer Day Camp which St. Pauls hosted. It was quite an exciting event: six weeks, mid-July through mid-August, Tuesday-Thursday, 11 a.m. to 5 p.m. with 120 kids ages 7-12 and 20 high school counselors and lots and lots of adults leading workshops.

Every Thursday we'd take a field trip, helping the kids [and the rest of us for sure] appreciate how great a city Chicago is. Being on the northside meant, of course we'd take 'em one day to Wrigley Field to cheer for the beloved Chicago Cubs.

The day was perfect…sitting along the left field foul line, the temperature about 75 and humidity unnoticeable, which in Chicago summertime was rare. The Assistant Director ailed that day so my solo responsibility was to make sure no one ran onto the field or purchased too many hot dogs.

The illusion of perfection [how silly but who would know?] took over.

Perfect until James got sick.

James was a 7 year old and lived in a broken down walk-up south of North Avenue. [In those days North Avenue was a mile wide. That is, African-Americans lived south of North Avenue. One of the joys of the Summer Day Camp is we bused 30 kids from that area for the program, giving Rainbow Coalition early evidence of being possible.]

Here comes Mr. Stupid-Decision. James was sick, so I took him to the corner of Addison/Clark/Wrigley Field and hailed a cab—gave the cabdriver the address and some money and asked him to make sure James got home.

Hello? Did I do that? Would I do it differently had I the chance?

No doubt. No double-doubt.

The more I thought of how absolutely absurd my judgment, I left Wrigley Field and drove to James' residence. A couple of adults were sitting on the porch. I asked, "Is James….here?"

They looked blank.

I died emotionally on the spot. Ohmygoodness, it's the wrong address, Trouble-City is now my residence. [My thoughts were not G rated in self-judgment.]

I looked at my address roster, saw the number over the front door. They matched.

With my heart about to stop, my legs shakily moving up the stairs, with fear abounding I knocked on the 3rd floor door. I could hear children squealing.

One of them opened the door. It was James. His mother, standing with him, "Yes, can I help you?"

James munched on a hot dog. It wasn't from Wrigley Field.

I started to cry. Relief never tasted so good.

But stupid does what stupid is. At least then.

The lesson was learned. Big-time.

And it could have been so much more ominous.

But it wasn't.

Grace reigned, fear subsided and a HUGE prayer of Thanksgiving echoed all my way home.

The Folly of Christmas…or is it?

Posted on December 4, 2010 by Mark H Miller

Through the years, my life has been blessed and graced by clergy colleagues. Upon many an occasion—I think now of my last pastorate when I met weekly [which was better than weakly] with two clergy, when we could share the intimacies of the struggles and never fear—never once—that anything would be made "unconfidential." In that same period, a time of particular stress and conflict, to meet monthly with clergy colleagues who also served large congregations as senior pastor—meant the world. It was never an ego-drill, never, "How many in church yesterday?" Forget, "Did the pledges increase?" Always the focus was upon the inner self and how we breathed without breaking up inside.

Today I learned a dimension of ministry-benefit that has always been there, but came to me with such clarity and value—that is, writings from a beautiful friend. Her name is Joanne Carlson Brown, a Methodist pastor in Seattle, who when I served as Transitional Interim Conference Minister [how's that for a crazy title—that ends up being TICM. Say it out loud and try not to laugh!], served one of our congregations that was United Church of Christ and Methodist. Joanne's now serving a Methodist Congregation in West Seattle…and serving it with such passion and skill and insight—especially into how the seasons of the year can be times of nurture and growth.

Today I read her Advent message…it came to my heart and soul and mind…so much so I now want it included in my Blog…she writes so well, even brilliantly. And yet, it's common stuff that stirs the soul and quickens the step. So, in advance, Dr. Brown Herself, thanks for this… and even more, for your abiding friendship to both Diane and me. It means the world to us.

Here go some powerful reflections:

She begins with the well-labored-complaints of Christmas: it's phony, it's too jolly, too commercial, too much too much, with the capstone those who find Christmas a lacking-value because it's a myth. This Christmas

85

narrative, how can you not be confused between the contradictions of Luke and Matthew? And the whole "virgin" thing and the "choirs of angels?" Really.

Joanne responds in this manner:

Yep, I agree, Christmas is a heck of a thing to base a religion on.

Because the Christmas story is about the most important thing in the universe—love. God's love for the world. God's love becomes incarnate in a little baby and in the love of a mother and a father. In the wonder of shepherds, and in shining stars. The Bible is a book of faith, not fact. It is the sacred story of how the world came to be and how we are to live our lives. It calls us to think, to imagine and to act out of trust in God. The Christmas story releases our spirit to fly and to remind us we are not alone. It introduces us to another world, rich with values and wonder, a sense of something beyond, more to life than possessions and competition, leading us to the God who loves us.

I believe that what isn't used, exercised, appreciated, becomes useless, dormant, dead. Without faith imagination how do we recognize the angel's announcement, the dream, the song, the call, in our own lives here and now?

Faith helps us ask: How am I related to Mary or Joseph, the shepherds of the magi, Herod or Simeon, John or Jesus? Why did Mary believe the angel's announcement? Why did Joseph believe his dream? Why did the shepherds believe the song of the angelic host? Why did the wise men follow a star, believing it would lead them to a king? By faith imagination we enter into the heart of Mary to hear the good news, "You will give birth to the incarnation of God here and now; into the heart of Joseph to hear. You must believe." Into the hearts of shepherds, "Be not afraid. Go and see what God has done..."

The Christmas story gives visible form to our faith. And when we see it with the eyes of faith and hear it with the ears of our heart we will know the truth of the story.

One of my favorite carols goes:

Love came down at Christmas; Love all lovely, love divine; love was born at Christmas; star and angels gave the sign. Love shall be our token; love be yours and love be mine; love to God and neighbor, love for plea and gift and sign.

This Christmas, hear the story and let it live in your faith imagination to become new in your heart and mind; hear the story and know its truth—the truth of love incarnate, the truth of Emmanuel, God-with-us. And let us live the gift of love for all, even the bah humbuggers.

Writing...more than a good idea

Posted on December 5, 2010 by Mark H Miller

Last week I had a delightful conversation with a newspaper writer of the Tillamook, Oregon Headlight-Herald. She had learned one of the novels, "Murder On Tillamook Bay," will be published in 2011 and since the venue is her city with the action taking place on Tillamook Bay itself, she wanted to learn what she could.

I was flattered by her interest. Even more, though, found her questions to be very helpful to help me think through why I enjoy writing and how it all started.

Not to narrate the history of my first novel's opening chapter, the question most highlighted for me was her asking, "Why do you write?"

I didn't hesitate, "Truth is, Laura, when I write I grow. When I write the thoughts get focused and the connection to our current pulse and the way in which we walk the human landscape makes more sense—at least to me."

I hope that for others, in the very least.

To the end of growth of one's life, the question for each person perusing these Blog reflections: why do you do what you do? Does it help you improve...does it help, as a friend once offered, to increase your stature?

The sadness I often experience inside where the soul pulses and the heart paces is when people say they are not happy [that's the polite public version] and then share privately, "My life is dreadful, I cannot find ANYTHING worth doing. " [They always say anything louder].

As a novelist once wrote about his main character who was losing at every effort, no hope in sight, "My life is one long suicide."

I don't know what to say...really what to say.

What Laura asked, though, triggered a hope. Especially now that it's Advent. The hope is this: somehow people are able to know their value is not what others think, is not waking up each new day, is not anything other than to know they weren't created for nothing.

When Laura and I visited, I found in her own world, a new world of being a newspaper reporter, she couldn't say how it would go. But she knew, and conveyed it in a gentle but clear and firm way, she would do her best.

So this. Even when things are bleak...and often Advent is that, which is why there's a Blue Christmas service in many churches on the longest day, December 21...I recall a cartoon...it showed a man, bulky overcoat and heavy scarf, walking through a storm. He looked down at his only visible foot, his right foot, and exclaimed, "Anytime now the left foot will come into view."

Sometimes that's all we can watch for.

But, you know what? That's better than not looking, not seeking, not wanting and not hoping. It sure is.

How about you? What makes for growth...and hope...and life? Is the other foot coming into view?

Parenting…when it splinters rather than strengthens

Posted on December 6, 2010 by Mark H Miller

The mother made it clear, caps for what I sensed, "DON'T YOU EVER LISTEN TO ME? GET OVER HERE! NOW! YOU NEVER MIND…WILL YOU EVER?!"

The boy, no more than 4, had walked aimlessly toward the mirror at the end of the fitness center—instead of going with his mother to the nursery.

Her intemperance was in override, her patience vacated. Her shouting got attention as folk stopped lifting weights and shook their heads in disbelief.

All the while she held the cell phone to her ear and ran at her son, pointed to him as if her arm was a sword, grabbed his arm and jerked it as his head snapped the other way. I'm glad his arm was secure to his shoulder.

She then talked into the cell phone, "Just a minute—we have an attitude here." Woman, I sure say so…AN ATTITUDE. Yours is reprehensible, unconscionable. My word…where's he going to go? He just liked seeing himself in the mirror…other parental tactics could have been more effective.

She still had the phone to her ear as she demanded the son to open the nursery door for her.

Yep, I thought it…I know EXACTLY where to put that phone.

Of course I thought against it, but then pondered, Gosh, if the apple doesn't fall far from the tree…I sure as the world hope that tree is on a steep hill.

About 40 minutes later leaving Target, I was still thinking about that miserable-acting mother [honestly I couldn't care less what the child might have done…her methods/manner was ugly—one of my prayers

90

would be that, "Dear God, may the child not grow up like his mother."] and then noticed a new dynamic leaving the store ahead of me.

It was a mother and son...they had finished shopping and the 6 year old was holding a bag. As the automatic door opened, the mother in a very gentle/loving manner tussled her son's hair and said, "Look! The door opened for us again!"

They then walked to their car with the mother's arm around her son's shoulders and the boy with an arm, hugging his mother.

They parked next to me. I couldn't be muted, getting the mother's attention, "Ma'am...I watched how you and your son left the store...how caring you were. That is probably very common for you...but it's a new picture of a mother and son for me today. Just wanted you to know I appreciated it."

What I bet...that tree is on level ground. Good.

Okay...what to do with this?

What I figure is certainly families need discipline...everyone in the family does. But what happens when it's the mother or father who needs more discipline than the children? Why? Because not every apple tree sits on the top of a steep hill.

And in the mix of it...maybe we can help...even those whom we don't know...to tell them when they've helped, "Thanks for that." Today the cashier and the guy bringing in the shopping carts from the lot each smiled. A kind word was said by a customer to each. I overheard both... and saw the appreciation.

I didn't say thanks to the lady in the fitness center. It boiled my blood. And I felt for the child...hopefully that exchange was exceptional...in terms of both its pattern and its frequency.

But, maybe not.

Which means then we hope for steep hills when apples tumble.

Yester-decades…never forgotten

Posted on December 7, 2010 by Mark H Miller

This is not the triumph of hubris. Rather, it is the exaltation of gratitude.

Mentioned previously, with cause not clear or necessary, I've done my best to contact friends of decades past to inquire of their well-being. No less, as you would imagine, to share the world Diane and I experience.

It has been the most wonderful experience…make that experiences.

For instance, today I heard from Linda—she and her husband Dave were youth group advisors for our church when I was leading the youth ministry program. Goodness, that was 40 years ago. Forty! And their daughter is one week younger than my son, Andrew. It was delightful to hear how they are doing…and it was the, as Texan imaging provides, the full enchilada, her coursing through life and death and all the breaths in between.

So many more have been kind enough to reply.

One caught me by surprise…a phone call, that began, a deep voice that almost sounded like it was being altered with one of those voice-changing devices always in murder/mysteries, "Bet you don't know who this is."

Since it sounded like no one I could even guess about, and since I thought if I named someone and be very wrong the conversation would result in a clicked disconnection, I agreed with his bet.

Turns out it was Neil…who lived a block away from our home in Portland. He learned my number from one of my Oregon fishing guides and called. We remembered various early child events, most of which would never make a blog, and probably truth pushing, a confessional. Still, decades later we could laugh, especially since he got all his marbles back [not a metaphor] when his older brother hammered on our back door and demanded them. Great memories reminding me

92

that to achieve perfection is not a worthy goal; to live life fully is, with or without marbles.

Then a high school baseball coach...still alive in his late 80's. And of all things, he remembered one night in Portland—summer American Legion high school baseball—when for reasons I'll never know, the fast ball zipped and the curve ball zagged and he said, "You've got it tonight!" He remembered that! I hadn't reminded him.

Followed a week later in a letter from a baseball teammate who was the relief pitcher saving victory in my last game pitched [circa 1962]... he was also my mother's boss with Northwestern Mutual Life and he agreed with my perception that Es Miller was an angel impersonating a human being.

One of my former church secretaries who was so competent and caring and who always had a greater willingness to understand than a need to judge.

Still another a former professor who counseled in writing novels to NEVER [he will appreciate the caps] use an exclamation point...if you write well you won't need it...who responded today with some editing help on a synopsis of a novel and then shared their family's joy their daughter has accepted a full athletic scholarship [swimming] to Stanford, to begin next fall. I couldn't resist by replying with everything in exclamation points on congratulating their daughter. Hope he got the humor!!!

On it goes.

Two reasons for focusing on this today...one, to hear that in each life there has never been a jump, to put it metaphorically, from Palm Sunday to Easter. Maundy Thursday and Good Friday are in there... always—but in each life there's been horrific moments, times of dread when it appears tomorrow's dawn is an uncertainty. In EACH CASE, though, my friends and former colleagues are living in the fullness of the day and giving thanks for their journey and testify by their current worthy manner of life, Good Friday doesn't win. Hasn't, doesn't and won't.

Second reason: to suggest that it's a good use of time to track down friends from yester-decades and say hello…maybe none of us knows Clint Eastwood, but still, *it's a great way to make your day…and theirs!*

Today–infamy and a new fly rod and radiation

Posted on December 7, 2010 by Mark H Miller

Ohmygoodness. Today is a day with a fullness of events and history… and in a moment, a discovery that will mean I need to buy a new fly rod.

Most importantly, today Diane begins radiation. She's done significant research on what effects radiation has, knowing, of course, each person is different. It is apparent, though, the most common consequence is fatigue, that tends to be accumulative. That is, at first it's not a factor. But what we've learned…in reading and in conversation with those who have walked in those moccasins…by the end of radiation there is the experience labeled fatigue-heavy.

We know that radiation is not optional. We are grateful chemotherapy will not be necessary, that the lymph nodes were clear and the cancer-tumor was 1 centimeter, less than ½ inch. We hope, pray and trust the radiation will be effective and the side effects minimal. However, for sure, Diane's so very strong emotionally and spiritually she will be the embodiment of resolution and tenacity that the radiation, though real for at least six weeks, will not be daunting.

Today in 1941, ten days short of my first birthday, was Pearl Harbor, with its devastating impact upon so many. In knowing this from reading—never did experience it through close family members—it had to be horrendous. The memory of that triggers what's deep within me: challenging the necessity of war.

A year ago while serving in an interim ministry the son of the organist stepped on a land mine in Afghanistan. His death [a West Point graduate—I only met him one Sunday a few months before his death—it was clear he was one of the finest people you could ever know] shook everyone. We honored him with two funeral services, which were very inspirational. And yet, down deep, I could only ponder the why-ness of our being in Afghanistan? That is NOT to disregard or disrespect Paul's faithful serving of our country. It is only to ask the larger question, triggered by this day, December 7, 1941, 69 years later.

I'm looking forward to lunch. It's with a former parishioner for whom I have such respect. It will be good to get caught-up. Included will be what I'm sure will be a helpful conversation on how radiation impacted him…he had prostate cancer and is now, at least conveyed by the recent tests, cancer-free. Well, as Diane informs me, none of us is ever "cancer-free" because the cells lurk in each of us. It's simply a matter for my friend the cancer cells cannot get along with each other. I know. That's not medical, but hey, if it works, write it.

Another part of today will be to look for a new fly rod and reel.

Cause for same, I have a commitment. Well, first it's a self-designation: I proudly acclaim that I will be EACH of my grandchildren's fly-casting coach. In the closet still, since the grandchildren are pre-casting-age, are five fly rods and reels. Well, we learned yesterday that Jason and Teela are expecting their third child next summer. They are parents to our 3 year old twin grandsons, Aiden and Jackson. And, I'm assuming that only one new fly rod should be ordered.

But, I think I'll wait a few months to make sure more than one additional fly rod will not be necessary!

Ingratitude management

Posted on December 8, 2010 by Mark H Miller

Not sure why, but the following has happened…and has not led me to clap and cheer.

Spent hours and hours combing through 70 years of pictures, grouped them for key family members and friends who can redistribute to their own children or buddies, went to a camera shop and had pictures put on a DVD and sent them. Lots of DVD's, which felt good, that a new album might result.

But it probably won't.

Discovered a very insightful Yahoo.com article about the ten most important questions teenagers are asking. Copied it and sent to a minister who works with youth, thinking it might be a discussion catalyst.

But most likely I'll never know.

Sent some copies of "Hooked On Life" to friends, listed as gifts. No invoice was attached or mentioned. Hope they enjoy the gift.

But most likely I'll never know.

And, in each instance, now more than a month later, there's not been one word acknowledging receipt of the package[s] or any gratitude.

Is that to be expected?

Are people too busy [read that engorged by their hubris] to recognize a caring gesture outside themselves?

Do I find the ingratitude to be a critical wedging event in a relationship?

Am I to forget [hardly possible but naively listed] and forgive, even if this is the 491st time? [Am sure you've figured that comes from the "forgive seven times seventy" biblical reference.]

Honestly, I am more into curiosity than contempt, although the latter is not unnoticed. For it could be that contempt and ingratitude have an undeniably intertwined relationship, no matter how hard my attempt to turn a possible mountain into a molehill.

Think even more this moves into the whole personal and more serious and more evidenced world, for me and everyone I know: How to manage anger and the folly of people not really giving a damn when they ask, "How are you?"

I remember…and when possible try to emulate…what a very wise Rabbi/Theologian/Therapist, Edwin Friedman, once counseled through his writing, "To be a viable leader, especially in conflict, it's crucial to be a non-anxious presence who stays connected and is always able to self-differentiate."

That's good stuff, so for now I'll lean in that direction…but also will not look away from e-mails or surface mail letters or phone calls that might obliterate any evidence of ingratitude.

Ever been in a short line that didn't halt time?

Posted on December 9, 2010 by Mark H Miller

Here's the situation: you are in a hurry [no stranger to anyone] and MUST deposit a check before anything else happens. The drive-up windows are open—5 stations, each of which is occupied, some with 2 cars waiting. You consider the most favorable line [read that, quick and out-a-there] and drive up.

Question: based upon your experience will you be the first "next" car making a deposit? Or, as you've found time and again, you chose the wrong lane?

Where the car ahead of you is unhappy and enters into argument with the bank clerk and the only movement you see is the driver ahead of you tapping in no apparent rhythm on their steering wheel...and then turning off their car?

This dilemma-reality can be transferred to the check-out lines at HEB as you wheel your overloaded cart to the one that seems to be the less-slowed.

In this scenario does it happen, again and again and again, that you've chosen the slowest, less paced than glacial flow line?

Because the person ahead of you made the wrong produce-choice and asks for the packaging person to go get it what was wanted initially...and then cannot find their credit card when the food has been tabulated?

New?

Not for a moment. And, with honesty pushing here, it comes to be what we expect...wrong line, delay when we are hurried [something about the faster I go the behinder I get]. All that changed this morning.

I had been told on Monday at the optometrist's office that my new glasses would be "delivered to us tomorrow, and I'll call you."

Tomorrow—that is in time yesterday—no call. Didn't really question that, since it had some proximity to the first two examples of this reflection.

As schedules would go, of course clueless on how to proceed in a non-pushy, non-aggressive, non-non-non-way, I just happened [that's the truth] to figure out I could simply drop in to the optometrist office on my way home from an appointment.

The lady..her name is Janis and she's as nice as the day is long, even though we're getting close to the shortest day—i.e. December 21—looked at me, smiled and said, "I am hoping your new glasses will be delivered today."

Friends and neighbors…it was better than a script…she no longer completed her hope-filled sentence underlined with anticipation, when a bell jingled, indicating the office door was opening. Janis looked up, "Talk about timing!"

It was the Fed-Ex delivery man delivering my new glasses frame.

Ka-ching.

Wadda ya know. An exception to the most-often-experienced-delay…

Guess it only goes to remind me that not everything has to be a yellow-light about to be red in the journey of life. Once in a while it's green and we don't expect it. But, that doesn't mean we shouldn't find the surprise a welcomed event.

You May Be Right...

Posted on December 10, 2010 by Mark H Miller

Great minds run in the same channel; but still greater ones take a course of their own. That was shared with our 8th grade Vernon Grade School class in 1953 by Miss Agnes Carter—a statement that holds with firmness and accuracy and verity today.

Mark, you didn't get 100; you got 95. Spoken by the driver's license examiner in June of 1956, because I had not looked over my right shoulder when shifting to a right lane, a penalty of 5 points. Using a signal light was insufficient. Today I cannot remember not looking over a shoulder when changing lanes. Even when I'm not driving.

You're going to be a good minister for you understand your authority is real but shouldn't be lorded over an office visitor by sitting behind your desk. That was said when Don Essig, a phD student at the University of Oregon, circa 1970, entered my office. As he came through the open door, without any prompting or honestly any thought I rose from my desk chair and sat with him in front of my desk. Never forgot his perceptive counsel.

Always know the difference between the language of religion and the language about religion. Stated often by my favorite seminary professor, Dr. Paul Holmer, indicating that religious faith is as much as the pulse of the heart as the grasp of the mind. Making it clear the language of faith is more into values than facts. I was honored when Dr. Holmer preached at my installation in my first parish, St. Pauls Church in Chicago in August of 1966.

Mark to use a computer you should first learn how to shut it off... often like as a good minister you need to know you have two ears and one mouth—essential ratio in communication. Said by my first computer teacher and valued friend, Tim Green, member of St. Peter's UCC in Elmhurst, Illinois. [I had been pushing a button, not kosher for any computer geek.]

When playing a fish, ALWAYS lift up and reel down. When I lost my first winter steelhead, fishing with guide Paul Hannemann on the Nestucca River in Oregon [circa 1956], when the line pinged [as in snapped] because I had pointed the pole at the fish and only reeled. Paul said it softly but I heard him clearly and have never forgotten or neglected to practice his advisory.

If you don't walk the talk what you say will be shallow and no one will follow. Said by Malcolm Gillespie, my colleague and mentor in campus ministry the academic year, 1964-65 at the Student Christian Foundation, Carbondale, Illinois, Southern Illinois University.

I spent the year as a campus minister intern. He said this as my car was loaded up with elementary school books, delivered to a Southern Christian Leadership Office in Hattiesburg, Mississippi, my first "walk" into the world of Civil Rights, during which I helped register African-American men and women so they could vote for the first time. Never did see a white-sheeted person, although I was on the look-out—not that I could have done anything about it.

Mark, you should learn e-mail protocol...when sending to a group, click on the CC button to get to the BCC button and put the names there. Takes too much room to put stacks of names in the CC slot. Said by a minister friend whose name I have lost. Guess a sign that aging sometimes means memory lapses, just like I couldn't remember if I locked the door last night or shampooed my hair during this morning's shower.

You may be right. Offered by a wonderful professor at the University of Washington, a course on "Writing Fiction Novels." James Thayer [himself a novelist with his new book, "The Boxer and the Poet—Something of A Romance" an excellent novel—I get nothing from the plug, other than to share his excellence! I include the "!" because he eschews it...he may be right!] said he offers that when someone disagrees with him vigorously on a writing principle. He said it's a good way to lessen the animosity or prevent a conflict that might ensue.

I'll have to remember that when people chortle endlessly about how absolutely horrible our current president is and how a resident of Alaska is the best next President. Reminds me of the bumper sticker, "I cannot wait for 2012 to get here."

They may be right.

Certainly there are more, but these "pop" right now. How about you? In your life, who are the people who planted at least one seed that is of continual benefit? Thanked them? Not a bad idea.

I could be right.

You think?

When the learning curve's steep

Posted on December 11, 2010 by Mark H Miller

The current situation does not change my loyalty—read that without pause—for the Denver Broncos. But, there's a deeper lesson that lingers. Will get there shortly.

Both my sons, Matthew and Andrew [you should see Andrew's video room—I doubt there's anything labeled Broncos out of the Broncos gift shop that Andrew lacks] and I give fervor its best definition in rooting for our beloved Denver NFL team.

Probably the classic moment indicating the passion was the moment the first Broncos' Super Bowl victory was in hand, Andrew called Matthew with this declaration, "Now we can die!" Is that supportive or what? Okay, extreme, but it's better than not rooting for anyone and spending the day looking at a mirror.

This year has been hapless and hopeless for the Broncos, now dealing with the temptation to lose in order to gain. That is, the more final games in the loss column the better their first round draft choice.

Hopefully that will not even be a murmur in their collective sub-consciousness, that to lose is to win.

But, the deeper trigger, on this Saturday morning, December 11, 2010, Austin, Texas, when the temperature will encourage t-shirts—something almost unsavory about moving toward Christmas on the calendar but not toward the sweaters in the closet—is what led to the downfall of their head coach, Josh McDaniels.

Yes, it was his arrogance. Yes, it was the spy-gate episode in England when his video man whom he had brought with him from the New England Patriots and who secretly taped six-minutes of the 49er's practice. Yes, it was their woeful record, now 3-9, but especially the slaughter at the hands and feet and shoulders of the hated Oakland Raiders.

I think it had to do with another aspect: **he didn't know what he was doing and was unwilling to ask what he needed to learn.** Pointedly, they asked McDaniels to do two jobs, neither of which he had done before. Complicated, demanding, almost like his personal tsunami.

In thinking about that this morning, it occurred to me: **every one of us needs to climb a learning curve**...and to recognize when the job demands more than I know...and in painful situations...than I can ever offer.

Sliding toward a personal side of this for a moment.

In all the years of ministry...both as serving churches as their pastor and as serving a conference working with ministers as their pastor...it was clear: the ministers who were the most effective were not the ones who dabbled and at times plunged into a world that was self-serving. Rather, they are the leaders who know their limits, who know what they do well and who know the areas in which they most need to strengthen.

And in the latter, it has been the case: either get someone else to do it or learn how to do it better or agree the call to ministry was misheard.

Certainly the last of this triad is harsh. But, given the demands of ministry, I don't consider it untoward.

Learning curve. The functional needs of a profession that need to be recognized and reduced. Admitting when you are in something over your head.

I share one example. No, make that two.

A minister friend has a passion for mission, for leaning his congregation toward the building of a new home in Mexico or Guatemala, in making sure the needs of the poor are neither denied nor neglected. He does this in an exemplar fashion. But, don't ever tell him a church member has been hospitalized. When he went, given no other choice, he stammered in his body language—never looking at the ailing person in the bed— and in his hesitance to say anything, let alone offer a prayer.

The goodness of this was the recognition that you cannot be a pastor of a congregation if hospital visitation is anathema. In that recognition the minister left the pastorate for ministry that had nothing to do with hospitalized parishioners.

Another minister went to his first solo-pastorate, which is to say there was no second minister [i.e. someone else to blame for problems]. When he got there he knew there were two challenges that HAD to be addressed: church growth in new parishioners and in financial giving.

He was pretty good in the former and utterly clueless about the latter. In fact, was it his choice, he would never preach the tradition first-week-in-November-stewardship-sermon.

Then it happened. At a meeting in early October with the church Trustees, the purpose of which meeting was to talk about how financial giving could be increased, when the question was asked of him, "Reverend, what do you think we should do?", he clutched his chest and collapsed to the floor.

Turns out it was an anxiety attack and not a heart problem.

The next meeting was to happen in two weeks, once his medical situation was understood—primarily by himself.

Recognizing, *I really want to keep this job but I need to learn…lots and lots of learning…about giving to the church*, the solo pastor identified the three ministers he knew who knew so much more than he—that honestly took hardly anything—about stewardship. He put his tape recorder on the table three times, pointed to it and said, "You have 30 minutes. Please tell me EVERYTHING you know about stewardship."

He found that the giving learning curve could be climbed. The first step was to recognize what he didn't know. The second step was to begin knowing. And the third step was to keep learning.

Back to the beginning. This is not to say McDaniels shouldn't have been fired. One of the options was to take one of his tasks away from him—a demotion. The decision was made to terminate.

Certainly there'll be plenty of money for him the next two years—unless the Broncos owner decides the termination was "for cause" [read that the video-taping in London], which I doubt will happen—but the real issue is for McDaniels to see how the mirror answers when he looks in that direction and asks, "What do I need to learn in order to be a better coach?"

Goodness, all this on a Saturday morning, when thinking through what makes for good leadership probes. And, hopefully, it always will. Always.

Words are really planted seeds...continued

Posted on December 12, 2010 by Mark H Miller

More seed-planters...they keep coming...

When you come to a curve slow down so when you're actually in the curve you can accelerate—thus having better car control—to keep your brakes when curving is not helpful. This came about 50 years ago from a sage cousin, John Sinner, who was a butcher so he knew about cutting corners, which he never did. His wisdom works, yes it does.

When driving, for greatest car control [read that, safety] put your left hand at 10 a.m. and your right at 2 p.m. on the steering wheel—the best possible control grip. Learned that when taking the Colorado Springs Police Department driving test to qualify when driving the Chaplain's Police Car. By the way, not a car with a siren or flashing lights, but we were connected to the dispatcher.

When backing up to launch your boat, put your hand at the bottom of the steering wheel. If you want your boat to go to the right, lift your hand up to the right. To the left? Ah, you can figure that out. Came from Kenny King AND Pete Cornocchia in Eugene, Oregon. Kenny was a fishing guide and Pete the Outdoor editor of the Eugene Register Guard. It was my first and last boat, giving credence to the mantra that the two greatest moments in having a boat: the day of purchase and the day of sale. Not sure who said that but I can witness to it.

Mark, realize that you and I and everyone else should not be someone else's opinion. Stated with experience and poignancy by Ernie Huntzinger, at the time the Senior Minister of the First Congregational Church of Elmhurst, Illinois, at a time when "opinion" was not exactly accompanied by clapping and cheering. Maybe someday there can be more on that. Only to say parishioners tend to believe what they believe based upon whether or not they like their minister more than whether or not verity is apt. No one said that, but it's true.

As a minister you're only as good as your next phone call. Said by George Otto, God rest his soul, who was Conference Minister in Colorado when I went to Lakewood. He knew, because most church members expect and expect and expect and most Conference Ministers spend most of their time listening to church members on why their serving pastor should be dismissed. Even when at 3 in the morning a pastor calls [this happened on my watch] to whine and complain because the toilet in the parsonage just dropped through the floor. He acted as if it were my fault. I grimaced…at him as much as for him, and saw to it the family toileting was soon on a better foundation. It is true, though as pastor, if you forget Aunt Hattie [as in Battie] had surgery, hence you didn't get there for a prayer, watch out.

Printed on a rock a Christian Education Director once gifted: *I'm me, I'm beautiful, I'm good…cuz God don't make junk!* That came from Lucy McCorkle when we shared in ministry at Lakewood United Church of Christ—Colorado. Lucy's now 96. I just received her Christmas missive…ah, what a great lady, one who brings grace and love and some quip that bears more truth than any sermon.

I'm finding it a good exercise to recall the word or moment that outlives itself, no matter the instability of the church or the minister or driving on the road or if a boat is purchased or a rock on your desk.

Just a word or two…and then…so much more…

Posted on December 13, 2010 by Mark H Miller

More quotes that mattered….

Are you really asking me that? Honestly, Mark? That's the dumbest question ever…how could you ask what you think you should be? Of course. Silly. You will be a minister, no question. Said the fall of 1956 [considering "fall" a time of year and not a theological condition] by Jeannette Butts, a fellow junior at Jefferson High School, a Sunday night after we'd spent two days in Ione, Oregon, meeting a new church youth group representing the Oregon Pilgrim Fellowship organization for the about-to-be United Church of Christ.

Jeannette's comment was a trigger point. At least as I remember it. For some reason—am clueless about such—I thought it important to know what you should do by your junior high school year. I went home and shared with my parents, waking them up. My mother thought it was a wonderful decision, whereas my father cleared his throat, may even have coughed once or twice, "That's fine, son. Get a good night's rest and we can talk about it in the morning." Great response from each. Hence, the steps toward ministry began.

I saw Jeannette at our 50th high school reunion and shared what she had said. She remembered it, "See, I knew what I was talking about." We laughed. It was a good laugh that was filled with gladness. Fact is I never saw Jeannette the intervening 50 years, but that didn't matter. I remembered that night in front of her house on the corner of 9th and N.E. Going…and how much it meant. More than much.

You should play professional baseball—that will mean you'll be a more successful preacher. And besides, you have the same initials as Mickey Mantle. Ah, my Stanford sophomore year it made sense: take an essay writing course because in ministry you have to know how to write sentences, paragraphs and complete sermons. The teacher was a great guy, Louis Ruotolo, Teaching Assistant getting his phD in English and a former Roman Catholic priest. He encouraged me to not attend seminary before throwing a few fast balls on the outside corner for a professional team. When both the Dodgers and Pirates had the same idea, I smiled and thanked them and went directly to seminary. And truth holding firmly. I sure appreciated my professor's encouragement. But even more, I KNEW I wasn't that good and simply didn't want to be cannon fodder for the next Mickey Mantle, toiling in White Face, Montana for a couple of dusty summers.

That Miller kid, he gonna be a minister? Well, the pitcher for the Georgia team's a Southern Baptist Preacher—will be interesting to see which religion's better. Said by the home plate umpire to my semi-professional baseball coach, just before our semi-final game in Battle Creek, Michigan, in pursuit of wanting to be the winner of the Semi-Pro Baseball World Series. Two days later I drove to New Haven, Connecticut for my first year in seminary. I laughed at the comment—it was shared AFTER the game, which we won, 4-3. But I must say it was a relief to not know it before my first pitch that day…just in case the umpire was Southern Baptist.

We're sorry, but the pilots are unable to fly your plane tonight. You'll need to get a ticket on the last Denver to Austin flight. Said by a flight attendant as I sat on my scheduled flight. Had to go a number of gates to get to the last-flight-tonight-gate. Standing behind me in the line to the get-your-ticket-counter was a lovely lady whose cell phone battery was dead. The conversation started…and last August it was ten years since that night…and Diane and I have loved every minute of it… whether or not the cell phone works.

Can you tell me how many are in your family? The question I asked Diane by the luggage carousel when we arrived in Austin on the last-flight-to-Austin. I didn't want to be too direct [cough here] and ask if she was married or engaged. When she said, "I live with my son," I thought, Great news, and handed her a couple of vacuum-packed salmon fillets—salmon I had caught just 12 hours earlier out of the Pacific Ocean off the mouth of the Columbia River. Now, talk about being fresh. That's in reference to the salmon.

Wing it! You're much better that way, so wing it! From Verne Fish, bass in the choir at Lakewood United Church of Christ, circa 1976.

What had happened is that I delivered my sermon from a manuscript. In the middle of a paragraph I looked up and a church member just arrived, sitting in the back pew. Seeing him triggered a segue, so I went for it. When finished I thought, I've got to get back to where I was in the manuscript, so looked down. I was in trouble. Couldn't find my place. Which gave "pregnant pause" a lengthy definition. The congregation became restless. At which point Verne bellowed his advisory. The verb is apt—don't think Verne ever whispered anything, anywhere, anytime. I responded, "No. I need to find myself. I'm lost." Verne didn't hesitate, "What's new?" Luckily the congregation's laughter gave me time to find my place. But, the seed was planted and years later, in fact when I started in conference ministry, preaching in a different church every Sunday, I never again carried a manuscript. Felt good, actually, all triggered by Verne.

And so it was...sermons became building a plane while flying. Well, not totally. There were some connections to the morning scripture and some stories. But, preaching in a different church each Sunday meant I could repeat a story—especially those "that worked." Where it became a problem was when I'd return a year later. I had to ask the serving pastor, "Did I tell this story last year?" I may have, but no minister could remember. Which, of course, brings up a whole new question.... for another day.

Monday afternoon...sun and shadows

Posted on December 13, 2010 by Mark H Miller

Many pulse-rate matters today—it's Monday afternoon.

Another radiation treatment for Diane. An interview in the morning with promise—the corporate world is inviting, which is terrific. A trip to the dentist to undergo their verbiage, "gum therapy," but which is really gum gouging. Many of you know I love alliteration, but also find euphemisms to be clever but not helpful. For instance, in my day it used to be "used cars," but now it's "pre-owned."

We had a lovely evening last night at First Christian Church in San Marcos—to appreciate their music ministry with choirs participating. Very balanced in terms of the choir's cantata—which means no one could be heard singularly or off-key!

What was really special, though, was the graciousness and affirmation by which we were received. Sometimes it's awkward [that's another one of those euphemisms] to come back as the former minister. For most people, though, that very clearly was not a problem. And they promised—they are good in keeping them—to see us again next Sunday morning...and even buy a book or two for Christmas presents. Nice.

What I appreciated the most was how great Diane looked...with the weight loss, her hair cut shorter, the new boots...yes, sir and madam, she looked fabulous. And people picked up on that. Made me feel better than good...great, in fact, to know the new day will be a better day.

Received a card this afternoon of a treasured friend who's very aware of our medical challenges in 2010, who wrote simply, "May 2011 be less difficult." Will hold that card as a guide-card for 2011.

Am wrestling, though. And that's part of this afternoon. Am not ready to blog-it, but am about to write for my own needs and will probably tear it up, a statement of some of my angst about people whose need to judge is greater than their willingness to understand. They have been harsh, even brutal, not sparing judgment, no matter its inaccuracy.

Maybe when I sort some of the shadows [I know, they are always there], I will have a greater comfort level in writing about them beyond my computer.

Now, though, it's to savor the day…and to appreciate an e-mail from another valued friend—my goodness, are Diane and I blessed with friends—richly so—who sent a message that made it clear: give thanks for kindness and caring friends…and pray for those who are not and who have acted in harsh ways.

Good, salient and prudent guidance. I thank God…virtually and endlessly…that the former list is SO MUCH GREATER than the latter. What a great imbalance…just great. Which makes for a better day, it really does.

So, it's to prayer…and that will be short…for the outspoken gratitude takes up most of my time.

And then, to write a letter to a friend whom I met in 1988 and let him know why I'm thinking of him today, why I admire him in his ventures, for he gives *entrepreneurial* its best definition.

Texas...more than tumbleweeds and Bonnie and Clyde

Posted on December 14, 2010 by Mark H Miller

My thoughts are on Texas today. Sitting here, a calm afternoon, Austin, Texas, a day when a T-shirt is what I grab, all the while wishing I could justify going into the closet for a sweater. Something's just not right seeing a cloudless sky, deep-blue, gentle breeze and a temperature pushing 70 in mid-December.

Before I came here to live I can remember my image of Texas—tumbleweeds cluttering roads, flat land without trees, lots of dust, cattle whose ribs could be counted, winds that re-arranged anyone's hairdo, even Jimmy Johnson, former Dallas Cowboys coach whom I swear used lacquer instead of hair-spray and that in abundance. In fact, I could wager that John Updike's "Grapes of Wrath" was more likely written for Texas than anywhere else.

And then it happened, my preconception, my *this is what I will find*, was cast aside as I drove into Austin, my new home. It was 1997, July, when the low temperature every day that month and into September was almost ALWAYS higher than the high in Portland, Oregon, my birth home.

I drove in to Austin and with no stretch in the imagination, even a twitch, I looked around and only thought, *Are you kidding*? THIS is Portland, Oregon, especially if you pay no regard to the humidity and torturous heat!

For anyone who's not been to Austin, you should change that. Yes, it is the live music capital of the world, no doubt the verdict of the Chamber of Commerce, and yes, the home of the University of Texas that is still trying to find some humility and the state capital where Ann Richards was once governor.

The reason I mention Ann Richards and none of her successors, has nothing to do with the Democrat-identity she reflected. It was her sense of humor, so lacking, even vacuous in politicians these days. To wit: once a secret service agent gave her a gun and told her to put it in her purse. She handed the gun back, "Sir, that won't work. If I put the gun in my purse I'd never find it."

The reason Austin and Portland could be twins is the hills and trees and rivers and lakes—my goodness, how lovely. And the bikes and the paths and all the half-marathoners—three out of four nurses, it seems based upon our medical journey this year, would rather run than breathe. Okay, hyperbole but not without accuracy.

Now, live oaks are not a match organically or visually for the statuesque Douglas Firs of the Northwest, but they are magnificent, full and stately in their own manner.

I bet. I bet if someone walked through Austin's Zilker Park and then walked through Laurelhurst Park in Portland, the images would be cloned.

Anyway, images of Texas were changed.

Until.

Until I was to visit a church in Friona, Texas. Now, Friona, in West… or maybe Northwest Texas is miles and miles from almost any city of size. Going there was my job, because we had a church there, a church that had diminished in membership from small to token. It was in a city [that's overstated] that could be seen in the blink of an eye.

The day before I was in Lubbock, home of Texas Tech University, and residence of another of our churches…smaller than Friona's, but heartier. That was a Saturday night. The worship in Friona the next morning was at 11 a.m., but the distance was so far between Lubbock and Friona I decided to split it, staying in one of the most "Texas-named" cities, Muleshoe.

A side-bar—what is notable about Texas is some of the city names. Ever heard of Old-Dime-Box? Or, Cut-N-Shoot? On that, I do patronize the Cut-N-Shoot hair salon in Austin…gotta blend in with the Texans, right? The name works, although I only ask for the hair to be cut and I'm nice about it, so haven't been shot....yet.

Ever been to a restaurant [giving restaurant the benefit of a doubt] where you are handed a menu AND a fly-swatter? I have...just outside of Zuehl, Texas. Not zeal, but Zuehl.

Back to Muleshoe.

Muleshoe was the Texas I had anticipated before I arrived in Portland...I mean, Austin.

Train tracks everywhere, tumbleweed pushed across the two-lane road, some wheat storage barns, some empty cattle-pens next to the train tracks.

And one motel, at least the one I found. I HAD to stay there...there were many rooms, each like an individual cabin, all logged-built. Everything was old, with keys the size of a hand to work the huge, rusty locks. The manager was still in the 20th century, early in it, because he used an abacas to add up what I owed, only reluctantly wanted a credit card and lifted an old cigar box, his money storage container.

Think it was about $25 for the night. How's that for 1998?

Glad it wasn't one of those places I had seen on the outskirts of Chicago once—rooms rented by the hour.

The manager—at least I assumed that his place in life[I was comforted he didn't look like Anthony Perkins in "Psycho"]—smiled, cave-like mouth, at least with the three missing teeth spaced around some still surviving. He looked like there was no dentist in town. I also figured he was a lifer because he didn't miss the spittoon. The splash was contained by the sides.

Luckily my cell phone still worked, so I called Diane to tell her that I had arrived at the Muleshoe Inn in Muleshoe, Texas, and in the morning I would get up and make it to Friona. Yes, oh boy yes, I was in REAL Texas.

And then I saw it. I knew the motel was old—the bigger than life key gave it away—but I went into the bathroom and there it was...carved into the log...THE initials. Said it directly, *B + C was hear.*

I called Diane back, excitement unharnessed, "Diane! You won't believe this! Guess who stayed in this motel room?"

Now, admittedly that was a stupid question. WHAT could anyone answer? Ann Richards? Davy Crockett? [Probably not because San Antonio and the Alamo were too far away.]

I didn't wait for her answer, "This is fabulous...and they left their initials, even though they obviously could have used some spelling lessons. This is double-fabulous: Bonnie and Clyde stayed here!"

Hey, you had to be there to appreciate it.

I know, I should have taken a picture. But I hadn't had my cell phone that long and didn't know how to take a picture with it. And I was more than sure Mr. Gap-Tooth Spittoon-Guy didn't have a camera.

I slept well, with some fanciful dreaming notions on what Bonnie and Clyde might have planned after they carved their initials. I was certain it wasn't to look up a spelling teacher.

The next morning, Friona the next stop, I was alone on the road. Sunday morning and no traffic.

The sky was a bright blue, the sun in all its glory and the breeze barely noticeable.

To my left and right were fields, freshly ploughed. Not being a rural guy I still imagined they were ploughed for a purpose, maybe planting seeds. See, you don't have to be a genius to figure some of these rural things out.

Then the second discovery happened, and to me it was as fresh as the new day. I looked to my left and right there....right there in the middle of a ploughed field, stood the most beautiful pheasant in the world.

Now, I'm no expert on pheasant-sightings, but I stopped the car, walked across the road and just looked at this beautiful pheasant...the reds and greens and dark brown. Wow. Right there...God's creation. In Texas.

......

So it is, now living into my second decade as a Texas resident, I remember the log-cabin motel, the pheasant in the field and what can happen...

It is certain, though, no matter how long I live in Austin and serve churches and meet new Texans, I won't learn the twang. For you see, a native Texan is incapable of saying a one-syllable word—for instance, yes becomes yay-es. That's okay, it really is. Because when driving around Austin, seeing the hills and trees and the lakes and rivers, it's a reflection of my birth home, Portland. And so, through my experience and imagination I can have both.

Not bad on a December day when the sweaters will remain in the closet.

Advent...more than the color purple

Posted on <u>December 15, 2010</u> by <u>Mark H Miller</u>

It's not the color, although purple, and when lightened, mauve, are favorites. And it's not the conclusion to each...for Advent it is Christmas, the birth of Jesus. And for Lent it's the triumph of Easter, that moment before and beyond all, when because of God's power and love, death lacked containment of the Holy Son, but even more on our futuring behalf, death will not be the end.

Certainly it is true...for Advent and Lent to not have the concluding triumphs, well, life would be different—too shallow, too sordid, too painful.

But there is more.

What is the more for me than purple is the deeper place of Advent and Lent: the prayer of confession and assurance of pardon...going deep within the self with honesty not deception or denial.

That's not easy.

Someone once said you learn more about a person when defeated than when triumphant, more through the loss than the victory.

That's probably true.

But, no matter the year, no matter the pushing stress of what has not been accomplished, the length of the list on what needs to happen, or the floundering, the four Sundays of Advent and the six of Lent—very important. Cannot gauge it on any scale.

So it is. This Advent the foe is cancer. With it, though, is the reality that perfection is not the goal, but cleansing is, coming to terms with the anger—and at times fury—of being ignored or used by others—and by failing myself to be better in the moment than I was—this Advent will be more than days on a calendar. It will be a time when truth is on the throne and hopefully my inabilities to deal with anger will lessen, maybe even be less apparent.

For whatever reason, since managing anger is my sternest challenge, I am called to follow this reflection, reminded a few times when attending chapel service at Yale University when William Sloane Coffin quoted St. Augustine, "It is your enmity and not your enemies that does you in…every time."

Now, how can that spoken truth from the 3rd century be my experience in the 21st century?

Gotta work on it…this Advent…and then into 2011.

And the first *work on it* happened yesterday. I had had a particularly difficult time—read that I was treated poorly—in a medical office. There are times when you feel more like a bank with limitless funds than a patient with medical difficulties. When sharing with Diane about my experience, finding that my understanding and perception were off-kilt, Diane only said, "Does it matter? Really?"

So insightful. I marinated on that a while and decided, *No, it really doesn't. I'll move on and not turn the mole hill into something bigger.*

Before I knew it, *poof,* the quarrelsome time evaporated and the air I breathed was clearer and the anger, even distrust, was no longer resident.

Ah, a good step toward lessening what needs to be lessened.

Goodness, that's a whole new way to lose weight…and maybe, just maybe I can be one of the world's biggest losers.

More than a football game

Posted on December 16, 2010 by Mark H Miller

I didn't see it when it happened. But, rest assured, anything extraordinary in the sports world can be seen, again and again, on ESPN within four hours.

However, **I think everyone's gone overboard on the culprit and paid next to no attention to the cause.**

This is about a terrible decision, even given the apparent spontaneity, by the New York Jets' assistant coach for strength and conditioning, Sal Alosi, who tripped a Miami Dolphins player during the game. Alosi put out his knee from the sidelines and the player tumbled to the ground, which kept him from tackling the opponent.

People probably feel good he was fined $25,000 and suspended the final three games of the league season. And then yesterday Alosi was "suspended indefinitely."

I've heard another claim [at times quite honestly it was chortled], "How horrible. Can you believe someone would do that? Guess it points out people will do anything to win. Probably happen elsewhere. Lots of elsewhere's."

Wait a minute sports fans, boys and girls. Another way to regard this. No, I'm not standing up for Alosi, because he would probably trip me. No, I'm not saying the penalty wasn't harsh enough…or too harsh. No, I'm not dosing tolerance when judgment pours down, even contempt.

What I'm looking at is not Alosi who put out his knee; I'm looking at the Jets organization who time and again puts out its chin and challenges you to hit it.

In my opinion **Alosi acted as the Jets are**.

Hello?

Consider this: The HBO "Hard Knocks" program taped the Jets during preseason…the profanity laced was more frequent than the profundity offered or evidenced and their arrogance, containing no license or sideline, was over-the-top.

Consider this: Their head coach, Rex Ryan is a jokester…and thinks his humor is funny. He's an "in-your-face" kinda guy, whose talk when walked is brazen and contemptible. He also gives the impression that the end always justifies the means.

In short, what Alosi did is not surprising…for it is the overall manner for the entire organization.

For instance, this wouldn't ever happen to the Dallas Cowboys. Nah, their owner had cosmetic surgery and their glitzy and classy style is all surface. But, to trip someone in order to get the upper hand? Never.

And it wouldn't happen to the Denver Broncos. They are so sorry these days, by most people considered the 31st best team [there are 32 teams in the league] it's enough for them to stand up when their inabilities tackle them every time.

It is the deeper issue of what are values.

Another example.

Cliff Lee said no to the Texas Rangers and the New York Yankees and signed with the Philadelphia Phillies…yes, for lots of money. But, another part of this—and it isn't pushed by the reality in 2011 they now have the best 4 starting pitches in the major leagues…and probably the least used pitcher will be the set-up guy who enters the 7th inning. No, Cliff Lee signed…and this is being suggested but probably will remain undisclosed because it's in the realm of intent…and who can verify let alone prove that? Cliff Lee signed, yes, because he played for the Phillies before. But his values said he needed to do whatever he could to take care of his young son whose leukemia is now in remission and the pediatric care for such is best in Philadelphia. And he's stated the needs of his family were of considerable influence. Besides, no one ever spit on his wife at a game—except when she was at Yankee Stadium.

Okay, it's true that I am simply pounding away today on the computer keyboard.

But, what's not okay is to think people do stupid things independently.

Almost everything we do and value is the result of family and culture… mainly family.

Another example. And I won't name the family because they'll be embarrassed and not want the attention. But. I know a family whose values are strong, whose caring for their children is exemplar, who work hard and expect their kids to do so. And who would never put up with any of their children acting in a manner that was untoward. They really wouldn't. It's a family that I can say…and will watch over the next decade…that the kids should grow up like both their parents.

Wish we could say that more often.

Some words about Preaching

Posted on December 17, 2010 by Mark H Miller

No one's asked the question, but I'm prompted to share, perhaps because I'm only preaching sermons in my sleep, or while driving to another doctor's appointment. How do sermons get written?

I realize this won't benefit the economy or give the Broncos more energy or calm the Yankees because they didn't get Cliff Lee. Oh, that last one was not truthful…am not a Yankees fan [that was for my friend Jimmy Cobb, wonderful former pastor at First Christian Church in San Marcos, whose only excursion along the road called mis-informed and badly warped in judgment is his uncompromised support of the Yankees—someone said he wore a Yankees hat to church when I was interim. I didn't see it, which is his good fortune.]

First of all the sermon is based upon one of two options other than blanket plagiarism [more on that later]: a sermon is either biblically based, which utilizes a lectionary, or topically based. The former relies upon a Catholic/Protestant calendar that lists four Bible passages for each Sunday: one from the Old Testament, one from the Psalms, one from Paul's Epistles in the New Testament and the fourth from one of the four Gospels, Matthew, Mark, Luke or John. The latter means a minister picks a topic and most often but not always, seeks a Bible verse that has some connection. It's mainly, though, what the minister's interested in and a response to current events.

The value of the former, the lectionary, is it keeps the minister from preaching one of three sermon themes, which is about all a minister really has, with variations given the season of the year.

When I began in ministry, circa 1966, I had no choice. At St. Pauls Church in Chicago the lectionary was preached. I knew this was the case even before I got there because the two pastors, Fred Trost and Herb Davis, conducted a 2-hour interview of me, most of which was focused upon what I might term biblical theology. I guessed a phD exam would have been more relenting.

One other prefacing comment. Karl Barth, a wonderful Swiss Theologian in the early 20th Century, whose Dogmatic books sometimes had 80 page footnotes [you can imagine its grueling "read"] made the case a good sermon is preached with the Bible in one hand and the newspaper in the other. I added to that, maintaining a good sermon requires the newspaper and Bible in one hand and the church roster in the other. A sermon must connect with the "where and how" the members are.

What about sermon preparation and delivery?

My first clue with this, because I never knew how any of my pastors as a child and youth or in college did this was when I was a student minister from '63-64 and '65-66 at Brookfield Center Congregational Church in Connecticut. The pastor, Ted Walker, had his sermon manuscript ready to preach the preceding Wednesday at noon. And, I would bet, although I never counted the word number, EVERY sermon contained, within 20 words, the same total word amount. The only time he changed his sermon was the Sunday following John Kennedy's assassination.

As was generally the case his sermons, if you wished, were printed. Although I don't believe in that, even though it was the case in my last three congregations: printed sermon manuscripts was the rule. The main reason for not believing in printed sermons is they are delivered to be heard and not read.

My next awareness of sermon preparation came from Fred Trost, the senior pastor at St. Pauls in Chicago and the most important mentor of my entire ministry. Fred preached at an early German-language service and then two English-language services. He felt he was better preaching German, so the first sermon draft was auf Deutsch and then he'd translate.

Herb Davis, the other pastor on our St. Pauls Church staff, had an unique way of sermon preparation. He would "marinate" the text he has chosen all week, then would show up at church 4 a.m. Sunday morning and begin writing the sermon! I can remember once Herb was still typing his sermon during the prelude. [We had the old-fashioned typewriters.] I came to his office, grabbed the sheet still in the typewriter, and said, "Herbie…make up the rest…time for worship!" Oh could he preach. I didn't care when he typed it up…he KNEW good preaching and he hardly referred to his manuscript. Hardly ever.

I knew another preacher—most popular, effective and well-regarded in the area—who would write his manuscript on twenty 3×5 cards and on Saturday morning would put each card in a different church school room and would go from room to room until his sermon was memorized. He was very powerful, but honestly I wondered about the time it took and what else might have happened in his ministry. But who am I to complain? He was a brilliant preacher.

I then knew a pastor who had been in a church for over twenty years. I would notice that EVERY sermon he preached had dates on the front page upper right corner…when he had preached that SAME sermon in that church. Some of the sermons had six dates. Then one Sunday he preached what I considered a brilliant sermon. I complimented him. He didn't respond. That night I noticed his sermon leather binder was on the secretary's desk. I thought it would be good to see if he had preached that before, because it seemed very current. He hadn't preached it before. But, to my chagrin, he also hadn't written it. It was a sermon from someone else Xeroxed out of a book, carefully cut so only the page numbers showed…nothing about the book or the author. Someone once said, think it was in a seminary class, "All work and no plagiarism makes for dull sermons." I don't agree.

My own style changed. Maybe even evolved. For the first 30 years I had a manuscript…and I can say 99% of the time I followed the lectionary and never once did I repeat a sermon, even though my lengthiest tenure as a church pastor was eight years. That doesn't mean I didn't repeat experiences or stories, but never twice in the same church. I may have been dull; but I was never repetitive.

That changed when I became a conference minister, preaching in a different church every Sunday for over ten years. In fact, all those years, serving out of Austin, Texas and then Seattle, Washington, not once was there a manuscript. Why? Mainly because I didn't want the sermon to be "The latest news from our conference," or, "We need more money," or

"We need more of your members attending our conference programs."
Never, ever, I am pleased to share.

I wanted the sermon to be just for them, which meant I needed to do homework before I got there on what the pulse [rapid or glacial paced] of the church was or what the community was dealing with or what the minister wanted addressed. And there were times when I got to the church an hour before the prelude and visited with people, asking them, "What do you need to have preached today."

And a couple of times, which I'm not sure was that helpful, I asked the congregation before the sermon what scripture passage gave them the most trouble. I always had at least 5 options, so it wasn't totally a stump event, because you could always count on a question about miracles… if they happened and where are they today?

During my conference ministry only once did I stay in the pulpit, because the minister would have been offended had I left it. [I would guess his shirts didn't lack starch.] I did what he requested.

Otherwise, the other 450 or so sermons, probably many of which were so-so, I walked back and forth in the chancel, and if it felt right and viable, I would go up the aisle. I wanted to make sure they knew I was there and had no canned sermon I was emptying.

Certainly everyone has their favorite sermon or favorite preacher. That's a good thing. And there are preachers you'd get out of a sick bed to hear. There are also preachers that cure anyone's insomnia, and there are preachers who are socially-connected but preach what I call cotton-candy sermons: fluffy and sweet but lacking substance.

For me the preparation of the sermon, not having a manuscript, goes like this: I look at the four lectionary lessons, read some research in preaching journals, figure out which Bible passage I will base the sermon upon and try to link it with the church where I'm preaching and the news of the day and then simply let it marinate. In truth I think of it almost constantly. In that reflecting there is what I call a "sense of fitness," and more than not, I can depend upon that. However, I cannot be locked in to the preparation. Because when I get there, everything might change, so the metaphor of building a plane while flying is apt.

And often, the first 33 years of preaching from a manuscript, my regular rhythm didn't always hold. I guess I tried to get close to Ted Walker and have the manuscript done before Wednesday evening. It would be printed up, but I would NEVER look at it. Stuffed it in a desk drawer to let it marinate on its own. Then I would get it out Friday afternoon, or maybe Saturday morning.

There would be a few times…yes, the truth rules here…when I thought it was pretty good and would go over it in my office Sunday morning, and about 30 minutes before the prelude would realize: This is terrible! Panic would set in and I hoped…lots of hope here…that Herb Davis would walk in and bail me out. He didn't and the people were kind and patient, even if the sermon was underwhelming…and all I hoped to do was to whelm.

Today–two key questions

Posted on December 19, 2010 by Mark H Miller

There are always two events each day in each life in each moment.

There is the activity event—what is done.

And there is the value event—what does it mean.

Reading the Bible is an example. I've always pushed, whether pastor of a congregation or working with clergy, the Bible can be read for what happened—that's the historical—and for the theological, what does it mean?

It is often the case people get mired in the "what happened?" of the incident and not of the "what does it mean?"

Certainly detailing the historical for its verity is important. But it should not preempt the importance of meaning. Just because an event didn't happen doesn't mean it isn't important.

For instance, there are those who cite Easter as only important if you can detail Christ's physical being after the tomb became empty. That's not helpful. What is helpful is to trust that Easter is a transforming event that indicates death does not end a relationship with God for any one of us.

Or, and citing the Apostle Paul becomes so helpful at this point: people questioned his statement of a bodily resurrection of each of us after we die a physical death. They wanted to know, "Paul, by what form will our resurrected body be?" [Reference is I Corinthians 15]

He responded with a "this is what it means" comment, "You are asking the wrong question. The question is not, 'By what form will our body be resurrected?' The real question is, DO YOU HAVE FAITH THAT GOD WILL MAKE SURE IT HAPPENS?"

Back to today.

130

It will be a busy day for Diane and me. We will attend worship where I served as interim minister, First Christian Church in San Marcos, Texas. Following worship will be a monthly luncheon, kids [of all ages I presume] visit with Santa and a book-signing for two of my books of pastoral epistles, the most recent of which includes many letters written to this church membership.

Following that Diane and I will drive to Kerrville, Texas, to clap and cheer for Andrew's Schreiner University basketball team, following which we'll have dinner with Andrew. Jennifer and Dylan and Taylor are in Seattle with Jennifer's family—Andrew heads there tomorrow.

We will then drive home…and look to tomorrow…primarily to 11:20 a.m. when Diane continues her second of five weeks of radiation treatments. Then there'll be a total lunar eclipse. And what else might happen.

That's today and a peek at tomorrow—what we anticipate will happen, the data, the facts, the moments.

But, what about the deeper matter, the *what can it mean?*

Of course we don't know…but there will be questions about relationships with former church members and staff, questions about coaching gifts, questions about driving safety, questions about what the book-signing can mean—will it trigger a deeper interest in starting a new book?

None of that can be anticipated. We have what we have in terms of where we need to be when.

And, I would guess, unless something very dramatic happens, the case with most people is they linger at the *what happens* and never get to the *what does this mean, what have I learned, in what way does the what impact the values of who I am and who God wants me to be—are they within sight of each other?*

131

Okay, this is Sunday morning, and it's early. But on this Sunday morning, as on every morning that dawns, to keep the double perspective active has one very significant value: it keeps a person from the accusation, *down deep he's shallow.*

Spurts of promise…do we see them?

Posted on December 20, 2010 by Mark H Miller

As indicated yesterday—Sunday—morning December 19, we considered what happens in our world from an historical and then "relevant" dynamic. The first is the front page; the second is the editorial page, to put it in journalistic function.

Or in biblical understanding: what happened in this incident and what does it mean—facts and relevance?

Yesterday the front page included worshipping at my former interim parish in San Marcos, having a book signing, clapping and cheering at Andrew's Men's Basketball game at Schreiner [they won by 31 points—perhaps the largest victory margin in the school's history] and then having dinner afterwards with Andrew and then discovering a new way from Kerrville [Schreiner's venue] to our Austin home. That's the front page.

Shifting.

The human pulse of people impacts—big-time. I learned of a beautiful parishioner—he and his wife have lost both their sons to cancer—who's now "in his last days" with cancer. How sad. I learned about other parishioners who are experiencing more of Good Friday than Easter and who have need for prayer and comforting presence. My prayers include them…very much so.

I learned of a beloved pastor—the most important minister in my life—who will celebrate his 75th birthday on December 30 and a chance to link-up with him and his family.

I learned how many parishioners still give value to our shared ministry—and their appreciation [just as much as any sermon ever preached] for how good Diane looks—and to know their prayers for her complete recovery will continue. That's special..the depth and value of friendship that transcends any professional level.

But most of all, I learned of players on Andrew's team, and a new player to join the team next week…stories filled with anguish, poignancy, hope and utter collapse.

Of course no names are included and I will not be too specific…but there are the ones who deceive themselves and carry that through their promise to others…about how well it's going and they flunk out of school or earn a failing score on a drug test…and end up with nothing and a grade point average that keeps them from any intercollegiate competition. To learn of a child who was six weeks in neo-natal care, had multiple heart surgeries, and some physical impairments, yet who has not been conquered by that, but has the inner spirit and resolve to make more of his life than chopped liver. And he has. What a great example of how we—each of us—when it gets down to it, has the most to say about how our life will be lived.

To see parents at Andrew's game, whose son is currently having some freshman college woes, who still drove almost 3 hours to cheer the team on—even though their son must sit out a semester. Goodness, talk about loyalty and support. Caring parents, for sure.

And then to hear from a friend about a job that didn't happen—he was the best candidate, no question—and yet another was chosen. He said it wasn't fair; he doubts he was considered for more than a glance. He then followed up later with this, *There must be a reason this didn't come through for me. I don't know what it is, but I refuse to get into an ego-drill on why I'm better. THAT'S beside the point…what isn't beside the point is to keep open to new job possibilities and know that my place and purpose in life, no matter what happens, is to be resilient and determined and caring. I don't want to become uncaring or hard or cemented because I wasn't chosen. Rather, God has something for me…and when I find out, world look out!*

That declaration—my goodness how strong—gave my day such a zing…and that's the final declaration on my editorial page….

Other…

[You knew this was coming]

The Broncos.

We had taped the game and watched it last night upon our return home. It was the first game for Tim Tebow—and it was against Oakland—the dreaded Bronco enemy—in the Black Hole—the description of the Oakland Stadium.

Tebow had a great game—for his first. So, maybe there's hope for the Broncos. Even though they were batted around, there were spurts of promise.

And, after all, were I editorializing, I'd make something of *spurts of promise.*

Because the spurts are there...if we will look down and know our feet are moving, look up and know we have purpose and look ahead to see... ah, good what we see when we don't give up.

Living the Hyphen

Posted on December 21, 2010 by Mark H Miller

I just viewed a very poignant and powerful [aren't they always linked?] video on the Yahoo.com web page. In short it's about Sabrina Parker who was too young to marry Matt Scozzari — but before she died, they found an alternative.

They were both teenagers. Sabrina was suffering from ALS, Lou Gehrig's disease, which had advanced. Everyone knew her days to live were numbered. Because Matt and Sabrina wanted to affirm their friendship [think how many at age 15 and 16 never think about friendship but about sexuality and then move on?], so they had a friendship ceremony with family and friends. Matt purchased a friendship ring. To enter into what I would call the covenant of friendship. It came through as a powerful and beautiful moment.

If you've ever experienced a friend or family member who's suffered from ALS, you know how unforgiveable it is. It is the muscle atrophy that cannot be halted.

I've gone through ALS with two parishioners, each of which finally couldn't breathe given the lack of muscles functioning their lungs. It's dreadful.

In fact, in one instance, it was the mid-80's when I was serving Broadmoor Community Church in Colorado Springs, I visited Doug who was spending his final days in a Veteran's Retirement Home in Florence, Colorado. I went to his room…well, I cannot even write this, his condition was worse than death, a death if it would only arrive would be a friend. As I stood alone in that room with Doug—no one had seen me, no one knew I was there, except Doug, but he had no strength to lift his head—it sank into his chest. It made it clear to me, death would be liberating, a welcome friend. As I stood there my prayer was for him to suffer no longer.

Sabrina had such a struggle—and as a teenager, my limited knowledge indicates that is very young to contract the disease.

She died ten days after their ceremony of friendship.

I was so touched by the caring…yes, teenagers can care…and at times more than some of us older ones, even those with white hair and left-handedness.

And I thought—about a lot.

Yes, my thought coursed, we each are going to die. In that I remember the great line from Morgan Freeman in "Shawshank Redemption," when he says, "Some people are busy dyin'; some people are busy livin'. It's better to be busy livin'."

I have another thought: anyone who's afraid to die is held back from living. I honestly believe that. I remember the time when I came to terms with my death. It was scary. I was alone. A time when uncertainty was as great as fear and both kept hope from my door. Quiet. [Yes, I can be that.] Reflective. Focused. I realized a great truth: we don't know, for the most part when we'll die, but we have one helluva lot to say about how we live. And then, because it's the undergirding truth of my faith, joining the Apostle Paul, *Whether we live or whether we die, we belong to the Lord*, I realized that if life is put in grammar, when we live, in the sentence structure of life and death, death is never a period or exclamation point; it is a comma.

Put another way, I do my best to "live the hyphen." That's what ends up on the tombstone: the date of birth and the date of death, separated by a hyphen.

How do you live your hyphen?

Okay. In less than a week it will be Christmas. In less than a week we will sing the songs of faith about the birth of God's love in the child named, Emmanuel, which means God with us.

And so we should be talking about birth.

And here I am talking about ALS, about a teenager dying ten days after a ceremony of friendship with her boyfriend.

I do this, because lately I've heard so much whining and people spending lots of energy holding their own pity party on how horrible the economy is, how horrible their future looks and the tentativeness, the ominous shadow of death that cancer brings.

And then I look to Diane…yes, who's got cancer. Yes, who's reflecting an attitude that is so far into hope and resilience and determination that whining and self-pity never have a chance.

She's living a great hyphen.

I try to do the same.

How about you?

Silliness of words…easier said than understood
Posted on December 21, 2010 by Mark H Miller

Tie the knot. Read that this morning, an incidental note about Hulk Hogan getting married. Now, I have nothing against Hulk Hogan….

…a sidebar triggered by "Hulk Hogan"…I remember when we had our first television set in Portland, Oregon, early 50's I believe, one of the programs on was pro wrestling. At the time I didn't know it was scripted and most "falls" were agreed upon. A favorite of mine was Red Berry. He'd get into hopeless holds and somehow, just like a Saturday matinee movie serial the next week, get himself out of it. He would then parade around the ring pointing to his temple, indicating his intelligence was his strength. For whatever reason, but probably because in my mind and experience my father was one of the smartest people in the world, I nicknamed my father, "Red." He never died his hair.

…a second sidebar…I consider boxing and wrestling as mired in muck as roller derby, none of which I watch. I do remember the only boxing match I attended, again with my father and some of his garbage-hauling sidekicks, was on a Friday night at the Portland Auditorium. I was maybe 8, which makes the circa 1948. The main event featured a Northwest Heavyweight, Joe Kahut. I now think someone made the name up for marketing. But not then. I do remember how repulsed I was by the blood, smeared across his body.

But even more I remember that following the fight we went to the Ringside Restaurant [guess that made sense given where we had been] for a late Friday meal. First I thought it special because it was waaaaaaay past my bedtime and I didn't fall asleep. Second, I remember we all had crawfish, one of my favorites. But then, one of the first major faux pas at eating: a waiter brought me a soup bowl filled with clear bouillon and a lemon. I took a spoon and started to enjoy it, only to be advised by my father it was a finger bowl. Hey, at 8 it looked drinkable.

Back to *tie the knot.* I realize it is often used to describe marital vows. But think about it. A knot? Quite often that's what ends up in a marriage—or any significant relationship—all knotted up, which indicates inflexibility and entrapment and snarls.

Occurs there are other things we say that if thought about, would be jettisoned.

Try these:

He knows that like the back of his hand. Think about it. I would wager more people than not wouldn't know the back of their hand if they saw it. I bet if you took off the rings and removed the ink, and pictured five hands on a page, identification would not be like the snap of a finger.

I love her to death. Hello? Why not *love her to life?*

Slick as a whistle. Are you sure? How about *shrill as a whistle?*

Bet you a dollar to a door nail. Think I made that up, but still, maybe it says a *slam-dunk bet.* Now, I know what that means.

Slippery as an eel. Okay, tell me…how many people whom you know have ever held an eel? Why not *slippery as a fish?* Haven't had that experience in too long…which indicates that a fishing trip should be *on the horizon…in the future…upcoming like the sun…looming ahead?*

All this on a December day in Austin, Texas, when the temperature will be *hot as a firecracker.* For December 21, 2010: 80 degrees.

Okay. *I'm out like a light.*

For now.

The best....or your best?

Posted on December 22, 2010 by Mark H Miller

America's Next Greatest Restaurant—The Biggest Loser—The Survivor—The Next Iron Chef—The Next Top Model—The Top Chef—Project Runway—Shear Genius

Maybe some of these are new to you...but I'm guessing not all. They are television programs in which people compete for the top prize.

As I've pondered these—and I have not seen each, but some—it occurs to me there are three key components that must be ingredient in each contestant.

They first must recognize a need. That means a good self-awareness, acknowledging within where the self is strong and where the self needs to improve [I eschew the word *weakness*]. This means self-confidence but not arrogance, this requires a love of self that doesn't find hubris out of control. Biblically the Great Commandment hinges on the end, "Love your neighbor as yourself." SO MUCH in how the self relates to the self guides, restricts, empowers, discourages ALL relationships... with the Holy One and with the others. For instance, the people I have met over the years, it is quickly evident how they feel about themselves. The self has eroded significantly when a person is more interested to complain than learn.

They must next have energy. That means half-effort is like no effort. The self must be willing to work hard, to sacrifice and not have alibis. It requires recognizing when the best has been given. And when it hasn't been. I know of no achievement that comes from thinking about it. In a direct, perhaps even offensive manner, I will admit, nothing...let me put that in a stronger manner, NOTHING, infuriates me more than ministers who are lazy, who believe their effort isn't needed...and to those ministers I have said, "You are taking grace too seriously."

But, perhaps most of all, and I've seen it in each of the above programs I've viewed...

They must each have passion. That is the will of the heart. That is WANTING to reach the goal more than anything. On a personal basis, when I learned almost a year ago I had Diabetes 2, I was overwhelmed with, *What in the world have I done to have this?* Luckily encouragement by friends, a great doctor, but most of all my wife, Diane, I decided a self-pity party was pointless and very selfish. So, learning what had to be done, lower the blood sugar and lose weight, my heart said, *Go for it*. Diane herself has had formidable medical challenges. Each day she greets as a possibility to get stronger, to deal with the cancer and to make sure radiation is a means to a healthier end.

It is the case more than likely none of us will ever be on any of the above television competitive programs. And yet, far more important: each of us has a life gifted by God, and each of us has days…today and tomorrow and all the tomorrows that are to be for us to see how discerned needs, galvanized energy and unfettered passions blend together to make each day more than a good idea.

Do dreams ever come true…really?

Posted on December 22, 2010 by Mark H Miller

I never thought about it—not really. Went to the fitness center, peddled away my routine, worked up some sweat and then started to exit. Which is different than exiting.

An elderly gentleman, his white hair matched mine, although he was tanner than I, which takes practically nothing. He had just registered at the front desk, turned and read my T-shirt, the one that is my attempt at humor, even though not above lameness for some, *Be nice to me…or I'll put you in my next novel!"*

He nodded, "Well, guess I won't be in your next novel…but, got a minute?"

I did…even more…"Sure, time's on my side."

Not aware how that slipped, but hey, spontaneity's no enemy to me.

"Are you really a novelist? I mean, do you have anything published?"

Not sure where that was headed, I figured truth was always the best policy, "Yes, I am. Nothing published yet, other than some books of letters I've written to some of my churches and clergy. But, a novel will be published next summer…that's for sure."

"Gosh, that's great. Might I ask your genre?"

Thanks goodness I paid attention to his lips [my hearing has gone south…way south in recent years…to the point my audiologist has used the word *severe* in describing the increase of loss from 5 years ago] because at first I thought he asked about my gender.

"Genre? I write murder/mysteries. Not in the league with Child or Patterson or Scottoline or Grafton…although I did get a personal Christmas card from Sue Grafton last week."

"That's more than interesting to me."

I didn't know if getting Sue's card or writing novels was his interest. He didn't reveal the backing for that as he continued, "Is this the only novel you've written?"

[This was going in a good direction and I was good, I didn't look at my watch…or my wrist since my watch was in my car.]

"No, in fact, it's not…I've written a total of 4 fiction novels, each has to do with ministry, fishing and murder, with a few comments about how life can be more shadows than light, but the shadows never win."

"That's more than interesting. Give me a couple sentences on each novel, first with the one that will be published."

I did…still wondering what his aim was.

He then inquired, "Do you have a contract with your publisher? Meaning, will they have the rights to each that you have written or will write?"

"No, we have a verbal agreement that I will honor to have the first one, Murder On Tillamook Bay published. Nothing more than that."

"Well," as he reached for his billfold and took out his card, "My name is………and I am the CEO of …….Publishing Company in Austin. I'm always on the hunt for Austin novelists. Can I ask you to first send me synopses of the other three novels…your description of them is more than interesting…and then I'll get back to you for the full manuscripts. Will want my chief editor to peruse them."

I knew what *peruse* meant so I didn't look like I had dumbed down.

I looked at his card after I got into the car…and thought, *Never in the world did I think the T-shirt would lead to this…but hey, I'm not against surprises.*"

. . . . . .

Then I awakened, was so tired I had nodded off at the bicycle peddling, an easy rhythm that can do that, and was pleased with the discovery and the conversation, even though it hadn't happened. But hey, don't think not dreaming is the 11th Commandment…and who knows how sometimes dreams become reality. You think?

More than good fortune...

Posted on December 23, 2010 by Mark H Miller

I had forgotten this, even though the two events said much about the ways in which life happens…and God brings hope.

What triggered the events tonight was a moment on television, an advertisement for whom I do not recall, but in the background was the famous Christmas song, "Chestnuts Roasting Over the Open Fire," by Nat King Cole. I figure it's okay to mention Cole, although most people under, what 30, would be clueless.

Scene: in my freshman dorm room at Stanford, about to take my last fall semester exam before driving with Portland friends to be with my family for Christmas. I was worried. My baseball scholarship depended upon getting a good grade in Biology…not my best subject. That's a gross understatement. I tried to study, but was wanting more to skip the exam and get home. I then heard, "I'll Be Home For Christmas" sung on my roommate's radio.

It got me. Right between the eyes. I lost it…at least emotionally and was very foggy on anything. Homesickness beset me—big-time. A friend down the hall dropped in [I thought later it wasn't an accident.] and saw I was somewhat distressed. He's also from Portland and took time, simply to listen and then to offer, "It will be okay. Keep throwing fast balls." [He had also played baseball in Portland—in fact we played against each other. But this night he was not an opponent—nor was I. Simply two freshmen trying to get through our first semester.] His words helped and I did okay in the Biology test, even though I learned something about multiple choice exams: never change your first answer. I had gone back over the test and changed ten answers, each change went from correct to….well, you can figure that part of it.

Then the drive home. There were three of us driving. From Palo Alto to Portland is a good stretch so we switched every three hours. We were north of Salem on Interstate #5. It was double lane both ways with a wide median, mostly of grass, some trees.

146

I had fallen asleep in the front seat passenger side. The following happened. The driver fell asleep and was driving onto the right shoulder. I leaped across the front seat and grabbed the steering wheel to correct us. The driver and I struggled and finally his yelling, "Mark, stop!", woke me up.

I looked around and wondered why we were still facing north but on the south side of the interstate.

What had happened is the driver was just fine…my horrible dream that the driver had fallen asleep triggered my grabbing the wheel and sending our car swerving across the median.

Fortunately the traffic was light, there was no accident and the car only had minimal damage.

The police helped us get back on the north side of the interstate. I stayed in the back seat the balance of the trip.

Amazing to me how two events could have gone another way. I could have lost it so badly in my dorm room that might have resulted in a blown Biology test, which would have cost me the scholarship. And, the grab of the steering wheel could have led to fatalities.

That was 1958.

Tonight, December 22, 2010, we are about to enter a new year. Even more for me personally, in two nights Diane and I will light candles during a Christmas Eve Service.

Because of tonight I will recall again both those events. And as I'm doing now, I will offer a prayer of thanksgiving to God…that neither ended up as it might have. To say my life is blessed is an even greater understatement than my difficulty with Biology.

It's not to be presumptuous about my good fortune. But it is to realize that each day is a gift…the second greatest gift from God. Of course the first of which, even our very own lives, is the presence of God-become-human, to let us know how life should be lived and that we are okay, whether or not we like Biology.

Lighting Candles and Dancing–a great partnership

Posted on December 24, 2010 by Mark H Miller

I didn't know Diane at the time. I didn't know there'd be a Diane. All I knew was I was in trouble—emotionally and spiritually. I had visited a dear friend who was in a coma…he would die in less than a week. As I saw him I thought to myself—not because I was at all sacrificial let alone noble or gallant—rather because I needed the release, I thought that I'd like to trade places with him.

That moment told me I was in trouble and needed to do something about it.

I had forgotten that moment until this afternoon.

A beautiful friend, Bob, who was a parishioner in my last pastorate, is now retired in North Carolina, sent me a video via e-mail. It was called "Boogie Woogie." [I don't know how to have you access it on the Blog, but the piece was labeled, **BOOGIEWOOGIE.wmv** the U Tube version]

I played it…I played it again…and again. And with it, suddenly a liberating moment was revisited.

But, that's the last scene.

When I realized I was in trouble I went to get help…the helper was perceptive and shared thoughts on what I needed to do…and made it clear the trouble was manageable, my future was not doomed.

That night I went to a rather formal dinner event. There was a band and suddenly a couple went to the dance floor and danced like I'd never seen before. I was mesmerized how fluid and together they were. My eyes sparkled at their beautiful symmetry, the way in which they danced. When they finished everyone applauded, for others had beheld the skill, almost magic, in their dancing.

148

I remember what a transcending personal moment it was…watching that and knowing that somehow, somewhere, sometime, I would experience that joy and harmony.

When I listened to what Bob sent [and he himself is having a tough time now because his beloved wife, Susie, died of cancer and Bob will be having critical heart surgery in January] I was taken back to that night so many years ago.

And then gave thanks the depression didn't win. No less a profound thanks to God for Diane…for the way we dance each day in our marriage covenant. To support, to care, to listen.

I don't believe for a moment we become whole unto ourselves. No. Never. Forget it.

I do not think we are to dance alone.

Tonight is Christmas Eve…we will sing of our faith and the birth of new life and the way in which a worthier manner of life can be experienced…."O Come All Ye Faithful," "Joy to the World," "Silent Night." And we will together, not alone, light our candles.."The light shines in the darkness and the darkness has not overcome it." And when pastoring a congregation, I added, *Remember, the light breaks the darkness into a million pieces.*

And then tomorrow we'll be with family…with Jason and Teela and Jackson and Aiden and with the new life to be born next summer [Teela's now pregnant.].

And may it be…not just tonight and tomorrow, but each tomorrow that dawns, we continue to dance, to celebrate life and to know the darkness doesn't win. It didn't years and years ago and it won't in 2011. Nope, it won't. That's a statement of faith, based upon the promise God made upon the earth's creation and upon Christ's birth and in each dawning day, "I am with you, no matter what, no matter what."

Seeing the Boogie Woogie and that young couple dancing...wow, how good they are. And how blessed I am. I didn't trade places with my comatose friend. Thank God I worked through it...and the first moment when hope was real was seeing the couple dance.

Now, Diane and I share the dance, and with God's love and presence, the New Year will be a time when each of us is healthier, and if we step on one another's toes occasionally, well, that's okay. Because we'll keep dancing, loving, caring, and yes, fishing.

I can sense it now...the trout in Colorado and Montana and the steelhead in Oregon and Washington are already trembling. But tremble they will, because they will never ever stop the music as we dance each day that dawns. Yes!

The ministry of mailing post cards…priceless
Posted on December 25, 2010 by Mark H Miller

This will take a while…more than a few paragraphs. It is triggered by the birthday event of my mentor in ministry, Fred Trost, who on December 30 will be 75. I'm calling him to affirm his day and tell him my indebtedness for his mentoring will never be repaid fully or adequately…but I'll do my best.

It started, unbeknownst to me, November, 1965, as I walked to the seminary refectory. Mr. Gaylord Noyce, an administrator, came out of his office as I passed by, "Hi, Mark, I realize you're graduating this May—what's next in the journey?"

I shared that I would begin seeking a ministry position in Chicago, triggered by an upcoming marriage, my fiancé an undergraduate at the University of Chicago.

His eyes had that *have I got something for you!,* look, "What timing! I just read a letter from a former classmate of mine, Fred Trost, currently the Senior Pastor of St. Pauls Church in Chicago—he and his associate, Herb Davis, are looking for an assistant minister to work with youth. Let me give you his contact number—I haven't posted the position yet on the seminary bulletin board."

One contact led to a new day—and a career I could not ever dreamed, let alone imagined.

That February Fred and Herb interviewed me for the position. I sat in the corner of Fred's living room, 640 Fullerton Parkway, they facing me, asking one question after another. It was as if I were questioned for a phD in pastoral ministry. I picked it up quickly, *These two were very focused on the practice and theology of pastoral ministry.*

They offered me the position which I had accepted mentally before it was offered officially.

That ministry began in July of 1966, prefaced by a rash of activities: My future mother-in-law died of cancer on June 14, we had a committal service for her at the cemetery the morning of Friday, June 17, that afternoon I passed my ordination examination and that evening I was ordained at my home church, Zion Congregational Church in Portland, Oregon. It was also my 26th birthday. On Sunday afternoon we had a memorial service for Shelly and the next Saturday was the wedding ceremony.

Arrived in Chicago an early July morning, Tuesday I believe. We were advised the FBI had left our vacant apartment the night before because of their surveillance of a national bookie across the street. The next Friday my car was stolen, the next Sunday I marched in a Civil Rights March led by Dr. Martin Luther King, Jr. and the next Tuesday Richard Speck murdered the nurses—think it was eight homicides.

Welcome to Chicago, welcome to ministry, welcome to...

Since July, 1966, Fred has been the most valued mentor...has never failed to care, to listen and to share his perceptions, always as balloons to consider, never as spears to pierce.

Of course there are zillions [not understated] of times shared...to list would be more than a book. We could laugh and cry, we could get furious at the lack of justice we beheld in our society.

I could not have begun in a better ministry—in fact, it was like another 3 years of seminary. Fred was the pastor and Herb was the prophet. And lucky me, I was in between them, grasping as many ideas as I could ever hold.

Of all the experiences, the shared times, the moments of learning, the indelibility of friendship, there's one event that is the capstone on what it means to be alive and not comatose in ministry.

It happened in 1968 as the National Democratic Convention came to Chicago and Mayor Richard J. Daley blew off the dust of a 1919 city edict, *All city parks are to be vacated by 11 p.m.* That was used to tear-

152

gas-out the thousands of hippies, who in their long-haired protesting rant insisted a pig be elected president.

The Sunday afternoon before it began, Fred and Herb and I met with some council members to recommend St. Pauls be a sanctuary for any of the protestors who wanted to be in a safe overnight environment.

So it was.

We housed over 2,000 hippies through Friday morning. Since I was the youngest guy, it was my responsibility to greet EVERY ONE of them before they entered the church to insist they give me any "meds" they might have and not to have contraband. I wasn't sure what that meant, but figured it meant any instrument of harm, so to speak. By 4 a.m. each of those days I was the most drug-laden guy in Lincoln Park, with no competition.

I made a decision to flush every "med" that wasn't in a prescription bottle, telling the youth the next morning, "It's for your good," when their "med" was no longer available.

Friday morning completed that very dramatic ministry, a time when I experienced, perhaps more than anyone could imagine, how being a prophet can happen.

But the drama of the week paled to the drama of Sunday morning. I told Fred that he should preach, because we three clergy [probably considered Moe, Shemp and Curly by many parishioners] were on the spot, so the senior minister needed to preach on WHY we opened our gymnasium, kitchen and fellowship hall to 2,000 rebels. Herb was scheduled so Herb preached.

Remember, Herb was the prophet side of that tandem—pastor and prophet. He compared the Chicago police to the Keystone cops—not exactly calming the waters.

But the drama and the huge waves of protest came forth during a congregational meeting following the uneasing worship. One parishioner after another hammered us. I remember one elderly lady, shaking her arthritic finger at us—she a life-long member—"You ministers have baptized MY church with a bag of urine."

Damn, I thought, *What a creative metaphor.* I thought even more, though, our days as pastors of St. Pauls Church were numbered. And the three of us agreed, if Fred was fired, we'd walk with him.

Then it happened.

Georgia Smith, I'm guessing about 30 years of age, stood to speak. She spoke softly so the room quieted. It was amazing how 300 people could be stone-quiet.

She shared, "My name is Georgia Smith. I was baptized and confirmed and married in St. Pauls and Nick and I hope our two daughters will experience the same. I am a nurse on the Geriatrics Wing of Bethany Hospital. Three weeks ago Frau Krieger, a life-long member of our church, was on my floor. I was assigned as her nurse. She was dying of hardening of the arteries. On a Wednesday night she received a post card from Pastor Trost. He was vacationing in Germany with his family. But he took the time to send Frau Krieger a post card which was written in German. I read it to her that Wednesday night. The post card said Pastor Trost was praying for her and he asked God to be with her as comfort and peace. Frau Krieger smiled. Her pastor had cared for her. She was grateful. The next morning Frau Krieger died. Knowing the love of the church and her pastor. So, please, don't any of you ever say these men are not our pastors."

You could hear people swallow and purses opening to retrieve handkerchiefs.

Then, one of the strongest protestors rose and started to sing the Doxology, "Praise God from whom all blessings flow...."

That was in August of 1968.

Today is Christmas day, 2010. On December 30 I will call the most beloved mentor in the world, to wish him a happy 75th birthday. And, as we have done for over 44 years, we will end our conversation, as 1,000 times before and still counting, "Pastor, remember to mail your post cards."

One extra fruit basket and a great lesson

Posted on December 26, 2010 by Mark H Miller

Still Christmas day...thinking about how special...to spend part of the morning and early afternoon with Jason's family of Teela, Jackson and Aiden and Teela's parents. Nice. To see the zeal of the 3-year-olds is wonderful. To talk with Matthew—gosh, what timing for his gift—delivered last night at 6 p.m. before we went to Diane's sister's home for a lovely dinner. Hopefully not too far into 2011 Diane and I can get to Winnetka to visit Matthew, Sheila and Laura in their new home. Later we'll talk with Andrew to see how he and Jennifer and Dylan and Taylor are enjoying Jennifer's family in Seattle.

Just moments ago I received an e-mail from a wonderful friend and colleague, John Thomas. He's one of my most favorite clergy friends—especially when I was Conference Minister and John, as President of our denomination, was my pastor—how much he cared for me, most focused in memory was when my mother died and then that horrible weekend in early May when one of our ministers and his wife were bludgeoned to death in their sleep by the Railroad Killer. Goodness, it had to be one of the most sordid times ever—and John was with me in spirit and in many conversations.

What I think about though, John mentioned that he worshipped last night at St. Pauls for their candlelight/communion service and how much it meant to worship where Fred Trost [very close friend of John's] and I had led worship and how inspiring the Widor's Toccata was in that magnificent sanctuary. It really is one of the most awesome worship centers. Yes, for sure.

In thinking again on St. Pauls and Christmas Eve, marking the conclusion of Advent, I couldn't help recall an experience that impacted my ministry. Actually as I recall 44 years of ministry, some of the most life-shaping and transforming moments happened in the 1966-69 window as I served with Fred and Herb Davis.

Let me set the Advent experience table. At St. Pauls we were committed to serve Holy Communion for those members homebound—either in

156

their own home or apartment, or more likely in some retirement facility, some of which were elegant and others—more of these—that you wondered how people could really live—the odors of urine and purex were always in competition.

During Advent the ladies of the Frauenverein helped us by preparing fruit baskets we were to gift when we served communion. The ladies were adamant ALL the baskets got delivered—45 of them numbering precisely the number of communions we had to serve. With their firm resolve to look over our shoulder, and at times when I walked in the kitchen one of them would point to the baskets and say, "Yes?" It wasn't a question—rather it was a, "When are you going to get to these?" Might even have been a 11th Holy Commandment they had, **Don't let the bananas get brown**. Damn straight we wouldn't.

Or so I thought. Being pretty organized [that's my understatement], I took care of my 15 [we were pretty mathematical about dividing up 45 by 3 pastors] the first 10 days of Advent. I noticed, about December 22 with the clock not slowing down, that Herb has his delivered, but there were 15 still there.

"Fred, might I deliver your communions for you?"

Now the truth was he wasn't lazy, just had a number of meetings downtown in the metropolitan church office—yeah, right.

He didn't hesitate, "Marky [my moniker], that'd be great."

So the next morning, I loaded up my car with 15 fruit baskets and my trusty visitation list. Off I went, probably down-deep seeking the Guiness World Record of number of home communions in one Advent day. Everything went fine...I even remember the clear blue sky that darkened about 4:30 p.m.....the 5 degree without the wind. The wind was about ten miles speed, so the chill factor...well, it was somewhere between very cold and totally cold.

I got to my 15th communion, did pretty well with the visit, the purex odor prevailed and returned to my car. It had to be about 6 p.m.

NO! I looked to my back seat and ohmygoodness, there was one remaining fruit basket. HOW COULD THAT BE!

Did I forget one? Is there one of the 15 who's cursing the night, *Why didn't I get a fruit basket?* I dismissed that because what I didn't want to do was to go back to the 15 and inquire. I then entered into a self-taught ethical discussion focused upon *What am I to do with this remaining fruit basket?*

It would be the wrath of the Frauenverein were I to return the basket to the church kitchen table. I couldn't take it home—that would be greedy if the word ever got out. You must remember this was my FIRST Advent, having been ordained just 7 months previously. I couldn't throw the basket in a nearby store dumpster, that would be wasteful and disrespectful, a cardinal sin.

So I asked what seemed like the only wise question: *Is there someone who would appreciate a visit from one of the pastors, to be served communion and to receive the last fruit basket, now minus the two bananas—they were brownish with yellow only a history.*

It then hit me…like bells, like a trumpet sounding, like drums pounding: Esther Selk. Yes!

A word about this gracious St. Pauls parishioner. Many times she couldn't get to church—diabetes was getting the upper hand. She endured one amputation of a leg—up to the hip, and had a glass eye, only squinting out of her good eye. And, I knew she liked me. So, off to Esther Selk I went, only two turns from where I was.

Since those weren't days of cellular phones or texting, I took my chances when I parked in front of her two-story house, with a faint porch light giving bare visibility to a porch that had buckled wood, some slats missing. So, walking to the front door had to be done with great care.

Now that was a problem, for I hadn't shared the for Holy Communion at St. Pauls we served port wine…and I had already drained all but a couple of small cups worth from the 2nd bottle.

In other words, as you've probably discerned, I was feeling no pain.

But, let not one's condition keep a new pastor from a world record in number of home communions in Chicago on a cold winter December night.

I was loaded, so to speak: fruit basket, home communion kit, almost-empty bottle of wine and my Home Communion Book of Worship.

I knocked, not realizing what was to happen has had as great an impact upon 44 years of ministry as anything I can think of.

I could hear Esther thumping to the front door…she eschewed her wooden leg and refused crutches and was still able by pushing a chair ahead of her, to bounce along on her remaining leg.

She opened the door, squinted out of her one good eye and saw me. You would have thought I was an angel from heaven, "Ah, Pastor Miller, it's wonderful to see you…I see you have a basket of fruit—and is that a bottle of wine?"

It's great what you can see out of one squinty eye.

I tried to say "Esther," but am pretty sure it came out, "Ether, can I come in?"

Of course the answer was yes, as she followed her chair to the kitchen, turned it and sat down at her narrow kitchen table. It had linoleum for its cover, but some of it turned up at the corners [that meant nothing could spill on the floor].

I took off my coat and threw it at a living room chair. I missed. Not a surprise.

I then sat down across from Ether—I mean, Esther. She sat there waiting for her favorite pastor in all the world, along with Fred and Herb mind you, to serve her.

Doing my best, I drained the remaining wine into the two miniature cups, took out the two wafers and then opened the prayer book to the "Home Communion" section, because even though this was my 16th home communion, all in one day mind you, I still wasn't sure of the words. Why? Because can you imagine the embarrassment of offering communion with, "Jesus took the bread and drank it and took the wine and broke it?"

Before I looked down for the word, I looked over Esther's shoulder and saw her wooden leg propped against the refrigerator. I also noticed the fridge door was opened slightly and right there, right there without question was the glass of water holding her glass eye and that eye, no doubt in my world, was beamed in on me, *Don't you screw up, buddy!* Or something perhaps less charitable.

Esther waited.

I then looked down, anything but clear of mind or memory and couldn't read the words. Oh they were there, but fright abounding, *what do I do?*

Esther gave *waiting and patience and hoping* its clearest definition.

What in God's name do I do now? Forget the Guiness World Record...how about a hint at survival, God?

Not to pause any longer, thinking this at least looked religious, I waved my hand over the elements, the wafers and the two cups of wine—that had to be very honorable and helpful I deceived myself—and said, "Ether, help yourthelf!"

She smiled, still squinting, reached over and squeezed my hand, "Pastor Miller, you must be very tired."

Never in my life did I appreciate an euphemism so much.

I only nodded...and of course it was my imagination, but I think I saw that glass eye wink.

Esther then reached with her other hand, took my book of worship and squinted down and read, "On the night in which he was betrayed, Jesus took the bread…"

And in that moment, that incredibly powerful moment, Esther Selk served me.

As I end my 44th year in ministry, I consider that experience valued because there are times when I am not the helper but the helped, not the minister serving but the one served. That's what ministry's all about—the covenant of caring in which we each promise to give our fullest, and when that's not always possible, may another reach over for the book and continue the lesson.

Television Quiz Show "glory...sort of"

Posted on December 29, 2010 by Mark H Miller

The Million Dollar Drop Show has come up in three different conversations this past week.

Not having seen the FOX program, which is not surprising because, candor prevailing here, the only program I watch on FOX is NFL games.

Especially I won't watch their news programs. Yes, I believe I am open and affirming, but their approach to what's okay in America is so far to the right...goodness, I am waiting for one of their newscasters to say he or she can see Russia from their news desk...that I find myself scowling rather than pushing with an appreciative inquiry. Guess that means I'm as bad as some of my Republican friends who under any threat or coercion would never ever consider a Democrat candidate to have any worth.

And I imagine the same "won't watch it" is said by FOX News devotees who wouldn't give Keith Oberman the time of day if he asked them.

Back to the new program...two triggers on that this morning.

First, there have been two pairs of contestants who gave the correct answer but it was declared to be incorrect. The host of the show offered this morning, "That doesn't matter if we made a mistake. They missed the next question, so they would have lost $800,000 anyway. Besides we invited them to re-appear on the program and they're uncertain because they indicate there's too much pressure. And another besides, the U-Tube clip circulating doesn't show the next question which they missed. It was all moot, so what's the big deal?"

Hey, buddy, hold it. How many people take that route? How many people never face up to the fact they've made a mistake? I know lots of people like that. No matter what it's someone else's fault, or it isn't a relevant matter. Not. They are the kind of people who never need an assurance of pardon because they've got no sin to confess, at least not verbally or consciously. Maybe that's why I was not happy when

162

worshipping at the church where I served as interim and they had excised the confession of sin and assurance of pardon. Hello?

Reminds me of the Nixon chortle, "I am not a crook," and Clinton, "I didn't have sex with that woman," and Simpson,….well, you can fill in his declaration. We shouldn't scoff because I'm sure our face wouldn't be blank if we held a mirror up to our own.

The second trigger is not political or theological. It's actually fun and humorous and it has to do with a television quiz show.

It was September of 1963, to begin my second year at Yale Divinity School. One of my very best friends, Richard Howard Davis, a phD student in ethics, said, "Mark, how'd you like to be on a national television quiz show?" Pushing all timidity aside [yeah, right if you know me] I inquired.

Turns out Dick had just been on the "Password" television quiz show and when he left the director said he was so effective that he should recruit classmates from seminary.

He conducted, "How you get on Password" seminars. He also pointed out the person in the interview who really made the *"You're on the show"* decision.

I went to Manhattan and tried out. Funny thing, I ended up on the elevator with the decision-maker, and again shoving timidity to the corner, caused her to laugh or at least smile.

I made it!

The program was taped a week in advance. Ironically the first taping was the week after John Kennedy was assassinated, so it was postponed.

But, it then became *Show Time*.

For those who have always been focused on really intellectual programs, or will only view FOX News, let me explain the program.

There were two contestants, each of whom had a Hollywood star as their partner. My opponent was the wife of a New York Jets player and her partner was Gary Moore. My partner was the comedienne, Dorothy Lauden.

One word would be given one of the partners and they could only say ONE WORD to see if their partner would guess it. First time answer garnered 10 points with the first to 25 points the winner.

What Dick Davis taught us was HOW you said the word or your body language made a huge difference. For instance if the word was "day" you could say "nighhhhhht?," stretching it out and leaving it as a question.

So, we began. The NYJ wife was good and I was down, almost for the count, 24-14. Talk about having pressure.

Oh, one other thing…we were televised on the one evening show, Thursday night, which gave more money for the first prize—think it was $500. Hey, it was 1963 so that was LOTS of money, especially for a seminarian. Probably not for the NYJ wife.

So, I was up against losing.

I got the word, "Lover." I looked at Dorothy Lauden, and with a sigh and longing, said to her, "Romeooooooooo."

She leaned back, almost falling out of her chair and said with a flash of fright , "Lover?"

Alan Ludden, said, "Mark, that's right! By the way, are you married?"

When I indicated I wasn't, Dorothy Lauden said, "Oh, Alan, of course he's not!" Now, WHY would she have said that???

I ended up losing because I knew more about theology than real estate. The word was "Deed," and all I could think about was Boy Scouts, even though I never graduated from Cub Scouts as a child. Actually truth on that—see I can confess, although most of my confessed sins are either trivial or humorous—I was to create a hamburger fryer out of a #10 vegetable can and my father helped me. When I admitted I had help I was booted from the Scouts. But, that's for another blog day.

I look at the word, "Deed," and said to Dorothy, "Goooooooood," of course believing she could immediately say, maybe not leaning back in fright, "Deeeeeeeed!"

She didn't. She said, "Baaaaaaad."

The NYJ housewife looked at Gary Moore…and said, "Scouts."

She said "Deed," and the show concluded.

Ah, my 30 minutes of fame, which when you think about it, ain't bad… double the normal 15 minutes of glory most people get.

So, here it is, Wednesday morning, December 29, with two more days of 2010.

Tomorrow night I'll call Fred Trost and I'll rejoice in his 75th birthday.

Even more, though, I'll be grateful that Diane's radiation treatments are moving toward conclusion. THAT will be a great day with hope the future for us both will be so bright we'll need to wear shades, even if we don't get on the Million Dollar Drop Show next year.

Hey, I got $50 for "Password Show" participation. It didn't break the bank, and it won't even breathe on immortality, but it was fun…and after all, life's supposed to have as much of that as possible, right? Even if we cannot see Russia from our kitchen window.

A 2011 project: adopt a phrase and go for it

Posted on December 30, 2010 by Mark H Miller

Lives based on having are less free than lives based on either being or doing. If you don't know what port you're sailing to, no wind is favorable. It is the weak who are cruel; gentleness can only be expected from the strong. We don't' seek things as they are; we seek things as we are. When I let go of what I am I become what I might be. If you don't create your reality, your reality will create you. Once the last tree is cut and the last river poisoned you will find you cannot eat your money. There is hardly anything in the world that some man cannot make a little worse and sell a little cheaper and the people who consider price only are this man's lawful prey. If you don't know where you are going you will probably end up somewhere else. When you come to a fork in the road, take it. There is no wealth but life. Every increased possession loads us with a new weariness. We must become the change we want to see. The workplace should primarily be an incubator for the human spirit. If what you've done yesterday looks big to you, then you haven't done much today. I've never seen a luggage rack on a hearse. There is nothing so useless as doing efficiently that which should not be done at all. Think how many great things have been done in life by people not aware they weren't possible. He knows most who says he knows least. A great man is hard on himself; a small man is hard on others. At the feast of ego everyone leaves hungry.

Not sure of the sources of all these quotes, but as the year becomes history and the New Year is yet to be born, EACH of these merits thoughts and a wonderment, *Does one connect to me particularly?*

What's interesting to me, as Diane read these quotes from a business journal, in almost every sentence, I can think of at least some people. That's only to mention that each of us is our own individual self. [That was declared once by my son, Andrew, when he had a protest to contined piano lessons—shooting basketballs had more promise…and now that he's coaching college basketball teams at Schreiner College and not receiving applauding endorsement at a piano recital at Carnegie Hall, that seemed to be a good self-discovery/affirmation!]

So, what is the dream...for each of us...the vision, the hope, the expectation?

I'm figuring that what is to be is not unrelated to what has been... although there may be some shifts and adjustments, how life unfolds is mostly the result of our attitude, our passion and the ways in which we can answer the question, "In what way can you get stronger?" [I prefer that to the query, "What are your weaknesses?"]

I'm saving the first paragraph. Others who read this may want to do the same. Why? Look at it this way: it might work if we each took one of the first-paragraph-affirmations and adopted it...and be like one family I learned about yesterday...

To go into the New Year, and this is a first-time act for them, they sat down and each wrote on a piece of paper what they hoped to learn and accomplish in 2011, sealed it in an individual envelope. They will be opened a year from now on New Year's Eve. A great idea.

So, about to wave farewell to 2010 and nod in greeting to 2011.

Walk well and safely...for each of us...and see how our lives cannot be focused on how much we have...but on how much we can give...of our energy and our caring and our resilience and of ourselves, resolutely...

Tomorrow–bring it on!

Posted on December 31, 2010 by Mark H Miller

I hadn't thought of it in a long time, the very helpful, powerful and poignant book by Rabbi Harold Kushner, "When Bad Things Happen To Good People." I came across it today in my reading.

The book was written in response to the Kushner family's son who died of progeria—a disease advancing age, so at the early age of 14 [this is from memory] he had the body of a very, very old man.

I've had two responses to this great book over the years—one, his philosophy on how to cope with the untoward, the negative, the evil: live in faith that God is not the cause of the evil, that God isn't "after you" because you might not have been as good as you wish.

The other response, that is not often considered, is this: the book title has an implication, certainly not one Kushner intends, nonetheless is implied—namely if you are good then nothing bad should happen to you.

In the journey of ministry I've known people who believe that. They believe a primary purpose of being good, a primary consequence of being faithful will be a relatively unblemished life.

Time and again I argue against that: the purpose of being good is life is more meaningful to me with that attitude and expression. I am not faithful in order to be protected, in order for the unseemly to not intrude. No, time and time again, no. Fidelity is not for protection; fidelity is for endurance.

I had an experience tonight of that in my mentor, Fred Trost. Truth is I know of no one in ministry who better reflects the pastoral and prophetic. He means the world to me. And yet in our conversation tonight, December 30, as I wished him the best on his 75th birthday, is what he and his family [18 of them gathered this week in Wisconsin] have experienced: they worshipped together on Christmas Eve lighting candles, his brother Robert died of cancer and Fred led his dearest

168

brother's Memorial Service, the family—each of them—contracted the flu, they celebrated the wedding of Paul, Fred and Louise's son, they took a sleigh ride this afternoon and today is Fred's special day.

Goodness, all in one week. It happened. Stuff happens. Good times happen. And in it all, my wonderful brother in ministry, Frederick Richard Trost, was a gentle, loving man who knows that in it all God was present with each of them as an abiding and caring and strengthening Presence.

As I've said but want to repeat it now...we don't know what the future holds but we know Who holds the future. In a little more than 24 hours the new year will dawn. And then on January 6 it will be Epiphany, the moment the wise men beheld the Christ Child. A moment of awareness. May that be our world in the new year, no matter where or how we are, no matter what happens, may we be aware we are never alone, that God's promise to be with us no matter what is always kept.

Faith—for endurance. Goodness—to fulfill life. Tomorrow—bring it on!

Bucket List started for 2011

Time and again—and that is an understatement—my wife, Diane, focuses relevance. Many would experience her being quiet and reflective. That's true. And for certain, now as we head toward our tenth wedding anniversary [I realize it's nine months ahead, but hey, what's a clock when you're having the time of your life in a relationship beyond dreams but not beyond your reality?] she would not be a screamer or sulk in the shadowed corner of silence. Had plenty of that and don't need it.

In reading through a recent blog, Diane asked, "Are you selecting a personal goal for 2011?"

I shared what that is and told her it was triggered by two questions she had asked. Questions that perhaps more than any other, in almost every instance, especially the untoward and conflicted but not short of the glorious are relevant.

Her questions: "Is this really important? Does it matter?"

A paragraph back story, almost mentioned, although surface-level factoring, in recent blogs: my management of anger is a Mt. Everest. Not sure it ever was a mole hill.

And if I wanted, I could identify one of its sources, a family member who was uncanny on never forgetting when someone caused a problem. Memory to the hour of the day of the year, even though it might have happened 30 years previously.

Might label it, *Keeping a record of wrongs.*

I know that I'm not alone in this, that almost everyone has trouble letting go when someone *tries to do you in…and succeeds!*

A record of wrongs. Probably the chapter heading on that book of woes and weaknesses [they are both, mind you] is when I've done something

170

for someone, not to be recognized in a bold way, but at least to get a glimpse of gratitude. And it doesn't happen.

Yep, that's what has been real, and at times wears the hat of tormentor: spending time, giving effort, focused in purpose all for another person and then not having one word of *hey, thanks for taking the time on my behalf.*

Now I realize the best revenge is doing some good and doing it well. And it may be, short of deep therapy this is only speculative, my taking time to thank others is a way of over-compensating for the times I'm left standing there unthanked, flooded by someone's ingratitude.

I share an example of my revenge and this is so trite it may border on silliness: we took my cousin, Molly, to Austin's most famous BBQ place, the Salt Lick. Classic—open pit as you enter, "all you can eat" menu and for sure, the world's finest blackberry cobbler, even in December.

Salt Lick was crowded, so there was a policeman directing traffic in order for people to check in. Now, that's a real definition of crowded.

I stopped and asked, "Does anyone ever thank you for helping the traffic flow?" His first response was almost a startled look, like I was a ghost. He then raised his eyebrows—maybe wanting to know my ulterior motive in asking that—then shook his head, looked down and muttered, "Practically never."

I simply said, "Well, then, this is an exception to the never-hear-it-syndrome: thank you. What you are doing makes it better and safer for all of us."

No big deal…but he looked and then nodded, "Wow, why did you stop for me?"

I smiled, "That will help the blackberry cobbler taste better, because I've regarded someone else."

I'm not really sure why I said that, but I did mean that I always feel better when I regard someone for something they've done, from which I've benefitted.

But, many don't or won't or can't.

So, back to Diane's question, "Mark, is it really important? Does it matter?"

Her questions will be my companions in 2011.

What I'm hoping…and even more, planning…is that when tomorrow morning dawns, January 1, 2011, those questions will be dominating… whether experiences are good or bad, beneficial or detrimental, helpful or harmful, "life-ing" or "death-ing."

For 2011 Diane's two questions will be my high on my bucket list…a bucket list of attitude and temperament and memory. And who knows, maybe, just maybe I can have selective memory loss.

Now, that's not such a bad thing, is it?

I Hope You Dance
Posted on January 1, 2011 by Mark H Miller

Of all the *go back and do it over—or maybe better*—one would be, LISTEN TO THE WORDS AND NOT JUST THE MUSIC. My grade would be zero if you named any popular song and asked me the words—I could hum the melody in most instances, but come up blank on the words.

That change-it-thought occurred this morning, while of all things, riding an exercise bicycle. Was watching the television, an ad came on. There happened to be words printed for those without ear phones and I read the words.

I'd heard the song before, but never heard the words…and I thought, *Those are really great words…in fact, a fine message for a new day and even, as today proclaims, the first day of a New Year.* Maybe you've heard it before—the words. At any rate, I find them filled with value, so want to be sure it gets blogged. Have a great day and no matter how we be, where and why we be, keep dancing:

I Hope You Dance
by Lee Ann Womack

I hope you never lose your sense of wonder
You get your fill to eat, but always keep that hunger
May you never take one single breath for granted
God forbid love ever leave you empty handed
I hope you still feel small when you stand beside the ocean
Whenever one door closes I hope one more opens
Promise me that you'll give faith a fighting chance
And when you get the choice to sit it out or dance

I hope you dance
Hope you dance

I hope you never fear those mountains in the distance
Never settle for the path of least resistance

173

Livin' might mean takin' chances, but they're worth takin'
Lovin' might be a mistake but it's worth makin'
Don't let some hell bent heart leave you bitter
When you come close to sellin' out, reconsider
Give the heavens above more than just a passing glance
And when you get the choice to sit it out or dance

Time is a wheel in constant motion always rolling us along

Tell me who wants to look back on their years and wonder
where those years have gone.

I hope you still feel small when you stand beside the ocean
Whenever one door closes I hope one more opens
Promise me that you'll give faith a fighting chance
And when you get the choice to sit it out or dance

Dance
I hope you dance

Time is a wheel in constant motion always rolling us along
Dance
I hope you dance

Tell me who wants to look back on their years and wonder
where those years have gone
I hope you dance
Hope you dance

Myrrh–who knows it? A helpful lesson with the children

Posted on January 3, 2011 by Mark H Miller

Not sure the lesson made it.

But, then, when a children's sermon steps beyond cutesy and humorous, do they mean anything?

Like almost never.

Reminds me of the time I asked the children, "What do we put in the baptismal bowl?" The immediate response, "Oatmeal," brought guffaws and a scowl from the minister toward his oldest son. But other than that, zilch.

Giving children's sermons is not a lost art, but in most cases, like almost every time, it should be a cast-aside-art. A waste of time.

Okay, it's a chance for the kids and munchkins to come forward, it's a moment when the kids can say they're included and the parents check their grocery list.

As you can tell I'm speaking from experience here. In fact, of the thousands of children's sermons I've given, there are no more than maybe a handful that I would repeat. If that.

Until today…and I'm not even sure the congregation got it or the pastor meant it.

But, that's besides my point.

In the children's sermon today the minister was working with the word, "magi," and the kids' responses [i.e. a robot] brought the smile as the adults left their shopping lists. For the blink of a moment.

But then, almost as an aside, the minister asked when mentioning the three gifts of the magi, *gold, frankincense and myrrh*, "Do you know what myrrh is?"

175

Hey, I bet they couldn't even spell it.

And then. Right then he said, "I'm not going to answer that."

He continued, "Tell you what…when you go back home after the worship service today ask your grandparents, your aunts and uncles, your parents. Ask them to tell you what myrrh is."

The laughter was not as full, which was really very appropriate. In fact, I'm not sure people laughed much at all.

Why?

Because the minister, whether or not a strategy or bigger game plan, made one of the best points from any children's sermon ever preached: HEY, BOYS AND GIRLS, PARENTS, GRANDPARENTS, AUNTS AND UNCLES, DO YOU GET IT? WE, YOU AND I, ARE IN THIS CHURCH WORLD-BUSINESS TOGETHER, IN THIS TRAINING OUR CHILDREN TOGETHER. I'M NOT HERE TO DO IT ALL BY MYSELF, TO BE ALL THINGS TO ALL PEOPLE, TO BE THE ONE WHO EXPLAINS EVERYTHING. NO SIRREEE. RATHER, YOU HAVE THE TASK NOW OF EXPLAINING MYRRH, WHICH REALLY IS THE SURFACE TO THE UNDERGIRDING REALITY OF CHURCH: COVENANT THAT WE EACH WILL DO OUR BEST FOR THE GOOD OF THE RELATIONSHIP. AND WHEN YOU GET HOME, TAKE A MOMENT AND LEARN ABOUT MYRRH AND THEN SHARE IT WITH YOUR CHILDREN. OKAY?

That was a very crystallizing moment for me this morning in worship. The minister got it. And hopefully, the children and the older children [read that adults with parental responsibilities] get it.

Never loved oranges so much

Posted on January 4, 2011 by Mark H Miller

Yesterday, January 3, 2011, was a day filled with good and not-so-good news. But, in reality, isn't each day filled, maybe not brimming over, but nonetheless with news on either edge?

The not-so-good news is that Schreiner's Men's Basketball Team lost its league opening game. They've been much better earlier this season, far more than since Andrew began his coaching tenure in Kerrville. I don't know what happened—was at home watching a certain football team toss oranges to each other following the game in southern Florida—but looked the stats up on line and saw that the team shot very poorly [that's the kind version]. I tossled some over that, because there's nothing that happens to either of my sons that is unaffecting to me. The good thing is this was the first league game and Andrew really does have some fine, quick and very passionate players—all dynamics helpful here. So, here's hoping the not-so-good changes to the so-good and then to good and then to...well, you get the drift.

The good news came in bunches, the best of which Diane is now employed as Project Manager at GTECH, a huge company with offices in Austin. She begins on Monday as a Contract Employee with the possible change to permanent employee in a month or two. She's signed a 6-month contract. In this day of high unemployment, to get such a fine job—GTECH oversees/manages the Texas Lottery—is wonderful. I'm proud of her, very much so.

That doesn't mean the vision to become a Hospital Chaplain will be jettisoned. Not at all. Although Diane will not attend Spring Semester classes at the Austin Seminary of the Southwest this Spring Semester. Important to see about the requirements of the job.

Other good news: I was delighted to see Stanford steamroll to victory in their Orange Bowl game last night. Yep, I clapped and signaled *touchdown* a number of times. During the game I remembered how woeful the team was—this is back in the early 60's [that's 1960 for those who might chide]—so much so that the football coach then, Jack Curtis, who was more comfortable with horses and snakes and tumbleweed, once said to alumni expecting the team to do great, "Gentlemen, this year we are not big; but we are certainly slow." Somehow I don't think the humor helped.

But, last night...sweet victory. Pride won't last; it shouldn't. But, for a little while it's so good what the Stanford Cardinal did. And I admit, I am curious if John Elway, the new executive-head-guy for my beloved Denver Broncos, had a persuasive visit with the Stanford coach, Jim Harbaugh, to move to Denver. And then, although there are many Tim Tebow fans who believe the future of the Broncos is in his hands—I'm not a Tebow fan in the long run, not at least until he has more confidence in his passing than his running—I wondered if Andrew Luck, Stanford's quarterback and the likely #1 draft choice, might come along to the Broncos with Harbaugh. I realize that won't help the Bronco defense, which is horrible these days, but when thoughts ramp up, this is what happens.

And then, more good news: one of my fly-fishing guides in Colorado wrote me to ask for a copy of "Hooked On Life," and there's a possibility he will want additional copies for his guide shop, where he's now the manager.

That is a curious relationship with Clint. I only fished with him once, almost ten years ago. It was the day before Diane flew to Colorado. I had taken a sabbatical leave and was working on my first novel. I said to Clint, "Clint, make me a hero to my wife...show me some publicly accessible Colorado River water, teach me what flies to use. My wife's coming up tomorrow and I want to be a good guide." Well, he did. And, I was. In fact, Diane and I look to that day as the finest day we've fished together...she couldn't miss and my new task was to net all the trout she hooked. Loved it. At any rate, Clint has been very good in staying in touch. That means a lot.

One of our pastor friends is contemplating, with his membership, the launching of a major capital funds drive and has asked if he can visit with me about how to take those first steps. That means so much. It's an area in which I have a high interest, so we'll see how his church can engage each other in such a major project. To have some input as he has requested…that's special. Not that I know everything, for goodness sake, but at least I know a few somethings on fund raising and why people give to the church.

Another *"and then."* Received the loveliest note from Margaret Trost, one of our most favorite friends. Margaret's the daughter of Fred Trost. Margaret is the Founder of the What If? Foundation, an incredible ministry in Haiti. Because of Margaret's missional spirit, she, with the help of many others, makes it possible to feed thousands of children and their families each day. It's a joy to support that ministry. Margaret was so gracious in her words to Diane and me and it's beyond heartening to know how much she cares and values our friendship.

Finally, I needed to see my dermatologist for a follow-up appointment. I was relieved a couple of warts were not malignant, but one remained and needed to be excised. The doctor, Stacia Miles, is a wonderful person, very skilled and caring. She shared with me her father is having a quadruple-bypass heart surgery this morning and asked for prayers. Of course. But, in that moment I felt good because I could do something.

So, one day.

A gift from God.

A litany of far more than *this and that*. A litany of how God can be present in the good and not-so-good, as One who never leaves us.

Today is Tuesday…and I'll still think of the Stanford Cardinal and how this football team is big and fast. I'll think of Diane and give thanks the radiation treatment days are lessening and a new corporate position has begun. I'll think of Andrew and be there with him on Thursday to clap and cheer and hope their shooting improves.

And in it all, give thanks to God for life, for ways in which we benefit and are challenged, and for oranges. Go Cardinal!

Does everything that happens have a reason?
Posted on January 5, 2011 by Mark H Miller

Time and again. Cannot remember when the declaration was muted. It goes like this, and I'm certain all of us have offered it, especially when something happens we don't understand or appreciate.

The question is this: *Is there a reason for everything?*

Most people I know would nod in the affirmative, "Yep, everything has a reason."

I would not join them. I really don't. Not simply because *we have neither the power nor the wisdom nor the insight to know why things happen* all the time. There are actions that happen, that puzzle, even miff.

Now there are friends who deal with this question in two ways, neither of which I agree. Want that up front.

The first is that everything is authored by God. Taking that another step the logic runs in this manner: God must have a reason to bring this to me.

It's hard to overemphasize that I don't believe for a minute that God has full authorship. I believe that God creates us out of love and grants us freedom in our living out of hope. It's hope we won't blow it. But, when something bad happens, that's not a sign that God is bringing us into a more disciplined life.

I learned this so clearly when studying with Douglas Meeks, my doctoral professor at Eden Seminary. Doug took that famous passage in Genesis indicating, "Then God said, 'Let us make man in our image, after our likeness…'" [Genesis 1.26a] Doug made it clear to be made in God's image means we are **authorized to represent God** and no other creature in creation is.

A step further, God does not force us to represent God. No, a thousand times no. God give us the **freedom** to choose that. If we didn't have

180

freedom to love and/or to sin, if there were no choice or option, if God had everything worked out, a blueprint of our life, how long we'd live and what happens to us, then God becomes the puppeteer and we the puppet. That's not the God I know and certainly not the God I would ever follow. Because God is a Choice-Giver, no matter what.

The other thing I don't believe, which is related. Ever heard it? "God does not give me more than I can handle." That's assuming God's authorship. It's one thing to believe God is present in our life. But, it's another thing to believe that no matter what, we'll make it.

I've known people that simply were not able to make it. I know that is dour and grim, but during ministry there have been friends and parishioners who have made a decision to not continue because the pain of the present was unmanageable.

Back to the original question: **What is the reason for what's happening, assuming everything has a reason?**

It's not the right question.

Therefore, I choose to go into another direction, asking two different questions, and they go like this when considering any dynamic. In short, they probe CAUSE and PURPOSE:

Taking them in order.

What caused this? Cause is almost always discernable. For instance, if someone runs a red light and hits a pedestrian, the cause is clear: irresponsible driving. If I oversleep because I haven't heard the alarm [that HAS happened, unfortunately] there are causes. You can cite your own examples.

Which leads to a second question that can ALWAYS be answered: *What is the purpose; what can I learn?*

I don't have to discern the cause but I can always consider the purpose. To put directly and personally, as I reflect upon my years of ministry—which has been a priority for me these past months of blogging—it's much more helpful when I discern the lesson in an experience.

For me, there's ALWAYS a lesson.

Now, I don't have to like the lesson, because it might be, heaven forbid, right[?] that I am the problem and I need to change, I need to take a different attitude toward the jerks in my world. It's not fun to learn I am the jerk, but it's an important lesson.

For instance, when someone slams me for something, the first instinct is to reject it, to not listen to it, to move on. The second instinct is to slam the criticism as being wrong, as being imperceptive. But, what I try to do and am not as successful at this as I'd like, is to ask the question, "is this criticism true? Am I the one who's the problem here?"

To summarize: What are the facts: what happened? And what are the lessons: what does it mean, how can it be instructive on how life can be better ordered.

For instance apply this to reading the Bible. There are two essential questions: WHAT HAPPENED? And the second, WHAT DOES IT MEAN?

Quite honestly, it doesn't matter to me, in an ultimate sense, if there ever was a Flood or Noah. I do believe there was a flood and I believe a man named Noah built an ark. But I don't know that it ACTUALLY happened. And I don't know how long Noah's cubit was. What the facts are we can ponder the days after days. In factual truth it may never have happened. But in spiritual truth—what is its value, its lesson, its instruction—it is essential.

What is instructive is that how am I going to face the floods of my life, the Tsunami's when I am up to my neck in alligators [please forgive the mixed metaphors here]. Down deep I don't care if Noah is apochrophal, I really don't.

I don't believe God floods me, but I do believe, not unlike Noah, God bails me out.

Another example: reading the newspaper. There's the front page, the facts of the matter. And there's the editorial page: what can be made of life. I find it most important to focus upon the editorial page in my living.

I'd be curious how you look at this…in looking at your life and what has happened to you…or when you really wanted something and it didn't happen…how does it unfold when you think about what caused it and then what is the lesson, what does it mean?

Not for a moment do I consider this academic as much as relative. For to be engaging of these questions really makes for a life that is never shallow and an inner self that is never unsettled.

A postscript: Know the length of a cubit? Everyone's cubit's different, for a cubit is the measure of distance from the point of the elbow to the tip of your longest finger [on the same arm!]. Wonder what Noah's was?

Handling unexpected conflict and other briefs in one day...

Posted on January 6, 2011 by Mark H Miller

Briefs:

John Elway joins Denver Bronco executive staff. I can remember, was serving the Broadmoor Community Church in 1983, when hearing the news the Broncos drafted John Elway, quarterback from Stanford. I knew in my gut he would be the real deal, his university notwithstanding [a dose of modesty here]. But, my gut this morning is in the form of a question: Can he judge football talent? Will he be willing to be an endorser of Tim Tebow? Will Elway have serious conversations with both Jim Harbaugh, the hottest NFL new coach prospect AND Andrew Luck, the #1 draft choice for this year's NFL draft—both at Stanford now? Will the Stanford Connection work? I'm sure they won't need additional support, but hey, alumni need to stick together, right?

Andrew's basketball team stumbles. I don't know the details but Schreiner's losing to Texas Lutheran on Monday came as a surprise. However, I know next to nothing about the game, other than the story of the statistics. Andrew's best scorer made 3 of 27 shots [that's south of miserable] and they were outrebounded and were under-turnovered. Part of me gleans *it's only the first league game and they have some talent, more than in Andrew's previous 3 years.* And yet, I fuss and toss and turn with every game for Andrew, for he is a day-brightener and a free spirit and I love that about him. Guess once a father always a father. That is, until I'm too feeble and inattentive that I become a son. That happened to me with my own father, but I hope I'm not an echo in a few decades.

A storming customer telling those around her, and the world I suppose, she was more than angry; she was furious. I was at Office Depot yesterday to fax some information requested for Diane's new employment with GTECH. [On that, I'm pleased they want her immediately if not sooner and they're indicating the contract position will morph into a permanent position. I HOPE that become words of verity.] As I was asking the clerk to help me with the fax, a lady customer stormed by me, hurled her long scarf around her neck, pointed to my clerk and shouted, "Stick it in your ass!" In a heartbeat I looked at her eyes, appearing almost red with rage and noticed about a 7-year-old boy standing close to hear what she clamored. I said to her, muffled customers taking it all in, "Lady! Watch your mouth. There are children here."

As she left the store—it was a good thing the automatic door cooperated, although I must muse it would have been interesting if it had been stuck—she turned to me with additional judgment. It was a two-word accusation illustrated by a one-finger salute. The boy's eyes saucered and the customers and other clerks shook their head.

These outraged and outrageous incidents probably happen with a frequency that would be greater than any of our guesses. Still, when people blurt out in such a public manner, thinking they've been mistreated, I wonder, can reason and perception ever take the place of screams?

The clerk thanked me and explained what prompted the outburst is the customer was offended because she had to wait in line. I asked if her explosion was merited and the clerk, obviously shaken, shook her head, and whispered, "No."

I then said as the clerk looked up—I noticed as she handed me the receipt her hand was shaking—"Ma'am, I am confident you are the victim and not the cause. I'm sorry you had to experience this. Please know I come to your store frequently, very frequently, and I've ALWAYS been treated with respect and from your manager to all the clerks, each time I experience competency and caring. Please don't take the outrage seriously."

As I left the store another customer followed me, "Mister, great call on your part. We all should have clapped and cheered."

I told him I had additional thoughts on what I might say, but am glad I didn't. The one declaration was sufficient.

Ah, a few moments in a day.

And in a few moments next Diane and I head for her radiation treatment, then to her new employer to have her first meeting. And then tonight I'll clap and cheer for Andrew's basketball team…and hope they do well, which honestly IS more important to me than winning, although, truth reigning, only by the slimmest of margins.

Life is more than following rules…much more.
Posted on January 6, 2011 by Mark H Miller

I've written before about bumper stickers. Today one triggered many thoughts, not many of which were positive. The declaration went like this: YOU CANNOT BE CHRISTIAN AND BE PRO-ABORTION.

I would disagree, but my disagreement—perhaps to some, contrariness—doesn't say that being a Christian and favoring abortion is what I want.

Because it isn't.

No less, I would be against a bumper sticker—fully without question—that said, YOU CANNOT BE A CHRISTIAN AND BE ANTI-ABORTION.

The disagreement has to do with an overall ethic. Before I expand, let me explain that I've never ever endorsed absolutes. I don't believe in rigid rules that leave nothing to the circumstance. No more than I favor what is antinomian—that is, no rules at all. That latter dynamic was developed in a brilliant manner in the book/movie, "Lord of the Flies," when what ruled was the holder of the conch. Nothing more, nothing less.

Back to the abortion mandating. What I would say is this, using caps for emphasis: A CHRISTIAN MUST REGARD ABORTION AS SITUATIONAL.

The trigger point happened early in my Chicago ministry. In fact, I didn't know the 15 year-old, but she was a friend of a couple of the girls in my church youth group. I only learned about the situation after it was said and done—tragically so.

This 15-year-old had been raped. Pregnancy resulted from the horror-filled event. She felt worse than evil because of what happened to her and wanted to not continue the gestation. No one counseled her; abortion was not an option. Somehow a quack [not inaptly applied] met her in a motel room and proceeded to kill her and the fetus, using a coat hanger.

She had no option, at least as far as society was concerned. A society that said then, *Abortion is wrong, always and without exception.*

I've never forgotten that horrid event.

Which leads to what I think it means to be a Christian, no matter the circumstance. That is **to regard the circumstance**. Which means when we consider what must be done, this question above all others must be asked: ***How is love served in this situation?***

Now I would agree that few people get that far—for the most part people WANT/NEED/DEMAND rules that tell them what to do. They really don't want to think. They think the best life is dumbing down to a list of rules.

In the specific point, when it comes to abortion, I reject pro-choice AND pro-life and only endorse PRO-SITUATION.

What is the particular situation—is life at stake with continued gestation?

Yes, I believe that God authors life. Yes, I believe that life is sacred and holy and of the greatest value to God. But as I embrace God—or better, as God embraces me [I'm reading currently a biography of the great German theologian Dietrich Bonhoeffer who would prefer God as embracer], **I want to consider the situation.**

I cannot think of any life-future-determining decision that stands apart in the best determination from situational ethics.

That has to do with abortion. That has to do with divorce. That has to do with euthanasia. That has to do with staying in a job.

Certainly we go from one day to the next never having to make major decisions. But, even in the minor ones, when we think of the manner in which love is manifest, the decision, ultimately right or wrong, is the best one.

Why "right or wrong?"

Because, at least it's my experience that when I ponder with energy and depth and sincerity the "love serving the situation question" and go with what I go with, I consider that finally, my life is guided and sustained by God's grace. And in EVERY situation, God will not throw me out. Even if I have messed up in the decision-caused result.

That's not license to do whatever I want. No, no, a thousand times no. But it is to give my fullness to a decision, to living, to growing and to loving.

And in the final analysis, the goal is not perfection, a 100% on the test. Rather the goal is fidelity—**have I been faithful to my calling as a child of God to not be impulsive, childish, arrogant or self-serving.**

In answer to that, not always, but my sense is more than not, I've been okay.

Allow me to share a post-scripting experience wherein I felt a decision was made with the situation prevailing. It happened my first July in ministry, 1966. St. Pauls was across the street from Children's Memorial Hospital. The hospital pediatric intensive care clerk called our office to see if a pastor could help them. A 4-month old child was dying of leukemia—it was imminent. The mother had not had her child baptized and they couldn't find a priest, to honor her Roman Catholic beliefs. The mother felt if her child died and wasn't baptized, the child wouldn't get into heaven.

Of course I didn't believe that for a minute, but didn't think time for theological jostling was at hand. I met the mother—she was devastated by the situation, as anyone would be—and then went to the ICU nurse to explain the situation. Shortly later the nurse indicated the child had died [The mother remained in the waiting room.]. They cleaned the infant and poured a bowl of water. The physician and the head nurse stood by me as I celebrated the Sacrament of Baptism—my first.

I had chosen to not have the mother present, but then went to the waiting room. The mother only had one question: "Did you baptize my baby?" I told her, "Yes, your baby has been baptized and would be held forever in the loving arms of God."

The mother wept in gratitude, for baptism in that moment gave her assurance that God would be caring for her child and she as mother could be comforted by having it taken care of.

It was the situation in which the ministry was to the mother—not to theology, not to principled mandates, not to holy writ. It was the situation that indicated the way in which love could be served was to perform the baptism. It was a ministry to the mother. I knew God would take care of the infant, baptism or not. In that moment caring for the mother was the reality.

Pain in every corner and on every face…

Posted on January 8, 2011 by Mark H Miller

I sit here, aside from the television, the words too low-volumed to understand. Even more, though, I'm not interested. Not because I couldn't care less about the news of this Friday morning. Rather, I am more focused on those sitting around me.

A man in a wheelchair, his left arm limp on his lap, the right arm lifting the arm to be more comfortable. An elderly couple sits next to his wheel-chair and the woman reaches over to rub the man's back. It then becomes clear: she is his mother, probably in her 80's and her son, suffering from a stroke and other probable ailments, sits without expression, leaning forward for his mother's caring hands.

Another man, wider than tall and he's not short, waddling at the call of the nurse. An elderly couple, nicely/neatly dressed, not sure which will be called next—maybe both. A young lady, maybe 30, scowling. It's not a *I am mad at the world scowl*; rather it is because of apparent pain as she shifts endlessly in her chair. An early twenty woman reading the newspaper, holding it close to her face and shifting to one side, apparently to relieve her discomfort. A woman just walked in, briskly and with purpose, to check in, looking at her watch, not a sign of being early. Another just walked in, chalk-white-face, eyes caved deep shaded dark, expression sullen, brow furrowed, eyes darting erratically, as if fear is about to pounce from the lobby corner.

I sit here, waiting for Diane, who is now undergoing a third back surgery, a procedure to cauterize the raw nerve ends mingling around her three lower-back degenerated disks, a procedure prescribed every six months.

A woman leaves the office, neutral expression, but nodding. The nod suggests treatment that benefits. Maybe not, because as she opened the door to leave, she then nodded from left to right rather than from north to south. Not a good sign.

Okay, so I'm reading body language and facial gestures. Still, there's a chance I'm closer to the truth than random guessing.

As you have figured out, this is the Austin Pain Clinic, where all the sorts and conditions of those suffering gather. People who would prefer being someplace else—perhaps at a job, perhaps volunteering in their child's elementary school class, perhaps sleeping in.

Dealing with pain, hoping the folk here, physicians and nurses and staff, can be pain-reducers if not woe-eliminators.

And then, once Diane's surgery is finished, we head to the radiology department at the hospital, so she can undergo her radiation treatment. Once that's finished it will be just ten sessions to go and what we hope, a cancer-free future.

I know what I will see there…people in much worse condition, people whose future will not require shades—at least for the most part. People whose link with more breaths is tied to a machine and the hope [not a promise] their cancer will not win. There will be the 19 year old who has brain cancer, the 80 year old with cancer of the stomach, cancer, cancer, cancer. There will be two 5 year old boys, not related, but each with the same menacing truth: brain cancer. There will be the radiation, the chemotherapy.

In the mix of that there will be the caregivers. Diane has commented how caring each person is at the Radiology Office—from the receptionist [Olivia, herself a cancer-survivor] to the guys who make sure the radiation is well targeted.

I sit here on a Friday morning, wondering. How in the world do people handle all this? How, when life seems to shift from lemonade to lemons, do they cope?

Of course there's the hope the medical treatment will work, will extend their life, will keep the pain down if not put it away.

I'll tell you how I make it, because there are times, truth pushing here with great force that I'm not sure I can.

I make it because of two blessings.

The first is faith…to know that life is never a guarantee and all we can do is our very best. With that to know that God is not the cause or source of anyone's pain. No. Rather, God understands and cares with a Holy Presence. Yes, it takes a spiritual "sense." For instance, the people who handle their misfortunes the best are the people who know that cancer is not judgment and their spiritual foundation is solid.

The second is God's richest blessing to me: Diane. She NEVER EVER complains, she does not rage into the night and she has, not once, offered, "Why me?"

Rather, she is cognizant of the medical issues, the cancer, the new stomach, the degenerating disks, and doesn't think for a moment she has been picked out for the pain-registry. Rather, and this is her beautiful insight, "Mark it is what it is, and I'm going to give my fullest effort." She has resolution and tenacity and a great energy that never gives up. And yet she is humble, knowing she cannot do this alone…and she doesn't. So many have shared prayers, cards, a phone call, a hug in the family. Oh yes.

Certainly the radiation causes fatigue. And yet, next Monday when she begins her new job as program manager in information technology, she will have energy and focus and will take first steps in her new office with great skill.

So it is this Friday morning…pain clinic, radiology office…life.

I don't see how anyone can do this alone.

As I've mentioned I'm reading a biography of Dietrich Bonhoeffer, a great German theologian of the 20th century who aligned with others to attempt to stop Adolf Hitler and his raging schemes. Bonhoeffer failed and was hanged shortly before WWII ended. And yet he didn't fail, for his writings, his witness that truth does not have to be on the scaffold and evil on the throne, is a great affirmation of how each of our lives can be for something.

Reading about him has been refreshing in how he dealt with the sordid realities.

No less, sitting here this morning in the pain clinic lobby, seeing the coming and going of people who cling to hope, is actually inspirational—because I know the purpose of our life is not to avoid the untoward, although we try our damndest to do that, and we should.

But, when life is lemon-from-lemonade, being in faith and in covenant with others, helps get back to the lemonade.

Lock and Load, America–how tragic!

Posted on January 9, 2011 by Mark H Miller

I am writing this Saturday night, January 8, with all the news of the Tucson tragic shooting incomplete. What isn't incomplete is how horrific it must have been that a young man, evidently firing with an automatic weapon, shot at least thirteen people, leaving 6 of them dead, including a 9 year old girl and a Federal Judge. The U.S. Congress Representative Gabrielle Giffords had one bullet fired literally through her head and brain. The physician, understandably guarded in his comments, indicated the surgery was successful and he is optimistic she will make it.

What to say? I was struck by Gabrielle Giffords' father's comment that the Tea Party, who tried to defeat her and almost did in the recent election, was against her totally. And her Tea Party opponent advised in military terms in his campaign rhetoric how she needed to be defeated. On that from Yahoo.com:

During his campaign effort to unseat Giffords in November, Republican challenger Jesse Kelly held fundraisers where he urged supporters to help remove Giffords from office by joining him to shoot a fully loaded M-16 rifle. Kelly is a former Marine who served in Iraq and was pictured on his website in military gear holding his automatic weapon and promoting the event.

Unbelievable.

Again, what to say?

An experience struck me as I tried to get the information and what this might mean. The experience was actually in an east Texas church where I preached when in conference ministry. The moderator of the church, choir member and bank vice-president in career, offered a prayer before we walked into the sanctuary to lead worship.

As soon as the prayer was completed, he looked at the choir and said, "All right, everybody, time to lock and load."

What in God's name was that, I mused. *Lock and load? For worship? Go away!*

I figured it had to do with hunting, but wasn't sure. I was hesitant to ask the voice about heading into worship, for fear he'd think I was really stupid. When I got back to Austin, a friend said two things, "Oh, Mark, it's a hunting term…to get the rifle read to shoot. But, second, that's simply east Texas…quite frankly surprised they even had you there to preach—you're too liberal for them. But, unfortunately in many venues it's the thought that if you cannot stand someone, you would lock and load."

Of course the shooting throws sanity out. Of course we find this tragedy horrific. But why is it…why is it the likes of the Tea Party, if they don't like what you believe, think the only resolution, if not to defeat the opponent in the voting booth, is to be destructive?

I'm sure there'll be all kinds of back peddling on this—it's already started with Giffords' Tea Party opponent's spokesman saying there is no relationship with the shooter. My Lord, you don't need to "have a relationship" with him to not be connected—in terms of your heinous words infecting this 22 year-old.

Of course the specific "causes and motivation for this horrific event" need to be plumbed much deeper, but the anger toward Giffords and her position on the health care legislation seems to be an obvious trigger point. Consider this: threats against her had increased significantly in the last year.

There's much to write and think and reflect on this.

Immediately from Huffington Post the following comment made lots of sense to me.

"As I write," says long-time author and social critic Gregory McNamee in Tucson, *"it is not clear whether Representative Gabrielle Giffords has been killed or has survived being shot, along with at least a dozen and perhaps as many as twenty other victims."* McNamee adds:

"*What is clear to me, at this chaotic moment, is that no one should be surprised by this turn of events. The bullets that were fired in Tucson this morning are the logical extension of every bit of partisan hatred that came spewing out during the last election, in which Gabrielle Giffords—a centrist, representing well and faithfully a centrist district—was vilified and demonized as a socialist, a communist, a fascist, a job-killer, a traitor, and more. Anyone who uttered such words or paid for them to be uttered has his or her name etched on those bullets. With what we have seen today, the rest of us must declare that we will tolerate no more lies, no more hatred, no more violence—and that never again will we spend a single dollar on the wares sold by those who perpetrate them. If not now, when?*"

Moral culpability cannot be neglected

Posted on January 10, 2011 by Mark H Miller

It is Monday morning, January 10, 2011, and I just sent a message to my Oregon friends rooting on the Oregon Ducks, for the national college football BCS title game is tonight. If only I could focus upon football and whom the Broncos will hire as Head Coach and whether or not Andrew's Schreiner University Basketball Team will win Thursday night in Belton, Texas.

But I cannot. Oh, I wander into those areas of special interest, but the focus is upon the shooting in Tucson and what to make of it.

Have some thoughts, but first some quotes this morning to frame them. I realize many if not most of you have read about this, but wanted to outline the characterization of the shooter, Jared Loughner, from Yahoo. com:

The friends' comments paint a picture bolstered by other former classmates and Loughner's own internet postings: That of a social outcast with nihilistic, almost indecipherable beliefs steeped in mistrust and paranoia.

"He appeared to be to me an emotional cripple or an emotional child," Coorough said. "He lacked compassion, he lacked understanding and he lacked an ability to connect."

Over time, Loughner became increasingly engrossed in his own thoughts — what one of the friends described as a "nihilistic rut."

Loughner, an ardent atheist, began to characterize people as sheep whose free will was being sapped by the monotony of modern life.

In a sense, he acted alone. And yet, which is the basis of my thought this morning, we never act alone. We are who we are as the result of more than family upbringing, more than schools we attend, more than food we eat and cars we drive, more than friends we cherish and people we despise. We are who we are based upon the totality of input and impact. And, none of us is aware of how our thoughts shared impact others.

For instance, it was twenty years after the sermon was given and I could not remember one word of the sermon, a parishioner told me they had given up on Christmas, but after worship made the decision to buy a Christmas tree. Their two sons were serving in Vietnam and they were depressed. But, the worship changed that. And in another parishioner, to learn a particular worship impacted them to change careers and enroll in seminary. Who would have known?

And sometimes it doesn't take twenty years to discover that what you say matters. Sometimes for the good and sometimes for the...

I have been aware in ministry that what I say has impact, and not always for the good. Thinking about the University of Oregon this morning I remember in June of 1972 when I was invited to deliver the commencement address at South Eugene High School, I was very committed to the election of George McGovern over Richard Nixon. I was also aware 1972 was the first time 18-year-olds could vote. In the speech, not without passion and insistence, I said this, "I urge each of you voting for the first time in this upcoming November election to vote for a peace candidate who vows to end the Vietnam War now with no bombs attached."

I didn't get off the next salvo, because in a furious response, a father of a graduate jumped to his feet and shouted for the whole world to hear, a fiery insistence, "Richard Nixon forever!" Another stood and began to sing, "God Bless America!"

And the next two weeks, after reading the editorials—it was my guess those who favored the speech were under 30 and those who didn't were over 30—you'd think I was a Communist, that I was a disgrace to ministry. I even got a phone call, anonymous of course, suggesting I would be better off leaving the country. [I couldn't help but think of a Chicago friend who described anonymity as the *ammunition of cowards.*]

At any rate it was no secret that what I said, even though I believed it fully, was incendiary.

199

I also remember when Conference Minister, at an annual conference meeting, challenging some church members of their contention that the only way to know God was through Jesus Christ. They chafed and scowled…some even walked out of the meeting. A week later I received a letter that did not lack clarity and furious demand, to come to a meeting and defend my heretical views. Whoa, fella, what's this about? When I got there, at least in my mind's eye what I saw in their hands was rope. *These folk are beyond anger.* Although no one said "Lock and load."

Back to Oregon a minute…one of the blessings of the Eugene ministry, circa 1969-1973, was the friendship of Senator Wayne Morse, one of two senators [the other was Senator Gruening in Alaska], who voted AGAINST the Gulf of Tonkin resolution, which granted our President full say on increasing our involvement in Vietnam. I remember visiting with the Senator about the fire and foaming on what I had said and he simply smiled, "Welcome to America."

Yes, it has to do with freedom of speech. But, and this is my case this morning, freedom of speech is not without responsibility.

Which is to say no one will be legally culpable in causing Jarod Loughner to do what he did, the height of being dastardly. But that does not mean we are not morally culpable.

Which means for me personally to be aware that what I say is important. Loughner did not act in a vacuum. In our country I am aware of radicals on both sides of the political aisle. I am aware I am not innocent in this, for it is my belief—make that conviction—there are some folk who say what they say because their narcissism fuels them. But if they are not aware of the moral implication of their impressing others to act in heinous ways, then what they say fuels the tragic.

People should not shut up. No. But, we each—and I will mirror this comment this morning in considering my own beliefs and verbiage—make sure what we say doesn't put someone in a corner, or encourage them to buy a gun. Rather, I will speak the truth, but give others the space and respect to offer their own ideas.

That sounds simple, but more than simple, it's necessary.

I pray for recovery for Representative Gabrielle Giffords. It will be a long road for her, but hopefully in her faith [which is Jewish] and all our prayers, recovery will be manifest. In the meantime, for our first step, let us acknowledge there is moral responsibility we must assume, without compromise, in how our beliefs become words.

Being a parent when shadows fall

Posted on January 11, 2011 by Mark H Miller

More to digest on the Tucson tragic shooting. I had been thinking about this, now triggered by the following internet article:

TUCSON, Ariz. – The parents of a man charged with trying to assassinate Rep. Gabrielle Giffords are devastated and guilt-ridden, a neighbor said, mourning their own tragedy as Tucson residents prepared Tuesday for a community memorial service and a visit from the president.

Jared Loughner's mother has been in bed, crying nonstop since the shooting rampage on Saturday, neighbor Wayne Smith, 70, told KPHO-TV. Amy and Randy Loughner want to know where they went wrong with their 22-year-old son.

It is not hard to imagine the despair, utterly so, of the parents. It is also understandable they are sinking [most commonly labeled cratering] into, "What did we do wrong?"

The imagery of apples falling from a tree comes to mind. So often we do see considerable similarity between the behavioral patterns of children echoing their parents. And as I wrote some time ago in a Blog, there are times when we see parents who clearly define *parental unfitness* we wish their tree was on a very steep hill or mountainside.

I pondered for a moment—*what if I were in that situation? Or, if my sons were in that situation with their children…or, not to be totally subjective about this, with their parents?*

There are two sides of this mult-faceted question I address:

#1. **What about our parenting?** I can illustrate both leanings on this—great parents whose kids never functioned in a healthy manner, or who got so off the track they needed electric shock to bring some corrective. Or parents who were, to be graphic, scumbags, whose kids approached the realm of being Rhodes Scholars.

My only answer is personal. As a parent I learned every year what it meant to be supportive but not suffocating, caring but not controlling. I NEVER tried to establish a co-dependency with Matthew or Andrew—probably more what I considered inter-dependency. And more than anything, I did what I could to "be there" at their various athletic or academic or musical events [yes, they did show up for their piano concerts]. And I did my best discerning effort to help with their classroom work—discerning means I stayed away from math and science and did what I could in English and writing. Now they are 38 and 41 and are doing just fine—at least that's my awareness. So I can look in a mirror and offer, "I really did my best and gave my fullest."

#2. But, here's the crunch: **what when their world breaks apart**, what when they lose jobs or get divorced [certainly I'm no innocent stranger in this regard!] or pick up a gun and fire away—their way of anger-expression—or find themselves at loose ends. I'm sure—pushing positive—were that to happen I would ponder, "What did I do to push them there?" I bet it's unreachable how the parents of the Tucson Shooter feel right now, for they, too, evidently, ask, "What did we do wrong?"

To that I have two responses: First, **I may have not done anything wrong.** Children are not children for ever and as my son Andrew once announced—probably at the age of maybe 12—standing up straight, his hands on his hips, "I'm my own individual self." Yes, they are, both Matthew and Andrew and Jason [Diane's wonderful son]. **As their father who they are is not condensed in how I treated them.** It has to do with culture, with school, with friends, with enemies, with goals, with….the list will never end.

Considering an unending list of what can go right and what can go wrong, I would hope…with all in my whole self, that no matter what might happen that is untoward, on which they might be totally responsible, I would stand by them as their father. Not to say, "Yes, you are screwed because of what you did." Or, "How could you be such an idiot!"

Rather, I would hope I would be more willing to listen and understand than judge/condemn/castigate and would hope even more that my prevailing response would be, "I love you and am with you; let's see how we can move forward."

And, no less, should I be the one about whom my sons are embarrassed or chagrined or really pissed off, I would hope they would look beyond my weaknesses and mistakes and offer, "Dad, we're with you. You can count on us."

Today on Colin Cowherd he discussed athletes who have messed up… and the tendency to blame others, to claim innocence no matter what. Cowherd said, "Hey, everybody has to deal with their situation. They must OWN UP to their own baggage."

I agree with that.

However, I would add, no matter what, as a father, I hope that helping them carry the baggage, unpack the baggage and when necessary, get rid of the baggage, would have a place.

You think?

The illness of racism refuses cure

Posted on January 12, 2011 by Mark H Miller

This is not easy to write. Not that feelings are dwarfed; rather because it's more subjective than anything. And, I'm not sure the culprit, racism, will ever fade into the historical abyss no one can find.

It was triggered yesterday in a phone call Colin Cowherd, ESPN morning talk-show host, received during his claiming that Michael Vick would not be one of his top 15 professional football quarterbacks today, and also claiming that he might forgive Vick for his "killing-dogs-show" of five years, but he would never forget it and most of all just because someone says they're sorry—which Vick did—doesn't mean they are any more intelligent in their next steps and decisions.

I'm white. When I heard Cowherd's claim I agreed with him…and considered it a statement of truth and not a revelation of racial bias. But not everyone shared my response.

The caller accused Cowherd of being Jewish [not sure why that would have mattered, unless the caller considered Jews lesser folk on the cultural/religious scale], of not knowing what it's like to be in the *hood* , and of accusing Ben Rothlisberger [Pittsburgh quarterback who was accused but not charged or tried on rape] of being just as bad and implying that dog-activities such as Vick pushed for more than five years, wasn't so bad after all.

Then Cowherd said that when he opined that "Vick was always hot news" because whenever he dissed Vick, which he does on a frequent basis, the callers are always black. I took his comment in a factual not racially slurred or pejorative way.

Racism—looking at someone in a critically disclaiming manner because of their color. Considering yourself to be elevated in importance because of your skin color—is probably more alive and well than any of us would either recognize or admit.

As part of the mix I've experienced racism used as a tool of self-elevation. In conference ministry there was a minister—yes, he was black—who claimed that any criticism of his ministry was evidence of racism. It was very unsettling and disheartening because he would never consider that he might be at fault. Which far more than not he was. In truth he should never have been in ministry—he had a ministry of atrophy and finally left in a huff claiming that I didn't support him because I was racist. He then went to another conference and peddled the same bias.

I don't consider that anything more than a negative experience. And, truth reigning, there were far more Caucasian ministers whose incompetency was their most evident characteristic. Wonder if I were black how they would have handled my concerns about their mishandling of parishioners?

I am not black. I do not know what segregation does to the inner core, what it is to have my own bathroom or drinking fountain and have that be racial judgment rather than social elitism. I do not know what it's like to be demeaned or neglected or discarded by a selection committee because of my race. When I've not been selected my first response is they got it wrong [see, hubris pops up for each of us] and then I see that the other candidate is a better fit. Takes a while but I get there.

It just strikes me this morning that race issues are not less today; we simply clothe them in new cloths, but down-deep blacks are more defensive than understanding and whites, and this is not a pleasure to write, are not color-blind and use that in their judging considerations/responses.

A thought just occurred: I'm glad the Tucson Shooter was white…and not black or Hispanic or Asian. If that were the case—he of another race—the dynamics today would be much different—and in the eye of my heart—more explosive.

I guess for these times, if I see any color, it will be red. And that is red as in blood and not as in rage. Wish that had greater representation in more people.

And then, in the mix of this, we have the Topeka, Kansas church and their minister, Fred Phelps, planning to picket the 9-year-old's funeral today. Why? Because they believe the Tucson Shooter was sent by God and Americans need to be punished. They say God has no place for homosexuals since all homosexuals are deviant—they held their condemning signs in picketing at an United Church of Christ General Synod—because we were the first denomination to ordain gays and lesbians. They found the same purpose in Katrina, judgment of God for the waywardness of our country. Sometimes religious extremists cause my blood to boil—they are idiots and their antics only prove they are self-serving folk who value the spotlight more than the truth. But, that, my friends, is for another day.

A possible path to civility

Posted on January 13, 2011 by Mark H Miller

It is Thursday morning, January 13, 2011. Primarily because I find the thoughts from President Obama last night essential, I devote my Blog to his comments. In summary, I was inspired by his hopes and the foci that came together in asking each of us to live up to the humanity that God wishes for. At least that's my take in connecting with what was said and the ways in which civility has its best chance.

This summary is from Holly Bailey.

Obama urges Americans to use words that heal, not wound

In Tucson to eulogize the victims of last weekend's tragic shooting, President Obama somberly called for an end to the political blame game that erupted in the wake of the tragedy and urged Americans not to use it as "one more occasion to turn on each other."

Instead, Obama told an overflow crowd of more than 14,000 people at the University of Arizona the moment should prompt Americans to step back and reflect on how they lead their own lives and how they deal with one another.

"At a time when our discourse has become so sharply polarized—at a time when we are far too eager to lay the blame for all that ails the world at the feet of those who happen to think differently than we do—it's important for us to pause for a moment and make sure that we are talking with each other in a way that heals, not a way that wounds," Obama said.

Referencing the finger-pointing that has taken place over the last several days, Obama warned of trying to find "simple explanations" in the aftermath. "Scripture tells us that there is evil in the world, and that terrible things happen for reasons that defy human understanding," the president said.

The truth, he said, is that "none of us can know with any certainty what might have stopped these shots from being fired or what thoughts lurked in the inner recesses of a violent man's mind."

The emotional high point came early in the speech, as the president drew an exultant cheer from the crowd by breaking from his prepared remarks to announce that Rep. Gabrielle Giffords, shot in the attack on Saturday, had opened her eyes for the first time.

"Gabby opened her eyes. So I can tell you, she knows we are here," Obama said. "And she knows that we love her and she knows that we are rooting for her through what is undoubtedly going to be a difficult journey." The president spoke shortly after visiting the bedside of Giffords, who was shot and critically injured while meeting constituents at a Tucson grocery.

Obama also used the speech to return the nation's focus to the six people who lost their lives last Saturday, noting that they were fulfilling "a central tenet of the democracy envisioned by our founders" by attending the Giffords event.

"The loss of these wonderful people should make every one of us strive to be better in our private lives — to be better friends and neighbors, co-workers and parents," Obama said. "And if... their deaths help usher in more civility in our public discourse, let's remember that it is not because a simple lack of civility caused this tragedy, but rather because only a more civil and honest public discourse can help us face up to our challenges as a nation, in a way that would make them proud."

In particular, Obama focused on the life of 9-year-old Christina Taylor Green, who was killed at the event. Green, who is the same age as Obama's youngest daughter, Sasha, attended the event out of her growing curiosity about democracy, the president noted, at times becoming emotional.

He urged Americans to view democracy and their role in the country as Green did in her final days.

"She saw all of this through the eyes of a child, undimmed by the cynicism or vitriol that we adults all too often take for granted," Obama said. "I want us to live up to her expectations. I want our democracy to be as good as she imagined it."

Muting the Cackle

Posted on January 14, 2011 by Mark H Miller

It never occurred to me before. It not only makes sense, but has some helpful advice and is true. It goes like this: *you can stop a fire by cutting off the oxygen.*

A fine example of this, stopping a possible fire of contempt and ridicule, follows:

By Greg Wyshynski

Elizabeth Hughes, 8, made her debut singing the national anthem at an AHL Norfolk Admirals [the Tampa Bay Lightning's affiliate] against the Connecticut Whale [New York Rangers' affiliate] last Friday night January 7, 2011]. Angelic voice, bundle of nerves ... and then after the words "gave proof," her microphone abruptly cut out.

What happened next might be something we've seen before at a sporting event, but that never lacks for inspiration (and maybe a misty eye or two). There's a moment around 1:30 into this clip that gives us hope for humanity:

An 8-year-old girl is about to suffer a moment of extreme embarrassment that's not of her creation. A woman in the crowd cackles at this moment; not laughs, cackles. You then hear someone "shoosh" those like her during the brief silence. You then hear the crowd pick up the tune in unison.

From Kim P., an Admirals season-ticket holder who sent over the clip:

http://sports.yahoo.com/nhl/blog/puck_daddy/post/Video-Hockey-crowd-sings-after-8-year-old-s-nat?urn=nhl-306789

The little girl did not lose composure at all and after a second the crowd took cue and started singing. But even the players were singing and did a stick tap at the end.

According to Elizabeth's mother Dorothy Shiloff Hughes, she was invited to sing at another Norfolk home game this season. Hopefully without incident; but if there is one, at least she knows hockey fans have her back.

It strikes me this morning cackling has become a national pastime. Shoot at you, shoot at me, shoot at him, shoot at her [in tragic cases not a metaphor, but in most it is.] Call it cynicism, call it an ego drill.

I've known lots of ministers who cackle. They are miserable in their attitude. One instance is not forgotten. A gathering of retired ministers [maybe they are the worst at this, no longer having a pulpit and no longer looked at for counsel] was considering how retirement can be viable and good. As the speaker, a wonderful consultant and ordained minister, was making one of his most important points, one of the retired ministers jumped up, stopped the presentation, pointed to the head minister of the conference and cackled on and on at how incompetent the lead minister was.

I read and hear lots of cackling on each side of the political aisle, each side of the religious aisle—my goodness, there is more than one aisle here, primarily because I am unaware of NO RELIGION that doesn't have an insulting and carping and cackling fringe section. It was certainly true, perhaps still is, in my beloved United Church of Christ.

This video inspired me…a woman cackled when the microphone failed and the 8-year-old was in a horrible position—as Wyshynski indicates. The cackle was not prevailing. In an instance, the crowd and the players joined in to support this lovely, first-time-sing-National-anthem girl. The crowd joined in. The players. And when it was finished the players *did a stick tap at the end.*

THAT'S what is needed today—a way to cut off the oxygen to the cacklers, to the voices of contempt whose need to judge and criticize and reject is MUCH GREATER than their willingness to understand. To cut off the oxygen is to take a deep breath and sing your heart out.

Besides, singing is much more helpful—and pleasant—than the cackling voice.

What we need today is living that results in stick taps. Lots of them.

You betcha.

What say you? Jesus the only way to God?

Posted on January 15, 2011 by Mark H Miller

Theology is the language by which we interface God with the human condition. Yes, it is more, using language to explain God—identity and purpose and will. But essentially theology is putting God and each person in the same room and then say, "Okay, how will each of you relate with each other?"

I realize that is somewhat condensed, and perhaps to some, off-center, maybe even startling.

But, stay with me on this.

The question: **Is Jesus the only way to know God?**

Today's reflection came to me by a bumper sticker that said *Jesus was the only way to know God.* But it stemmed from an experience I had when beginning conference ministry. The conference I served included 100 churches spread throughout Texas and Louisiana and the social mission project, Back Bay Mission in Biloxi, Mississippi.

Now, when you think religion and Texas [read that, SOUTH], a case can be made that if the South is the Bible Belt then Dallas is the buckle.

I knew that. But, I also knew the United Church of Christ was anything but Bible-belted. Which in many cases was a problem, for many clergy [yep, it's true] and church members wouldn't know if Philemon is in the Old or New Testament.

And I knew there were pockets of religious conservatism in my conference. But I didn't expect it to hit me with a tirading scourge.

It was my first annual meeting to which all the churches were encouraged to attend. Maybe 65% of the churches showed up. I went to a general discussion group, just to listen. That didn't last long because a minister made the case that *if you are not a Christian God will have no tolerance of you*. His phrasing.

I won't print what I thought, other than to say I disagreed. It's hard to describe my indigestion. At any rate, my vow to be silent and observant was broken.

I shared how much I disagreed with the thought that accessibility to God was limited. That is, the claim the follower of Jesus was in a trumped position on getting to God just didn't fly. And, I said, there's NO biblical support for this.

Ever thought your first few weeks of work might not lead to years of service? That was pushing me as I left that annual meeting, thinking, *Wow, if the sentiment of God-accessibility is held firmly in this conference, I'm in trouble.*

That possibility took on more than an academic curiosity when I got a letter the following week, demanding I show up in a church near Waco to defend my heresy. Gulp.

I got there...only women waited, each of whom smiled with restraint when I sat down. I found it more noticeable how they each had scowling brows, as if a chorus line. As I've written in an earlier Blog I looked at their hands and imagined they each held rope.

The leader got out her Bible [I knew this passage was coming] and referred to the cementing [for them] passage in John when Jesus is quoted as saying, "I am the way, the truth and the life; no one comes to the Father but by me."

She closed the Bible ceremoniously, although I knew she had memorized it, so believed it was only for authority she even held the Bible, and said, "Okay, Dr. Miller [I appreciated the entitled respect], explain yourself... how can you say anyone can know God aside from Jesus?"

It was so quiet you could hear a spider burp. I know, that's not the best metaphor, but at least it indicates quiet beyond silence.

At first I was tempted to unpack the John passage, indicating Jesus was not referring to himself as a person, but to his manner of living—which meant that God would be known when we lived as Christ lived—and people of all religions hold that manner of living as more than exemplary—they held it as a necessity, to regard others as you wished them to regard you.

But I said more. In so many words I shared my faith, that for me the best way I can know God is through Christ, because I believe with Reinhold Niebuhr [who was out of their original denomination, the Evangelical and Reformed Church] who wrote, "Jesus Christ is the Supreme Revelation of God's Love."

I also gave them some Bible study indicating that the Gospel of John was written more for persuasion than historical truth, that when the 4th Gospel was written after 100 A.D., Christianity was in dire straits, and fading quickly. The Gospel was written to encourage Christians to not give up. Therefore, John was to be looked at not for historical truth; rather, John was to be held highly for religious truth.

They weren't convinced. I then said, "If you believe God can only be known through Jesus, what say you about Adam and Eve and Moses and David and Jeremiah….?"

I went even more to say that I simply couldn't believe in a God who was so provincial, who would only accept people who accepted Christ. In a word, to believe single accessibility was through Jesus, made God myopic.

Nonetheless, I made it clear: Jesus is my Lord and Savior. I considered that, however, as I consider EVERY religious truth as descriptive and not prescriptive. But, what should I have said at the funeral of my closest friend, who dropped dead when we were both 36 [of a brain aneurism]? He was a practicing Jew. His Rabbi and I shared in worship leadership. Was I to say that Ullmann would not be held dearly by God in the afterlife? Or, what about the first baby I baptized—aged 4 months—who was dead when I baptized her? Or, how can we say that God is so narrowed? In fact, I believe if you believe only the Christian knows God, you have shrunk God so small no one can know God. J. B. Phillips wrote about that, "Your God Is Too Small."

I believe God cares for all and is not preferential to anyone. **There is no religion of privilege. There is only religion of fidelity.**

The Bible? I do not believe in biblical inerrancy. As Marcus Borg said in his book, <u>Meeting Jesus Again for the First Time</u>, "the Bible is to be considered seriously, not literally."

Well, they were kind to listen. And they offered me a nice dessert.

But that meeting told me there are those whose beliefs are so narrow and cramped, they will never allow others a freedom to find God…or as happens mostly, to allow God to find them.

Basically I hold this: For me Jesus is my primary access to God. But not exclusively so. And for others, leave it up to God and each person to discover their relationship.

What we don't need on our earth in our day and place is for people to chortle away on a belief that reeks of contempt and condemnation.

I end this with a humorous anecdote—at least I think so. In my third ministry—Lakewood, Colorado—in the 1970's, I was in a group discussion with other United Church of Christ clergy. One of them said how they couldn't stand the iron-clad-opinions of Southern Baptists. One in our group—Bill Davis stood to speak. Ah, Bill. He was savvy and clever and caring, shown by the fact he had a horse named Calls, so when someone called his office his secretary could say, "Pastor Davis is out on calls."

Bill said, in his southern drawl, and reflecting his own Southern Baptist roots, "Hey, you have it wrong. I give thanks for Southern Baptists, for when they grow up theologically they join our denomination—and they never forget how to tithe." Ka-ching to Bill.

I'm sure this positioning on the many ways in which God is known is somewhat rambling, maybe even circular. And it may be the case that, "Who cares?"

But in my heart of hearts, one of the greatest woes of God today is how we think our religion is the only and best and are willing to kill to defend our position. That's wrong in my view, so I hold respect for all ways people discover God, but for no way someone must take a gun and fire away in front of a Safeway store at a political rally in Tucson or in a high school or....

The many faces of grief and death

Posted on January 17, 2011 by Mark H Miller

A news bulletin from Yahoo.com

Some question pep rally atmosphere at Obama speech

What was billed as a memorial for victims of the Arizona shooting rampage turned into a rollicking rally, leaving some conservative commentators wondering whether President Obama's speech was a scripted political event. Not so, insisted the White House and host University of Arizona.

Rich Lowry of the National Review wrote that "the pep-rally atmosphere was inappropriate and disconcerting," although he admired the president's speech. .

I can appreciate the "this isn't right" response to President Obama's speech at the Tucson Memorial Service.

And, it's more than *Listen, whatever he says or does, people will chortle and reject and speculate it is simply a political ploy. That it is disingenuine.*

Really. No one who is public and notable will ever have 100% endorsement and appreciation and validation. And, in the course of the world turning and how that ends up, such negating even applies to sermons!

What is deeper, though, is the perplexing question: **How do we respond to tragedy?** Name any.

My experience with this is people respond how people respond. And it is both inappropriate and imprudent for any of us to prescribe managing grief and the horrific.

All I can do is share on two fronts.

One of the most personally devastating deaths was when Ullmann died. It was 1976. Stephen Ullmann was a "truth friend," which meant he was a Las Vegas-slogan: what was shared with Ullmann stayed with Ullmann. How important that was to me, to have someone with whom I could share both the light and shadows of my journey.

He was one of those guys who lived beyond the edge and I loved that, and at times, committed the sin of envy, if only I could be that daring. You bet. For instance, he wanted to learn skiing. So, we went to a Colorado Ski Area, Copper Mountain, for him to learn. I had already learned skiing, which quite honestly was an overstatement. I always went for the green slopes [for beginners] and snow-ploughed down every slope. That simply meant my legs were a moving V, ski tips creating that letter.

Ullmann, who was not an economically strapped person [that's euphemistic], hired a private guide and said he'd meet me at noon.

After lunch he said, "Okay, let's go."

I assumed it was green slopes all the way. Not. He took me to the blue slopes—more than a grade more difficult and challenging and off he went. I gasped, *Good Lord, he's already skiing with skis parallel; no V for him!"*

Ullmann was a very kind man…he once came to Lakewood, Colorado and took Matthew and Andrew to Target. It was December. He gave each of them a shopping cart and said, "I'll meet you at the check-out."

Certainly there was some question about, *Should there be a limit to generosity?*, but I only thought it. I was pleased neither cart brimmed over with stupid things—everything was good.

Then it happened.

Ullmann wanted to ski Vail, so he arranged for three days. He paid for the room [Tom Beaudette was nowhere to be seen, believe me.], the meals AND our own private ski lessons. Talk about generosity. I never did understand why he preferred steak tartar, but it wasn't for me to criticize the appetite of my truth friend.

Ullmann got on the plane Friday afternoon, returning to Chicago. His wife, Judi, was to receive her phD in Russian from the University of Chicago on Monday, so we thought it would be nice and affirming to send flowers to her on Monday morning.

Saturday morning at 11 a.m. the phone call came. "Reverend Miller?"

I indicated I was he.

"Reverend Miller, I have very bad news and Judi Ullmann wanted me to call you and your wife right away. Stephen died this morning."

He played in a YMCA basketball league and dropped dead, dead before he hit the floor, caused by a brain aneurism. Bam. It was all over.

I cannot even begin to share—and here it is more than 30 years later—how that devastated me.

Judi wanted me and their Rabbi to share in Ullmann's service. [I always called him Ullmann.]

To prepare for the service, I met with six of Ullmann's friends, buddies since they were in a pre-school program at the University of Chicago. We sat for hours the night before Ullmann's funeral service...and the reactions were all over the chart, telling stories about their time with Ullmann. There was great laughter and somber sadness.

Five months later my family was eating dinner at home in Lakewood. Out of the blue my son, Andrew, having just celebrated his 4th birthday, started to cry.

"Andrew! What's wrong?"

He looked at me, "Dad, don't you know? Ullmann's dead."

Ohmygoodness.

We walked through that, trying to help him cope. And trying to help me cope, for sure.

All this is to say, no one can know the depth of relationship and pain and torment and gratitude [ALL of that is there] when someone dear to our heart and journey dies.

As I listened to Obama's reflections at the Tucson Memorial Service, I was moved beyond words at the truths he shared. I found it inspirational and when people clapped, and even cheered, it didn't bother me for a moment.

Why?

BECAUSE IT WAS THE MEANS BY WHICH PEOPLE COULD GET THROUGH THE HORROR OF WHAT HAD HAPPENED.

Yes, some will criticize. That is to be expected.

But, what I experienced was a very real, authentic and powerful speech... and even more, the responses of the 14,000 gathered I felt were not only honest, they were very therapeutic.

Each of us copes in different ways. It's not helpful to look at someone else's response and slam it. What is helpful is to look in a mirror and answer, "How am I dealing with this?"

And along the path of life, something will happen, it always does, when we are reminded of a friendship that is of the memory and not of the current day...and it hopefully will bring us a nodding smile and a short prayer of thanksgiving, for the ways in which someone who no longer lives physically, does in memory and spirit.

That happens to me whenever I go to Target...and see the shopping carts.

What we eat…does it matter?

Posted on January 18, 2011 by Mark H Miller

This reflection will lead to vulnerability—lots of it. Still, I am curious.

Probably verity resounding, but the question pushes a little this morning: **Does what we eat matter?**

After squinting in disbelief, give me a few words.

Now I know, *Of course it does.*

Learned that a year ago, almost to the day in January, when I was itching all over and couldn't understand why. Mosquitoes are not known for January-molesting, so that was ruled out. I went to my all-time favorite internist, Laura Johnson Guerrero, to find some good scratching medicine. She had a hunch, called in one of her nurses to "check your blood, Mark."

When the nurse's eyes had that, *Uh-oh* look, I knew my problem wasn't mosquitoes. Dr. Guerrero, whose candor is always cushioned in kindness told me I needed to see an endocrinologist. I wasn't sure what that meant. She continued, "Your blood sugar is higher than we prefer. The high number for all of us is 140; yours is more than 3 times that."

I've never been a math whiz, but three times 100 [I figured that additional 40 was not essential for knowing my situation.] equals 300 and 300 is sure higher than 140.

Ah, there are times when my wisdom exceeds my humility.

Dr. Paul Moore, the endocrinologist, stayed calm, although he said the D word. He said it was not academic; it was "the truth." I wondered if academic and untruth were related. He continued, "But, I don't know if it's Diabetes 1 or Diabetes 2."

The more he explained I rooted for D2, as if my vote mattered.

"Spice drops," I muttered.

"Pardon me?"

"Dr. Moore I have an unrequited passion for spice drops...love the sugar hit."

He smiled, but I could tell he was not happy.

"Well, it may not be that, but I recommend you attend four Diabetes classes and reconstruct your eating pattern."

I know he didn't mean when I ate but what I ate.

So, a late-January resolution was, *NO SPICE DROPS, LOSE WEIGHT, EXERCISE MORE AND LOWER THE FRIGGIN' BLOOD SUGAR NUMBER. GET UNDER 140.*

Well, the fast-forward on that is my anti-spice-drops strategy worked, so that a 3-month's test last summer revealed I was finally in a normal range for blood sugar. It's nice, at times, to be normal.

So, that's under some management, but I cannot say I don't sneak a peek to see if anyone's watching when I walk through the candy section at our grocery store. Hey, glancing is not the same as taking...and forbid eating the spice drops.

What I'm really curious about, though, is the greater question—finally got there. In what way, really and truly and for the love of life and its endurance, does diet matter?

What I think about is my mother died at 89. Alert to the end, even telling her new minister to NOT pray she keep living, but, "David, thanks for your prayer, but really, please focus upon your other members; I'll be just fine." She died with less unfinished business than anyone I've ever known because her last item on her bucket list was to hold her first great-grandchild. That happened when less than a week after she was born, Zeli Grey, was held by Esther Miller. Good stuff. My father died at 84. Them is pretty good life-time-spans.

And, not for a moment did we ever keep the freezer door closed to get ready for dinner. It was a freezer that bulked with beef. My father, a garbage-man, had a great customer, a small butcher/market/grocery and the butcher would always tell Dad, "Hank, it's time to come down— why not tonight—and I'll prepare a side of beef for you."

In fact, in those days, we never heard the word *cholesterol*.

And rarely, if at all, did we not have at least a 3-course dinner—each night—and Sunday was always the fried chicken [think my mother did that in a large pan holding the Crisco] and mashed potatoes, beans with bacon and gravy that was smoother and tastier than words could even give justice to. And for dessert, the apple crisp blessed [blessed?] with melted butter and partnered with ice cream.

I know, the descriptions are less than tweaking your appreciation.

At any rate, this morning I read of an actress who's pregnant and is a vegan. I wasn't sure what that meant…thought maybe a description of inter-planetary-folk…so looked it up: **a vegetarian who omits all animal products from the diet.**

Probably if I were really prudent I'd take some of this "non-meat" stuff more seriously. And pay more attention to what else is eaten.

But, for some reason, since my cholesterol is well under 200 and the blood pressure, except when the referee makes the wrong call in Andrew's Team's game or the Broncos lose, is actually pretty good, I'll nod to the vegans and appreciate their commitments.

And, when the question comes up, "What about supper?", I'll head to our small freezer and look with a smile. Because there won't be any meat—a nod to the healthier options that lie there on the freezer shelves: many pieces of vacuum-packed-filleted-salmon-or-steelhead and take one, fire up the barbecue and go for it.

And I wonder…if I were a vegan, could I eat fish—which I believe is not the same as an animal product?

But, maybe I'm wrong. In which case, I'll smile, grab my keys and head to the fitness center. Because vegan or not, the exercise is important.

And then, when the packages of fish lessen, it will be a sign of the times I need to arrange another fishing trip. Now, how's that for rationalization!?

And, at 70, I do wish to keep going…especially since Diane and I have this minimal goal: to be married at least 30 years. We were married in 2001, so I've got it figured out how to reach our goal. Especially without spice drops.

Keeping Promises

Posted on January 19, 2011 by Mark H Miller

Keeping promises is not academic. I learned as a child and youth, *Be good for your word.*

And truth holding fast: I had forgotten the promise I made.

Some back story.

In 2005 Diane and I moved to Issaquah, Washington, an eastern suburb of Seattle. It is a lovely area, somewhat distant from the downtown Seattle world, about 15 miles east from the business district [where Diane's Washington Mutual office is]. It was also closer to the Yakima River, the best fly-fishing-trout-water in Washington. No surprise there.

We wanted to fish a river north a few times, the Skagit River, known [fishing guides at times extend the truth, but that's okay] for its abundance of salmon and steelhead.

I remember wanting to catch the first steelhead of the season, the day after Thanksgiving of 2005. As we drove north on I-5, Diane and I had a debate on who would catch the first steelhead. Actually debating that was somewhat useless, since she is always *on to the fish first.*

I then looked in my rear-view mirror and the red and blue lights were flashing. I was hoping the state patrol car was heading to another car. But, since our two cars were the only ones on that section of the interstate, my hope was groundless. I looked at my speedometer and realized...well, you can guess.

The officer came to the passenger side and asked about our speed.

I indicated we obviously had been speeding and he nodded.

He then asked, "Where are you headed and why were you speeding; it's still dark."

That gave me the chance, "Well, officer, I was speeding because my wife and I were disagreeing on which one of us would catch the first steelhead of the season. I was making my case that I would be first, and as a result, paid no attention to my speed."

He didn't hesitate, "What? You are going steelhead fishing? Where?"

I explained.

He then closed his ticket book, "Oh, the Skagit. Great river and lots of fish. Well, please drive more carefully. Gosh, wish I could go with you. Have a great day."

He then looked at Diane, "Make sure you whip him real good!"

We loved fishing with the guide, John Koenig. The Sauk and Skagit Rivers were abundant…in fish. I can remember one time in the fall we never made more than 2 casts without getting a fish. Ah, the joy of such repetition.

A few times that winter and the two winters to follow I would go up by myself to fish with John. Each time, his best friend in the world, Warnie Johnson, would join us. Warnie lived in the area—was my age—a great guy.

On one of the trips, out of the blue, and certainly not something I ever anticipated, Warnie asked, "Mark, when I die, I wonder, would you conduct my funeral? I don't have a minister…but seeing how you fish and hearing your stories, some of which are actually interesting and even a few humorous, I'd love for you to do my funeral."

I promised him I would.

That was 2006.

I didn't expect Warnie to die.

But.

Yesterday afternoon John Koenig e-mailed me, "Mark, we need you. Warnie died yesterday. It came sudden…he had two blood clots in his lung; he died on the operating table. You promised to do his funeral. Can you?"

Hey, a promise is a promise. Yes, in deed…and in word.

I then called Thelma, Warnie's widow, to make the arrangements.

Warnie Johnson. I really didn't know him at all well, but still, I am honored to help the family.

John said I can stay with him and his wife and daughter in their new log-cabin home.

So, I'm headed to Seattle, then up to Concrete, Washington.

And, in addition to the prayer book and Bible and a good notepad [so the funeral connects with the family—super-important] I will also pack some steelhead fishing clothes. You never know.

Guide In Training
Posted on January 20, 2011 by Mark H Miller

"Welcome, GIT, thanks for comin'."

I had forgotten—my moniker from John Koenig, our Skagit River fishing guide, *GIT*. He, his wife, Corinna and daughter Angelica, welcomed me last night to their log-cabin home in Rockport, Washington.

Although fishing is on our agenda—if the river drops to a fishable level—my main reason for being here is to officiate at Warnie Johnson's funeral, which will be on Saturday.

The *GIT* title came from a time when John and Diane and I were fishing for coho salmon—one of those days when the casts never went to three consecutive without a salmon hammering our jig-bait. At one point—probably my sub-conscious finding its voice—I looked at the distance between John's boat and the shore and commented, "John, aren't we too close to the shore?"

Before he could answer Diane responded, "Fish on!", at which point she brought a beautiful 15 pound bright, mercury bright, salmon to John's net.

Raising the fish-filled-net John only responded, "See? You try it!"

That cast brought in another fish…and then another and another.

His smile never became a smirk—it's not his persona—and he offered, "Mark, I'm now naming you my GIT."

He explained, "I know, you are trying to help us and probably deeper I bet you've wanted to try your hand at guiding. I can help, so, you are now named my personal Guide-In-Training."

GIT was born.

He and his family welcomed me and I was overcome—maybe *stunned and amazed* would be more apt—as I drove to their home—nestled in a valley along the Skagit River, all lighted like a realtor's show home—the largest and most beautiful log home I've ever seen. And over it as illumination and blessing was a full moon.

I then learned that John PERSONALLY built his home—took him ten years. Incredible home. All logs that he has felled and de-barked. I know that's probably not how to put it, but stick with me on this, your blogging city-slicker.

I don't know how long it took for my eyes to return to normal.

What a great achievement, a fabulous goal.

Their next goal—they call it a hope and remarked, "Mark, how can anyone live without hope?" [Gotta preach that some day.]—is to build two cabins and start a Bed & Breakfast. They cannot miss. His wife, Corinna, is a great cook and NO ONE [caps for accuracy on his skills] fishes the Skagit and Sauk Rivers better than John Koenig.

But this morning, Thursday, there's no fishing. River's too high, so we'll give-it-a-go tomorrow. I sit in the Hi-Lo diner in Concrete, Washington and am reflecting upon the gathering last night of Warnie's family—his wife of more than 50 years, his three daughters and their husbands and families and three great-grandchildren.

I listened for over two hours as they shared their lives in the ways in which Warnie impacted them—very much for the good. It was a time of tears, flowing from pain and laughter.

No need to detail, but it was remarkable how Warnie impacted every single one of them for the good. Of course he—and they—wasn't perfect. Still, the joy and affirmation were so real—authenticity and gratitude were in charge. A good thing.

After our sharing John and I returned to his logged castle and we took time to catch-up. Corinna and Angelica tuned in about their own experiences.

I had no idea what they had been through—during the construction of the log-home—the medical issues, the surgeries, the mishaps, the accidents—everything.

They even reminded me how they wanted me to officiate at their wedding and scheduling didn't work.

They then said, "Mark, you promised us about being our wedding preacher and we understand the scheduling log-jam. Now, you are keeping the promise to lead Warnie's funeral. That's a good thing. But, we ask you as a make-up call in missing our wedding—down the trail—hopefully no less than 10 years—will you officiate at Angelica's wedding?"

I promised—along with fishing trips I added. John, who doesn't miss a beat—"Yeah, but only if you bring Diane along."

And then as I pondered the time yesterday—all that I've shared—I couldn't help but think of so many of my friends whose aches and tragedy and mishaps and derailing has impacted them. And then I thought, yes I really did, of the Apostle Paul who said we may not know "what kind of body" we'll have in the hereafter, but the real question is, "Do we have faith that God will cover that base?"

THAT'S what came through last night—in the mix of everything, the "fish on!" and the "Warnie's got two blood clots in his lungs," [said just before the surgery during which he died] and everything in between— the need, the incredible need, knowing that life is unpredictable and at times onerous and unnerving, the need we have for hope and faith and love.

All three—a glorious trinity of hope and faith and love—flowed last night as people wiped tears from their cheeks and continued on about Warnie—and John and his family did sharing when their own journey.

I'm grateful to be here this morning, 32 degrees, flakes of snow dotting the landscape—even in the Concrete Hi-Low Diner—and am already thinking of making a reservation for the Koenig B&B. And, Angelica's wedding. And becoming a better GIT.

Thoughts about Goose Calling

Posted on January 21, 2011 by Mark H Miller

It started with an International Goose-Calling Champion. Now, truth pushing here, I wouldn't know a goose from a duck, let alone how to tell a good goose-caller. Now, I know the difference between a goose-caller and a goose-called, but what in the world difference does this make?

Let me explain what I read this morning and the trigger-point.

Each morning I go on-line for the Denver Post. On Wednesdays and Sundays I click first to the Outdoor section, because my friend, Outdoor Editor, Karl Licis, has his articles available. This morning he writes about a Metro College [Denver] left-handed pitcher who just won the international goose-calling championship. I so respect Karl's writing gifts—taking sporting events and interfacing them with people and what they do well.

In the mix of reading this, I thought, *Isn't that really something—to be good at something?*

I wrote Karl to thank him for his wonderful article, but then the trigger got pushed: **What is excellence in each person?**

Have you thought of that? What you do well? What I do well? Are there an awareness and a focus about that?

Suddenly [these thoughts pop more these days because of pondering the life's journey on the human landscape] I thought of "doing well" at checkers and rigged telephones.

It was 1964, I had arrived at the Student Christian Foundation in Carbondale, Illinois, home of Southern Illinois University. Their nickname was the Salukis, although I wouldn't know a Saluki if I saw one. [Do you know what it is?] I spent the academic year as a Campus Minister Intern, taking a year off of seminary to consider campus ministry as my field of direction after ordination.

One of the students, Ross, came to every meeting, even attended two university classes I taught—Major Prophets and the Language of Religion—and went on our field trip to Menard State Penitentiary. I'm getting too far ahead and afield.

Ross was a struggling freshman [aren't most of them?] but had one expertise that he valued: winning at checkers. He was truly amazing, without question. No one ever beat him at checkers. I tried but didn't even get close—he always finished with at least 4 ahead. He never pounded his chest. But you could tell, it gave him value and in his mind, credibility: an expertise with a passion. I loved that about Ross.

But even more was the expertise of my boss that year, Malcolm Gillespie. Mac was an ordained minister in our United Church of Christ and excelled at Campus Ministry. But, his more evident expertise came from his undergraduate education in electrical engineering.

In this manner. He and his wife, Kathy, and their children, Alan and Grace, lived in a geodesic dome [designed by Buckminster Fuller] on campus. Years before when Kathy was pregnant with Grace, she contracted polio. In those days treatment for same was in an iron lung. Kathy was able to deliver Grace, but the polio left Kathy paralyzed. She had rotating use of her arms, but nothing more.

Mac used his undergraduate background and wired the house so that Kathy could turn on almost anything electric by dialing the telephone. Amazing.

She could dial the telephone and all the dishes and silverware came down a pole over the kitchen table...she could reach each plate and set the table. She could work the oven. Dialing the telephone...presto, something came on.

Because of an expertise.

I don't know if Mac could call geese with a whistle or ever beat Ross at checkers. But, his expertise. Ah, how special.

I think of that this morning as I now fly to Seattle, to celebrate Warnie Johnson's life at his funeral service this week.

I'll be with my guide-friend and his family, staying in their new log cabin that John built. Then I'll probably, if the river's not too high, spend a day casting for steelhead. But, most of all, I'll share about Warnie's life—a beautiful person who brought value and humor and understanding—every time we shared in fishing with John. John Koenig—one incredibly good guide and log-cabin builder. And, he probably has called a goose or two to northern Washington lakes.

And, I'll wonder. What is it? That each of us does well? What is it we are passionate about?

Important. Even if we never win at checkers and couldn't call a goose.

Postscript:

I then remembered Sarah. She is a member of a church I served back in the 80's. One Sunday I told a story about Melinda—a 7 year old who had a terrible self-image. She wanted to be in the grade school play. Her mother dwarfed at Melinda being rejected when trying out. But, she still encouraged Melinda to give it a try. After the try-outs, Melinda came home, bouncing into the kitchen. "Mom, I made it! I'm in the play!"

Her mother was beyond delight, "Ohhhhh, so great, honey! What will your role be?"

"It's great, Mom! I've been chosen to clap and cheer!"

After the service Sarah came out, eyes teary, head shaking, looking down. I took her hand, "Sarah, thanks for being here this morning."

She muttered, "I'm the one who's been chosen to clap and cheer."

About two months later Sarah and I visited, "Hey, Sarah, we have a need. We are working with other churches to resettle Hmong people from Southeast Asia. Care to help us with that?"

236

She accepted and over the next four years helped—her personal energy and commitment and charisma and passion abounding—settle more than ten Hmong families. Wow, what a way to clap and cheer!

How about each of us?

Second postscript: A Saluki is an Egyptian hunting dog.

When Rules Are Broken
Posted on January 23, 2011 by Mark H Miller

Maybe you read this…or maybe someone shared…or maybe you heard it along the way. This, to me, is an example of what it means to be more focused upon a situation than any rules. I share it—from yahoo. com—about a Southwest Airlines pilot who acted in a very caring and supportive manner and was commended by the SWA leadership. Yes, the plane was 12 minutes late and yes, I'm sure people looked more at their watches than their heart, and yes, I'm sure judgment for some [hopefully not most] was greater than understanding and empathy. But, underneath it all, surrounding it all, was a caring spirit that recognized and reduced human need. THAT'S what it's all about…yes, it is.

Please read…then think about the last time you did something for someone that was unexpected and that brought them benefit and you value—for you see, you cannot have one without the other.

Here it is:

"Last night, my husband and I got the tragic news that our three-year-old grandson in Denver had been murdered by our daughter's live-in boyfriend," she wrote. "He is being taken off life support tonight at 9 o'clock and his parents have opted for organ donation, which will take place immediately. Over 25 people will receive his gift tonight and many lives will be saved."

So early in the morning, after what must have been a torturous night's sleep, Nancy and her husband arranged for him to fly from Los Angeles, where he was traveling for work, to Tuscon, where he would step off one plane and immediately onto another one headed to Denver. "The ticketing agent was holding back tears throughout the call," Nancy wrote. "I'm actually her step-mother and it's much more important for my husband to be there than for me to be there."

Mourning the loss of his child's child, and no doubt worrying about his grieving daughter, he was likely in no state to travel. Airport stress only compounded his despair. He arrived at LAX two hours before his scheduled

238

flight time, but quickly realized that delays at baggage check and security would keep him from making the flight.

According to Nancy, he struggled to hold back tears as he pleaded with *TSA* and Southwest Airlines staff to fast-track him through the lines that were moving like molasses. Even though missing his flight could mean missing a final chance to see his grandson, no one seemed to care.

Too much was at stake to simply roll over and cry. When he finally cleared security – several minutes after his flight's planned departure – he grabbed his computer bag, shoes and belt, and ran to his terminal wearing only his socks. The pilot and the gate agent were waiting for him.

"Are you Mark? We held the plane for you and we're so sorry about the loss of your grandson," the pilot reportedly said. "They can't go anywhere without me and I wasn't going anywhere without you. Now relax. We'll get you there. And again, I'm so sorry."

It's hard to underestimate the courage of the pilot's decision. The flight, which ultimately departed 12 minutes late, likely had hundreds of passengers rolling their eyes in contempt. And given that any delay has knock-on effects for passengers at the destination airport, his decision placed Southwest at risk of facing the wrath of travelers, and more than a few demands for compensation.

Elliott, who brought the story to the blogosphere's attention, approached Southwest about the story, half expecting the airline to be outraged by a pilot's refusal to push the on-time departure.

Instead, they told him they were "proud" of their pilot, a man who clearly understands that taking a child off life support has consequences that run deeper than a flight taking off late. As Nancy wrote: "My husband was able to take his first deep breath of the day." Hopefully, over time, his daughter can do the same.

Slow down…and look up

Posted on January 23, 2011 by Mark H Miller

Blog Prologue:

Ever been in a situation when you didn't know whether to laugh or cry? Came to me yesterday as I drove along a large field of Christmas trees, probably ready for next December. Northern Washington, Rockport to be exact, not far from the home of Warnie and Thelma Johnson.

I smiled about what the trees reminded: It was Chicago, December, 1966, still enjoying the first year of my ministry at St. Pauls Church. My mentor needed a tree for his apartment as did I. So, hey, partnership in hospital visitation, Church Council meetings and worship. So why not cutting our own Christmas tree? Well, we ended up not cutting one, but it sounded good as we left. Wrong possibility about cutting, but hey, Fred Trost, the best mentor in the world, didn't have everything right all the time. Almost, but not always.

I brought the tree home. Unloading it, not sure if it would go up three floors to the apartment, Fred asked, for sure very late to ask this, "Mark, did you measure the apartment ceiling?"

My blank look gave him an answer. Always positive, "Oh, I'm sure it will be just fine," he counseled.

I had purchased a tree stand and that fit. Then, the reality came without compromise: the tree was probably one foot taller than the front room where it was to reside.

Now, how to get it fittable? Somehow that was accomplished. I then used wire to hold the tree to the French doors—my move toward security.

Until about 3 in the morning when a *CRASH* made it clear: the tree was stronger than the French doors. Not a good picture: all the ornaments askew, most broken, the tree lying on the floor as if it was wanting Christmas to be over RIGHT NOW.

Main Blog:

Warnie Johnson was a lumberman. His specialty was a tree feller. [I'm trying to remember the lingo.] I didn't know much [that's an understatement] about felling trees happens. I knew one of my fishing guides out of Forks, Washington, got hit by a falling Douglas fir tree, barely escaped with his life, but had a back so messed up he couldn't row a boat…ever again.

I knew Warnie could fish. But, I didn't realize he was the "best damned feller" in the county. That referred to his "tree felling."

No one expected him to die…as quickly as he did. The two blood clots—one in each lung—evidently the size of thumbs—did him in. The CT Scan was too late to help. Not good.

In visiting with his family and fellow "fellers" I learned one thing… more than impressive and preachable and livable.

Actually learned it from a wrestling coach. My great fishing guide friend, John Koenig, through whom I met Warnie five years ago… and on that first trip Warnie said, "Preacher, if I go before you, do my service." I told him I would, never expecting it to happen very soon. One reason is Warnie is 12 scant days younger than I.

At any rate I went to a wrestling match with John—he's the assistant coach. My only "fare of wrestling" was once on television—WWA or something like that—and it smacked of phoniness.

John explained to me that it takes intelligence to wrestle—to know the moves and to know the next three moves you need to make. It was beyond me, but I watched and found myself caught up in rooting— clapping and cheering—for all his players from Concrete High School. Boy. Couldn't believe how intensity took over, for everyone. Quite something.

Just before that match, the coach came up. His birth name—on his certificate—was David Dellinger. But everyone knew him as Goob.

Not sure what to make of that, but everyone smiled at the funeral when I quote the Goob guy.

Turns out Goob and Warnie were the best of friends, had felled trees for years, even decades. He told me, "Warnie was the best, and we all followed him and paid attention. And when we screwed up, we knew it. No one's raised eyebrow said more. That's when we had done more than 'oops.'"

I inquired, "Goob, what was Warnie's best lesson for you?"

His eyes got larger, "Oh, it was a great one. I had messed up felling a tree—hadn't got it down yet, but somehow I hadn't paid attention and bark from everywhere came at me, almost covering me completely. I had only looked at the root of the tree and the ground around it."

Warnie found me in that mess, helped uncover me. He then said, as only Warnie could, few words and great meaning and value: *Slow down and look up.*

As shared at Warnie's funeral, *Such wisdom and truth! Right now we can slow down and look up—for Warnie and even more, for God. But, in each day/hour/minute of our life—and I'm preaching to me as well as for any of you—slow down. Don't try to get it done so fast! And be sure to look up.*

I'll remember that. Far more than a Christmas tree that needed shortening. Why? Because I figure if I follow Warnie's advice, it will mean my life will not be shortened. And, that's a good thing.

Six Seconds

Posted on January 24, 2011 by Mark H Miller

Have a theory—never proven but often experienced. It is this: **when something good or bad happens [it can go either way] the most important part is what you do with it, how you react, what's its impact?**

For a few blogs I share some "for instances."

For starters, an example that happened in six seconds.

My son, Andrew, is the head men's basketball coach at Schreiner University. A word about the school. It is a small university, no more than 2,400 students I believe, located in Kerrville, Texas, about 50 miles northwest of San Antonio. Kerrville, a population of 20,000, dwarfs almost every city circling it for 30 miles. In other words, for the folk in that area, Kerrville is metropolis, baby.

In terms of classifications for athletics, Schreiner is Division III, the smallest of all the divisions. The key sport is basketball because they've dropped football.

And yet, it's not really a fan favorite, given their record over the last 12 years, never winning more than six games any season. On a good day there'll be 250 fans in the stands.

Recruiting by a Division III school is tough—they provide no athletic scholarships and it probably costs at least $30,000 each year to attend, given tuition, room and board. For the most part, Andrew and his fellow Division III coaches get the "last of the options," [that's the polite version] in recruitment. However, truth is Andrew's excellent in recruiting…winsome, focused and very energetic. He'll drive 8 hours to recruit a shooting guard or a rebounding forward.

They've had an almost .500 season, losing just two games more than they've won. Which put their overall record at 6-8, with ten games to go.

Then came the six seconds.

It was a home league game, which made it more important.

With six seconds to go the opponent scored a basket tying the score.

Andrew's best guard made a 3-point shot with two seconds to go.

The team was jubilant. The opponent called a time out.

In enthusiasm [but not knowledge] one of Andrew's two assistant coaches ran on to the floor to greet the players. Still, two seconds to go.

That meant a technical foul, giving the opponent two free throws, both of which were missed.

But, something more crucial in basketball. With the technical foul the opponent got to put the ball in play near their basket. If there'd been no technical, after the time-out the opponent would have had to go the length of the court—so, that was formidable.

The technical took away that formidability and as you can guess, as the horn blew to end the game, the opponent made a 3-pointer, putting the game into overtime.

A game Andrew's team finally lost by ten points, going south with their shooting in the overtime.

I read about that game [was in Washington for the funeral of my friend] and thought metaphorically, *What a terrible loss—must be like a funeral for Andrew and his players.*

Six seconds. Unlike any six seconds in all of Andrew's life—and the players—and the assistant coach.

I talked with Andrew the next day and he explained the dynamic and how he tried to stem the tide. He did EVERYTHING he could as a coach.

Six seconds…snatching defeat from the jaws of victory.

How would he and the team respond? For Andrew knew it was not the loss but the reaction to the loss that would be crucial.

Two days later, last Saturday, they played a very strong team…and WON, 83-82, when the other team's best shooter [he ended up with 32 points—huge for Division III] missed a 3-pointer at the end of the game.

The response was more than commendable by Andrew and his team. In my metaphorical language, they moved on—as Andrew's college coach used to advise, *Keep on keeping on*.

Seven victories. The first for Schreiner since 1999. And to think, they have lots of games to go. Andrew's goal is not 8 victories. Andrew's goal, shared by the team, is to reach the league playoffs.

Whether or not it takes six seconds.

Sculptured Butter

Posted on January 25, 2011 by Mark H Miller

A second example of my theory—never proven but often experienced: **when something good or bad happens [it can go either way] the most important part is what you do with it, how you react, what's its impact?**

It was hard for me to imagine more going wrong for Blake. He was in the 9th grade, attended junior high, and a member of our confirmation class and youth group. To say he was shy and withdrawn was an understatement. His older brother got lots of awards for academic and science projects. Blake was always shadowed.

He never missed a church youth group meeting and had perfect attendance for confirmation. Did his assignments but never participated in discussions. Nice, quiet, but almost hidden.

He then asked, "Would you come to my house? I'd like to show you something."

I was amazed. Blake had built his own soapbox and was entered in the city's soapbox derby that next Saturday. His soapbox was smooth and sleek—looking at it you could tell, *what a beautiful creation—built for victory.*

I stood with his parents—and older brother—at the top of the hill, the starting point. We clapped and cheered and gave him as much encouragement as we could, "GO Blake! We're with you!"

He nodded, but I wasn't sure if a slight grin made it.

He then took off, zooming down the hill. At maybe thirty yards, his front right wheel broke off, the soapbox careened off the road and into a thicket of blackberry bushes.

Dreadful.

We helped carry his trashed soapbox derby racer to his dad's pick-up.

Blake looked down, tears coursing their way to the street.

Dreadful.

If anyone needed a victory it was Blake. Especially Blake.

Fast forward a year, in my office. He shared that he had just been diagnosed—at the age of 14—with testicular cancer. The surgery was set, his future possibility in ever being a birth father dashed.

Dreadful.

And yet, Blake continued his faithful attendance and silence.

The youth group had a one-week-field-trip to San Francisco, to see how churches ministered to the poor and struggling. Reminded me a lot of Blake..well, not poor economically, but poor in spirit and emotion.

We stayed and ate meals in a welcoming church.

At each meal, without saying a word, Blake got a cube of butter and began carving it.

What was this?

I thought, *He's doing this, a good thing. But, a butter carver?*

Fast forward again.

We rode our chartered bus back to our home town, leaving San Francisco, so much the better for seeing the ways in which the church can give arms and legs to the Gospel [my version at least].

Half-way home, Blake asked me, "Could I make an announcement to the group, using the bus' speaker-system?"

"Sure, Blake, have at it."

I was beyond clueless, but hey, Blake was going to speak to the group.

He got the microphone from the drive. There was something stronger about his body language, his shoulders didn't slump and his head was strong.

He then said, "I have an announcement to make. I'm making this announcement on behalf of my fellow union members. I am the chairman of the Union of Butter-Carvers and want you to know that we reserve the right to butter carving. I am a butter carver and proud of it!"

Stunning.

Butter-carvers!

The bus erupted in applause and Blake returned to his seat, high-fiving everyone.

What a moment. What a great moment.

Two years later I left that church to pastor a new congregation. As the moving van loaded up I noticed this sports car drive up.

It was Blake.

He got out, held a package, handed it to me.

"Mark, this is for you. Thanks for the church not giving up on me. Thanks for the youth group not giving up on me. And thanks to you for not giving up on me."

He pointed to the package, "Go ahead, open it."

I did.

Now my tears hit the driveway.

Blake had created it.

It was a plastic tube of carved butter.

I have had that gift from Blake on my bookshelf for over forty years now.

In two weeks I'll be preaching in Dallas and will bring it along and will share about Blake's beautiful testimony of the ways in which the future can be lived, no matter the present, whether or not you've ever carved butter.

Life is Instructor…no matter what.
Posted on January 26, 2011 by Mark H Miller

A third example of my theory—never proven but often experienced: **when something good or bad happens [it can go either way] the most important part is what you do with it, how you react, what's its impact?**

My father, Hank Miller, died, in 1994. Mother, Esther Miller, continued to live in their retirement home.

My mother, energy-re-visited every day, even though she had macular degeneration, INSISTED on walking in the neighborhood each morning, rain or shine.

The truth is, no secret to anyone spending any amount of time in Portland, Oregon, the rain was more frequent than the shine. In fact, one of the NW mantras is, "You don't tan; you rust."

It was February 14, a dreary, rainy, cold morning—they always went together in February. Mother walked the sidewalks by her retirement home and crossed the street.

She *thought* she was at an intersection, not realizing that walking between two parked cars indicated otherwise.

But, hey, with her macular degeneration, she could only see peripherally, and with that, not well. It was dark, she was not wearing orange or yellow—a dark green rain suit.

As she crossed the street—mid-block—she didn't see the car and it didn't see her. It hit her full-blast, knocking her up over the hood, crashing into the passenger side of the front window and then hurled to the street, with two bones compound fractured below the knee.

The blood started its own path from her leg, mixed with the rain water.

250

Another pedestrian saw this, ran to my mother's side.

She wasn't unconscious. Dazed, but not unaware that something very horrible had just happened.

He looked down at her, "Ma'am, are you all right?"

My mother nodded with an immediate response, "Goodness, this is some way to spend Valentine's Day."

That's Es Miller.

Okay, this happened, but we've got to move on. Yeah, I should have known, but I now have learned. Is the driver all right?

The next day I arrived in Portland [was in Chicago at the time]. The surgery dealt with the compound fracture. Other than that, no internal damage it appeared.

I walked into her room.

Mother looked like it was a train and not a car that hit her—no mystery something terrible had happened.

One of her first comments was empathy for another patient she saw down the hall, "Mark, there's someone on this floor who just lost a leg."

That's Es Miller.

And then, she got a great laugh.

As I sat with her a second patient was placed in the adjoining bed. It was also an elderly woman who suffered a pedestrian accident—she was about my mother's age.

Two of her grandchildren in their twenty's came with her.

We hadn't a chance to exchange accident details when the nurse excused us to the hall way.

One of the grandchildren looked at me and asked, "Can you tell us what happened to your wife?"

My mother loved it. As she loved all of life—no matter what.

If life wasn't always good, it was always instructor.

Protect and Serve–constant vulnerability

Posted on January 27, 2011 by Mark H Miller

Prefacing note: Today is Thursday, January 27, 2011. Wanted to share this reflection about the life, world and swirl of the police. The series on Life As Instructor will continue in a couple of days.

I'm not an expert, by any stretch of the imagination or experience. But the perspective was more than nudged recently when I heard on CNN that ten policeman were shot in recent days, most of whom died.

It triggered more than twenty years ago, circa 1980-88, when I was a pastor at Broadmoor Community Church [United Church of Christ] in Colorado Springs. Six of those years I volunteered as a police chaplain. There were 30 of us, ranging in every "religious stripe," from Catholic to Protestant to Jewish. The one rule was when we were on duty we could never share our personal business card or mention our church. It was truly a non-denominational witness.

We would ride with an officer one night a month—with 30 chaplains that made the rotation easy. And then, we would share a 24-hour pager for two weeks, which was 24/7 duty.

On my night I would arrive at the downtown police station about 9 p.m. and ride with one officer until about 3 or 4 in the morning.

I remember my first night—riding with Sue. We no sooner got in her squad car and the directive was clear, *Robbery at Sampson Dry Cleaners...*

We took off like the veritable rocket and before I knew it we were in an alley behind the cleaners—it was part of a strip mall—with the cleaner's back door open. Sue got out, pulled her gun. I sat, doing my best imitation of a rock. She leaned in, "Pastor, come on, we're in this together."

I blinked, "Not now...it's no fair, you've got the gun and the bullet-proof vest," to which she replied, "Oh, but don't you have a bullet-proof faith?"

253

Got me. Besides, that can *really* preach.

Then another time I rode with a sergeant, just off of 2-years of vice and narcotics assignment. We were called to a motel where a farmer in from the edge of the county had been bilked of his money and his watch by a prostitute. His anger was greater than his embarrassment so he reported it. The cab driver knew the prostitute would be in this motel room... didn't know her well, but said she was pretty new in town and went by the name of Brown Sugar. The sergeant got out his photo album [they were not his family pictures] and asked the farmer and the cabbie to see if Brown Sugar was in there. I looked it over, "Pastor Miller, why should you care about this?" the sergeant asked. I shirked, "Oh, just seeing if there are any parishioners."

Never did find Brown Sugar but when I got home and told my wife where I'd spent the last 4 hours she advised, "You'll find a 2-pound bag of brown sugar in the kitchen."

But, bullet-proof faith and Brown Sugar is not my main point.

My main point, shred of humor and anything but shallow is this: After serving six years as volunteer chaplain with the Colorado Springs Police Department [besides, the captain was a member of our congregation], I cannot say strong enough: *It is simply not possible to have too high of respect for our police.*

Oh, of course, there are exceptions and variances.

But, ride in a police car sometime—in the front seat and not in the back handcuffed—and when there's a traffic stop and after the officer has done a background check on the car, see how your gut feels when the officer gets out to meet the driver.

To the point, last week in Waldport, Oregon, along the Oregon coast, a policeman stopped a car, approached and was shot and is barely holding to his life. The assailant escaped in battle fatigues into the woods and is still being sought.

254

Or, when there would be a domestic conflict and you never knew how explosive that kitchen would be. As chaplain that was the worst-case scenario. I would take one of the couple and the officer the other—in separate rooms, to be about the business of quieting and learning. Or, going to deliver a death-notification at 3 in the morning—did that once, only to find we were given the wrong address. Or, to go to a bar at 4 in the morning and see three bodies on the floor, a man and woman and the man's son…and not sure there wasn't a 4th somewhere in one of the side rooms.

I've had the privilege and honor—those are not quickly or lightly chosen words—to know many policeman and policewomen in my life…and I can say, I respect them, I appreciate them…and although just a little here and there…have considerable awareness of the difficulties and challenges to uphold the law as their cars say, "to serve and protect."

Whether or not Brown Sugar is ever found.

Janie's Story

Posted on January 28, 2011 by Mark H Miller

A fourth example of my theory—never proven but often experienced: **when something good or bad happens [it can go either way] the most important part is what you do with it, how you react, what's its impact?**

At first I only knew Janie. She was in one of my first youth groups, a struggling teenager [that's never an oxymoron, always a redundancy, right...at least for most adolescents] who never went to a scale she appreciated and she maintained they disliked her. In addition, frequent appointments with the dermatologist were always not mentioned, although I did know of them.

Having taken that trail myself—including the dry ice on the face—I did understand.

Just before I left that church I met some of Janie's friends—but only through Janie. She began to share about twelve other friends, each of whom had taken residence within Janie's life and body and psyche.

I really didn't know much about multiple-personality-disorder, but Janie began the teaching.

Of all her "persons," the one who was incarnate evil was Jane. Jane tried—with effort and constancy—to get Janie to go into the garage, turn on the car after making sure the fuel tank was full—and KEEP THE GARAGE DOOR SHUT.

Janie was able to thwart those efforts, only making Jane furious. Jane was constantly harping and chiding and trying to kill Janie. Thank God it never worked.

Some of the others were only about goodness: Carolyn took flowers to gravestones of Janie's friends. Karen went to nursing homes and asked the manager which residents had no visitors, and then Karen would introduce herself and begin visiting.

One time Janie visited our family. After breakfast she went out on our porch for a cigarette. I came out later and looked at her. It was a different person. The eyes were caved, the scowl unchanging...bitterness abounding.

I got it and honestly, not knowing if I was doing the right thing, launched, "You're Jane, aren't you!"

The sullen face nodded and smirked, never meeting my eyes.

I then gave it my best effort, told Jane she was unwelcomed because of her terrible demands of Janie.

Of course I was unsuccessful. But hey, couldn't be accused of giving no effort.

Years passed, but Janie kept in touch, phone calls, nice gifts for my sons, lovely cards. Each card was signed *Janie*, but I think Carolyn and Karen had a hand in it.

Janie then went to a special treatment center in Philadelphia. From what I had learned, this is the finest treatment center for Janie's difficulties.

And then. What a wonderful *and then*, through not giving up, through not giving in, Jane left. And somehow, I don't understand, but you don't have to understand to appreciate and affirm and celebrate, the other eleven personalities blended into Janie.

Today Janie is terrific—centered, focused, one single ordinary [and yet very caring and connected] person.

It's a joy to know this, to see the healing has happened.

That doesn't mean shadows don't lurk.

But what it means, it's Janie who deals with them...no hand-offs to others.

A joy to behold.

Thank you, dear God, for Janie...and for the ways in which your Healing Spirit makes for goodness and beauty and value...and for continued delivery of flowers to nursing homes and for taking the poor and disenfranchised to the medical clinic.

Playing the Blame Game

Posted on January 29, 2011 by Mark H Miller

I have lots of reasons not to like Jay Cutler. When drafted by the Denver Broncos the hopes were high. Not that he was born in Christmas, Indiana, and certainly not because he went to Vanderbilt and won nothing. But, because he has a great arm and was tall enough to make it big-time.

When the Broncos hired a new head coach, Josh McDaniels, from what was revealed recently, Cutler wanted out of Denver. He went to Chicago with derisive comments sending him along his way.

That was nothing compared to what happened during and after Sunday's National Football Conference Championship Game in Chicago as the Bears and Packers battled.

Cutler played through one series of plays into the third quarter and then sat—due to a "leg I cannot plant when passing because of a twisted knee."

The cameras [reminded me of Candid Camera] found him riding a bicycle, sitting by himself, never talking to the 3rd string quarterback who was sent into the game, no encouragement, nothing. For the most part it was imaging of aloofness, indifference and boredom. In the championship game!

Then the comments flowed, a virtual tsunami of negative shots at Cutler—and, of all things, mainly from fellow NFL players. His own players defended him staunchly, saying he's not a quitter, fights to stay in the game, had to be injured badly to stay out of the game. The Bears lost the game, which turned out to be incidental, although I would be curious what reaction would have been with a Chicago victory.

A MRI revealed some damage to the knee, a level 2, which meant he had little mobility and strength, especially when passing or getting away from oncoming Packer linemen and linebackers.

And then. A report on what happened Sunday night. Cutler and his girlfriend and 11 other friends got together at a Chicago steak house, gathered in a party room just for them. Makes sense.

Except.

The party room was on the second floor and Cutler refused the elevator and *walked the stairs.*

From which all hell has broken loose.

As the writer ended his article, *Or maybe the whole MCL tear story is an elaborate ruse to divert attention from the fact that Jay Cutler started the O'Leary fire, helped throw the 1919 World Series and actually is Steve Bartman.* [Bartman became infamous when he reached over the Wrigley Field left-field foul line and snatched a fly ball, keeping it from being caught. The Cubs lost, thus failing to reach the World Series and the culprit was Steve Bartman.]

Honestly, I find all this very typical—in the rush to judgment, the need to find reasons/causes/culprits keeping victory from being achieved. Ever considered the frequency with which people find someone else to blame, never holding a mirror to themselves? It's never ever their fault! From the beginning when Eve lambasted God, "If you hadn't given us the snake we'd never be in this mess." We're much better at indictment than acceptance, that for "whatever" we may be culpable.

I still don't like Cutler…and not for what happened Sunday. And not for dissing the Broncos. Rather, the quarterback for a NFL team NEEDS to show leadership. In truth the whole first half of Sunday's game was one of Cutler's worst. He was sluggish, overthrew key passes and just didn't have it. He, simply, is not a leader.

Then when the knee injury benched him, he became disengaged. That was obvious.

Perhaps next year all the harping and chiding and castigating will be lost in new victories. And yet, as commentary after commentary happens, it's clear Cutler has dug himself into a deep hole.

Some will want to hand him a shovel so he can dig the hole deeper. I wouldn't.

My own response is to see again the news looks in the wrong direction. For four days the key/lead story has been Cutler—and now *climbing stairs*, in which critique someone chortled, "I'm surprised he has 11 friends."

Give me a break. It's a game. It happened. Moving on is better than all the banter. It really is. Green Bay was better than Chicago for the NFC championship game.

Let it go.

If Cutler came to me, I would only say, "Tough time…care to share?"

Does there ever need to be more? Not that I consider—since understanding trumps judgment every time if moving forward can ever happen.

Just a notion from a Bronco fan.

We'll get to Tim Tebow later.

Pitching and Swinging–Life's Pulse

Posted on January 30, 2011 by Mark H Miller

A fifth example of my theory—never proven but often experienced: **when something good or bad happens [it can go either way] the most important part is what you do with it, how you react, what's its impact?**

Right on the edge of success—just a few innings from victory—it happened. It was early August in 1961, Portland, Oregon, the last semi-professional baseball game for our team, Showboat Lounge, before the Northwest Tournament. I was to pitch 4 innings and then start the first playoff game.

It was at Skavone Field along #99E in Portland. All went well, the score tied at zero. We were up and the first batter hit a single. I was next at bat, given the sacrifice sign by our manager. Made sense.

It may have been the best—and as it turned out the most fateful— bunt of my career…the ball slowly moving up the first base line, not wavering a moment, not to go foul. The first baseman charged and in a heartbeat, or less it came to me, *quit running, make the first baseman chase you back to home plate and maybe, just maybe the runner can get to third—what a great deal: one out and the go-ahead run on third. Good thinking, Miller.*

I stopped in my tracks, which wasn't too difficult since blazing speed would never describe me. Oh, I was pretty good winning the church picnic carry-the-egg-on-a-spoon-race, but never a sprint on the base path. I can still hear [and this is 50 years later] the snap in my knee. I collapsed to the ground—no challenge for the first baseman. My leg was locked bent, couldn't move it. Needed help off the field.

The next morning in the hospital, Dr. Hopkins the orthopedic surgeon, gave the verdict, "Mark, you have a torn cartilage. It has wedged into your knee space—so, let's take a few days with therapy to try to wedge it out—then we'll do surgery."

Not the news I wanted. Good-bye semi-professional baseball and my teammates on the Showboat Lounge team. Hello, surgery.

Those were days well before arthroscopy, which meant a few hours removing the torn cartilage and then 5 days in recovery. The first day after surgery my mother brought me a greeting card from my Stanford girlfriend, Dinny. We had dated all my junior year. She was a freshman from Dallas. We had a great time...until I opened the card to read she was leaving Stanford for SMU in Dallas and returning to her high school boyfriend. Not a fun time...no baseball, no girlfriend and lots of ache...in more than my knee.

I was happy, though, that my teammates made it all the way to Battle Creek, Michigan and ended up winning the World Series of semi-professional Baseball. That was great news. [In those days the rules were you could have five players who were former professional baseball players—the rest of us were in college, mostly along the west coast.]

I recovered—well enough that fall to begin conditioning for my last baseball season in college. Could even run up the stadium stairs [110 of 'em as I remember] three times. That was great.

And the season, my last, went well. Even did better than ever pitching, could paint the outside corner of the plate with my fast ball and had learned a slider pitch—almost always resulted in a ground ball.

I was *good to go*, and had been told by my coach, "Mark, I want you to start the league opener next Saturday in Los Angeles against UCLA—just pitch 3 innings today for a warm-up." That was Tuesday, about 3 p.m.

About 4 p.m. all went well. The opposing pitcher was up and kept fouling off 3-2 pitches. My catcher, Bob Overman, came to the mound, "Come on, this is the pitcher—blow it by him!" [I took some offense at that, his suggestion a pitcher couldn't hit. But, hey, I was to pitch and not anything else.]

I threw what may have been the fastest pitch of my life. And, as it would result, my last pitch at Stanford. The snap in my arm alarmed me. The pitcher whiffed, but little did I know, so had I.

My arm was numb—no feeling. I didn't say anything, figuring it was no big deal. Went to the mound for the next inning—hoping all would be well so I could start the next Saturday—took the ball and threw it to Overman.

Picture this: home plate is sixty-feet-six-inches from the pitcher's mound. I doubt the ball reached 30 feet, bouncing lamely to the ground.

Verdict: a torn nerve casing in my arm, putting me on injured reserve for the season. I got lots of practice rooting on my teammates that year, my last, but the ache, again, hurt.

Not wanting to close down playing baseball entirely I decided to join another Portland semi-professional team, Archer Blower & Pipe. A few of the Showboat Lounge players were there, but half the team was new.

I couldn't pitch so played outfield, because I still knew a little about hitting.

Then, in mid-July, our pitcher didn't show up. Our coach, Milo Meskel, handed me the ball, "Miller, still know anything about pitching?"

That was more a challenge than an inquiry and I accepted it.

My mother said when she saw me take the mound she almost fainted. Fortunately my arm worked and the outside corner of the plate was still a friend. And mom stayed conscious.

Wins for Archer Blower & Pipe started to happen.

Before we knew it, after winning the Northwest and West Coast tournaments we were on our way to Battle Creek, Michigan.

I had made it so far. No snapped arm, but was able to have a snap in my curve ball and the slider still got grounders.

There were eight teams in the Battle Creek Semi-Pro World Series, a single elimination event. We won the first game.

Milo Meskel gave me the ball to pitch the semi-final game.

You can only imagine all the images that scooted in and around me—the torn knee, the Dear John letter, the torn nerve casing and about to start my final baseball game.

Whoa.

Then, just before I went to the mound—top of the first inning because we were home team—Milo pulled me aside. "You need to know… the umpire just asked if you were going to Yale to become a minister. I told him that right after these games you were on your way to New Haven. He said the opposing pitcher for the Marietta, Georgia team is a Southern Baptist minister."

As I walked to the mound for my first pitch, I had two hopes: that I could pitch my best…and that the home plate umpire was not Southern Baptist.

All of that, my goodness.

….think about the ups and downs, the good pitches and those that are still in orbit when my fastball found the middle of the plate, nowhere near the outside corner and the batter hit like Mickey Mantle.

I now look up on my desk over this computer and there it is: the baseball from that 1962 World Series game. And just a month ago I exchanged correspondence with Tom Becic—a great guy and terrific pitcher who was our relief pitcher that day in Battle Creek, preserving our 4-3 victory.

We went on the next night to get the trophy for first place.

Crazy world…two teams from Portland, Oregon, winning in consecutive years.

Down? Yep. Up? Yes, sir. Keep pitching? As much as I can…it's called life…every day and every swing of the bat.

Hapless as a Fishing Guide

Posted on January 31, 2011 by Mark H Miller

My wife, Diane, who gives "alert and affirm" depth, pointed out my Blog coursing is breathing on 100. Today's the 99th…so, for today and tomorrow, a 2-part series, I share what probably is the most instructive, disheartening and exhilarating experience in this journey called life…

Here goes…

A sixth example of my theory—never proven but often experienced: **when something good or bad happens [it can go either way] the most important part is what you do with it, how you react, what's its impact?**

Five days. The chance never before offered. To verify my interest to become a fishing guide was not only veritable, but workable.

It was mid-80's, Tillamook Bay, October, Monday—Friday. Had some cousins aboard my father-in-law's boat, whimsically labeled the African Queen Two. It was big and bulky, looked more like a barge than a fishing boat…and maneuvered like it.

But, we were not in a speed contest. Nope, as we slugged our way across the various Tillamook Bay holes—in front of the Coast Guard Station, the Ghost Hole, the Picket Fence Hole, the Sheep's Corral [it's important as a guide to name the holes—the clients cannot help but be impressed]—nary a bite, a nudge, and as one of the cousins offered, "Man, I'm not sure the fish even breathed on us." His attempt at humor was almost as lame as my fish guiding.

But the truth is, you can name every hole—even make some up—but if you're going to be a guide, if you don't shift from fishing to catching, well, you can guess.

Now, my cousins were polite and as they left for home Friday afternoon, nets emptier than unfilled [what?], they didn't offer, *Great time fishing with you.* Rather, with no spice to their thought, and I imagined their limp wave good-bye only foretell the future: *see if you'll ever get us to do this again.* You'd think perhaps a comment of anticipation: "Maybe next year." Not to be.

I then thought that Saturday would be my day. Okay, I accepted that fish-guiding was not my thing, giving credence to sticking with my day job. But tomorrow! Ah, my deliverance was at hand. I had a trip scheduled with Keller, my erstwhile fishing guide. Truth is I had fished Tillamook Bay with Keller every October for 12 years and NOT ONCE did we not land a chrome-bright, sea-lice laden fall Chinook salmon. Think the smallest one topped 17 pounds. The sea lice was important as a freshness scope—indicated the salmon has just come in from the ocean.

I could hardly sleep—the possibility of deliverance does that to me, knowing, living in a world of verification, *Tomorrow is my day!*

I got to the dock early—that's my nature anyway. Was never one to make sure I arrived at a parishioner's home for dinner even five minutes late. Someone once said *promptness* was one of my mantras.

I looked down at Keller getting his boat ready. It wasn't a barge, but a 22-foot sled boat with a 150 horse jet motor and a 10-horse kicker—used for trolling. See, I know the lingo.

"Hey, Keller—a great day!"

He looked up and what he said next was like the worst thing in the world, "Mark? What are you doing here?" It was like, *you have five minutes to live, there is no treatment for your condition, you might as well forget fishing forever.*

Emotionally I was comatose.

Keller continued, getting out his tattered datebook, "I have you down for next Saturday, not today."

He then shook his head—that shake that says everything and offers nothing. "Sorry, but I have a full boat—the maximum of 4 clients—they come down from Portland—have fished for years."

My ears became deaf…

He then raised his hand—just like we do in preaching to make a point, "But, Mark, don't leave. Sometimes my clients, especially one of them, parties very late on Friday night and are too drunk to make it. So, wait, maybe last night he binged."

Truth? It's the first time in my life I prayed for someone to be drunk.

And, as 3 guys came to the dock, Don looked at me with a thumbs-up, then pointed to the 4th seat. "This is your day."

One of the three said, "Keller, we think he will make it."

Damn, I hope not! I hope he had a flat tire. I hope his alarm didn't work. I hope a cop stopped him and hauled him off to jail after the breathalyzer.

All hopes were dashed with the slam of a door—and I couldn't help but think a slam to my day.

The 4th arrived.

"Sorry, Mark, it just isn't to be. Can you get back here next Saturday?"

My nod was lame, but I was sick.

Keller blew it. My calendar had the truth. If I do anything right it's to keep a calendar. I've never shown up for a wedding or funeral on the wrong day. WHY DID KELLER DO THIS?

Yep, Keller blew it…and I was the blown-upon. The storm crashed my day and battered my hopes. And, that's not just preacher-talk-lingo.

That was truth on the throne and fishing on the scaffold. Forget the catching part of it.

What to do?

The drive from the Oyster House [south end of Tillamook Bay] north on #101 through the cities of Tillamook and Bay City on my way to the north rim of the bay and my residence, the less-than-famous Tilla-Bay Motel in the sleepy fishing village of Garibaldi, took forever.

I didn't walk to my cabin—I slinked to it, opened the door, sat at the rickety-kitchen table, table topped with cracked linoleum. It had one short leg so it was hobbled and off-balanced. That was my story and I didn't want it to stick as well as it did, for I don't think I've ever been more hobbled…

….to be continued tomorrow…

One hundredth blog–net no longer empty

Posted on February 1, 2011 by Mark H Miller

A sixth continued example of my theory—never proven but often experienced: **when something good or bad happens [it can go either way] the most important part is what you do with it, how you react, what's its impact?**

Wanting to lessen the self-inflicted pain and torment and grief and agony and brokenness—hey, don't make fun unless you've fished five days like I had and came up with not even a whiff of a bite—I took a couple of sugar packets to keep the table stable.

At the moment it was all I could do, having failed at my impersonation of a fishing guide for my cousins. At least the table stopped its hobble.

I looked around room #7 [the one I always rented, had done so for over ten years and EACH year salmon were caught...but not this year] and noticed it had aged—the calendar was two years old. And THAT'S exactly as I felt—a 2-year-old who had just lost his favorite dog. I know—harsh—but in #7 at the less-than-famous Tilla-Bay Motel [Tom Beaudette would not have had anything to do with it], life was un-squeezable lemons. Pretty bitter.

And then it hit me. One of those DUHHHHH moments. The truth muttered this: **I knew of no one who ever caught a fall Chinook salmon in October in Oregon from a motel room.** And. To make the point secure, my boat still was tied to the dock at the Garibaldi Bay Marina.

So off I went. Give it a go by myself.

A few words on the formability of that. As mentioned previously the boat was a barge, hence the name African Queen Two. Humphrey Bogart and Kathryn Hepburn would have loved it. It had a steering wheel up front and a large outboard motor that hardly ever went at trolling speed. To help the boat slow down a bucket was dragged behind the boat. Bulky. Awkward. No one ever cruised by and took my picture.

271

But, off I went, was able to slug my way out of the dock area, barely missing four moored boats.

Got to an area where there were lots of boats, always a good sign, let out my line tied to a copper spinner with a red feather hiding the triple hook. Put the pole in the holder at the back of the boat right next to the motor. Let out the bucket—hey, maybe it would be a sign of a virtual bucket-list [Mine was to catch a Chinook that week]—went to the front and turned on my tape-recorder to play what had to be the best song in the world—Billy Joel's "You're Only Human." That was little consolation, but it worked for me. And I knew the first words, so apt, "You're having a hard time lately and you don't feel so good; you're getting a bad reputation in your neighborhood...but, that's all right."

Well, I wasn't sure it was all right, but I was singing to the heavens. Again and again and again Billy and I did my version of a duet, just trolling along.

A boat across from me was waving and shouting. I smiled and kept singing. They persisted so I muted my melodic offering and listened, "Hey Mister! Turn around! You've got a fish on!"

I turned and about fainted. The new song was from my reel, zinging and zinging, the rod bouncing up and down like tomorrow would never make it. The rod was doing its version of an epileptic seizure.

I shifted the motor into neutral and ran for the rod, grabbed it. Whoa. The fish wasn't stopping. I looked down at my reel, thinning quite fast of line and thought, "Damn, I'm getting spooled," which meant...well, you get the idea.

For some reason—maybe in appreciation for my singing, who knows?—the fish turned and came at the boat.

Suddenly images of "Jaws" struck me and I wondered if maybe this was version #2 and it was really a shark. The African Queen Two could take it, I was sure.

Nevertheless, I reeled like my life was depending upon it…and was able, not sure why or how, to keep the line tight.

Now, even I knew in playing a fish, two dynamics must ALWAYS be in place: NEVER POINT THE POLE AT THE FISH, AND WHEN BRINGING THE FISH IN, ALWAYS LIFT UP AND REEL DOWN.

I then saw Mr. Salmon…and almost stopped breathing. Boys and girls, this was a fish…I mean, A FISH.

Mr. Salmon saw me and no doubt thought, "What is this?" Turned 180 degrees and ran again…and again…and again.

It then slowed down so my brilliant technique of lifting up and reeling down was winning.

The net.

I looked for the net and there it was—stuck in the side of the boat intertwined with my extra fishing rod and a spinner caught in it.

It was the other side of the boat. How to get it?

I let out line, snuck away from the fish and pushed and pulled and jerked to get the net free.

The handle was aluminum, which wasn't a good idea. Wait, you'll see why.

I then went to the fish-side of the boat, fully armed, net in one hand and rod in the other.

I laid the net at my feet to pull the fish to nettable-reach.

That worked. I thought.

I then held the rod sky-high, took the net with one hand and dipped for Mr. Salmon.

Didn't realize in all this battle my hands were sweaty. Too late, the net slipped from my hand and began its own version of *drop to the bottom of the bay.*

I'm sure it was a scene for the ages.

I barely held on as I leaned over the boat's side and as my head hit the water, was able to reach and barely seize the dropping net.

I'm sure at this point Mr. Salmon knew he was being played by the world's craziest guide and he started to flee again.

I barely had the rod in hand as I got back fully into the boat.

The net lay at my feet—still empty.

The rod still dipped and at least I had the decency to keep the rod up and not reel as I lifted.

It was now SHOWTIME, sports fans, as the fish was on its side, idling by the side of African Queen Two.

I knew the net was too slippery for my one-hand technique, so I decided to risk it.

As fast as I could, although I'm not sure there was one energy-cell left in my body and the adrenalin had left long ago,

I had the audacity to lay the friggin' rod on the bottom of the boat, grab that net with abandon, reach over the side and net Mr. Salmon.

THERE HE WAS! Netted.

Now. A problem. This was Mr. Salmon and not Mr. Sardine.

How to get the fish in the boat???

I grabbed the rim of the net and Heaved with my biggest Ho.

Mr. Salmon bumped the edge of the boat but stayed in the net.

And in one amazing swooshing moment, there we were lying on the bottom of the boat: Yours Truly, Mr. Salmon and the net.

The motor was still in neutral and since it was the peak of high tide, we hadn't gone very far.

I then heard applause.

What was that? Was I asleep? Am I still in room #7. Is this the world's biggest joke…simply a dream?

I sat up and looked over the side of my beloved barge and there they were—about six boats had encircled my battle.

And I thought, *Okay, so you can applaud and laugh. But, why didn't one of you jerks come aboard and help me?*

I never said that—stood in response to the applause. Never in all of football history had a referee ever signaled a touchdown with such enthusiasm.

I zoomed back to the Garibaldi Bay Marina. Well, "zoomed" is way over-stated, but hey, I was on a high above the highest mountain.

The dock-boy took Mr. Salmon. Another crowd gathered. It was hard to look humble, but I honestly did try…well, not much, but at least some.

I couldn't see the scale; it was turned. But, I heard the gasps of those who saw the scale. And then looked as the dock-boy brought me a hat, "Congratulations, Mister. Great job."

Oh, yes, if he only knew.

I then looked at the hat, "Garibaldi Bay Marina—50 pound class."

I couldn't wait. I put Mr. Salmon back in the boat and went south to the Oyster House—I knew Keller would be there.

I pulled up to him and showed him my hat...then Mr. Salmon.

He loved it, "Ah, the Preacher scores again—your Preacher's luck still works!"

We laughed...I didn't tell him about the previous 5 days.

Got to remember that, though, to keep the perspective. And for sure I was right: didn't catch Mr. Salmon in room #7.

I then came home and a parishioner gave it his perspective, when hearing the story [it really can preach, I am sure you have figured out], "Mark, I betcha lots of people will see that hat from Garibaldi Bay Marina listing 50 pounds and think the Marina is a diet-center."

Mark holding 50 pound salmon

Violence Without Borders

Posted on February 2, 2011 by Mark H Miller

The headline comes from a newspaper, but the reality impacts the heart and every breathing moment:

Ore. town getting back to normal after manhunt

I haven't been there in over fifty years…and yet I AM there emotionally and experientially. What I remember of Lincoln City, Oregon, started with our United Church of Christ congregation there—small, maybe 30 in worship, mostly retired, a reflection of the sleepy community. The apt description of the area is an enclave for retirees and vacationers. In fact, most of the Oregon coast is sleepy and retired, save a few fishing guides and lumbermen and city or school employees.

It's where you go when the world of *not-so-fast* is needed. Where you go where you don't worry let alone fuss about locking your door at night or leaving your porch light on. If you're from Portland or Eugene or Salem, it's where you go to catch fish or crab or enjoy a nice weekend. Away from the swirl, mayhem and dangers of life.

A week ago that changed for the residents of Lincoln City and Waldport. The calm and beauty of Alsea Bay was shattered, the stormy winds of violence making for white capped water on the bay and white-knuckled fists of the residents.

A policeman stopped a car for a vehicle violation…and the horror happened. The policeman was shot, almost mortally and a police chase ensued. The policeman, now being treated in a Portland hospital, will make it. But, if the horror-filled-moment had happened a few miles down the road, he wouldn't have.

The bad guy escaped. He's been identified, a 43-year-old from Portland, about whom his family states, "He lost it, was way-off because of pain medication." For four days, tiny Waldport swarmed with dozens of police as three SWAT teams combed for clues about the whereabouts of 43-year-old David Anthony Durham of Portland. The "lost-it" culprit escaped and no one knows where he is—lots of vacation homes closed up for the winter are in the area. The family says he made his own camouflage clothes and knows about surviving in the wild.

The chase continues.

And then I read this from one of the policeman, "Normally this neighborhood is nice, quiet, beachy," Williams said. "It's an excellent neighborhood. To have something like this happen just reminds us that there's another world out there."

All of that struck me…"reminds us that there's another world out there." For, I'm not so sure for anyone, there's ever a "world out there," always apart from our own place and time.

The thought on that is about the time, more than ten years ago when the small town of Weimar, Texas, was invaded by the "world out there." You may remember the culprit, the Railroad Killer. I was Conference Minister in Texas at the time. One of our pastors, Skip Sirnic—had been the pastor at Weimar for over ten years—dearly beloved—and his wife, Karen, who was the Secretary of our Governing Board, were bludgeoned to death in their sleep on a Saturday night. A 16-pound sledge hammer was the weapon.

They lived in a parsonage on the church property—off to a corner. Skip was also pastor of a neighboring church seven miles down the road, New Bielau, and preached there at 8 a.m. When Skip didn't show up for the Weimar service it was thought he had an emergency—or had to remain a while longer at New Bielau. So, some of the Weimar church leaders started the worship.

During their worship the Moderator left the service to check at the parsonage. Found the horrific scene, called the police. The Moderator then had to tell the congregation their beloved pastor and wife had been murdered.

I was notified an hour later, had been attending a national church meeting in Cleveland. I couldn't imagine the Weimar homicides happening. Even when I arrived Sunday night to visit with Skip's and Karen's families and church members. Horrifying.

As you may recall the Railroad Killer was captured, tried and sentenced. And yet, from what I have learned over the years, the shadow never leaves completely. It simply doesn't.

The Lincoln City/Waldport scenario brings that back…all too clearly.

But even more, it is the case—wherever we are in whatever time of our life—the world is both "out there and with us." I realize that…it's not a world of smooth roads and unblemished experiences.

It's life…and the world in which we live…which makes the case bad things happen. Everywhere and in every time. Good things do, too, although they tend to be less memorable and impacting. Sad about that.

BUT.

It also makes the case you and I can live in and through all of life… no matter what. Because, and this is the most basic faith foundation I experience and can share: God's promise to never leave us is never broken, God's promise to be with us no matter what is always kept and Paul's affirmation that *whether we live or whether we die, we belong to the Lord,* is true and abiding. Okay, that's preachy in a Blog. But, hey, it's my life and my experience and it's my story and I'm stickin' to it.

Storms of life–not always a metaphor

Posted on February 3, 2011 by Mark H Miller

Storms. Any time of year.

February has started, greeted by a furious storm—snow, ice, wind chill—throughout most of the mid-west, as is reported, and more: from Maine to Texas. Read that Denver didn't reach zero all day, noteworthy even for the land of mountains and skiing. My favorite Colorado guide, Matt Krane [my personal "Rabbi Guide," who's also on the Breckenridge Ski Patrol] sent a picture indicating a temperature of minus 20. And I thought, *It's 45 degrees warmer than that in Austin and yet, it's really freezing.*

That caused me to laugh, because at times in August, the Austin weather-guy will say something like, "A cold front's coming in tonight—will drop from 79 to 72." Go figure, right?

Back to this stormy reality, because it is serious and incarcerating.

Schools closed [One professor had classes canceled and needed the "snow day" to revise the semester's curriculum pacing and assignments], kids at home, parents trying to cover bases if they can get to work, and especially if there's no "okay, stay home" alert from their office, roads closed [read that Lake Shore Drive in Chicago, right next to Lake Michigan, got closed, but not before dozens of cars were stuck—no relief in sight.].

Not fun. Sure, staying home has its benefits—kids relax—and for some, hey, it's a truth, check the maternity wards in 9 months. Yep, life happens.

In hearing about more than 20 inches of snow in Chicago, I first worried about my son, Matthew, his wife, Sheila and their daughter, Laura. They have Sheila's family nearby in Winnetka, and are very responsible and reliable. Yet, "Are you all right?" is always the first question. And they are. Matthew said his neighbor trudged to their front porch to borrow their snow blower. Out of luck because the snow blower was in the garage and the blown snow made the garage hard to even find. Well, that's a tad overstating, but the point of being deluged is not lost.

All of this triggered something about storms—how people deal with them.

It was my first super-storm, at least non-metaphorically. First winter in Chicago, January, 1967, labeled the "Super Storm." Snowed over 27 inches in one day. All parked cars were only minor humps along the curb.

Some people dug out their cars, but because street parking was at a premium, often left for work or groceries and put a chair and sign, "Mine!" for their return.

I then noticed a beautiful moment—a man across the street, Fullerton Parkway to be exact, was digging his car out. Sitting on a stool because he had only one leg—a victim of diabetes–he was still able to clean off some of the snow. Then, some neighbors came to help him, because he had a tall car and reaching the roof was not possible. Got the car cleared out.

I didn't see if he moved it, but found the next day, each car uncovered of the blanketing snow—which added up to about 25% of the cars–had parking tickets on them. City ordinance enforced that you cannot park on that street when snow exceeds 8 inches—or something like that.

I noticed the ticketing police did not clear through to the snow-laden cars. They were untouched, hence unticketed. And noticed the cars were ticketed at 4 a.m. Are you kidding me?

I got my ticket and was told by my Alderman [went through them in 1967] that he couldn't help, but I needed to protest my ticket.

Got to the courtroom some weeks later. The courtroom was standing room only, no smile anywhere, each of us for the same purpose and some court-room strategy. At least all but one of us.

We were advised by friends and in some cases, by attorneys, "Challenge the ticket…they'll need to dismiss it because the 'law was not enforced uniformly.'"

I had also been told dismissal could be received if the ticketing police officer wasn't in the courtroom, "Dismiss, your honor, because of want of prosecution." Or something like that. That advice was my short-term-version experience of law school.

I chose the dismissal for lack of prosecution and the judge didn't blink, "Dismissed." The ticketing policeman wasn't there…probably issuing… well, you know the end of that thought.

I then noticed the one-legged neighbor, waiting his turn.

I chose to remain, standing in the back of the courtroom.

My neighbor didn't receive any counsel, so all he said to the judge, "I'm not guilty, your honor. I'm a victim like the others."

The judge gaveled, "You're guilty. You go pay your fine."

The ruled-guilty neighbor, shouted, "What? How can you do that. Everyone else is off the hook and now I'm hanging. That's not fair! You're excluding me from justice." Or, something like that.

The judge looked to an officer, "Remove him…disorderly conduct. Jail's his choice and I didn't offer it.."

And off he was escorted. They didn't bring out the handcuffs. Guess they reasoned a one-legged guy would not run very far…or fast.

I got home and pondered, *How to deal with this…gross injustice.*

Ended up writing a letter to a very popular, and yes, controversial Chicago Tribune columnist, Mike Royko, detailing the whole episode of my one-legged-snow-clearing-off-his-car-neighbor.

About a week later I received a call from one of Royko's assistants, indicating they'd like to publish the letter. I told them to go to it.

Nothing.

And then, a month later another phone call, "Reverend Miller, this is ...., Mike Royko's assistant. We're sorry, but we cannot publish your letter. Your neighbor's an employee of the City of Chicago and has refused permission for the letter. Because he's certain such action would get him fired."

Turns out he wasn't jailed and a lawyer friend got it all thrown out.

Still, I thought, *Storms bring out the best..and the worst.*

Hope these days as people get out from this Super Storm, the best will be far more prevalent than the worst.

A footnote as I think back upon the '67 storm.

Although I had removed snow from my car, driving was next to impossible. A funeral home needed a pastor. I told them if they could pick me up I could help. The pick-up spot was in front of the library, some blocks west on Fullerton at Southport. I walked—really I sludged—to meet the funeral home car. The director had said they'd pick me up in a hearse.

What a time—standing on that corner, wind chilling the body and probably the soul, holding my pulpit robe in one hand and my briefcase in the other. Waiting and waiting.

Ah, the hearse arrived.

The red signal light stopped him. I walked immediately to the hearse, opened the passenger door and jumped in, hauling my wares with me.

The driver, very surprised it turned out, furrowed his eyebrows [luckily the light was still red] and asked, "Who in the hell are you?"

Oops. Turns out it was the wrong hearse.

Got out…and soon all was well.

Super Storm.

Good.

Bad.

Ugly.

Humorous.

Just like the rest of life itself.

Hearing God's Voice

Posted on February 4, 2011 by Mark H Miller

Every protester had their own story of why they came — with a shared theme of frustration with a life pinned in by corruption, low wages, crushed opportunities and abuse by authorities.

A short paragraph from a news-item about the current protests in Egypt—more than 250,000 people, peaceable in this instance, indicated their demands for new leadership needed attention and support.

The paragraph struck me...*every protester had his or her own story*...at the deep truth in that.

After four decades in ministry, now stepping, but not as firmly as I'd like, into my own 7th decade of life, I can recall...example after example, how almost every parishioner and minister with whom I've shared in ministry, had something very traumatic happen to them.

The incidents.

The moments, the experiences when we weren't sure which would win...life or non-life...breathing or not breathing, making it or getting broken.

Sure, I can give a litany of 'em, but the point is not to dwell on those moments when life cratered me and all I wanted to do was crawfish away from them. [Learned that verbiage in Texas.]

The point is, okay general but hopefully not unhelpful, **What do we do with the negative moments?**

And, no less, *the positive moments?*

As I've tried to offer in recent Blogs, the response is actually more important than the event. A friend wrote that, "Mark, your Blogs lately have made it clear—HOW we respond is the crucial point."

I agree. And then, as I've mirrored some of those moments of untowardness for me, it's not always been the first reaction that was pivotal. It was perhaps the second or third response when the reaction was indelible, in terms of how I managed to keep on keeping on.

What I think about this morning, and I'm not sure why, is that I'm preaching next Sunday at a friend's church in Dallas. It's going to be a sermon on *How do we know God's voice?*

Not that I'm an authority—but as I answer it myself, the moments in my life which were pivotal, the occasions when I JUST KNEW something more than the voiced person was involved, was when I knew in my heart's eye and my soul's center, *God is involved in this.*

The one moment I'll share in the sermon next Sunday will be when I was 16 and asked a friend, "I don't know what I want to be when I grow up."

Her reaction, immediate and convincing, set me on my way, "Mark, what a stupid question. Of course you know. You will become a minister."

Somehow, beyond the crazy reason I thought at 16 the future should be prescribed [that's terrible theology but I didn't realize it at the time… for it takes away any spontaneity], I knew…down deep in an indelible manner…that ministry was the best option.

Especially when I never figured my hitting or pitching a baseball had "future" labeled, and for sure, since I struggled miserably with science and math, knew a technical world would always be stranger.

Of course that's a positive example.

No less important, with certainty clear and unchanging over time, I can list particular moments when I was judged far less than good or thoughtful or caring or useful. I was declared without purpose, other than to be the worst person my classmates ever knew.

I didn't give in to that. Although to say it lacked impact would be untrue. What was true, the most negative moment turned out to be great inspiration...to prove the judgment of others was both mean and not true.

Interesting, isn't it? How a moment—when good not to get too prideful, and when bad not have it get too controlling—can result in a new day that is known for its growth and vitality. Even at 70.

Or, hopefully, especially at 70.

Life is more than "Good Friday Events"

Posted on February 5, 2011 by Mark H Miller

This is not a complaint. Well, maybe it is. Not intended. What's intended is to push for *balance*.

The question I pondered this morning, when hearing recently it was the 25th anniversary of the explosion of the space shuttle, Challenger, is *Why is it the deadly—at least more negative, even dastardly and tragic—that gets more of our attention?*

Happened to watch part of the Oklahoma State/Texas college basketball game recently. At half-time there was recognition of horrible plane crash ten years ago–the 10th anniversary–in which OSU's players and coaching staff were killed.

That is not to say honoring the dead, memorializing the dead, citing important dates when history didn't just lean it tilted, is not helpful or good.

I cannot even imagine the extent to which September 11, 2011 will be noted.

As it should. And yes, we should NEVER FORGET what happened to the Challenger—and in all the other events that have not only impacted but in many ways have re-directed so many in the way by which they live.

And yet**, what about the good events?**

Do we celebrate them—beyond birthdays and anniversaries?

The end of a church camp when I was in the 7th grade, when the camp director, a minister in Oregon, pulled me aside, handed me a pocket cross, "Mark, you will have a great future." Not sure what that meant, but he continued, "Ministry is a vocation you should consider." Didn't think that was an option to ponder in the 7th grade.

And then when 16, when my great buddy, Jeannette Butts, high school classmate, laughed when I asked her what she thought I would be,

"Mark, at times you can ask really dumb questions. *What you will be?* Of course it's clear, you're going to be a minister."

Or, perhaps the best moment of all, the day, even the moment, Diane and I first met...in the Denver Airport...trying to get on the last flight to Austin after the previously scheduled flight was canceled. Of course I remember her birthday and our anniversary. That's important. But what about the "trigger-moment?"

There are others.

My point—it's so often the grim events garner the headlines and galvanize our attention. And I could, along with everyone who reads this, list all the "Good Friday Moments" in our life, for I contend NO ONE avoids them. But I won't.

Let's not get lost in those, however. Let's not have the macabre get overloaded, so much so we forget, or if not forgotten, give no attention to the good events, the times in which, as a clergy friend used to announce, "AHA!"

In fact, they don't know it—unless they get to this Blog—but after a recent funeral the family handed me a package, "You said something about liking scotch."

I looked puzzled, "Did I?"

"Yep, when talking about Dad when we mentioned how much he loved blackberry brandy you made it clear, *Hopefully there's single malt scotch in heaven—along with the fly-fishing.*

I smiled, "Got me!"

That night the two small bottles of single malt [the size you used to get on airline flights] didn't have a chance. As I sat in the clearly undistinguished Red Roof Inn across from the Seattle/Tacoma Airport, getting ready for my early flight the next day, I toasted my buddy, Warnie, and gave thanks for him...AND for his family, especially his wife, Thelma. How courageous, pioneering and caring they are.

I'll not forget that day...special and as meaningful as any I've experienced as a pastor.

Even loved it when the funeral director took me to his office and pointed to a picture, beaming beyond description. It was a picture of him holding a beautiful winter steelhead caught with a fly rod while fishing the Klickitat River.

THAT triggered another cherished moment...because it was the Klickitat River where I caught my first steelhead with a fly rod...guided by Joe Willauer, another wonderful guide friend.

What does all this mean? Well, it's more than another scheme to include fishing in the narrative.

It's meant that we should not deny or ignore the anniversaries of the crushing, defeating, tragic national events—even the ones only personal to our individual families or to our individual selves.

But, **make sure there's a balance**...to remember the great times, the moments that have changed our lives for the good.

And to know...they are not only what we remember looking into the rear-view mirror.

They ALSO WILL BE the great life-shaping events that are still to happen as we look through the windshield.

For, I believe in my heart of hearts, what is a wonderful event is not only contained by history; it's unfolding in the new day.

You think?

I hope so.

Be ready.

Value...and at times, the folly of prayer

Posted on February 5, 2011 by Mark H Miller

NOTE: IT IS NOW ABOUT NOON IN AUSTIN, SATURDAY, FEBRUARY 5, 2011. SENT A BLOG EARLIER THIS MORNING... BUT ANOTHER MADE ITS WAY TO MY COMPUTER, HAS TO DO WITH WHAT MIGHT BE SPOKEN TOMORROW MORNING IN A SERMON IN DALLAS. SO, TODAY IT'S "two for the price of one," on blogging. CONSIDER THIS SUNDAY'S BLOG A DAY EARLY...OR SOMETHING LIKE THAT.

I'll pray for you. How often have we heard it? How often have we said it?

I remember, although I wasn't there and at times the legendary stories about William Sloane Coffin were questionable, but once he met with some Southern Baptist ministers, each of whom, in the words of a professor friend of mine, "Hated him with a perfect hatred." When Coffin left the SB pastors said, "Dr. Coffin, we'll keep you in our prayers," to which Coffin retorted, "How can I tell between your prayer list and your shun list?" Oh, boy.

Or when he met his first wife's father, Arturo Rubinstein, the famous Polish-American concert pianist. Rubinstein, probably in a genuine *I have heard good things about Coffin manner*, said, "Oh, Dr. Coffin, you preach like Billy Graham." To Coffin that was anything but a compliment. To which Coffin replied, "Mr. Rubinstein, you play the piano like Liberace." Double-oh-boy.

Back to prayer. What does it mean?

I'm working on some sermon ideas for the first Sunday in February and the idea of prayer is included in the Old Testament lectionary passage for that Sunday, Isaiah 58:1-12, to be exact.

It talks about fasting and prayer and when illustrated, both are considered more alienating than coalescing in relationship with God. Primarily I gather, because of the self-serving nature of the fasting and prayers… me-focused, me-benefitted, me-served.

I can appreciate that.

The initial illustration I'm working with comes from a question I used to get often…*Do you pray that your sermon will convert people*…or when in college, especially for people who knew I had hoped to become an ordained minister…*when you pray, is your prayer before your first pitch for victory?*

I may have, but honestly…and I don't think my memory lags on this one…I don't think so. When I preach…when I pitched a baseball game, I did not preach to convert people or strike-out batters. I really didn't. Mainly because I don't believe the primary purpose of a sermon, let alone the essential ministry of any church is to convert the hapless soul as much as it is to help people transcend themselves.

Purpose and function of prayer.

What comes to mind, referenced in a recent Blog, is when I pitched in a national game in Battle Creek, Michigan and the opposing team's pitcher was a Southern Baptist preacher. I did pray that the umpire was not Southern Baptist. [Don't think he was…called fair and square.]

Or, my favorite prayer request over the decades—because, I suppose, people do think ministers have a special God-pipeline—came following a wedding rehearsal. More often, but not always it was the bride's mother. She'd ask to visit privately and then make it clear, "Dr. Miller, we EXPECT good weather for my daughter's wedding tomorrow." To which I replied, with what I tried in kind firmness, "Ma'am, I'm in sales and not management." That *worked* every time, I think.

Or the time I went to a very special dinner the night before the Academy Awards. A couple in our church was very proud and with justification. Their son was nominated for his first Academy Award…they asked me to offer the meal invocation, added by them, "And, please put in a good word for Gary." Hey, that was preferable than praying for Gary receiving the award. I tried to phrase the prayer with consideration but not a preferential bias, "Dear God, we celebrate Gary's gifts tonight—may he not do poorly."

Think that was okay. And, he did win his first Academy Award… because of his skills is what I contend.

Prayer.

Rabbi Harold Kushner who authored, <u>When Bad Things Happen to Good People</u>, defined prayer as *Conversation with God*. I would hope so—a DIALOGUE and never a monologue. For I do believe, and I'll try to share this tomorrow, that God does speak to us…at least in my own life and time, primarily through others. Evidence for another Blog and day.

But even more…the prayer focused: whether it's preaching or pitching… not for converting or good pitching. Rather, that I give fully of myself, that I have trained and prepared sufficiently and that my effort is as strong as I can give. That I be focused and determined and make sure if we don't do well it's not because of my lacking or compromising effort.

I'm pretty sure that's what is meant in the Isaiah passage…pretty sure. WHATEVER WE DO, it's not for self-elevation but for the benefit of others. And, we are as consistent in that as possible.

Where this gets faulty is when someone preaches about tithing and gives nowhere near that in his or her personal pledge money gift…or when a church time and again talks about helping the poor, clothing the naked and feeding the hungry…and their own annual church budget gives no more than 5% to others in what is called benevolence. Hello?

I guess this comes down to each person unto himself or herself. For prayer is essentially a private experience. The public part of it is whether or not the talk is walked. Or, perhaps to be offered in this manner: is what you say not a stranger to the manner in which you live?

One more note—not for closure but simply a personal approach. When I'm in the hospital—before surgery or following with recovery for the friend facing apparently a lonnnnnnnnnnnnnng road at least, I pray the friend "knows the healing, comforting, peaceful and strengthening presence of God." And then follow-up with contact—personal visit, notes, calls, whatever it takes to be what I find most elemental in ministry, a *caring presence.*

That does not minimize the value of prayer; it simply asks God to be present with me and others.

George's Story–43 years later
Posted on February 7, 2011 by Mark H Miller

I don't honestly remember the date. But, the circumstance, to every word of the conversation, remains indelible, never to be forgotten.

For time-reference it had to be 1968 or 1969. The youth group at St. Pauls church in Chicago for whom I had pastoral responsibility [read that *youth minister*] was a wonderfully mixed group, in terms of culture and race and religious leanings. We were German Caucasian [the ethnic founding for the church in its first steps in 1843], African-American, Korean, Japanese, Hispanic. It was great.

Brothers, Leo and George Blevins, made it across mile-wide North Avenue from their Green-Cabrini Homes [read that north side ghetto], to be in our youth group. Often one of us took them home. No problem. Leo and George were part of us. Period. End of conversation.

Then one morning, very early—had to be the summer of either '68 or '69 [and as you can imagine racial conflict was incredibly raging in our country]—my home phone rang. I squinted at the alarm clock: 3 a.m.

A slurred voice, "Mark, this is George. I need your help."

"George! What's the problem? Where are you?"

He asked someone near, "Where am I?" Still slurred.

He returned to the conversation, "Addison Street Jail. I'm in big-shit trouble. I need you."

"George, let me get dressed and I'll be there."

One attire comment: whenever I visited jails, which was more often than I ever anticipated, reminding me that not everything in preparation for ministry made it to the seminary class rooms, I wore a clerical collar, so my professional identity was clear.

296

I approached the desk captain, "Sir, my name is….and I'm hoping to visit George Blevins. I'm his youth minister at St. Pauls Church. Can I see him? I have no idea what the problem is."

"Reverend," as he slid me a sign-up book, "You'll learn soon enough. But, get ready. He's in deeper shit than you could ever guess." I wondered, *when trouble moves from lurking to reality why is vocabulary limited?*

Even more, I must say that trembling thoughts of *suicide, armed robbery, rape* pushed. I pushed back.

"Thanks, officer. Where do I see him?"

I looked at George—and cannot find words to describe what a mess he was…but I had figured out it must be serious because George only had one phone number to call…and he didn't call his Momma.

George wouldn't look up as he whispered, "Mark…I didn't do it."

"What, George, what didn't you do?"

"I didn't throw any paint in that apartment."

I looked at his boots—and it was no mystery how quickly innocence was out of the question: fresh white paint covered most of the boots.

"George, let me see what more I can learn."

It was obvious that George had too much bubbly and speaking intelligibly was questionable at best.

I went to the desk officer again, "Sir, something about white paint. Do you have any details?"

He pointed to the corner of the precinct, where stood a man about my age with a face that gave *wrathful and fury* a clear definition. "Go see that guy, Father. He can tell you everything."

I learned, in about one hostile paragraph that George and two other teenagers broke in to a brand new apartment building—it was to open to new residents on Monday—found 5-gallon buckets of white paint and decided to re-decorate by splashing paint everywhere. They left. The police didn't need a detection or seek-find credential. They simply followed the fresh white-paint footprints.

I thanked the owner.

Fast-forward a week.

Was able to take George home with the bail-out, took him to Momma. She was constrained and thanked me for getting George home.

George was one of my favorites and I knew his hope was to become a Chicago policeman. Now all that had less than no chance.

A thought hit me a few days later. I went to the damaged apartment and spoke to the owner, explaining George's relationship to our church [which was only about 5 blocks down the street]. I also explained that I had heard of the other two but didn't know them. And from what I gathered neither of the other two would surprise anyone about what they had done.

But, George was a surprise. He had made a HUGE mistake. But, I asked the owner if he would give George a second chance. The charges couldn't be individualized, so whatever was decided would affect all three.

I didn't know what the two owners would do as some weeks later we all stood before the judge. We had a public defender and the owners had their two attorneys.

The judge asked the owners, "Is there anyone here to press charges."

Neither owner spoke. Anticipation heightened as the roar of silence continued.

Then one said, "No, your honor. We ask for the charges to be dropped."

As the judge gaveled the dismissal the other two "free-painters" clapped and then sneered as they left the courtroom, slapping each other.

George shook his head, "Mark, what just happened?"

In the car I explained it wasn't over. "George, there is more."

I hadn't told him I had worked a deal with the owners. We went back to the trashed apartment. One of the owners stood there. I introduced George to Don Gale, "George this is the owner who has just saved your world and dreams for your future. He's now going to hire you at a very good hourly wage. They've figured the total cost of damage caused by the paint. You owe one-third and Mr. Gale will take it out of your wage...but you will also have some of your wage, to save up for school to become a Chicago cop."

....
....
....

Friends. That was more than 40 years ago.

I had lost track of George and his brother, Leo. I had lost track of most of the youth in our group and the leaders of the Summer Day Camp.

An important segue-note: Two months ago when I preached at St. Paul's Church in Dallas, a regular worshipper contacted me. Pam had been a member of our youth group, 1966-69 and now lived in Dallas. It was a joy to re-connect and learn how she is.

This morning Pam and her husband walked up to me. Pam was beaming. "Hey, Mark. Don't know if you can handle it," as she handed me a piece of paper. "I did some homework; look at the paper."

My breath wooshed, my eyes got all blurry, and I looked at her, "You've got to be kidding!"

"Nope, he wants you to write him."

Friends and neighbors, on that piece of paper was the name, *GEORGE G. BLEVINS, JR., HIS E-MAIL AND WHAT HE'S DONE... MARRIED, A COLLEGE GRADUATE AND WORKING IN THE WORLD OF MEDICAL SCIENCE WITH A DEGREE FROM THE UNIVERSITY OF ARKANSAS. HE ALSO HAS JUST UNDERGONE BRAIN SURGERY. LIVES IN ARKANSAS.*

I shared that with the congregation—HAD to work it in the sermon— and besides it fit very well as I shared what I think it means to be the church...a matter of faith...and surprises. For, who knows how a church's life and mission comes around...even more than 40 years later?

Just had to share...and now I connect with George...what a joy. What an incredible joy.

Thanks, Pammy. You done good, woman!

The Future: Catching over Fishing

Posted on February 8, 2011 by Mark H Miller

Presumptuous? No doubt.

Audacious and even high-fluting? Likely.

Hopeful? More than any of the above.

Let me explain.

Now that Diane's working in Project Management with a new company, GTECH, in their Austin office, and the radiation treatments are over, with hopes 2011 will be both cancer-free and surgery-free [She's had seven surgeries in less than the last year.], my thoughts turn to the fullness of our relationship as we head to our tenth wedding anniversary.

But, who's counting?

The presumption and audaciousness and hope came about two months after we met. I asked her, although it was probably more declarative than inquisitive, "Diane, it's important to me that I be with someone who is willing to go with me to the Northwest to catch steelhead. How would that be for you?"

She never hesitated a breath, "Mistah, you teach me to catch steelhead and I'll whip you every trip." [Well, it was not EXACTLY like that, but you get the statement's purpose!]

We exercised that fishing option and wadda ya know? Less than a hour drifting the Wilson River [flows into Tillamook Bay near Tillamook, Oregon], Diane cast, bounced eggs along the bottom of a drift, hooked, played and landed her first steelhead.

As she and the guide held the fish, she looked at me, "Mistah, are there any other questions?"

Since then, ten years ago, we have had great trips, and truth on beam, she HAS whipped my butt doing more catching than fishing.

I think of that now. With hopefully the cancer having fled never to return, hopefully the healing of the burning from the radiation to happen within the month predicted by the radiologist, and anticipating her new project management position will not require 24/7 at the work place, we will find some time to see about the imbalance of catching over fishing.

Here are a couple pictures...the first is Diane ready for her first "go at it" of casting on the Wilson River in Oregon, and the second, her first salmon just three days before we were married, caught out of the mighty Columbia River as it is greeted by the Pacific Ocean. Yes, indeed. Beautiful—the bride-to-be and the salmon—in that order every time!

Future, here we come...and the bumper sticker, "When the fish hear our name, they tremble," is not misspoken.

Diane on Wilson River

Diane holding salmon in front of Cannon Beach Motel

303

George's Story—2 days later

Posted on February 9, 2011 by Mark H Miller

No matter the word—beautiful, incredible, phenomenal—they'd be understated. Could never be hyperbolic or exaggerated.

A couple of days ago I shared "George's Story," about how I had been given George Blevins' current e-mail. The last contact with George was November, 1969, when I moved from the near north side of Chicago to the rainy climate of Eugene, Oregon. I shared the story about George, a member of our St. Pauls/Chicago youth group, his rather blatant attempt with two others in repainting an about-to-be-opened apartment, the owner of the apartment giving George a second chance and George's hope to become a Chicago policeman.

I wrote him. Many of you asked, "How did his brain surgery go? What have you learned?"

Well, it was THE George T. Blevins, Jr., friends and family…and this will go in my Blog tomorrow, but I wanted to give you a heads-up.

Amazing story. Here's an African-American, maybe 16 or 17, living in the ghetto-binding of Green-Cabrini Homes, near north side of Chicago. What kind of future does that foretell?

Well, his story has touched my soul and given me as much hope and joy as any I have ever experienced as I course my way through my 45th year of ministry.

I will have you know it is Dr. George T. Blevins, phD. WOW. Goodness sake's alive. Off the charts.

Here's his response…and it plays its own music—triumphant and jubilant and fabulous.

From George:

Hello Mark,

Yes, that would be me. I now live in Little Rock, AR and have since 1993. Married to Paulette for 39 years now. Four children, 3 grandchildren and 1 great grandchild. Have been everything from delivery boy to bus driver, prison guard, medical school professor, state-wide grant program director and now entrepreneur.

My brain tumor surgery (the 3rd in 9 years) went well. Tumor is gone hopefully to not return again. I am just home resting now.

Sorry for the delay in responding. Just a little tired now. Great to hear from you and that life is going well for you.

Best regards,

George T. Blevins, Jr., Ph.D.

The song to sing, with joy and profound gratitude: *Rejoice in the Lord, always, again I say rejoice! Or, perhaps the "Hallelujah Chorus"!*

Flooding Benefits

Posted on February 10, 2011 by Mark H Miller

David Johnson gets it.

First, some background. David is one of my fishing guide buddies. He fishes out of Tillamook, Oregon, and is terrific in catching steelhead and salmon and sturgeon. I would even wager he, with timing and river conditions right, could catch one of each on the same day.

Never asked him that.

David was our guide when Diane and I fished together the first time… and he helped Diane catch her first steelhead. That was something, since I believe the way it goes with catching steelhead is this: 10% of fishermen catch 90% of the steelhead. Of course, there's no guide who will ever tell you that percentage is the same for women. EVERY guide has told me, for reasons no one seems to reason but cannot deny: *Have a woman on the boat and she'll catch more fish.*

Just ask Diane…I can recall Diane and I floated a river with a guide outside of Billings, Montana. We were using the very same trout-nymphing gear, and wadda ya know, Diane caught ten trout to my one. I loved it, though, assigned the "clap and cheer and take good pictures" responsibility.

Back to David. The reason *he gets it*, and this can preach—in fact, were I still a Conference Minister I would send it to EVERY one of my clergy—is because of the following comment he posted on his web page:

That last big high water has really made some changes to our rivers. Some for the worse and some for the better.

It's sad when the old favorite holes change and fill in but it's all part of steelhead fishing. Because what the river takes away sometimes the river gives back. And part of what really makes steelhead fishing

fun for me is learning new spots and figuring out how to fish them.

I get such a kick out of looking at a new piece of water, saying to myself, "that looks fishy, it should hold fish." And then figuring out how to catch the fish from it.

Sometimes it takes several days to make it work. Sometimes you have to try it from one side of the river and then from the other side. Try different techniques. Sometimes a new spot won't work out at first, sometimes the river has to get lower; sometimes it has to get higher.

If you are going to hit the rivers anytime soon, be prepared to do some re-learning and have some fun doing it.

Thanks, David. Your insight is helpful—more than that, it's necessary for each of us as we walk the human landscape…for no day is the same. Storms come and go. Rivers change. What we did yesterday may not work for today.

The choice is ours. We can find the "old sure-catch-fishing-holes" gone and do the *woe is me* drill. Or, we can keep floating the river [living the life] and find new places to fish.

Why?

Because there is no trout or salmon or steelhead or sturgeon who flips out of the river to find somewhere else.

The river is the river. Life is life.

Keep fishing…keep living.

FISH ON!

Here's pict of David and his wife, Tesha:

Electronically challenged…the polite version

Posted on February 11, 2011 by Mark H Miller

I am aware of the need to be technologically current. But not without self-constraint.

Way back in computer-time—probably 1991—our church office got "networked." An IBM instructor was going to help us learn the system. I had only one request, figuring to learn all the tricks of networking and working my word processor [not a computer] was not for me, asked to see the teacher first. My staff thought that was workable.

I then said to the teacher—and had it written down to protect against faulty memory—*these are the three things I need to do in my word processing.* And, presto, I was good to go.

Then a wonderful church member, Tim Green, who was *beyond-guru* in computer savvy-ness, said, "Mark, you need to get a lap-top computer and start working the internet. Because he was very cognizant on these matters, I agreed. He even had me to his home-office to expand what I knew. That took nothing since my knowledge was just a little north of zilch.

Crazy, but what I learned—at least what struck me as more helpful than anything—was how to turn off the computer. He showed me the "shut down" tab. Hey, once I could start and turn-off the computer, that was advanced from my starting point, I could be trouble.

Fast forward to today, which probably will reveal little, other than I'm no geek.

First of all, what I don't do.

I don't text. My excuse, lameness visited, is that my fingers are too big for those stupid little letters.

Second, my cellular phone is six years old. I figure, if it's important, call me.

I love e-mail—I do that a lot. And, because my wife, whose world is Information Technology, knows so much in internet matters, suggested I start blogging. At first I thought she said, *flogging*, and I thought she meant the roll-up rugs in the house. Wrong.

So now into my second 100 blogs, it's probably the most beautiful time of the day, each morning to put a few thoughts together.

And, because of the books being published, friends said I needed a web page. I was south of clueless on how that happened, but signed up with Lane Boyd, who really is phenomenal in starting web pages. He asked what I wanted—I sent him picts and some script and woohoo, it came to be. If you want to learn about the publishing stuff—and even access the daily blog, please be my guest, www.drmarkhmiller.com

And, while mentioning books, I'm so pleased my Cincinnati publisher WILL [not maybe but WILL] publish my first murder/mystery novel, "Murder On Tillamook Bay," this summer. And no less, one of my friends, about whom I learned edits novels, said he will "give the novel an edit-scan" the next few weeks. Once "Murder..." is a wrap, dare I hint to the publisher there are three more novels written?

But, I don't Twitter and even more—here I don't know why I ever did it—I have a Facebook account but I do my best to not go there.

On this I'm never entering anything—probably because when I see what some people put on their Facebook account, it's embarrassing. Particularly professional people—honestly, I don't need to know if their young child didn't sleep last night or they fell asleep in a prayer meeting. But actually falling asleep in a prayer meeting is pretty unnoticeable—just seems like you're praying.

The Facebook "thing" is really stupid, at least as I see it. I do agree with Michelle Obama on this—not letting their daughters have a Facebook account—good call. And, I bet. I bet if some ministers spend less time with twittering and facebooking and more time preparing a sermon... well, wouldn't that be nice?

What else?

A blackberry? Nope—unless it's in a cobbler [sorry, that just slipped over the computer keys].

Can't you tell that I'm a nightmare for any advertisement on the new "gadget?"

I could be wrong—and no doubt many will assure me of that—but right now I think I have what I need—a working cell phone and an e-mail account, a web page and a blogging account with WordPress. com.

Yet, I still get these unwelcomed text-messages on the importance of my dialing a certain number to get $5,000 instantly. And it really irks me when the beep-beep-beep of the received text message goes off at 3 in the morning. Or the text message that if my last name is between the letters of A and N, I can call today. But, if between the letters O and Z, call tomorrow. Hello? Almost tempting to figure a 28th letter of the alphabet—or is it 29—to give a third time to call.

Just give me my computer and my printer and my e-mail and my internet. And every once in a while I'm really old-fashioned and send a letter the time-proven way—surface mail. Heck I started that when stamps were five cents—or was it 8?

I just remembered—at least one indicator I'm not totally without 2011 information technology. Diane gifted me an Amazon-Kindle. At first I wasn't sure…but now, most of my reading is with the Kindle…portable, convenient with book pricing low. The Kindle's a keeper. Not, to coin the fishing verbiage, catch and release.

Living into our Gifts

Posted on February 12, 2011 by Mark H Miller

I realize there are people who wish they could, perhaps just for one day—one hour—one minute—whelm life. For them, way too often self-reflectively, their world and their experience considered lead to one unrelenting conclusion: they are underwhelming.

That's not to say some people—perhaps at times, yes, definitely at times you and I, as a friend once offered, "Think their life is one-long-suicide, or at least, a month of Good Fridays."

Yes, it is true. Some people are so *down* they never look up. Reminds me of the cartoon [although it really isn't funny] of a man draped in a too-large-overcoat, slumping along, looking down at his left foot. The caption quotes him, "Any minute now I think the right foot will come into view."

I do know people, and I'm not a stranger to this myself, who look in the mirror and remark, not without some *truth-factoring*, "You know, when people look at me their only remark can be, *There's less there than meets the eye.*"

It's a continued cycle of underwhelming that dwarfs the self-image and diminishes the possibilities of whelming.

Into this world of shadows, which at times we may feel has arms and hands to seize us and keep us hovering in the corners, I read a clergy buddy's church newsletter editorial.

My clergy colleague, Joanne Carlson Brown, serving a Methodist Church in West Seattle, gets ministry. She's gifted in writing. Even more, she's gifting in ministry—her world touches so many people and graces and blesses their hearts [and give them a new willingness to walk without a down-cast glance]. She's able to be preacher, prophet, pastor.

In her most recent newsletter she addressed the issue of doing more than whelming life. It points out that EVERYONE is gifted. I like that.

Consider what Joanne offers as she quotes <u>Creative Power</u> by Hughes Mearns:

Each one of us has a gift.

There is the gift of courtesy often concealed in clumsy action, a gift of reticence when speech might hurt, a gift for withdrawal while the acquisitive are pushing to the front place, a gift for dispassionate conclusions in the midst of partisan heat, a gift for the understanding of minorities, and a very special gift for the understanding of children.

There is the gift of the quiet word that stills the anxious heartbeat, a gift of social grace that stoops to make life bearable for the awkward...There is the gift of living together, lost so often in the attachment of worthless possessions.

There is the gift for raising the mass spirit to worthy endeavor...

Joanne, in her own giftedness and wisdom concludes her sharing: "While this was written in 1929, it speaks to us today even in its slightly arcane language. Let us live into our gifts."

Living into our gifts.

Nothing with trumpets and cymbals required on this.

And we—every single one of us—can start...by looking at someone and in that view, see every "other" as a gift of God, as one whom God has given life...a life that has purpose to do so much more than whelm.

Think of that—I know I do with as much frequency as I can muster—to recognize and affirm others. THAT doesn't need to be anything more than opening a car door for your family or getting the mail and thanking the postman, "Thanks for all you do for us." Or not fussing when we check in for our next flight.

<u>Living into our gifts.</u>

Thanks, Joanne. You are such a great friend—the best. Has anyone made mention of that to you? I hope so. I hope your church members can spell *gratitude* more often and with more conviction and perception than *presumption*.

May that be true for every one of us, because life is and can be and WILL BE more than wondering if the right foot will ever come into view. In word. And in deed.

Joanne and her trusty companion, Royal Thistle Flower of Scotland

Confession of Sin/Assurance of Pardon—not optional

Posted on February 13, 2011 by Mark H Miller

Be assured I never write standing [or sitting with pomposity!] in a field of innocence. I have never pointed a finger at ANYONE [even those for whom I have not even a glance of respect] and maintained I am better in all phases. And what I hope, nothing I say or do—or don't say or don't do—will merit the wrathful accusation, *Damn, he's more arrogant than intelligent.*

In the liturgical language of worship I've always been unsettled when preaching in a congregation as Conference Minister, or serving a congregation as interim [meaning I'm in between settled pastors, which might make my ministry "unsettled!"] that has no Confession of Sin and Assurance of Pardon.

And it is not a happy moment—which happened in my most recent interim—within a few breaths, actually in less than a month—when the church removed the confession and pardon.

This leads to experiences in ministry that have perplexed—that's the polite version. For a blogging entry I'll leave it at that.

Some examples clergy have shared with me:

In one pastorate the spouse of a member came to church the first time—he had never met the minister before—and as the spouse left worship he refused to shake the preacher's hand. He jumped back, clicked his heels, thrust his arm stiffly in the air toward and spoke to the minister with derision, "Sieg Heil!" [Turns out the wrath was triggered because in the pastoral prayer that morning there was no inclusion of military serving our country. Actually was perhaps the first Sunday in more than 2 months when that omission occurred.]

The next day the minister told the family, "Give me a phone number." The family pleaded for no confrontation. The minister agreed not to do so. And then, less than a month later one of the family members sent an e-mail to the entire congregation lambasting some staff decisions, the written tirade filled with inaccuracies.

Ah, *justice*, why were you hidden?

Or, in another parish when a member barraged with accusations of molestation by one of the pastoral staff that held no truth whatsoever. At the end of the onslaught this church member indicated all was wrong, the parishioner had been to therapy, and wanted to apologize about these incorrect and inappropriate accusations and "be a friend." The pastor shared with me he explained to this person she was a church member period and left it like that.

Two months later the chiding parishioner wrote a 10-page letter detailing her inaccuracies about the pastor as if they were heralded truth and sent the letter to the 10 eldest members of the church.

The phone started to ring...and it took months for the clarification to be provided and the disquieting parishioner to take her family and go to another church. My pastor friend shared, "The irony of that is one week after they joined the new church the minister left abruptly taking his church secretary with him into their future."

And a third instance. A clergy friend of mine was divorced. A year later he started to date. While dating the ex-husband of his new friend contacted church members to say his ex-wife had been in an intimate relationship with this minister for twenty years. None of it was true, but word got out about the accusations and my clergy friend was told to sign a letter of resignation based upon the false accusations.

Justice and truth, you are hidden too often.

Why muse on this?

Because of a new learning in my denomination of how a Fitness Review was handled of a dear friend—the whole scenario was made public—before my friend had a chance to respond and agree or disagree with the prescribed next steps.

Truth? I don't know the details and don't care to know. I'm not saying my friend was in the right or the wrong. What matters is how the leadership failed to act in what I consider to be a responsible manner in processing the entire review and decision.

Okay, no one is perfect. Agreed.

Okay, I'm as capable as the next person in living well and at times stumbling badly.

And yet.

Make that and double-yet.

Life is never smooth, the road never without potholes and hidden rocks. It would be so nice if people were more in touch with their own vicissitudes and mistakes and were willing to admit them rather than spewing lies about self-perfection, or at least heavily weighted innocence.

One more contention, on why I *need* the Confession of Sin and Assurance of Pardon to be included in the worship service. *You never know what each worshipper brings to that service that is unsettling, perplexing, and yes, even sinful.* Because of that, and I've known this to happen because parishioners have shared with me privately after the worship, it may be only ONE parishioner who needs to confess their sins and NEEDS to do it in worship—as a personal moment with God and with no other. You never know. So, it's better to include Confession of Sin and Assurance of Pardon and not have anyone need it than not include it and have someone literally at the "I'm too unworthy to live because of what I've done" need it desperately.

Thought of all that this morning when listening on XM to the Catholic Channel. It was a worship service from St. Patrick's Cathedral in Manhattan. The priest shared in the confession and the assurance of pardon. As did I.

That was good…and necessary.

I only wish more people would agree.

Valentine's Day...

Posted on February 14, 2011 by Mark H Miller

Today is Valentine's Day...and that's a good thing. And, tomorrow is February 15, and that's a good thing. And Wednesday is February 16 and it's the third Wednesday of the month, which means Social Security checks are deposited. And that's a good thing.

It seems to me—even though I'm tempted to cite various Valentine's Days, and as I muse over same, there've been terrific days [the day I opened a letter of acceptance in what seems like ages and ages ago to a seminary] and days that more resembled the negative than a heart-shaped moment—**it seems to me to consider the "good-thing-ness" of the day is important.**

For in no day is there all one or the other—all good or all bad. Of course it's a special day, and I assume for any of us when considering the relationship that matters the most, we affirm, perhaps a card or a gift that makes it clear, *You matter.*

I read this morning a quote from Michelle Obama on what is essential in her marriage. This is important:

"I think a lot of laughing," the first lady said Tuesday at a White House luncheon with reporters who asked about the Obamas' union. "I think in our house we don't take ourselves too seriously, and laughter is the best form of unity, I think, in a marriage.

"So we still find ways to have fun together, and a lot of it is private and personal. But we keep each other smiling and that's good," she added.

...don't take ourselves too seriously. Some of us, myself certainly not excluded, may find that to be difficult...or inconsistent at best. Maybe it's because of a competitive spirit, maybe it's because we live with the delusional belief that ultimately, life, relationship, happenstance is shaped by our effort.

319

Yes, in many ways, that's true. But, down deep, it's delusional, even arrogant. Effort is important, but life doesn't hinge on that. A personal comment or two about what matters. Not in any preferential order…

I agree that laughter is good medicine. Diane and I are able to do that… and how important given the various medical challenges this past year. Cancer is not a ho-ho matter. And yet, I cannot help but recall the story from a doctor who did his best to keep a woman alive [pancreatic cancer was the culprit] for her daughter's wedding. She was able to be the radiant mother-of-the-bride. The next month during her check-up she advised the doctor, "You need to know I have two more daughters." Truth with humor—very impacting, even necessary.

Actually Diane's better at this than I. She keeps the perspective…and when I'm pretty intense—could that be a significant understatement???— she's able to be realistic, "Mark, you're doing what you can…what is will be what is. Got it, mister?"

Yep, I get it…and do smile…other reasons relationships work.

Our marriage is God's gift. We never lose track of that. Honestly, it's at the *no matter what* depth. When I learned of the Diabetes 2 reality, Diane simply made it clear: *time to look at the menu and get to the Fitness Center.* With her seven surgeries, I tried to keep spirits up, which happened in large part because of Diane's tenacity and resolve. I did what I could…and will continue that M.O.…to point out there's still many a river to fish. For us that's both reality and metaphor.

Laughter. God's giftedness. Tenacity joins in.

Call it what you will…tenacity..grit..courage…resolve…perseverance… it is so ingredient to not only a viable relationship but a strong self. And then this…knowing the list will never be totaled or complete for Valentine's Day or any other…knowing how to make the perfect peanut butter sandwich. That means in terms of *what does it take*, it's to do what we can for each other that helps the day be. A day with value and goodness.

320

Now that Diane's re-entered the corporate world, being house-husband is my current love. Yes, that's right…love…not tedious chore or task. That doesn't mean much to others…but hopefully can illustrate a good relationship is where EACH PERSON does something to make life more alive. Now I realize peanut butter sandwiches is really no big deal. But, honestly, it's to us a simple sign of being together in all things. That means the work place [fun to put notes with the sandwich… remember that as a kid?], the home place, the family-visiting place, the travel place.

Perhaps and at least finally for today, what is most celebrative about this Valentine's Day…is the combination of simply being together and knowing that the healing presence of God is impacting Diane from her recent surgeries. And, no less, because of God's blessing and our trust that God's with US no matter what, when we contemplate the future, we trust in it to the point of reaching for sun glasses.

Mark and Diane in front of Williams Fork River

New value for a new day

Posted on February 15, 2011 by Mark H Miller

Today is the day after Valentine's, on the calendar the 15th of February. But for me, at least if I take a myopic position and be self-focused [that's different than self-delusional or self-aggrandized, I hope], it is a day of discovery—one that took 23 years. But, who's counting, right?

For all these years, for a reason I will soon explain, many 14th days of February have been more onerous than wondrous, more of an arrow than a heart.

It was Valentine's Day night 23 years ago, about 11 p.m. in Portland, Oregon. I had officiated at the funeral of my wife's grandmother. The overnight, red-eye flight was to leave in an hour. My parent's phone rang. It was the moderator of the church I was serving.

My thought, *It's 2 a.m. in the Eastern Time Zone; someone must have died.*

I had no idea the call was not for me; it was about me.

The moderator advised there would be a meeting with me and four members of the council because a new member of the church alleged misconduct.

The coursing of that was everything was cleared up, the allegations were nothing more. The member admitted it was not true. Details are not necessary other than to say I went through many emotional moments of agony in order to have the truth win. It did.

But for these 23 years I've lived with what I will call the shadow of Valentine's.

Then something happened yesterday. Honestly, I've never considered this before, but it worked.

322

Rather than identify or bemoan the shadows, I, not knowing it at the time, decided I would do whatever I could to create more light.

And I did! It was as much fun [and some laboring] as I could ever have imagined. What happened is I tried my best to be a whirly-guy at house-husbanding. The whole drill of cleaning, dusting, washing…in Texan verbiage, the whole enchilada.

Then, a lovely dinner and a great chocolate cake baked by Diane…

And then. I sat down and realized: twenty three years ago is no more—it's gone! No more remembered notification phone call. NO MORE. POOF. SEE YA.

This Valentine's Day, circa 2011, was a difference maker. Not that I ever imagined it…but made this discovery: each of us…you…I…those whom we know…don't have to be caught up in the cages of what has happened. At the very most…or least…we do not have to be trapped by anything!

Why? Because in the new day we can be co-creators of good news… co-creators with God…because we can…and God…well, I believe… God hopes for it. And which of us would ever want to let the shadow of yesterday cloud the good effort of today or tomorrow?

Ah, let the sun shine!

There's a fabulous scene from the film, "Thousand Clowns," when Jason Robards and Barbara Harris ride a bicycle built for two through Central Park, singing their hearts out, "Yes, Sir, that's my baby; no sir, I don't mean maybe; yes sir, that's my baby now."

A new *baby* was born yesterday. My heart sings that truth…and I hope, pray and trust, you can know the same exhilaration in the new day… for yourself and for those who matter in your life.

History in ministry re-visited

Posted on February 15, 2011 by Mark H Miller

One of the realities of retirement—and those who share this senior status know of its verity—is a day [or days] arrives when it's no longer a "tomorrow task." That is, to FINALLY [emphasis intended] go through the boxes and boxes of pictures, old sermons, writings, to see what's keepable. In doing so, I came upon pictures that reminded me of some of the, for want of a better phrase, "extremes in teaching," that congregations and I shared over the decades.

So, in order to put this all in one place—here are some pictures with brief annotations:

I loved Noah, dearly loved him. Not that he figured out immediately how long a cubit is, but because he knew something about how to respond to God's command when a flood was imminent. Have never seen a picture of him, but hey, imagination is both a wonderful [read that, unlicensed freedom] and risky thing. So, we had our "Noah" worship service, which gave me a chance to put on the all-weather togs. No, I didn't bring a fly rod along—that was too modern. Noah's appearance came during the children's cantata, "100% Chance of Rain." Meet Noah:

Mark as Noah

Another "go at history" series of worship services was to re-create, literally because we had the historical documents, the first worship services of the root gatherings of the United Church of Christ founders, which included services from the 17th and 18th centuries, honoring early Congregationalists, Evangelicals, Reformed and Christian Churches. It was most interesting [and amusing] to do the early Congregational service, because the preacher used an hour glass and it was deemed an average sermon if the preacher only turned the hour glass once—and who wanted to be "average?"—and for seating in the sanctuary, we put the women and children on one side and men on the other.

The amusement lost some of its savor when some of our older members—read that, very old—were not allowed to sit where they've sat for 9,000 worship services. Plus, for the Congregational service we had a Tithingman, all dressed in Victorian-type togs of course, who had a long stick with a feather on one end and point on the other.

The Tithingman would patrol the worship and "enable awake" anyone who might have nodded off during the sermon. It was such a treat to share in the beginning services and theology of each denomination creating the United Church of Christ. Meet Reverend Boehm and some of his historical brethren, including my first [and I think, last!] attempt as a *Fire/Brimstone kind-a-guy:*

Fire and brimstone

Broadmoor church honors preachers

"Famous preachers of American history" will appear during the month of January at the Broadmoor Community Church, 315 Lake Ave.

The Rev. Mark Miller has announced he will present the Rev. John Philip Boehm, "an 18th century Reformed Church preacher" at the 9 and 11 a.m. worship services Sunday.

"It will be Boehm's second visit to Broadmoor in recent years," Miller said. He added that the liturgy will be exactly as the one used at an 18th century worship services by Reformed Church members in 1725 at Faikner Swamp, Pa.

Miller explained the historical connection, in that the Reformed Church eventually joined the Evangelical and Congregational Churches to form the United Church of Christ in 1957 to which the Broadmoor church belongs.

The liturgy of the other churches will be used on succeeding Sundays.

On Jan. 22 Miller will portray the Rev. Friedrich Schmid, an early 18th-century preacher of the Evangelical Church. Portions of the service will be conducted in German.

On Jan. 29 Douglas Adams of the Pacific School of Religion of Berkeley, Calif., will portray the Rev. Charles Chauncey, an early Congregational preacher. The service will be conducted according to the Puritan tradition, with men and women "strictly divided" and a tithing man with a long feathered stick will encourage sleepers to wake up. As it was the custom in the 17th century, the wearing of

18th-century John Philip Boehm returns to Broadmoor Community Church.

red-colored clothing is forbidden at a Puritan religious service.

In conjunction with the three historical services, adult seminars will discuss the traditions of the denominations which make up the present United Church of Christ. The lectures will be given by Rob-

ert Rupp, a teacher at the Colorado Springs School.

Also at the seminar on Jan. 29 Douglas Adams will portray the Rev. Henry Ward Beecher, famous early-day Congregational minister.

327

Winning is not everything

Posted on February 16, 2011 by Mark H Miller

He corrected it. Vince Lombardi was once quoted, "Winning isn't everything; it's the only thing."

When asked later, he said, "This is what I mean: What counts, winning or losing, is to know you have given your best effort."

My guess is he probably said both, but making a choice it would be more about effort than victory.

Listen, make no mistake. Being competitive to the core, winning is much more fun…and rewarding…and exclaiming…and notable.

I've never seen anyone going around in their own parade celebrating being #2. Other than Avis and that was for marketing purposes. For instance, there will be a victory parade for the Super Bowl triumph in Green Bay…not in Pittsburgh.

This is not a complaint.

But, it is to make a case that winning is not the ultimate, although it helps.

Where is this going? It's going to Kerrville, Texas, Schreiner University, Men's Varsity Basketball to be spot on.

My self-interest in this is not academic…let alone distant.

My son, Andrew, is the head coach. This is his 4th year.

It's Division III, which means his league consists of teams with very small university enrollment.

There are no athletic scholarships. Recruiting doesn't really begin until after all the Division I and II schools make their choices.

That doesn't make them bottom-feeders [yes, rather direct but not lacking perception] of college basketball players. Let me put it this way: maybe one Division III player in the country would even make it to the overall draft-board-options for any professional basketball team.

The point being, recruitment is at the last minute with the player-quality less important than player-attitude. That is, *does this guy really want to play college basketball???*

Andrew's team—for more than the last ten years, in any season, has not topped six victories.

This year has been different—they have an honest-to-goodness chance to arrive at double-digit victories. Four games left with eight victories on the board.

Even that's not my point.

Last night when I left their game in Kerrville, a city with 20,000 people which makes it huge metropolis to anyone living within 40 miles, a game which they lost, my thoughts were focused.

It was close, one-point behind with 4 minutes to go, but losing by 7: *a tough loss, but down deep a victory.*

The reason I came to that conclusion, which doesn't mean I've had an objectivity by-pass and ANYTHING Andrew and his team do is just fine—because it isn't—is because last week Schreiner played this same team and literally got blown out of the game, losing by 25 points.

Last night was different.

Oh, before the tip-off, "another blow-out" was written all over the game. Why? Because Schreiner's best scorer and ball handler couldn't play because of an ankle sprain.

I'm sure the other team figured, "Hey, all we have to do is show up. Game, point, match."

But no.

Many no's.

Andrew's team played their hearts out. They scrapped and ran and passed and shot with great success.

At the 4-minute mark it was anyone's game.

Okay.

The final score indicated Schreiner needed 8 more points to win.

And yet.

Make that, and double-yet.

I left there so proud of Andrew and his team. Effort, at least in the eye of my heart and the pulse of my life, was THERE.

They didn't give up. They didn't give in.

And, after all, isn't that what life's all about?

Sure, victory would have been sweet.

But with that effort, all the sweetness didn't escape.

And, I hope, as they hit the road [no airplanes just chugging along in a bus for over 5 hours for their next games], they'll know...they'll know very deep inside that Vince Lombardi got it right the second time...

A postscript: On the way home I visited on the phone with John Koenig, my northern Washington fishing guide and very valued friend. John coaches wrestling at Concrete High School [the high school version of Division III]. His women's wrestling team, the first in the school's history, had hoped to send four of the girls to the state championship matches. But, it didn't work that way. The girls were very upset...John didn't know how to encourage them. He then decided. "Hey, listen to this, team. What you can value…what you can always be proud of… what you can never forget…you will always be able to say—every one of you—were a member of Concrete High School's FIRST Women's Wrestling Team. Celebrate that."

A second postscript—written on February 16, 2011. Last week Schreiner won BOTH games, so they now have a double-digit-victory record, with two games to go. I visited with Andrew last night and they have more than a fighting chance to grab the last two games for the W column. Still, the deeper point is growth…for Andrew and for his team.

I love it.

Fishing awaits…yes!

Posted on February 18, 2011 by Mark H Miller

One of my morning drills is to check out some fishing guides' internet web-pages to see the latest fishing results. This morning I logged on to David Johnson's site. I've mentioned David in earlier blogging as a guide who gets it.

I came across this picture—and what a memory it triggered. Here's the picture, taken on February 16. David and his clients floated an Oregon coastal stream, fishing for steelhead.

Wilson River

The temperature, as you can guess, was below freezing and the snow was from the day before. When it snows along the Oregon coast, that's news..even when it's barely measurable.

The memory may show I'm either insane or crazy—probably both if they can be distinguished—when it comes to fishing.

It was in January of 1972, Eugene, Oregon. A neighbor, Bill Wilson, Eugene architect, was an inveterate fisherman. He invited my father and me to fish with him, the invitation for mid-week. Dad drove down from Portland the night before.

We weren't sure we should fish because the temperature was predicted for a high of ten degrees. The prediction held; it was not overstated. Bill insisted upon fishing, making sure we had warm enough clothes. I was set in that regard, for I had bib overalls—the bib was in the back up to the shoulders, protecting the back very well—and a hooded jacket. They were made by Frigidaire for people who worked in freezers—very apt for the day.

We drove to the launch site and it was covered with snow—on the North Umpqua River, a very fishable Oregon coastal stream.

I remember we had to slide the boat—a 16 foot double-bowed McKenzie boat—over ice to reach the river.

We only fished one hole that day—for about 4 hours. Luckily the breeze was calm [cannot use "gentle" at 10 degrees!] and of all things, we caught three steelhead. My Frigidaire gear was great, so I never was really cold. However, make it clear, it's hard to be cold and frostbitten when a running steelhead, darting and zigging and zagging and leaping causes the reel to sing and the blood to flow. Yes!

I thought of all that this morning…on a day in February in Austin, Texas when it will be at least 70 degrees.

And then I thought—a great thought of the future—in early March I will get to that Oregon coastal stream and fish five days—actually in Oregon and the Olympic Peninsula in Northwest Washington. The steelhead better be wary. And, I'll bring the necessary clothing, but down deep it won't matter. Because once I'm on the river and making those casts…well, it's showtime with the fish and my guide buddies.

Here's a picture of what I hope to accomplish…a winter steelhead. Ah, the blood flows, the adrenaline kicks in and the reel sings the greatest song in the world. I'm excited. Can you tell?

Mark holding steelhead on Wilson River

Thank you, Catherine

Posted on February 18, 2011 by Mark H Miller

48-72 hours is what the note said. Not that it's unexpected, but still, when a doctor declares something like this, the reaction lessens from, "Everything will be all right."

The notification came this morning from Catherine's daughter. Catherine has pneumonia and lots of other ailments, has been placed in Hospice.

This hit me pretty hard today. Let me explain.

Catherine Klemme and I met over her husband's body. She and Klem were members of the last church I served in Elmhurst, Illinois. She called, "Pastor Miller, Klem just died. Please come to help me."

He had died of a massive heart attack and Catherine awaited the EMS and related support people. They and I arrived at the same time.

After the funeral [that was 20 years ago] Catherine shared much of her journey, the tough world of the early 20th century, how she met every challenge of those who said she "should keep on your apron, Catherine—you owe it to your husband," in order to become a pharmacist. She worked at the Elmhurst Hospital with Klem. They raised their children, one of whom is a college professor.

Catherine maintained the family's interest in religion stemmed from Klem's death and funeral and something that was said at the graveside. Honestly, I cannot tell you for a minute what was said, because whatever the impact, it was well beyond me. For me it is evidence that God's Spirit did whatever needed to be done. Her son became active in a church and is proud to be a key layman, in addition to church involvement for all of Catherine's grandchildren.

What was special about Catherine is her support of my ministry and her caring for me, my sons, and then her delight when Diane and I got married. Catherine would do medical research in recent years to give me "Your friend Catherine's opinion!"

It was amazing to me that she became a pharmacist so early in the 20th century. Even more amazing was her uncompromised support of Native-Americans, especially with key leaders in North Dakota. She corresponded with them and gave money-contributions in support of their educational programs.

Her letters were always hand-written—very legibly so, I might add. She wanted to know how Matthew and Andrew were—she cheered from Lombard, Illinois for Andrew's Schreiner basketball team.

She loved the books of pastoral epistles and would read some of them to her buddies at the retirement home.

But, most of all, Catherine was a friend. Devoted, caring, understanding.

Oh, some politicians had other responses than that. She never ever let a key issue pass without giving "those silly leaders in Washington" more than her two-cents-worth. I loved it. Honest. Strong. Direct. But, never condescending or disregarding or disrespecting.

It may be by the time this morning, February 18, 2011, when this hits my daily Blog, Catherine will have, as she understands it, "moved on."

It hit me hard today.

There won't be any more letters from Catherine, no more news items on the victories of Native-Americans, no more copies of letters to set a senator or representative straight, no more questions about how Diane and my sons are doing, no more, *the novel published yet?*

But, there will be the memories of a cherished friend—one of the best—Catherine Klemme. Wow, how blessed I have been...and hopefully the better for her friendship. Yeah, that "better be," or I know I'll hear about it from Catherine.

May God, the God who keeps the promise to be with us forever, take good care of Catherine. I know that will happen. I just know it. Yes!

As I complete this reflection, I stop. Following the re-read I looked up.. and on my shelf is Catherine's gift to me—one she treasured more than words could convey: a white marbled statue of an angel, with caring arms extended to embrace and comfort and strengthen. Embraced by an angel. For in the best sense, Catherine Klemme to me is an angel impersonating a human being. How very special.

Catherine Klemme

A Revival for faith…sort of

Posted on February 19, 2011 by Mark H Miller

Recently there was contentious debating on whether or not President Obama is a Christian…a Muslim…or somewhere in between.

This blog will not take a position, other than I'm not sure it matters. I realize such a statement—*maybe not matter*—will be contentious unto its self.

There's a deeper question, at least for me: ***In our own life what matters the most to be religious?***

An experience to share…and then hopefully a point or two.

Early in life—read that before I decided to seek ordination in ministry at the age of 16—that is, I chose ministry but knew some intervening steps were required to qualify, such as high school, university and seminary graduation. At 16 I didn't know you could send $25 to southern California and receive *an official ordination certificate*—and I didn't know that in Colorado you didn't need a minister or judge or justice of the peace to get married…

I'm off track…back to the *Early in life*…I had one "religious experience" that was instructive if not helpful…or at least didn't encourage my anticipated ordination.

I was in the 8th grade when my buddy, Doug, invited me to go with him to hear Billy Graham, a person widely regarded as the most persuasive and authentic Evangelist of any era. Dr. Graham and his Crusade were to be in a field across the street from Benson High School in Portland, Oregon. Doug's mother took us. But didn't stay, "Doug and Mark, you stay together…I'll be back to pick you up when the service is over."

That sounded just fine.

Turns out Dr. Graham was ill, so George Beverly Shea, his soloist, did the preaching. Of course there was "alive" music—that was much more interesting than the dirge-like music in my German Congregational Church, when the only highlight was the summer of 1955 [that same summer] when Mrs. Anderson sang a solo and when she hit the highest note, which would have shattered the windows, but they were open for cooling of the 100 degree heat, suddenly a house fly darted into her mouth and stifled the song. I always thought that was an act of God since Mrs. Anderson did a terrific imitation of a squealing church mouse who had a hernia.

Don't remember anything about Mr. Shea's sermon until the end, when he asked us to join him in prayer. He told us about how to pray, remain seated, keep our feet on the ground, fold our hands and place them on our lap [that made no sense, as if I would have been tempted to put my hands on someone else's lap] and make sure we keep our eyes closed.

Okay.

Then in the prayer—like it was yesterday—Mr. Shea asked us to raise our hand if we loved Jesus. I worried that to do that I had to loosen my folded hands, but then figured this was okay…and since I loved Jesus [in fact, I NEVER remember not loving Jesus], I raised my hand.

He kept on with the importance of keeping our hand up, but I put mine down because my arm started to ache—think a cramp was coming on.

He then said, "Now is the more critical time. There are many of you, particularly you young people [I knew it! I knew he would get to me probably sooner than later] who need to give yourself to Jesus more than ever before. In fact, NOW [raised his voice] is the time to give it up for Jesus. I know YOU are ready to do this…so, open your eyes, stand up, and come forward. Jesus will be more than pleased."

I stayed seated, because I figured that Jesus and I were just fine. One reason was I was the Sunday School pianist and played the offertory every Sunday morning. I didn't tell anyone I only knew three pieces, so ended up mixing and matching them, which made for something different. And besides, my Uncle Johnny Schnell ALWAYS came up at the end of the 10-minute service to say it was the best piano playing he ever heard. I actually felt sorry for Uncle Johnny because of his poor judgment, plus I figured he didn't know anyone else who would play, so encouragement was a good retainer.

So, I'm seated because Jesus and I get along. Feet on the floor, hands back to folded position, eyes closed.

Then suddenly I felt movement next to me. I felt the earth rumble. Something serious was happening. Very serious, as serious as whether or not the Saturday afternoon matinee at the 30th Avenue Theatre would continue next week.

It was Doug. HE GOT UP AND STARTED TO GO FORWARD, ESCORTED BY A VERY PRETTY YOUNG LADY. Now, I didn't know where she came from, and honestly I really didn't care. She was way too old for Doug. But as I saw Doug walking up front to be with Mr. Shea, all I could think about, *THERE GOES MY RIDE!*

.....continued tomorrow....

Revival of Faith...sort of...continued

Posted on February 20, 2011 by Mark H Miller

It was Doug. HE GOT UP AND STARTED TO GO FORWARD, ESCORTED BY A VERY PRETTY YOUNG LADY. Now, I didn't know where she came from, and honestly I really didn't care. She was way too old for Doug. But as I saw Doug walking up front to be with Mr. Shea, all I could think about, *THERE GOES MY RIDE!*

So, I went up, catching up with Doug and his personal escort. Before I could even look around, we, along with quite a few others, were ushered into a side room, were handed a little red book, and were told, "This is all you need to know Jesus. Congratulations."

And that was it.

I never asked Doug about that day. 1955 was long ago.

The book? It was the Gospel of John...which made sense because I learned in seminary John was called The Evangelist. And I learned that the Gospel of John, real author not really verified, wrote about 110 A.D., more than 30 years after the first three Gospels of Matthew, Mark and Luke. When John wrote it was risky to be a Christian. That meant his writing had to make sure Jesus was as real and persuasive as possible.

Back to my inquiry: *What matters the most to be religious?*

It is probably the case—never for me to doubt or deny—that on that particular Crusade event, there WERE people who became "religious" as never before.

But, what has happened in my life...is NOT that an important converting event is necessary in order to understand the place of God and Jesus in your or my life. For instance, I can cite many—not a zillion, but many, many—times when I KNEW God was trying to get my attention. Primarily through others and mostly when I was cared for, when the "other" had more an interest to understand me than need to judge me. But lightning didn't crack with resounding authority and EVERYTHING has never changed with drama and decisiveness.

Goodness, I wonder if that makes me boring?

How goes it with me? Writing this Blog as a retired clergy? Thinking about my next fishing trip, but focused even more that my wife, Diane, will be completely healed from her recent surgeries and that she enjoys her new job and that our sons and their families, including spouses and grandchildren, grow and are...as well as they can.

It goes just fine with me...and my most profound gratitude is that Jesus and I are just fine. God and I are just fine.

But, there's something more.

Not sure how to write it, but bear with me a paragraph or two more. Because it's important to me.

I put it flat-out: **I don't think the primary purpose of the church is to convert souls.**

In fact, I've never had an altar call [think that's the correct verbiage.] And truth bearing itself clearly: In the last two years I've served as interim minister in two Christian Churches [Disciples of Christ], wonderful congregations with laity who very evidently were with God and with Jesus and with one another in indelible and profound ways. However, in each worship service, because that is the *way, the truth and the life* for them, just before the closing hymn there was an invitation to join the church.

I was uncomfortable with that. Maybe another Blog can expand why beyond my contention joining a church should not be on the spur of the moment or because of a sermon that may have brought some new light. Nope. Joining a church should be when learning and living in the congregation's life and mission to make sure this is not a blink of an eye and lasts just as long.

As I consider the years—read that decades—I have served as minister and in conference ministry, I have considered religion and church and the purpose of both to be this: **Not the conversion of the soul but the transcendence of the self.**

I like that…more than a lot. I see church/worship/life/mission as the means by which a person becomes stronger and more committed to recognizing and reducing human needs. Transcending, becoming more than the self. So you are not considered *the world's smallest package*, the definition of which is this: *the world's smallest package is the person all wrapped up in himself or herself.*

I've never wanted anything less or more…growth in the person, so it's never said, "There's less there than meets the eye."

Conversion? I consider that to be God's business.

Transcendence of self?…yes…whether you are a Christian or Jew or Muslim…what matters to me is how the person and God are…and how the self does anything but stagnate.

Remember, the Sea of Galilee is alive and vibrant…because water flows in and through and then continues on.

The Dead Sea is not alive because there is no flow; it's only for retention.

I'm sure if you had a choice—and you do no less than I do—which Sea you'd like to be.

That's the business of transcendence. God's far more effective than I in the conversion moments. I mean, truth is it was God and not Moses who parted the Red Sea.

Real Value? Not about your [my] checkbook

Posted on February 21, 2011 by Mark H Miller

A cold pushing frigid day in Austin, Texas. That's okay, it really is.

For reasons not totally clear or sourced [some don't need to be], a comment made by Patrick, one of the staff at the Fitness Center, stuck. His comment thawed a very cold, windy day.

He was no longer at the welcoming desk, having said something a month ago about being shifted. He explained yesterday, "Hi Mark. I'm really happy in my new position—I sign up new registrants. It's a little more money, but that's not the value. The value is welcoming new people and helping them appreciate our exercise equipment and encouraging them in the decision they've made to become more fit."

He smiled and asked about Diane, "How's she doing? Finished with the radiation treatment?"

Wow.

A number of appreciative notes about Patrick.

He always welcomed me by name when I came to the Fitness Center. I know he saw it when I signed in the first time, but HE MADE A NOTE OF IT.

Good stuff: to remember your name.

That meant I was more than a face.

Ever had your name not remembered…or offered incorrectly? That happened recently—to a new friend I'm always "Frank." I go along with it.

And to another I'm "Zark." Now, I know where that comes from. My signature reads more like it starts with a Z than an M. Because long ago in Eugene, Oregon, the clerk in the Lane County Marriage License office called our Office Manager at the First Congregational Church to inquire, "I'm sorry. But I need help. I've received a marriage license signed by evidently one of your pastors. We've looked through our clergy listing and we don't find a Zark Ziller." One of my buddies likes Zark better than Mark. Hey, how's the saying go, "Call me anything as long as it's not late for dinner."

Remembering your name. Patrick does that.

And.

He remembered about Diane. Early last Fall [and I try to always refer to "Fall" as a time of year and not a theological condition—sorry, that just slipped] shortly after Diane's breast cancer diagnosis, when Patrick asked how I was and how Diane was [we often exercised together], I let him know about it. He never forgot to ask. How I was and how things are with Diane…important. That was special.

But, moving from the helpful and special to the really significant.

It's a little more money, but that's not the value.

Friends and neighbors and Blog visitors, Patrick's thought can preach.

I remember when Doug Meeks was my wonderful teacher and mentor and friend during my Eden Theological School classes in preparation for the Doctor of Ministry degree. Doug said, "Money and value are not the same. And society doesn't get it. Society has this mantra, *The more you have the better you are.*"

Doug continued, "That assumes that possessions and wealth declare value. But, that's not true. Value is not correlated to wealth. Value is a direct reflection of caring and giving. Here is what is of essence: It's not how much you have, but how much you care, how much you love."

Patrick gets that. Which doesn't make economic realities a yawning insignificance. It does, however, give the perspective on how life has meaning and worth.

How much are we worth? It's not how much we have. It's how much we care and connect.

In that I recall, perhaps as financially wealthy a person I know. He said to me, time and again, "Mark [he didn't know the Zark moniker], I LOVE making money. But, I even LOVE MORE giving it away—why? Because I've never seen a hearse with a luggage rack."

I think Patrick gets that. I know my generous church buddy gets that. And, I hope I do, too.

Value? Not the bank account. Nope.

Value? It's the giving experiences, the connecting, the making a difference for the good in someone's life.

You think?

Noise was the introduction

Posted on February 22, 2011 by Mark H Miller

All—or at least mostly all—that I remember is the noise. If you held a glass of beer or wine or whatever, it wouldn't last. It would shatter in your hand.

Not sure of the year, but it had to be no later than 1950 when I was ten. One of my cousins, Dennis, LOVED [not overstated] car racing. He said I couldn't turn his invitation down. I smiled and agreed, with a reluctance I couldn't identify. At ten years of age, most reluctances are a blur, unless it's being told dinner wouldn't end and the apple crisp alamode wouldn't arrive until the liver was eaten. Just eating the bacon covering the liver didn't count. Pushing the onions aside was not a problem, but leaving the liver under the crumbled napkin fooled no one, especially not my parents.

Back to the Portland stock car races. Dennis and I went, probably a couple more cousins joined us. All I know the racetrack was just north of main Portland and the track seemed pretty small. I could hear the noise from the parking lot. Fierce, really fierce. The earth seemed to shake.

Dennis loved it. I thought it was stupid. Racing in circles. I probably was the only one in the crowd who didn't clap and cheer. Spoiled brat was probably an apt moniker. But, really? Cars racing like that? The noise stuck.

Then another time Dennis took me to a Destruction Derby. It was not misnamed. Old cars smashing into each other with the intent of being the last car with four tires not deflated and a motor still keeping the car in movement.

Not memories I would ever recall.

Until yesterday.

Driving home from the Fitness Center I heard some excitement on XM's ESPN station. An announcer saying something to the effect, "There are 40 laps to go…this may be the most thrilling Daytona 500 yet."

That sparked curiosity, so I turned FOX on when I got home.

It was the first time in 60 years I paid attention to car racing. And for the next hour I found myself considering the NASCAR world as if it mattered.

I don't know why..but it trickled into my thought: *this has some excitement*—and all those people…and then I tried to figure out the strategies—cars going 200 mph about two inches from each other. Something about "pushing" and "draft pull."

And then to learn a "kid," who the day before celebrated his 20th birthday, won…and something about a "Wood Brothers Team" won.

But, what impressed me, even though I didn't realize at the time the WHOLE NASCAR IMPORTANCE was adding up points during the racing season, was the class each driver had, especially those who hadn't won. And a couple of drivers allowed how they "screwed up; it was my fault, I should have gone to the outside then. I cut over too early." [Never hear that from a coach, something to the effect, "The referee made a good call and I didn't." Nope, not at all.]

I was also caught up in the incredible dancing joy of the winning team.

Now this is not a claim that I'm "locked and loaded" for NASCAR.

But, it prompted me to send an e-mail to a former Conference Minister colleague, a great guy who's now a seminary president and used to make sure he got to cities like Indianapolis and Dallas and Daytona—and it wasn't for conference ministry meetings. I told him I had a whole new consideration of racing, even though I understood so very little.

But, what I understood the most was the class of the drivers—not that they never fuss and throw beer bottles in anger—and the values they shared. Not that it reached panache, but hey, it kept my attention.

Crazy world, for sure.

And then this morning, the day after Daytona, I read that the earth will not be the same in some years because of seismic activity.

That can be for another day.

Now it's to share a new discovery—and to know another race will be shown next weekend. I then will look at WGN's schedule to see if the Cubs will be on for a Spring Training game, and to ABC to see if the San Antonio Spurs will have a televised game. A guy's gotta keep his values straight. Doesn't he?

Yelled lately?

Posted on February 23, 2011 by Mark H Miller

The points I now share are focused upon "being a good boss," or more pointedly, what it means to be a bad boss. I thought, though, *hey, these are points in any functional relationship, they really are.*

Which reminded me of a sidebar once from a minister buddy who described a couple in his church who kept trying their best to enact the hang-from-the-chandelier-scene in "War of the Roses," *That couple is trying their damndest to get the "fun" back into dysfunctional.*

A good relationship? Whether it's the workplace, the bowling alley [not sure where that came from because I was only good at hitting the gutter—hey, that's not a metaphor of self-description, all right?]— and family dynamics. And, of course, being a minister or the chair of a church board. Which might lead to another thought: the worst trouble I had in relating to parishioners and/or clergy I supervised were the passive-aggressive ones. You know, the ones who smile when their thought is, *You are an idiot and I will NEVER listen to you, let alone respond with my honest thought.*

Back on track—stay with me a few paragraphs—here is the listing on what makes for poor bossing…and hemorrhaging relationships. The list with a comment or two or three:

Most of your emails are one-word long. [the humorous anecdote was an employee got a response to her idea from her boss: he only wrote the letter "Y." She wrote a full essay elaborating on her insightful suggestion. Because she thought he was asking "Why?" When his "Y" was for "Yes."]

I can appreciate the value—it's often a time-economy issue—of e-mail. But, too often that is more than abrupt. It's impersonal. I believe a telephone conversation is better than e-mail and when possible, a personal eye-eye visit is best. It was always impacting of me when reading a biblical story how connected a person was when "he looked into the eye" of the other. When it's eye-eye, THERE'S connection and value.

Also remember a parishioner who never told his wife he loved her. She asked him about it. He responded, not looking her in the eye, "When we were married 30 years ago I told you I loved you. I also said if anything changed, I'd let you know." *Argggh,* I think to that.

You rarely talk to your employees face-to-face. This relates to #1... my take on it is, not that I'm into my 7th decade, but because I believe, we can get too technical and that can lead to too impersonal. Sure, there are dynamics, particularly in families—and I consider "church" a family, as well as some work places—where talking face-face is onerous. And yet, to not talk forever is lame at best and erosive at worst. I'm no doubt not writing from an innocent posturing on this.

Your employees are out sick — a lot. This applies more to the work place, I agree. Yet, often "illness or not feeling well" is more an excuse than a reality. It's a common way to create distance rather than resolve differences. A comment in the text suggests, "Employees will fake sickness to avoid a bad boss."

Your team's working overtime, but still missing deadlines. There are "deadline-make-for-sure" people and "it can wait another day or so" people. What's hard is when, say in a marriage or family or close-working group, you have extremes in various players. I am guilty of this. Using the personality-inventory Myers-Briggs, the "organized" and "get to it later" categories are J for the former and P for the latter. It was always a challenge for me, being, what my wife labels, "Capital J" [at times I'm "Doctor J" and that has nothing to do with basketball!] to have people on my pastoral staff who were capital P's. However, when I discovered the different manners of organization and deadlines, it was easier.

You yell. Ah, this is a relationship disaster. Now I realize certain cultures value the primal scream—obviously an exaggeration. But, yelling is really a form of control, of getting your way. What's important is to not lose civility. What is worse than corrosive, it's malignant, is when the boss, or the minister, or the choir director, or the spouse, or the parent, resorts to yelling. And, as the article intimated, "speaking loudly" can be just as harmful. I have never considered that speaking loudly was for emphasis and importance. It was once shared as humor in a seminary preaching class, although I know clergy who practiced it, to write on the sermon manuscript, "Weak here; yell like hell!"

The article put it more appreciably, "Even if you aren't screaming angrily at your employees, speaking loudly can damage workplace morale. Employees will constantly feel like they're being reprimanded and they'll avoid you if there's ever a problem."

Another employee offered, "My bosses would shout freely across the office, even when they weren't necessarily angry," she says. "It charged the atmosphere and really killed productivity, especially when you were trying to figure out who you should be listening to."

So it is, in a day and time when the headlines talk about the internal rupturing of nations—i.e. Libya, of the New Zealand earthquakes, of the 4 Americans slain by pirates, of Rush Limbaugh blasting Michelle Obama because she ate bbq ribs in Vail.

Each of those realities don't make our day…but they certainly impact our lives. And yet, in an echo of the song, "Let there be peace, and let it begin with me," we may not have a word or impact upon the great world events, but we can have an impact upon our own life…and the lives of those intimate or work-place folk in our life.

GET IT!!!!! [oops, lost my point for a moment.]

Today–a potpourri of mostly good news

Posted on February 24, 2011 by Mark H Miller

It's Thursday, February 24, 2011, with lots happening, most of which is engages the good. But not everything.

...find the tirading in Libya not new. For more than decades Gadhafi has been the imperial tyrant, which is much different than the imperial wizard. It seems, though, everywhere we look there is tumult. I wouldn't want to be President of our country—would you?

...find it disheartening, even devastating about the earthquake damage in New Zealand. Two of our closest friends have a daughter and family living there. They weren't affected—they live far distance from Christchurch, but the brother of their son-in-law and his family had their house demolished. They weren't hurt, but goodness, how difficult.

...are unions any good? I come as a child of unions. My father, a garbage man in Portland, Oregon, an independent operator, was a member of the Local Teamsters #220. I didn't know much about it, other than my father had a good support system for pricing. Although he rarely charged a going rate, especially when people had extra brush or boxes to be taken.

...It is such good news the reports show Diane's cancer-free. Such good news. We certainly hope and pray this year will be relatively scarce in terms of medical issues. 2010 was overbearing with the seven surgeries for Diane and my diagnosis of Diabetes 2. It seems the latter is behaving itself. I've been pleased to exercise almost daily at the Fitness Center.

...have had conversations with friends, even some clergy buddies, each of whom pays no regard and has even less respect for Facebook. I go to Facebook for one selfish reason: to get the most current catch/release reports from my Oregon and Washington fishing guides. Other than that, I agree with my friends: Facebook is intended to be a social networking, but the extent of personal information is really no one else's business, especially if the "Face-booker" is a professional. I don't worry about it, but others have told me Facebook tends to be a negative impacter.

...yesterday was a first-step day, actually a two-step, although it has nothing to do with the Texas-two-step-dance. I connected with my publisher about the novel, "Murder On Tillamook Bay," which he will publish this summer. We will talk again next week about his editing suggestions. I'm also more than pleased a good friend and very competent literary critic has agreed to read through "Murder..." for more editing suggestions. In this regard, I have been in good contact with the novelist, Sue Grafton. She sent me a letter recently affirming my efforts in writing and then shared the editing steps/phases for her alphabet murder/mysteries. I couldn't believe, but know it's true: there are probably 4 professional editors who work on her novels before publishing. *Yikes*, I thought. That's probably necessary, though, for someone of her stature. I was thrilled she wrote a personal letter. She's been very helpful to my novel writing—actually with three of the four novels that have been completed. Cannot go wrong with that, right? I remember one suggestion to my third novel, when I had my protagonist in a 6-month coma. Sue jumped all over that indicating the literary license I had taken was absurd. I never wonder what she really thinks!

The second step yesterday has got me fired up. These past three months blogging each morning there has been a lurking thought. Yep, lurking: how about a 5th novel? Well, yesterday was its beginning. Actually the day before, while getting dinner ready, I had a revelation on how to begin the novel. Let it marinate overnight [as the souse chef in our household "marinate" is appropriate verbiage] and then yesterday morning the novel got launched. I'm staying with my wonderful protagonist, Tricia Gleason, who has been a homicide detective for the Oregon State Police, a fishing guide in Tillamook, Oregon [venue and occasions for "Murder On Tillamook Bay"], a first-year seminary student in Berkeley, California along with being a seminarian working with Stanford students at a Congregational Church in Palo Alto.

In my new novel, first blush of two chapters written yesterday, she'll be a summer intern minister in Frisco, Colorado. She thinks/hopes/prays it will be a summer of low humidity, comfortable breezes, reading scripture each Sunday morning and teaching the junior and senior high school youth how to fly fish. The novel title, "Shattered Hope," gives a clear statement that all she'll get will be the low humidity. Seems she simply cannot walk away from the shadows of murder, and in this novel, homophobic trashing.

I'm also getting revved up for a fishing trip that will begin the first March weekend. Really pumped for that. I will be fishing with one of my favorite guides, Zorba [aka Chris Vertopoulos]. We will fish three days on Tillamook area rivers and then two days on the Olympic Peninsula in Northwest Washington. Then, a real bonus: I've arranged a fishing trip on Friday with a new guide, Ian Premo. We will fish the Clackamas River just south of Portland. The reason I'm so enthused about that trip with Ian is it was the Clackamas River—and we will fish the same river section—that I caught my second steelhead, probably in 1957 at the growing age of 17. And no less exciting, Zorba and I will probably fish the Nestucca River just south of Tillamook where I caught my first steelhead in 1956. Wow, how about that?

Another part of the Oregon fishing trip is that I will have coffee with a newspaper reporter in Tillamook who wants to know more about "Murder on Tillamook Bay." Laura says her staff is enthused a murder/mystery will be published with the Tillamook, Oregon venue. She didn't stop her interest when I told her about the first chapter, that a minister gets whacked at the end of the first chapter after he's caught a very large fall Chinook salmon. She wanted to know if there would be any more ministers killed. I demurred.

Back to the home front, I'm so very pleased how well Andrew's Schreiner University Basketball team did, am going to schedule a Chicago visit with my son, Matthew, and Sheila and Laura, and our daughter-in-law, Teela, is expecting their third child in August. Good family news.

But even more, it is good news that Diane's enjoying her new position in project management with GTECH, working out of their Austin office on the Texas Lottery. We've also learned GTECH manages international casinos which presents a possible overseas venue for her project management leadership. I've already—gotta live with some dreaming, right?—contacted a couple of my guides to learn which country, Peru or Argentina, has better trout fishing. Hey, gotta tag along as souse chef, right?

All this Thursday morning…yes, a potpourri but even more the good rhythm of dancing in the new day.

Now to the third chapter of "Shattered Hope," in which Tricia will learn a couple of new things about her summer internship ministry—dynamics she was never told about. If only the surprises would be good. But they aren't. Sorry, Tricia, but no good novel leaves the protagonist without trouble and fret and big-time frustrations. Gosh, just like life itself. Go figure.

Dealing with Death

Posted on February 25, 2011 by Mark H Miller

Death is an unwelcomed visitor. Most of the time. Yes, I am aware—and instances for footnoting for sure—there are times when death is the better alternative. There are times when death is friend and not enemy. There are conditions experienced that are worse than death.

What comes to mind are two instances where ALS [Lou Gehrig Disease] won the day. Gruesome and unaccountably insufferable.

But, for the most part, death is not something we await with joy and exaltation.

I remember in seminary pouring over and through and into the thought of Kubler-Ross on the four general responses to death. Not that they are ordered…but they tend to be experienced.

And I've seen people react to death in ways that seemed either tardy or puzzling. At least from my perspective, which very much could be smothered in myopia.

This morning I read about two deaths—one person I knew, the other only a name on a movie market flyer.

The first, a cousin, Eleanor Pitzer, died. Her mother and my mother were sisters. Her son, Paul, wrote to share the information. What I remember about Eleanor was so very uplifting. She was one of those rare persons who asked how I was doing in ministry and would NEVER be satisfied with the socially dominant response, "Fine, thanks for asking." Nope, not Eleanor. She waited. For more, for some details on the exigencies that illustrated the "Fine, thanks."

The second gave me some extended thought. It was an article about Liam Neeson in this month's Esquire magazine, in which he discusses—the first time since his wife, Natasha Richardson's death in 2009. She died from a skiing accident.

358

He describes trying to see her in the hospital emergency room. Terrifying moments.

What got my attention was his comment on how he copes with her death:

"I think I survived by running away some. Running away to work. Listen, I know how old I am and that I'm just a shoulder injury from losing roles like the one in 'Taken.' So I stay with the training, I stay with the work," he continued. *"It's easy enough to plan jobs, to plan a lot of work. That's effective. But that's the weird thing about grief. You can't prepare for it. You think you're gonna cry and get it over with. You make those plans, but they never work."*

What strikes me the most is, "But that's the weird thing about grief. You can't prepare for it. You think you're gonna cry and get it over with."

In a way, I would hearken others to those words, *You cannot prepare for grief.*

This triggers two notions, that don't obviate Kubler-Ross' positing about denial and anger and wagering and accepting of death and its impact when another dies.

The notions go like this: We should NOT prepare for grief. Rather, we should live each day as if breath will not continue. I don't consider that macabre. Not at all.

For the most part, and I've shared this at many a funeral, for the most part we don't know how long we will live. But, we have so very much to say about how well we will live. Please don't consider this brazen or arrogant or indifferent. But, I'm not afraid to die. I'm only afraid I won't live fully enough. I'm not afraid of stopping breath…I'm afraid of stopping the dance-step of life with each passing day.

With this, a wise pastor once counseled me, "Mark, it is my belief that until a person comes to terms with his or her death, they are not really—in the greatest sense—set free to live fully." His sage thought carries the day...at least for me.

One of the greatest quotes comes from Morgan Freeman in "Shawshank Redemption," when in prison he says to Timothy Robbins, "Some people busy livin'; some people busy dyin'. Better to be busy livin'."

Second notion is connected to the first, to be more about living than dying. It is this, agreed based upon only the experience in ministry in planning funerals, whether or not I ever met the deceased. **I contend people die essentially in the manner by which they live.**

I've shared this before, but it's clear in my mind now.

My mother, Es Miller, knew her days were diminishing. The only item on her bucket list was to see her first great-grandchild. Zeli Grey was born in San Francisco. With the obstetrician and pediatrician's blessings, Brian and Paige flew with their precious Zeli to Portland. It was a bucket-list-joy for mother to hold her first great-granddaughter.

Mother knew death was around the corner. It never bothered her. Never. Because as she contended, "Do you know anyone who won't die? Guess not. So, we live as long and well as we can, then get ready for the next experience."

Reminds me of the parishioner who told a clergy friend of mine about her funeral: *In the casket I want you to place a fork in my hand. That's all...a fork.* My friend was puzzled, "I'm sorry, I don't understand...a fork?"

Yep, cause I love dessert. And I know that in heaven it will be the best dessert ever...ever, ever, ever.

Keep living...nothing more, nothing less.

Paying the price…considering the value

Posted on February 26, 2011 by Mark H Miller

Some facts I know. Walked on the Stanford campus for the first time the freshman day of registration, circa September, 1958. The freshman convocation, with a class of approximately 1,500, caused me dread when the university President J. Wallace Sterling told us, "You have quite a class. Over 90% of you received straight A's in high school and your SAT's were higher than any previous class, over 1,400 on the average. That's the good news. The *other news* is that we're counting on your integrity with the Stanford Honor Code, which means a professor or assistant will not be in the auditorium or class room for any test; therefore, we count on you to not bring notes or look at another's paper, especially the multiple choice examinations. Although as a heads-up should you be tempted to test the Honor Code, for each multiple choice examination, there will be at least three different tests distributed. The real *other news* is to advise—which is not to be considered as a warning: WE grade on the curve, which means that at most only 15% of you can earn straight A's."

I remember the day was hot, the speech both stifling and intimidating. Why? Because I was one of those who definitely brought down the average SAT and didn't get straight A's. My high school basketball coach, although he appreciated my basketball passing, appreciated my effort in Physics, but since I never got an A on any test, made the final grade a B. I think he offered once, "Gosh, Mark, if only your physics knowledge matched your basketball skills." Hey, cannot have everything, right?

Some facts, I remember, at least a close recollection: the cost of education. Fortunate to have a baseball scholarship that covered most of tuition. In addition to books and commuting home on vacations, my only *out-of-pocket* expenses for my education that my parents provided was $335 for each quarter for lodging. That meant $1005 per year for 4 years. The food wasn't priceless in terms of quality, but was in terms of expense because I was a hasher, which meant I served meals in freshman girls dormitory. Hey, I wasn't stupid, especially when I went from being a dishwasher to a table-server, even wearing a white coat. House rules, okay? Not a bad deal, after all: free meals and dating options.

Now, fast forward more than 20 years. When my son, Matthew, graduated from Dartmouth there was a graduation-day celebrative brunch with Matthew's nine friends, each of whom connected their first week at Dartmouth, four years earlier. Even today, circa 2011, they are the best of friends. That's really impressive. During the brunch, one of the fathers asked all ten guys to stand up and face us parents and families. The father then commented, "Parents, look at these ten great sons of ours. And realize, there stands $1 million we have provided."

Where is this all going?

A couple of places.

First, I just got a "please contribute to help our students" letter from Stanford, as I do quarterly from my two seminaries—one for the basic degree and the other for the doctor of ministry degree.

And then I looked at what Stanford's one-year-expense is for a non-scholarship student, not to include books and school-home-school commuting: More than $55,000.

Okay, it's one of the higher expenses. But, even state universities [i.e. University of Texas in Austin] have raised tuition, meals and lodging.

And gas today, Saturday, February 26, 2011, unleaded regular is at $3.25, and according to some analysts, on its way to $5/gallon by Independence Day. Goodness.

Honestly? I'm not sure how this can be managed.

And yet. A very deep and profound *and yet*. Can anyone dismiss higher education and say it is insignificant? Hardly.

Where this goes is to worry a lot. But, where and when and if it can be, I think one of the most beneficial recipients of our money is toward educational funds set up for our family [and in my own case, additionally with fishing guides' children] so at least some of the resource-toward-education is manifest.

Hopefully each reading this will have it all figured out. If not, consider how your gifting can help the younger generation, no matter their school, whether they ever serve a table at a freshman girls' dormitory. It's important..make that necessary...we don't neglect the younger ones... and help where and how we can.

Agree?

Falling coconuts…and more

Posted on February 27, 2011 by Mark H Miller

I knew her as Jeannette Butts, a Jefferson High School classmate in the Class of 1958. She's the friend who said it was a slam-dunk I would enter ministry—at the age of 16 her words were first shared. We didn't connect over the years, through marriage and children and grandchildren. I always found Jeannette to be creative and energetic, more than a tad unpredictable. It was refreshing, for I like wacky people, pushing that in a positive manner.

One of our common friends gave me Jeannette's e-mail so we've picked up on each of our worlds. There's been more than a 50 year gap, but hey, who's counting in friendship?

Her world is more than fascinating, living in Hawaii with her husband, Vilsoni Hereniko. They joined their efforts in creating a film, "The Land Has Eyes." Jeannette sent it to me. This Blog is about the film, which can be ordered at www.thelandhaseyes.com. [No, I'm not part of their marketing team.]

Here's its story: About Viki, a young South Pacific Islander inspired and haunted by the island's mythical "Warrior Woman". The lush tropical beauty of Rotuma, an island of Fiji, contrasts with the stifling conformity of her culture as Viki confronts notions of justice and her own personal freedom.

One reviewer offered this, *This quiet, stunningly beautiful gem of a movie…plays like a kind of cultural window, presenting to the world a vision of life in the distant Pacific from the very imaginations of those who live it.*

The detailing of how Viki deals with deceit, hope, death and a future open to her does not need any detailing.

What I thought after seeing the film is how nothing has changed! The culture doesn't matter. The venue doesn't matter. The era doesn't matter.

Consider this. From the very first breath of Adam and Eve, of Cain and Abel, there's ingredient in the human journey sibling rivalry, refusing to take responsibility for faults [Is anyone different, when push comes to shove and the precipice of the cliff is a step away?]. Consider Eve. She offered to her sin, "God, let's face it. If you wouldn't have created the snake we wouldn't be in this mess."

The movie was compelling, even haunting, because in every human being there's longing to experience transformation, a battle between hoarding and being generous.

It doesn't matter that Viki's family can only make it—yes, theirs is a primitive world, but that's MY point, that doesn't matter—by harvesting coconuts and making reed fans and mats. There is deceit and death and evil. There is goodness and caring. There is bonding and the tearing asunder of families.

Just look around us today...can anyone not spell, L I B Y A, can anyone not know the challenge of escalating gasoline prices, the taxing economy that creates tsunami's of agony for our country and our states, and yes, I would know, our education and our churches?

When I finished the film I wrote Jeannette to share the film's strong, impressing value.

And then, I remembered, at least this morning, the last Sunday of February in 2011, as Viki sails to Fiji, made possible because she's the best student in her class, she is living her vision. A young boy stands on the shore waving good-bye. The boy found Viki to idealize what it means to be valued. The camera focuses upon his face...hopeful for her but saddened because she's leaving their island. Then the camera lowers to his hand, in which is a new ball point pen that he meant to gift her. But didn't.

That struck me...we don't always get to what we intend. There are times when we simply didn't do it.

But, I'm going to wager the boy will not lose the ball point pen. I'm going to wager there will be a day when the gift will be shared. He won't lose his intent and get caught up in the next falling coconut. He just won't.

Memory lane—joy behold

Posted on February 28, 2011 by Mark H Miller

This can be labeled, *The Joy of Memory*. In other words, *what we should not forget*.

This past week a clean-up decision was made—and it's not even March 21 yet, for Spring cleaning: go through a guest bedroom and make it sleepable. That means it's a storage room now more than anything else.

I had at it.

And now that I've learned to work the scan to produce e-mail-able pictures, it was a treat. Brought back many memories that had been dormant. Especially two pictures—one of Matthew playing in a Colorado State High School Tennis tournament and the other of Andrew, #24 it was!, dribbling a basketball past a defender. Was able to send each to them…what a treat, for hopefully it sparked "days of yesteryear" for them in a good manner.

I then found a box of Diane's memorabilia. Last night she shared a dairy she had written when her son, Jason, was born.

Honestly, I knew of the heart problems Jason had at birth…and the subsequent corrective surgeries. I knew he was born in Germany when Diane was serving in the Army there in Special Forces.

But, when she shared her own narrative, written more than thirty years ago, I was amazed at how tough that time was, the decisions that needed to be made, who would do the surgery and its impact upon Diane and her child, Jason.

It was so valuable she had written all that down, for now I know it clearly…and as a result, appreciate Diane even more. She'll share it with Jason so he can appreciate his earliest days, the time he first sat up on his own, plus making it through five surgeries.

Yes, I realize individual memories are with zillions of people. But it struck me so powerfully last night…and no less, this past week, to see a picture and remember.

For instance, I had forgotten my first steelhead, caught in the Nestucca River—I think I was probably 16. I had forgotten rowing my own drift boat on Lake Creek in Oregon, wearing a French beret. Wow, it actually looked pretty classy, even with the mustache. I had forgotten my first Tillamook Bay fall Chinook salmon, caught with Jon Winter. [I scanned the picture and mailed it to Jon and Patti—Jon called yesterday to remind me the fish was caught in 1983, where it was caught and what we used for a lure. Wow, right?] I then found a picture of our Archer Blower team, September of 1962, right after winning the Semi-Professional Baseball World Series. The smiles were unrestrained—and even though I couldn't name EVERY player, I could remember almost every pitch.

And then I saw something that reminded me how stupid I was—perhaps the stupidest thing I've ever done—saw some stamps—and remembered that I used to have a stamp collection that turned out to be priceless—not because of its value, but because it was worthless. What I had done was to lick every stamp and paste it in my book…impossible to dumb-down from that, right? Hey, stupid is what stupid does.

But, through it all—to add that now the guest bedroom is far more living up to its name—what sticks is Diane's dairy and who she is and how much I appreciate her.

Better to remember the more valued memories, right?

And then this afternoon I'll go to my "fishing room," and begin packing for my 5-day fishing trip to the Northwest. Yeah, I don't leave until next Saturday, but in my way of doing things, it's never too early to get ready. Does that mean I'm pumped, or what? And, hopefully it will be a splendid time to create new memories…even if the fish don't know it yet!

This was taken more than 50 years ago–the short hair and all–first steelhead–

Jesus shopping for groceries–sort of

Posted on March 1, 2011 by Mark H Miller

Yes, willing to admit, memory is not always the best partner in thinking. And, truth pushing, lately remembering such silly things—did I shampoo my hair this morning, where DID I park the car before entering H.E.B. for shopping—strike at me. But, let's everyone be honest…does anyone ever look for their glasses only to find them perched on your head—or your car keys to find them still in the ignition?

But, this isn't about memory—just a teasing first paragraph.

This is about moments, surprise and stopping the clock—when it may be that God's speaking to us.

My wife, Diane, gave the best first-statement about hearing the voice of God, "Mark, it doesn't happen if people don't listen." Ah, another reason why it's a good thing she's including Hospital Chaplaincy in her futuring vision.

Back to memory and God's speaking.

One example I think about on a morning when Austin's closed down—sheets of ice and 1" snow can do that, when ANY snow's a headline.

Happened in 1976. Serving Lakewood United Church of Christ in Colorado. Honestly, of the churches I've served, Lakewood was perhaps the best partnering. For reasons I may never understand but always will appreciate, creativity and trying the new was always encouraged. To the point we designated one Sunday monthly to have, for want of a more creative label, "The New Service."

I had this idea. Remembered a film, believe it was called "The Parable," produced by Canada and shown at a World's Fair, that was really a film about Jesus. The world of the circus was the stage…with various vignettes showing people being oppressed, controlled, not able to be who they wanted to be. It was the lady with the magician whose role in life was to lie in a box and be cut in half, a man carrying buckets of

370

water to elephants with no one saying a word of gratitude or giving even a glance of recognition, a man walking a tight-wire never knowing if he would fall—and as he looked down, no safety net.

Into each of these scenes a mime entered and set each person of enslavement free, either taking their place, or leading them to a new future. There was no speaking—only calliope circus music, playing with great zest when the Mime entered as Liberator. The mime was in all white, painted face, white clothed.

Of course the Mime was Jesus.

Some of us at Lakewood saw the film and decided to do what we could to have that theme be one of our New Services.

I really did object, but probably because I had a pretty heavy black beard, the team asked if I would be the Mime, the Christ-figure. Certainly hubris played some of this, but actually not a lot. However, since it had been my initial suggestion, I agreed to play the Mime.

Note, it's to "play" the Mime and not "be" the Mime.

The service could not have been more effective if we wished. The magician [one of our youth did know magic tricks] and the tight wire and the bucket of water...everyone did well. And when the Mime entered, our organist did his best calliope impersonation on the organ.

That unto itself was special, because our organist and choir master, James Yeager, was earning a phD in Organ Performance at the University of Colorado and could have waved us off. Because it wasn't Bach or Widor for sure. But not, Jim. He was the most skilled and supportive Minister of Music one could ever know. [Probably another Blog, but James took our small/modest choir of a dozen folk and taught them to sing an 8-part cantata accapella. "Peaceable Kingdom" was a glorious moment/experience.]

Back to "The Parable."

Everyone loved it. The Mime liberated. People smiled, even laughed, and teared up a lot. I'm sure it was because the message rang true and clear and connected, "Every single one of us needs to be liberated from something or someone or some place."

At the end of the service everyone was gifted a bright-colored-helium-balloon. We, all 250 of us, went to the church courtyard—which could hold no more than maybe 200 people, squeezed together, and at the end of "Hip, Hip, Hooray," released the balloons. The smiles, laughter, joy echoed as the applause crescendo made appreciation and value and affirmation indelibly clear.

I went home exhilarated. Removed the white-turtleneck, white painter's overalls, white shoes. Washed off the white paint and red cross on my forehead and took a shower. Did remember to shampoo my hair.

The next day, mid-morning, I needed to do some shopping at our grocery store. Still had the bushy, black beard, but no make-up, and I trust, no pretense. Hey, it was role-playing for a church worship service.

As I got in one grocery check-out line, in the next line over stood one of our church members and her daughter. The daughter looked in my direction. I smiled and said, "Hi there."

The daughter, no more than 5, tugged her mother's sleeve and pointed to me. "Oh, Mommy! Look! There's Jesus!"

I wanted to clear up her confusion.

But, I didn't.

Because what I heard in her affirmation was not that I was Jesus. I heard, though, that I could live in the manner of life Jesus urged, upon each of us. To recognize and reduce the hurt. To do whatever can be done to set people free from the enslavement forces in their life. To simply—and in moments when being a Mime is adequate, words are never necessary—be kind and caring and above all, listening.

In a way I'll never forget…that child's voice came to me as the voice of God…encouraging, lots of that, to do what I could to "go and do likewise," whether or not I always remember to shampoo my hair.

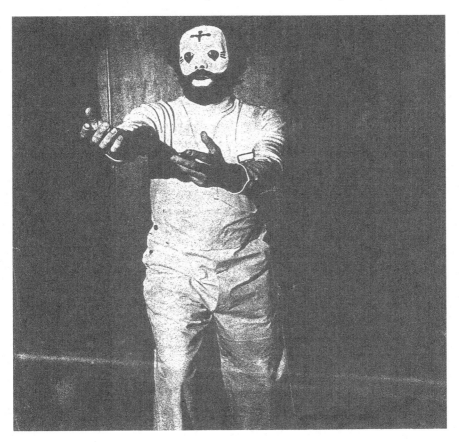

Fishing? Maybe. Maybe not.

Posted on March 2, 2011 by Mark H Miller

It brought back an old memory. As indicated in recent Blogs I'm enthused to fish next week in Oregon and Washington—my annual effort to catch [and release, mind you] winter steelhead. Everything's ready for packing—will have the necessary rain gear and insulated jacket. Of course my Indiana Jones hat will be included. Will give me that rugged, *can handle anything* appearance. We'll get to the humility later.

Then, this afternoon my guide wrote that it's raining upon rain in Oregon and we may find rivers unfishable. Now, that doesn't translate into *my heart will be inconsolable*, but it will be disappointing. Which is an understatement. I realize some of you shake your head as you smile [just don't smirk, ok?] at my unlimited passion for fishing. Well, look, it's better than looking at map, as some of my boring friends do and muse, *This is better than being here!*

What Zorba [my guide and valued buddy] wrote triggered another experience, and as these matter go, quite unpredictably and unexpectedly, not without a pleasant surprise.

I was seven; it was late August or early September of 1947. My father had arranged for us to fish with friends of his on a commercial fisherman's boat. Goodness, my first time ever to fish in the ocean, for fall Chinook salmon that I imagined weighed what I weighed. Well, not exactly, but hold with me a moment—a seven-year-old imagination should never have limits.

We drove to Cannon Beach to Ray Grimshaw's house [Dad's friend]. There were two other men, making a group of five, plenty of room in the fisherman's boat. I went to bed with thoughts about nothing but catching the biggest fish in the world. I was toilet-trained but almost slipped on that. If you know what a 7-year-old excitement can lead to. It didn't.

But, that wasn't the only "it didn't."

Dad woke me up about midnight—I remember it seemed the alarm clock only had one hand. He spoke with his own regret, profound disappointment, "Mark, I'm sorry, but the commercial guide just called. There's very rough weather coming in so you won't be able to go. He doesn't want to have a child on the boat, so you'll have to pass on this trip. But, I'll make it up to you."

It is one of the first times I remember crying myself to sleep.

I could hear the 4 hearty guys have breakfast and then leave.

The quiet was loud for me, the tears still not finished.

It turned out to be a fabulous day, weather-wise.

Mrs. Grimshaw asked if I wanted to go sailing. She said she'd have to show me.

We went to the surf's edge, just south of the greatest place in the world, Haystack Rock at Cannon Beach, Oregon. She took a huge pillow sheet, ran against the wind as the sheet filled with air, then closed the open end, so it had turned from a pillow sheet to a large balloon. She then ran, I remember her cheering herself on, to the start of the breakers, leaped on the new boat she had created, and rode the surf to the beach.

She then ran with me, urging me to fill my own pillow sheet, which somehow I did. Not sure how, but her encouragement helped considerably.

I remember floating on that new balloon…maybe it was a commercial fishing boat…and let my imagination run wild.

I think I caught about four salmon that day, each bigger than what anyone else caught.

I was okay. Mrs. Grimshaw showed me a new way to be alive and creative and have a great time.

Dad and his friends returned mid-afternoon. I was taking a nap. The tears had dried. Thoughts of more than sugar-plums danced in my heart.

When I woke up I saw the guys cleaning their salmon...they caught their limit which in those days was three each.

Dad was still disconsolate, explaining the weather report was wrong... the sea could not have been calmer.

I told him I was happy and then explained my new skills of catching air and making something of it.

.....

I thought of that day sixty-three years ago as I read Zorba's note again.

Will I get to fish next week?

Maybe.

Maybe not.

But, "whatever happens," there's bound to be good news, for at 70 I trust I am still able to make the most of every day, whether or not the rivers and ocean are fishable.

"Yes sir, that's my baby…." Oh yes, oh very yes!
Posted on March 3, 2011 by Mark H Miller

The recent Academy Awards program, and maybe you were one of the billion who took it in, triggered some memories, long lying dormant. This is not the first time I've watched this program. Paying more attention was triggered by my son, Matthew, who gave family members a test, to see who could predict the most winners.

To say I was guessing would be an understated truth. I know Matthew knew his stuff, because "Film and Journalism" were two of his foci in college and graduate work. He knows his stuff, believe me.

I put down answers to be a cooperative spirit and learned this morning that I was close to last in accuracy. But, that's not the prompter.

The prompter is to think about film in my life, admittedly not a major theme, but still it has a good place.

Here goes.

Two memories early. My parents, both hard working, still found, maybe once each month, a family movie night. The film that first struck me as having great power, almost a hypnotic impact was Orson Wells in "The Third Man ." I found the film more than interesting and am beginning to think, especially because of its twists and turns, how it might have been the unconscious seed planted to my launching the world of novel-writing, with novel a noun and not adjective.

I then remember a cousin, Jack Matlack, God rest his creative soul, who was the manager of Portland's JJ Parker downtown theatres, probably numbering four. Once in a while Jack would invite our family to a private screening of a movie, to arrive in theatres in a couple of months. It was always Sunday night in a very small theatre in NW Portland. I don't remember any particular film, other than what I think was called, "Man from Planet X." Didn't impress me, but somehow it was memorable.

Then, in the course of all that, actually in a much younger time, was the 30th Avenue Theatre Saturday matinee. Was cheap babysitting, I figured, maybe two-bits for admission. I loved it, though, with 4-5 cartoons [Mighty Mouse was my favorite], a Western [thought Gene Autry was wimpy] and then a serial, which kept us coming back. I do remember a yo-yo contest in which I proved I was incompetent, because my yo-yo string broke, sending my yo-yo into the cheering crowd. Last time for that.

From then to now it's not really unusual, not that it has to be. However, what strikes me is to recall the movies that impressed me the most… and why?

The answer to that question comes with a program I offered to some churches I served, called it "Theology of the Movies." We would have supper, watch a film, then discuss the film, looking primarily for what I called, "The Christ Figure." That meant, *who in the movie sets people free, recognizes and reduces the human pain, so people can become who they are meant to be?"* Was great fun.

The movies that impressed me the most—and my family could probably list them for me, include *Thousand Clowns* [I could never be Arnold Burns, but love forever the Central Park bicycle ride with Murray Burns singing his heart out, "Yes, sir, that's my baby…" or having a morning conversation with the recorded weather message.], *One Flew Over the Cuckoo's Nest* [the "moving the water table scene" preaches, big-time, plus the resurrection scene at the end with Chief hurling the marble water table through the window, then fleeing.], *Cool Hand Luke* [probing what it takes for communication], *Graduate* [the movie has many "boxes," in which people are trapped, including the swimming pool, the "fish tank," the school bus AND the church. Not to mention how in many deniable ways we think, make that ARE "plastic."], *Shawshank Redemption* [can never quote too often Freeman's counsel to "keep livin'."], *Stand By Me*, [probably because it was filmed in Cascade Locks, Oregon, which has a special place—venue for my first, albeit disastrous, attempt at baseball pitching], *River Runs Through It*, [certainly about trout fishing, but also about Norman McClain, who is writer and Dartmouth graduate, just like my son, Matthew.], "Wizard of Oz" [Ministry is a continual effort to help "tin people" find their heart.], "Zorba the Greek," [Image of dancing in the coffin is worth celebrating.]and "Deliverance," [more than the dueling banjos and possibility of merging cultures—a modern-day version of "Lord of the Flies," in which the more basic tendencies flaunt indulging of self and hubris.].

Interesting to me there's no film circa recent years. That probably says more of my movie-attending than anything else. Still, the films I value each has helped me understand more of what it means to walk the talk along the human landscape and not stumble and fall so often.

Loved yourself lately?

Posted on March 4, 2011 by Mark H Miller

I reserve the right to be wrong. But I also hold to the possibility I may be correct.

It goes like this.

I maintain the Great Commandment of *loving God with your heart, mind, soul and strength and your neighbor as yourself* hinges mostly if not totally upon the last two words: *as yourself.*

Of course it is vital and vitalizing to love God, no matter your religious connection. As I've stated in earlier blogs, Jesus is not the only way to God, but the life manner of Jesus manifests the "God-Connector."

My contention is this: I **know of no one who doesn't live in a manner that indicates the love of self.** And in too many cases, its excessiveness [ego/hubris unlimited] or its paucity [hardly at all functional] is the driving force to relationships.

Have an example, but to protect the guilty it will stay in the field of anonymity.

I knew a minister who had a church member who was very rich. That member split a $2 million gift—half to the church and half to the minister to do whatever he wanted with the money. The minister, focusing upon himself, kept the money, none shared altruistically. "It's for me," was his declaration.

I knew him from a distance—he was in another denomination and we only shared the same city—but didn't really know him. I happened to meet him once at a ski resort, too brutal a wind to ski, and I asked him how his ministry was going.

A mistake.

He spent the next hour, literally, speaking only in the first person, literally using the self-designation adjectives, "great, superior, impressive." I couldn't excuse myself fast enough—besides if I were smart I would have kept the conversation to the proverbial 15 minutes of fame. I thought, though, what an ego-maniac, one for whom the key question for all his decisions, *What's in this for me?*

Another minister—sorry, but that's my most familiar example vocation—whose ego dwarfed his heart. He was literally merciless, ran everything, thought being democratic in leadership was a gross weakness. In fact, when he retired, he violated a clergy retirement code [which states you should absent yourself at least a year after serving the church, especially retiring from an extended ministry] by returning to the church the NEXT Sunday, for goodness sakes, and greeted people. A couple came that had not attended a few years because of their dislike for the minister. He greeted them, "Oh, you've decided to return."

He also had ALL the keys to the church and refused to give them up. Boy, LOVE OF SELF to a fault, what I call a healthy imbalance.

These extreme examples echo in people all around, most of the time laced with subtlety. A good example, look for people who are never wrong, whose best skill is in scapegoating. It is the love of self, people about whom the Apostle Paul warned, "He [she] thinks of himself more highly than he ought to think."

And yet the flip-side of that, to belittle the self, to find the self underwhelming, to think we've always got to reach up to touch bottom because of our unworthiness, has too many examples. Way too many.

It has been my primary function in life, and for a good part of it in ordained ministry, to pay way more attention to those who don't think they have any value.

Why? Because I believe there IS value in each life or God wouldn't have created each person to begin with. To be blunt if not crass, God would not waste time making junk. The lament we turn ourselves into junk is too apt with people who KNOW they are less than meets the eye.

To that perception and value and truth—we DO have value—I owe a profound word of gratitude to a very special lady, Lucy McCorkle, who resides in Denver, pushing 100. She and her husband, Ev, were members of our Lakewood United Church of Christ in Colorado, circa 1973-80. She helped in Christian Education. But her real benefit was to help people know they had value. She gave me a rock once, well before Pet Rock was a rage. It said, "I'm me, I'm beautiful, I'm good...cuz God don't make junk."

I think of that these days...because almost every place I go...and it's not the classroom or the sanctuary. It's the grocery store, it's the store parking lot, it's the fitness center, it's the gas station where the lady in the office needs your card before you gas up, it's the restaurant with the waitress who never looks you in the eye—ALMOST EVERYWHERE, I sense people who think less of themselves and don't think that will change.

Hey, I'm no genius on this...nor am I one who can make a difference. That's the truth.

But, if I can say a word, or offer a little help to someone, maybe—just maybe—that moment God's Light will be evident. Not because of me, for sure. But, yet, maybe God and I—more important to me, God and you—can be a partner on this...to bring a little goodness to someone else.

And you know what? THAT ends up—the act of generosity and kindness—helping your own self feel a whole lot better.

Only if you've helped one person have a better day...or at least a better moment.

Reminds me of that wonderful story of a boy who looked for starfish along the ocean's edge—there were dozens of them on the sea shore—to toss them back into the ocean. A stranger came along, "That doesn't make any difference, throwing that starfish back—not at all. Look around, there are too many other starfish."

The boy, wise beyond his years, only responded, as he held up one starfish and tossed it, "It makes a difference to that one."

Good for him.

And good for us, in each blink of the day. To do what we can, and it never fails to reciprocate a good feeling of your own self, when you don't worry about whether that lady emptying her grocery cart has just inherited $1 million and you walk by and inquire, "Ma'am, I'm not an employee of H.E.B., but. Could I help by pushing your cart back?"

That "Thank you, mister," is a lovely moment. You should try it. Does wonders for making the last two words of the Great Commandment have value and not be excessive.

Intensity, when a dilemma
Posted on March 5, 2011 by Mark H Miller

These are new thoughts, although they may have had a subconscious streaming for more than a year or two.

The bubbling-to-awareness trigger was watching a television program last night on HGTV, something about purchasing a home in upscale Manhattan, certainly a redundancy.

I found myself caught up in one of the realtors. Hadn't seen the program before, although it's one I happen to enjoy with Diane.

Hey, she brings all kinds of newness to my life—reading a Kindle, appreciating "What Not To Wear," which is really a great program on transformation, and the many real estate shows. Now, that doesn't mean we're going to move. In fact, my accountant breathed more than one sigh of relief when we told her "we are staying in our lovely Austin cul-de-sac." She had been conditioned to include real estate transactions in recent 1040 returns. Truth holding firm there were six new home purchases—consecutively not simultaneously—the last eight years. That doesn't mean we're conditioning for a Witness Protection Program, not at all. It just means we moved from Austin to Issaquah to Lewisville to Austin, all part of our work-hire-transfer-realities.

I'm digressing. Back to upscale Manhattan's realtor.

As I've mentioned I hadn't seen the program before. But I found, short of Diane's alert, one of the realtors was offending. It didn't take a minute to say, "What's with this guy—he's awful, just so pushy and forceful."

Diane, as she can do so well, said the summary of why this guy was offensive in one word: INTENSE.

That was it. The guy couldn't say anything without a feel he was making the world's most important statement, without a "I'm the guy with the better perspective; LISTEN TO ME."

Damn, his eyes glared, never blinked. Actually about the 11th minute I hoped he was a manikin without a pulse or heart beat or more statements.

After I thought about it, I wondered, *what is wrong with intensity?*

My first answer was how much people with the opposite tendency cause me discomfort. Label the antithesis what you will, apathy, indifference, laid-back with no inertia, it seems to me that is being irresponsible.

But, what about intensity?

My first "take" was there's a synonym that gets this guy off the hook, ENERGY. No doubt about it, this guy had energy.

Then, and I didn't realize it until a day later, what really bothered me was the subconscious moment when the television screen turned into a mirror, I wondered, *Am I more like this intense guy that I would ever admit?*

Now, in self-defense I don't think such a self-discovery and self-disclosure's all bad.

But, I wonder. Is my intensity of appreciable value?

In writing this new novel I've thought of myself as resolved and focused, really determined to practice a new tact in writing novels—to write a chapter a day, but before that, each morning to edit what was written the previous day.

That may not be good for everyone, but it makes me feel better about writing. Why? Because I have friends who are better in writing than I who will help me with the editing. But, down deep, both initially and ultimately, it is MY RESPONSIBILITY to burnish the finished product.

Where is this all going?

Maybe it's a somewhat rambling way to say about the principle that "opposites attract" with the opposing reality that *like people don't*.

Maybe THAT'S why that guy last night on HGTV was so bothersome—maybe the Shadow didn't know the truth as much as the mirror.

I really don't know.

But, I do know that I want to think about my intensity/energy. I don't want to ever just bowl people over. Maybe I do, an unwanted and unintended consequence of intensity.

I do know, if given a choice to be a bowling ball or a pin or the alley and gutter, I don't want to be any of those. I simply want to be the bowler who does his very best.

The Genesis of Writing a Novel–Part 1

Posted on <u>March 6, 2011</u> by <u>Mark H Miller</u>

Writing a novel. Where did it start, the possibility? I'm not really sure, but a thought was when as a child I saw the Orson Wells' film, "The Third Man." I found the twist in the end intriguing. Maybe a writing seed was planted.

It was clear to me, writing novels notwithstanding, that I needed writing skills if ministry was a serious option. Yes, I had the educational value of my 8th grade teacher, Miss Carter. Oh we could—and at 70 I still am able—recite the linking and being verbs and EVERY preposition. But, more than that it was her mantra, "Great minds run in the same channel—but still others take a course of their own."

Not that I knew what that meant, but for sure, learning to write might lead to a new direction. What gave me strong encouragement in writing—not only technique but a willingness to keep going with it—was a teaching assistant at Stanford. Dr. Louis Ruotolo and I met once a week for a full quarter. There was always a pattern, that brought me new learnings as well as some laughter.

He and I would go over the weekly essay [which, of course, is better than a weakly essay] for 30 minutes, then we'd talk baseball, with his encouragement I sign a professional contract before going to seminary. He was clear if not perceptive or let alone a judge of my modest talent, "Mark, you should be a major league baseball pitcher—that will mean you'll be more popular as a preacher. Besides, you have the same initials as Mickey Mantle, so you cannot go wrong." He was much better in helping me to conjugate verbs correctly.

The writing in the early ministry years, which was essentially sermon manuscripts, seemed to go okay. I was better at writing than editing, although some of Dr. Ruotolo's teachings stuck.

In the last few weeks I've gone through all my papers since my 1966 ordination. I had forgotten that I had written some extensive essays, mainly about experiences that made some theological impact. I know, that's pretty fancy, but it is what I re-discovered. All of that, until I came to Austin in 1997 to become a Conference Minister, was pretty brief in length…and probably pretty shallow in depth.

Anyway.

An Austin friend said to me, one of those questions that is really a suggestion, "Do you think you'd ever write a novel?"

I allowed that I enjoyed reading murder/mysteries, my favorite genre, but hadn't thought of being a novelist myself. The friend said, "I think you should seek more guidance, because as friends have told you, and I agree, you are a pretty good writer."

That was tempting, so I signed up for a 5-day "Learn to write your first novel" seminar, held in a wonderful retreat center in northern New Mexico, "Ghost Ranch."

I got to the class and thought I was in the wrong place…there were twelve students…nine of whom had published at least one novel. The other two were housewives; they were just like me—never had written a novel. No less, they and I were there to consider the possibility of writing a novel, but more curious than anything else.

I'll never forget the last class on Friday morning. Our teacher, Mary Robertson, a Pulitzer nominated novelist from upstate New York, a tremendous teacher, asked each of us to read the first chapter of a new novel.

Ghost Ranch is in the desert, so Thursday afternoon I walked…and walked…and walked. And two things didn't happen, one of relief and the other of frustration. The former was I encountered no rattlesnakes. The latter was I had no idea how to begin a novel, no clue in the world.

Then, it happened. I cannot explain, but a novel began to happen.

I sat there in class that Friday morning and listened to the others reading their first chapters. *Ohmygoodness* was the polite version. *Holy shit* was the more guttural. Hey, being a minister isn't always a posturing of eloquence. The first chapters read by my classmates were dazzling, smooth, impressive, fascinating, mind-blowing, curious, compelling.

I was as creative as I could be to not be chosen, making sure I never looked into Mary's eyes. Finally it was up to me.

I looked at my watch, "Oh, gosh, I don't know that I can. I might be late for my flight out of Albuquerque."

Mary pointed, "You can do it. It's just 6 pages, right?"

It was.

So, I read the first pages of the first novel I had ever written.

Then something totally unpredictable happened. Two of the class members got up from the round table and walked to the windows and looked out. Mary reached for a handkerchief, touched her wet eyes.

What is this?

One of the class members slapped the table, "Mark, that is spell-binding. What happens? Does he kill himself?"

I looked at her, "I have no idea. I was lucky to get to page six."

"Come on," she protested. "You have this minister in a horrible situation, sitting in his car wearing his pulpit robe, puts the key in the ignition, looks to make sure he has a full tank of gas, throws the garage opener to the floor and starts the car. And that's it? Come on!"

Truth was I was totally unsure what page seven should say.

It was time to leave....

......to be continued tomorrow...

The Genesis of Writing a Novel...Part 2

Posted on March 8, 2011 by Mark H Miller

I looked at her, "I have no idea. I was lucky to get to page six."

"Come on," she protested. "You have this minister in a horrible situation, sitting in his car wearing his pulpit robe, puts the key in the ignition, looks to make sure he has a full tank of gas, throws the garage opener to the floor and starts the car. And that's it? Come on!"

Truth was I was totally unsure what page seven should say.

It was time to leave....

I came back to Austin finding the whole experience remarkable. Not because of what I wrote, but because Mary Robertson was great as a teacher. It was simple, direct and understandable teaching. Will never forget she said, "In writing fiction, make sure you know what you are talking about; never write on something that is no more than a hunch. And, for me at least, I never have anyone in my novels whom I don't know...but I embellish the character so they'd never recognize themselves."

About two weeks later I received a surface-mail letter. It was from Mary. She wrote encouragement to continue the novel—very affirming. AND. She offered to edit the writing...as a contribution.

How could I not continue?

Well, that was the start.

Along the way, from that day of discovery at Ghost Ranch in 1999 until now, I've had a great time writing novels. Along the way some great editing help. Particularly my Dallas friend, Al Day. The class work honing possible skills was mainly crafted by James Thayer, through three quarters of "Fiction Novel Writing" at the University of Washington. Both Al and James are beautiful friends. And then, my newspaper editor friend from Colorado Springs, Joe Barber [he's now working on his own.] and currently my friend and attorney, Jim Blume give me valued editing suggestions.

What was surprising is that Sue Grafton has taken some interest in my novels, offering very helpful adjustments. For instance, in my 4th novel, "Mask of Sanity," Sue thought it was writer's license but unacceptable that I had my protagonist, Tricia Gleason, in a 6-month coma. So, it got reduced to two weeks. Thanks, Sue!

Today is March 4, 2011. And something new is happening. I feel fortunate to have completed four novels and am about to have the first one published, "Murder On Tillamook Bay."

I have been mumbling in my sleep about getting to the first chapter of a fifth novel. Nothing focused.

Then, BAM. Less than two weeks ago, actually while doing my souse chef work at the back porch barbecue, I got an idea, then another, then a chapter.

The next morning, "Scattered Hope" began. And it's been fascinating to me. My erstwhile protagonist, Tricia Gleason, with a background as homicide detective, fishing guide and now seminary student, is spending the summer after her first seminary year as a summer minister intern in Frisco, Colorado.

She anticipates it will be humdrum, reading Sunday worship scripture, praying once in a while, visiting the sick and elderly, leading a youth group and conducting occasional fly-fishing classes.

The first day she arrives in Frisco, a Tuesday, the minister informs her that he and his wife are leaving town for the summer so his wife can heal from major back surgery—plus he's exhausted so needs sabbatical rest—all of which means Tricia will be "it" as the minister of the church.

The surprise wears off without any relief because of two church members have just disappeared, a college youth has been arrested for an armed robbery and a parishioner has intent to be destructive.

And that's just in the first 20,000 words. So, we'll see where that goes.

I wanted to write all this to share how much fun I'm having…and I'm good to Mary Robertson's counsel, writing about what I know, for my novels are all about ministry, fishing and murder, but not always in that order. And to emphasize all this, occasionally I wear a T-shirt a church member gave me, *Be nice to me…of I'll put you in my next novel!"*

I wore it recently, an elderly gentleman saw it, stopped in his tracks, hoisted his arms to the ceiling and proclaimed for all in the grocery store to hear, "I'm nice!"

Gotta love it.

Go, Tricia!

Life is more than fishing...

Posted on March 10, 2011 by Mark H Miller

Some good lessons to share, and some surprising clues on new possibilities.

Let me deal with the latter first, some of which may be unhelpful, so you offer, *are you serious, that's not helpful to me.* I'll take that chance.

...best day to make a plane reservation is Tuesdays.

...when you fly and the announcements are made about passenger safety, grab the flyer in the seat pocket about the safety information. I flew recently and sat next to a CEO who flies everywhere always...who told me she looks at the flyer DURING the announcements and twice, since she was the only one doing so, was given free round-trip coupons. How about that?

...best time to catch fall Chinook in the Columbia River is during the outgoing tide.

...the preferable tides for catching fall Chinook in the Columbia River is when the height of the high tide and the low tide is marginal. In other words, the lower the difference the better the bite.

...the sturgeon population is in serious atrophy, but no one wants to put new limits on catching same, other than what exists, which is minimum and maximum size.

I write this morning, having made some additional discoveries. I'm in Garibaldi, Oregon, the sleepy fishing village on the north shore of Tillamook Bay. For almost a year [I'm not a last-minute, "why don't we?" guy.] I've had a six day fishing trip planned, shared with my wonderful friend and fishing guide [great to have both!] Chris Vertopoulos, who for me is Zorba the Greek. It turned out, as to no surprise, weather impacts such a trip, for in March in the Northwest, rivers can be "knocked out" by rain and storm. [One of the mantras from the Portland Chamber of Commerce is, *In Oregon you don't tan, you rust.*]

The discovery is this: it is easy to harp and whine and even spite when plans don't work well. If I were to do that, I would offer immediately how bumpy my flight was to Portland, and that it rained and blew so hard that I am not able to fish this day or tomorrow [Friday]. The rivers are "flows of mud."

But, that's not what is chosen. Rather, the fact is, and this would be "luck upon fortune," I was able to fish four days, and each day, was able to connect with fish. In fact, when fishing with my friend, Zorba, on Monday, I was able to cast, bounce eggs, hook, play and land a beautiful 14 pound hatchery steelhead. The reason "hatchery" is mentioned is you can keep a hatchery steelhead, but not a native steelhead.

And since I hoped to bring steelhead home for dinner tomorrow night, I have been able to keep that promised hope for Diane.

And then the last two days when fishing in Northwest Washington on the Olympic Peninsula, got into some more steelhead. In fact, yesterday it was beyond anything I could hope, for I hooked into 8 steelhead–go figure, right?–it was a blast.

So, rather than lament not fishing today and tomorrow, I will GIVE THANKS for the 4 days of wonderful fishing with valued guide-friends, especially Zorba.

The second discovery is I must admit, and honestly it's not a stretch to go here, I am no longer physically strong enough to fish more than a few days. That's okay...so, it's actually a good thing today and tomorrow will not be fishing. Yes, I wrote that and mean it!

Today will also be a special day.

This afternoon I will meet Neil Kristiansen. The reason this is fascinating is the last time I saw Neil was 1958 when we graduated from high school. He happens to know Zorba and Zorba mentioned my name, that we are friends. Neil called me, is living in Tillamook. He said his mother, Agnes Kristiansen, is still alive and lives in a nursing home in Tillamook. This afternoon I will meet Neil and visit with his mother.

Crazy how life comes around. I imagine we'll see if we can recall incidents "way back when."

Then later this afternoon I will visit with Laura Ruggeri, who's a newspaper columnist with the Tillamook newspaper. She wants to learn more about the novel, "Murder On Tillamook Bay," indicating she and her staff are more than pleased a novel will be published that has Tillamook as the main venue. I look forward to that visit.

So it is, this new day. Lent has started. My life is blessed. And I will fly home tomorrow, which will be the best part of all. To go home is better than anything...including fishing.

Yes!

Tsunami Strikes

Posted on March 11, 2011 by Mark H Miller

It was a new wake-up call. The droning siren was the voice of warning and alert. No less than 30 minutes later Diane called to say a tsunami was headed toward the sleepy fishing village of Garibaldi. I needed to be aware of potential trouble, which was certainly at least in its possibility, an understatement. Garibaldi awakened suddenly from its sleep. So did I. You bet.

My host, Zorba the Greek [aka Chris Vertopoulos] because as a very conscientious fishing guide and wonderful friend it was his business to know all about weather, said the tsunami was headed toward the Oregon coast—pushing from Japan to Hawaii and then to the western United States, further saying folk should be more than ½ mile from the coastline and above 50 feet. He said his Garibaldi home was 213 feet elevation. [I thought, *I NEVER could tell you the home elevation, except in Colorado Springs when it was 6,200 feet.*]

Here was the first devastating paragraph from online news:

An 8.9 magnitude earthquake off the coast of Northeast Japan spawned a ferocious tsunami that's caused massive destruction; flattening whole cities, starting raging fires, and killing hundreds. Nearly 88,000 people are reported missing, according to the official Kyodo news agency.

What a horrific impact—beyond tragic.

Needless to say, I packed my bags and got out of Dodge. Zorba assured me he would be okay, knew how to climb higher should it be necessary.

The thoughts, driving well ahead of wind and storm [learned later the wave height lessened], were not random; they were very focused.

Most importantly, how special is Diane? Goodness, on a caring and be careful scale, on a 1-10 she's well above 16. She wanted to make sure "her guy" was aware. That is special. She considers it no big deal, but I consider it a beautiful gift, to make the call and make sure I knew what was happening.

Next thought, *how quickly life can change.* Certainly each of you is aware of that and probably can cite footnote after footnote when in the blink of an eye, and certainly without any warning, life has changed for you. The personal note on that, please indulge me because it is illustrative of sudden *life can change moments,* is when suddenly a fish strikes, the pole is almost jerked loose from your hands and the river explodes in a flurry of spinning cartwheels, the beautiful 14 pound steelhead giving a great example of high jumping. I cite this because the *quick change of life* doesn't always have to be evidence of Good Friday shadows.

It also reminded me of the need to never take life or relationship for granted. EACH day is God's gift, and there will be tsunami's, almost always for us inlanders understood metaphorically and not experienced literally, that happen. To thank God for life, for the gifts of relationships and for a new day...never can that be over-expressed.

And finally...to pray not only for ourselves, but for others, asking God to be both present and known as Spiritual Presence whose promise to be with us is always kept through tsunami's, through each new day, through fish caught and lost, through friendships discovered and sustained...and sometimes broken...through IT ALL, is never forgotten. The prayers for Presence...ah, THANKS BE TO GOD for the dawn of a new day.

So be it.

I flunked Cub Scouts

Posted on <u>March 12, 2011</u> by <u>Mark H Miller</u>

I flunked Cub Scouts. Not sure of age, but the moment is indelible. I had earned my Wolf badge and was working for my Bear badge. The assignment was to take a large vegetable can [think it was #10] and make it into a hamburger grill.

To say I was less than competent in creating a hamburger grill was an understatement. I didn't know how to cut/carve/bend the bottom of the can to grill anything let alone a hamburger.

My father, who knew more about these things than I, helped me. That's wrong. He built it for me.

I brought it to the Den meeting and the Denmother showed her appreciation, something to the effect, "Mark, that's one of the best hamburger grills ever."

I smiled.

She then asked, "Did it take you long to create it?"

I could have just answered, "No, not long."

But no. Truth pushed me into telling her, "My father made it for me."

That was my last Cub Scout meeting. Ever.

I must admit that I have not remembered that story—easy to either forget, neglect or deny some of the more vulnerable moments in one's life.

Until Thursday afternoon.

Staging of same is that I was in Tillamook, Oregon for some fishing… and visiting of friends, that included Neil Kristiansen. Neil and I were born the same year, went to the same grade school and lived one block apart—he on the corner of 25th and Highland and I on the corner of 25th and Holman, Portland, Oregon.

Through mutual friends, Neil called me a few months ago and started the conversation, "I bet you don't know who this is."

He was right.

When he introduced himself I was stunned…it had been more than 50 years since our high school graduation and the first contact. Goodness.

He indicated he and his brother, Jerry, two years older than he, both lived in the Tillamook area, he had heard I was coming to town and wondered if I could meet them and visit their mother, Agnes Kristiansen, now 99 and living in a care facility in Tillamook.

Of course.

When we got together this past Thursday, to coin Texan verbiage, it was a hoot. My oh my, how good it was to revisit some of our earlier escapades, what has happened to the old neighborhood—and quite frankly who is still living.

You can only imagine how special that was.

And their mother, Agnes. I can say, without any doubt, she is as alert and quick witted and clear in memory as anyone I have met who is 99. Now, that is not a legion of folk, but it does reference a pretty good list of former parishioners. Sharper than sharp—and the laughs and good memories abounded.

Then it happened. I didn't mention it because quite honestly I had not gone to that Cub Scout moment, it seemed at least, forever ago.

In a talk about favorite memories when we were young, Jerry mentioned how he loved to camp with the family…and then he added, "What I liked the best is we cooked our hamburgers on the #10 vegetable can I made into a grill in Cub Scouts."

He then looked and pointed to his mother, "And, we had the best Denmother imaginable. Mom, you were great!"

Have you ever had a WHOA moment?

It hit me like a thunderbolt.

I looked at Agnes [remember I said she had a great wit] and did my own version of pointing, "You! Agnes, you were my Denmother and you didn't accept my hamburger grill because my father made it. I never returned to Cub Scouts."

We laughed...for it was really humorous...

But, to think, to think again, what a remarkable moment—60 years later—our own version of Cold Case, and it all had to do with not earning a Bear badge.

Crazy world.

It was beyond wonderful to visit—to appreciate the Kristiansen's, even if I never made it through Cub Scouts. At least I made it this far in life to wrap up that very old event with some humor and "AHA!" Yes, indeed.

Nostalgia revisited

Posted on March 14, 2011 by Mark H Miller

I am nostalgic tonight—have just finished listening to the PBS fundraising concert with Carole King and James Taylor. I remember…oh do I ever.

First, accept my bias: I find no music more valued and pulsing than what they sing, along with one other.

Let me speak of the "one other."

It was the fall of 1964 [I refer to "fall" as a time of year and not a theological condition.] when I began a one-year internship in campus ministry at Southern Illinois University. The singer for whom I had the highest regard was Nancy Wilson. She gave a concert at a St. Louis concert hall. I was too late to get a front row seat, but was close enough to appreciate her voice and her beauty.

A surprise first act happened that I need to mention. The announcer said, "Ladies and Gentlemen, put your hands together. You will love this comedian who will be famous, very famous some day. This is his first time on stage—welcome….Bill Cosby."

How about that?

Then Nancy Wilson sang…fantastic. I knew most of the words but age has lost them. But not that night and the thought, *Gosh, I wonder if she'll invite me up to say hello?* [Hey, at 24, why not?] She didn't, but that didn't keep me from appreciating the beauty and value of her person and music. Goodness.

Then tonight to hear Carole King and James Taylor. One item on my bucket list is to see James Taylor in concert. Some day.

I remember, though, the night with Carole King. It was I and about 8,000 attending her concert at Red Rocks Amphitheatre just west of Denver. Wow, what a concert.

Yes, grass that you smoke was passed along. I didn't imbibe, but right then it didn't matter, for the music soared my spirits and fed my soul. I do remember that I was so smitten with Carole King ["You've got a friend"] that I couldn't remember where I parked. I did figure, though, everyone else could find theirs, so it was simply a matter of elimination. Hey, logic didn't fail.

At any rate, this night, March 13, to hear their PBS concert sent me into a wonderful realm—and to give thanks for how THAT music continues to reach, inspire and empower me.

So much to remember. I pray it never leaves me…never.

When Pain Visits…without knocking.

Posted on March 15, 2011 by Mark H Miller

I'm not an airport groupie—or whatever entitlement to those who fly more than they drive. It is of interest, though, when sitting at a gate to learn if "standby" means "you've got a seat, enjoy your flight," to observe the various folk who walk along.

What I've noticed today, about to fly from Dallas to Austin, is a series of folk who have crutches or wheelchairs.

Of course I don't know anything about "how did this happen?" and even more, it's none of my business.

However, across from me is a man with a sweatshirt and levis who leans against a wall on crutches, with only one leg. He cannot be more than 25 years of age.

And then a man literally strapped into a wheelchair, looking confused, and a friend—maybe a brother?—holding his shoes and an oxygen tank.

And then a father, literally running from one end of the gate area to a window—which is better than an escalator right?—to nab his crawling son. He said nothing but honestly he needed to scold himself. How could that happen?

Please hear this as observation on a Friday night in an airport—this one named Dallas/Ft. Worth International Airport.

What it prompts is this: do I give enough thanks for my health, my family's health? Probably not.

So many different options occur in one's life in terms of threatening one's health and then deeper, one's well being.

I wonder now how many people didn't survive the tsunami today—especially in Japan, but I wonder about other areas? I wonder if our daughter-in-law, Teela, is going to be okay in her pregnancy, with their

403

child to be born in August. And, personally, I wonder if I will continue to hold an upper hand on the Diabetes—it's so easy to forget about it, to "get to the blood sugar measurement" later. Shame on me.

I remember in this moment, having spent some time at the cemetery to be with my parents, Hank and Esther Miller, to recall how my mother ALWAYS looked at any mishap, *Mark, this has happened* [She had been hit by a car, the accident resulting in a double-compound fracture of her leg], *but you know, when I was in the hospital I saw a woman who had her leg amputated—much worse than I. I am lucky I will heal, so complaints have no place.*

What a great attitude—hopefully many will emulate that—because it's true: stuff happens, weather changes and planes get delayed. Some of this is trivial. But when it's more than trivia-revisited, can we keep a perspective—I like the word *balance*—at all times…or at least almost always at each happenstance? Can we spell whine without an 'h' so gratitude prevails? I hope so. At least it's a worthy goal, which makes it more than a good idea.

A postscript—the above was written this past Friday morning, March 11, 2011. It is now Tuesday morning, March 15.

Another venue where the struggle of people walking the human landscape came often this morning as the doors to the Austin Pain Clinic were opened. Diane continues to address the pain of the dangling nerves around her lower back degenerated disks—her monthly appointment.

I sat there as people came for their appointments—the registration of pain on their faces and in their eyes is beyond description.

Then to see on CNN the ominous build-up of radiation spewing in Japan…and to see individual stories of fathers finding their daughters who have been pulled from the rubble.

Hopefully this does more than take our breath. Hopefully it generates new—much deeper than imaginable—prayers and commitment to be agents of caring and benefit.

Not for any particular reason, other than I'm now crafting a new novel and it got mentioned, there's a powerful passage in Genesis 1 I think of, when it offers, "Let us make man in our image, after our likeness," spoken by our Creator God. My wonderful doctorate professor, Doug Meeks, then at Eden Seminary, explained that passage, *To be made in God's image means we are authorized to represent God.*

I like that. A great deal.

So may it be. No matter where or how we are, may we seize the day in a manner that gives thanks for life and asks for strength to get through all the shadowing Good Fridays we encounter.

Shalom—the inner well being of the soul—to us all.

Did God author the tsunami and earthquakes in Japan?

Posted on <u>March 16, 2011</u> by <u>Mark H Miller</u>

March 16, 2011

It is morning.

But, also mourning for the millions of people in Japan.

The pictures and narratives are there, telling of the joy of finding a 4-month-old-crying in the rubble, in a blanket suit. Words fail to describe how joy and relief abound as the infant and her parents are reunited. Or the father walking through the rubble, had to be numb in shock and fear, to learn his daughter made it.

Or the horror of having lost all of a family…or a village, not to minimize having nothing left in house and possessions.

Then the radiation, unseen but more than dangerous to breathing; even more to living.

In the mix of all this, and perhaps this is because I gravitate toward the theological in life's happenstance, I read of a response offered by a Japanese government official, who in so many words said the earthquakes and tsunami were God's responses to "the sins of our nations."

When I read that I cannot pass over with only a wince. It is more, for I believe such commentary is tripe, so uninformed and unhelpful.

My initial response is, "I want no part of that kind of God, a God who is wrathful, vengeful, even capricious. A God who is mean, enraged with acts of retribution and destruction. None."

But, there is more to share.

I do understand where it comes from, most often Genesis 6-9, the Noah narrative about God wanting to save only Noah and his family. Is that so?

Risking the wrong I maintain God wouldn't do that. Yes, there is a corrective later when God's quoted to say, "I will not do that again."

The wrongness has to do, in every instance, especially the untoward, the tragic, the devastating, when in a moment or two or three, EVERYTHING is torn asunder, with the answer to the question, "Who is God?"

Nothing more, nothing less.

Through my blog I ask each reader to be engaged by that question.

Briefly, I don't believe God authors floods and tsunamis. I don't believe God authors cancer. I don't believe God authors relationships torn asunder. I don't believe God's a record keeper. The image of God as referee with a whistle is insulting.

My God?

…when the people suffer, God's heart is the first to break.

…when I feel like nothing, when I am not sure if tomorrow has a chance, when I sense in my gut no matter what I do the future is bleak and Good Friday looms, my God, ever present, says to me, "I am with you no matter what. I am the God of Hope and not Devastation."

That doesn't mean we look willy-nilly at every event. That doesn't mean we are arrogant thinking who we are and what we do makes no difference.

Japan hurts beyond words. I know a lot of people who inside, in the heart of the soul, hurt beyond words.

My prayer, literally in the *no matter whatness* of life, "God, help me be the best I can be. Help me not give up. Help me always remember Good Friday never wins. Help me in my faith and join me in my efforts to be a presence of value and goodness for others. And, if at all possible, help me be a window, through whom people can get more than a glimpse of your Love, your Hope and their Faith."

Zorba my friend

Posted on March 17, 2011 by Mark H Miller

For years, read that decades, I've benefitted from friendships with fishing guides. It all started in the middle 50's when my father and I floated the Nestucca River outside of Hebo, Oregon with Paul Hannemann, who became a state of Oregon House of Representative for his Tillamook County.

They are too many to mention, but today I think of one, a very special friend and guide, Chris Vertopoulos, whom I call with respect and affirmation and endearment, Zorba the Greek.

Yesterday, Wednesday, March 16, 2011, Zorba launched his "business boat" into a new direction.

He's been a fishing guide for twenty years. For more than half of those years, I was privileged to salmon and steelhead fish with him along the Oregon coast, in the Columbia River and in the Pacific Ocean.

Just last week Zorba and I fished the Wilson River by Tillamook, Oregon, and then two days on the Olympic Peninsula in northwest Washington with two guide friends of ours.

On Tuesday Zorba sold his brand-new drift boat and many of his fishing rods and reels. He has cancelled most of his scheduled trips, handing his clients over to guide buddies.

Why mention him? In one vein because he is as competent and humble a guide as can be. Many guides have one characteristic or the other. The combination of competency/humility is part of Zorba's DNA. I know of no guide...and many of them get close...who works harder for his clients.

But, he never ever says something to the effect, "We will get a fish in the next hole—guaranteed." Never. He might say, "Everybody be ready—this could be a 95% hole," meaning simply he's caught fish there before. Always a hope but never a promise.

He's a great personal friend—we discuss theology and the practical joys and frustrations of daily events.

The reason I think of him is he is one of a legion…too many to count… who must seek new avenues of work because of our faulting economy.

It saddens me this is happening.

Oh, he did learn he will have Tuesdays and Wednesdays off from his new position [at least 40+ hours each week] as Assistant Manager at a new outdoors/fishing/hunting store in Tigard, Oregon, southwest of Portland. I've already signed-up to fish with him the last Tuesday and Wednesday of April, to spend what hopefully will be two great days back-bouncing eggs for Spring Chinook salmon.

I admire Zorba. I find him to be very special, in terms of he's doing his best to understand his situation and make the most of it.

He has a great dream that someday may happen. I believe it will. It's a dream he shared confidentially, but as I tell him, my prayers will continue for *dream manifest*.

I tip my hat to Zorba—I'll miss not fishing with him this late summer in the Columbia and next winter in the Wilson. But, the friendship is solid and my respect for him will continue without pause or qualification.

How many others do both you and I know who are finding new pathways for employment?

My admiration is for those who refuse to look down, throw up their hands and say, "The hell with it." I applaud those who refuse to give up or give in, who keep seeking a new day when their sunglasses will be needed.

I attach a picture of Zorba and one of his clients, having fished on Tillamook Bay. That's a Fall Chinook salmon in the center. Zorba and I are the ones without the gills. Go for it, Zorba, just like your namesake. Keep dancing and singing your song, a song of hope and energy and resolve. Tight lines to you…for every day.

My best.

From your favorite Padre, who will keep his promise, should wedding bells ring, even if in Athens, I will be there. Whether or not salmon fishing is in season.

Consequence Management

Posted on March 18, 2011 by Mark H Miller

Two words. In the plethora of reports—my reliance is primarily CNN and yahoo.com, both of whom I consider reliable and accurate—a comment from our government with regard to the increasing dangers of radiation in Japan got my attention.

Not that the entire scenario—more the grist for a horror film than one could ever imagine—isn't ominous and onerous and all other adjectives that birth fear.

Here's the statement, *"The president briefed Prime Minister Kan on the additional support being provided by the U.S., including specialized military assets with expertise in nuclear response and consequence management," it said in a statement.*

CONSEQUENCE MANAGEMENT.

I have no doubt, not even a blinking wince, we have specialists who know more than the rest of us in dealing with the travailing realities caused by the earthquakes and tsunami.

To say this is worth our concerns is an understatement.

And yet, as I think about life—not only my own but all I know if even for a moment—EVERY ONE OF US HAS THE RESPONSIBILITY OF *CONSEQUENCE MANAGEMENT.*

Isn't that synonymous with living each day? Each moment? Each comment? Each muted thought?

Question posed on this St. Patrick's Day—which I greet wearing a green bath robe, even though my DNA and heritage are total German—how do we cope with the more devastating occurrences?

For better or for worse, what occurs this morning are two notions—actually one notion and one image.

Both of which are needed for coping.

The first is the best guidance I've ever read or heard on how to deal with crises. Tough challenge, but worthy. Even more, necessary.

I learned it from a Rabbi therapist, Edwin Friedman, who said in so many words, "As a minister or mediator, the key is to stay connected with each person, be a non-anxious presence who is able to fully self-differentiate."

That's not academic gobbly-gook. It says, profoundly yet simply, *never lose touch with your own identity. Remain steadfast in who you are, your value, your essence, your personhood and your persona.*

To me that's a veritable insight into being a *consequence manager.*

For every day, every single day. Every yesterday and every tomorrow, we spend dealing with the what was, the what is and the what to be.

The second coping guide I saw yesterday on CNN—maybe you did also. It was a video clip from a Japanese station.

Lacking translation, verbiage was unnecessary—totally so.

The video clip showed a wounded dog...barely able to lift its head. It was on its side next to the rubble of destruction. Sitting next to the dog was another dog. Both were shivering and no doubt, overwhelmed by hunger and thirst. The well dog REFUSED to leave the wounded dog. Faithful. Present. Protector. Care-giver. Consequence manager.

I was overwhelmed by the imaging...very much so.

And it occurred to me: THAT'S what it takes to cope. Be faithful. Be caring. Be steadfast. Never compromise, never give up, never give in. Know who you are and those for whom you care.

Two lessons on this day, when the world is not on a steady axis, at least the stability of being okay.

But, in reality, no day is okay. Unless we are non-anxious, self-differentiating and linked through love and devotion to those who matter.

I believe that.

Okay, day. Let's get it on.

Healing Options for a Fractured World

Posted on March 20, 2011 by Mark H Miller

Perhaps this is too trite, simplistic, even pedantic.

I ask, probably only in the mirror in my house, *What is most important when the world seems to be headed to significant destruction?*

Rattle off these names and it's hard to believe goodness will not atrophy: *Libya, Afghanistan, Haiti, Japan, New Zealand, NFL Lock-out* [okay, could be omitted, but let's face it, the National Football League not having a season 2011-12 is disheartening].

From earthquakes to imperialistic leaders to continued famine and thirst, my gracious.

I mentioned previously the need to self-differentiate and be non-anxious.

This morning, Sunday, the first day of Spring according to the calendar, a time, at least in south central Texas, when buds are bursting on trees and the high yesterday was 82 degrees, I think of additional verities, that can *make our day.*

Not in any order.

Financial gifting. Our monies are part of our identity. And, for sure, we each can claim we don't have enough. Consider that a given.

But, to donate money to an organization, a need, a cause is one way in which we can know in our heart we have done the right thing. For us, gifting to a salmon hatchery, a church, our dear friend Margaret Trost's *What If? Foundation*'s Haiti food and education program, gives us a sense we have not muted or blocked out the world's maladies.

There's another, though, that seldom receives support: *be genuine, give an honest effort, be full in your effort and caring in your living.*

414

The people I find the most admirable, commendable and if I may, followable, are those who don't have the most money, who don't have all those educational letters after their name, but are the ones who are full in their genuineness. They live honestly, a transparent healthiness. No hidden agendas or duplicitous manner.

My life has been blessed by legions of folk like that. Not to mention names, but to affirm that to cope with the world we first must cope with ourselves and answer the question, "Have I given an honest effort, within my abilities and resources, and maybe in a moment or two, even beyond them?"

Perhaps another way to consider this, especially as the menacing world of Libya now takes a fractured center stage, a question in a much smaller room I urged clergy, and hopefully myself, "Is my heart bigger than my ego?"

Is yours?

It may be the answer to that question—ahem to ALL politicians and world leaders—could pivot the current direction we seem to be taking.

To put this in a way I've maintained would help—yes, it's fanciful and maybe even silly—would be my request that EVERY world leader, before making a decision to crush the foe—EVERY world leader, not make any decision about war without holding a new born baby in his or her arms.

Because? The child born today has no chance for a life birthed tomorrow, if ego dwarfs the heart, if power crushes understanding and if firing a gun or sending a missile prevails over, "What can my life do to increase the value and worth and health and future of all of life?"

The key to all this is to make sure our impacting considers the other in the following manner: as a child of God and not a step to the future. Or a threat to our wholeness. For the most part, the fracturing of self is when the ego and heart are strangers to each other, when the ego calls the shots and the heart says, *Why not?* To not let that happen is a profound healing option.

415

Change. Not the tingling coins in one's pocket. Rather, doing things differently. It is hackneyed but often maintains its verity: *insanity is doing the same thing over and over but expecting different results.*

It struck me this morning how I've changed—not knowing for better or ill—simply changed, which came about without any game plan or self-evident need.

It has to do with novel writing. The manner/style of writing itself.

I remember my very insightful professor at the University of Washington, James Thayer, himself a well respected novelist [think he's published nine novels], telling us that one novelist had something like five "writing" rooms, each of which had a novel under construction. Others create a full outline of the novel and then have at it. Others build the plane while flying.

Matter of style.

I think this morning, as I'm in the cauldron of deciding whether a suicide will happen in the next chapter [it was game planned but I'm having second thoughts this morning], how my own writing style has changed.

The first novel—the minister who thinks the future is hopeless because of wrong charges against him—was building the plane while flying. Which is to say one chapter led to another. But, it was written, almost in the dark, certainly only my editor knew what I had written.

Happened about twelve years ago. I was in conference ministry, officed in Austin. Had no associate, so the 100 churches, with various pushing force, needed my attention. They stretched more than 1,000 miles, so most days were full…and exhausting.

Yet, I wanted to write my first novel. I lived alone in a lovely home in NW Austin, on a placid street, Comfort Cove. My roommate was Mercy, my incredibly beautiful, wonderful, precious English Cocker Spaniel.

It made sense when someone once told me that Mercy always loved me, no matter what. I wish my clergy echoed that. How silly of me.

When I'd come home her body shook its greeting and then she'd walk to her food tray. No less, even when it wasn't feed-time, EVERY time I'd open the refrigerator, she'd be there in full expectation.

I'm off track.

I'd get home, slump the briefcase in the corner of my home office, get a snack—for me and Mercy—then very deliberately close my office door, pull my shades, sit down at my desk and labor away. Almost like I was creating the next world's greatest novel. Hey, scripture has it right: if you have no vision you perish.

I can remember one night shouting—literally. Not in joy. The minister [in the novel] had a favorite parishioner, one of those he'd never wish to trade. She had a stroke, was in a coma. The minister raced to the hospital, couldn't see her, sat disconsolately recalling the many times she'd encouraged him, told him it was un-pastor-like to give up or give in.

Then it happened. It just happened. Damn. As my fingers raced along the computer screen, the ER physician came to the waiting room and told the pastor "we couldn't save her."

Right there. Bam. She croaked.

How utterly....

Well, you can fill in the completion.

That was twelve years ago.

Change has happened. In writing the novel.

This one, "Shattered Hope," has pulled me in a new writing style.

I actually have built the plane before flying. I know who gets whacked, who the whacker is, what incidents happen on a private fishing stream… and whether the protagonist, Tricia Gleason, once a homicide detective and fishing guide and now seminary student, in this novel experiencing the vicissitudes of summer intern ministry in Frisco, Colorado, makes a firm decision to stay in ministry.

Yep, my buddy, Tricia, has one Good Friday after another, to coin a Holy Week image.

Knowing where I'm headed, at least in the writing, I have followed this schedule: write a new chapter each morning after editing the chapter written the previous morning.

It seems to work, a tighter, better connected and more sensible development of Tricia's world.

I feel better about character descriptions—physically and emotionally—and find lots and lots of humor sprinkled. Hey, without a sense of humor, life gets vacuous. Or something like that.

Now, to edit yesterday's chapter and then see if Tricia's premonition—she has a Wrong Meter, a powerful intuitive sense of things gone hay wire—that Blake's depression gets the upper hand, is correct. The Shadow knows…and I think I do too. Let's see…..

A War On War

Posted on March 22, 2011 by Mark H Miller

Not afraid to admit what I don't know.

Recall what Bill Coffin once said, "The only dumb question is the one not asked."

So, at the risk of announcing the vulnerability of dumbing-down or being really stupid, here goes: I don't know what a "pingback" is.

Once in a while it happens to the morning blog.

My hunch is there are systems out there which pick up key words... for instance, the *pingback* this morning has to do with the blog, "Life is more than fishing..." The response indicates where you can fish, big-time, in half a day.

I trashed it.

But, if I'm in the vicinity of defining a *pingback*, words that trigger a response, then I'm all in.

With just one word this morning: war.

I'm sure everyone has their own war with war. From *we don't do enough of it* to *it should never be.*

If the former is a 10 and the latter a 1, I'm brushing up against a 1.

I am heartened by some congressmen who push President Obama on what the goals are in Libya.

Although I'm sure it's impressive, maybe for many laudatory, I found myself wincing when it was noted yesterday the accuracy of our missiles, bombs. They are "smart."

Okay, that doesn't make me a tyrant-supporter. But it is the case, at least personally—and theologically I must add—war is the least, when it comes to an avenue to peace.

Another question, triggered by the bomb's accuracy, a bomb that hit the roof center of a building: *why cannot we be as precise in our caring, our feeding, our educating, our getting along in our own cul-de-sacs of family?*

But, the *pingback* for me, having been never in support of Vietnam or Iraq or Afghanistan military involvement, is one word, NECESSARY?

It is the case, in personal terms of ancestry, when my great-grandparents left Germany to reside in Norka, Russia, along the Volga River [called White Russians or Volga Russians], it was because of three promises: 40 acres for farming, freedom in worship and no conscription. I would have been pleased to migrate with them.

What I don't know—and for my *pingback* notes this morning, I don't know how we get to dealing fully with the question of war's necessities, in an era when one's intelligence provides smart bombs and not well educated children.

For I worry about that with five grandchildren under 8 and a new gift of life due in August.

Yes I do.

Know what you don't know–that's the smart approach

Posted on March 23, 2011 by Mark H Miller

I wouldn't know Brad Stevens if he knocked on our door. But, his Athletic Director made a statement that echoes well in my heart, *"I'm smart enough to know good coaches when I see them," he said. "Each year we have a decision to make that allows us to extend the deal by another year, and boy, do we want to."*

Brad Stevens, at the young age of 34, is the men's basketball head coach at Butler, a team that defies all predictors to reach the 16 NCAA teams still vying for the national championship.

The point pressing for more attention is the first notion, *I'm smart enough to know good coaches..."*

The parlay of that is to be smart enough to know what you don't know.

When in conference ministry, time and again the question was asked of our clergy, "What do you need to know that will make your ministry more effective?"

I was disheartened—never devastated because it's their opinion and posturing in ministry that must count in the final realities—when most clergy said, more I wagered out of politeness than honesty, "Let me think about that."

Maybe I smiled, muffling a laugh, *Gosh, you will benefit by looking more seriously at an answer to that question.*

What triggers this are two arenas, one pretty ancient, the other current.

In that order.

I remember my first meeting with the Trustees of Lakewood United Church, Lakewood, Colorado, circa 1973. LUCC was my first "solo" pastorate, having completed seven years in Chicago and Eugene as an assistant or associate. In somewhat humorous but honest consideration, to be a "solo" pastorate meant if something went amiss, there was no senior minister to blame.

At that first Trustees meeting the question was not ambiguous, "Pastor Miller, our greatest need is to strengthen our financial giving. How will you help us with that."

I'm sure I muttered something, but it was gibberish in my own skin. Truth was I was virtually clueless about stewardship, the world of giving and generosity. I had never been given that responsibility my first seven years in ministry. Never.

In one church it was never necessary, because the church had some members who would, before the year's books closed, "make up any difference anticipated." In the other, some very competent laity made sure we never spent more than we had. They should have been politicians, right?

So, that night, after my gibberish [the Trustees smiled but I think also knew we were in deep trouble here], I thought, *Who are the ministers whom I know who know the most about stewardship?*

They were the easiest to identify. I made 1 hour appointments with each, told them my needs, looked at them in their respective offices, clicked on the tape recorder, looked at my watch, "I need your help. You have 60 minutes to tell me everything you know about raising money."

It was the best 3 hours I could have spent. I was no longer in a world of duh-ness and jibberish. I even knew whom to contact to raise money to pave the parking lot. I mean, really, how's that for a bonus?

The latter has to do with my house-husbanding in cooking.

Hey, I know how to start the Weber grill and make sure the hamburger or chicken never get too done.

But, now with a Crock Pot, making sure the right ingredients join the baby-back ribs [that was easy yesterday, just a slab of baby-back ribs, some diced onions and 3 cups of bbq sauce. Wahla, it was pretty good.].

But the week before the pot roast was a different situation. Me? I would have put in the pot roast, throw in a few potatoes and carrots and sliced onions, add a can of cream of mushroom soup, maybe sneak in a few mushrooms [freshly cut, of course] and clicked on the Crock Pot for slow cooking. Put everything on the plate in 8 hours.

Diane offered an alternative. And boy oh boy, how cool was that. It was my first cooking school class, making a special seasoning to rub on the roast, making sure everything else was done in good measurement. I learned. And I learned. And, for sure, at the risk of casting humility to the side, it was better than good pot roast. Because Diane helped me climb a little up the learning curve.

Now, I still need to learn the difference between a dash and a pinch, but otherwise, I now KNOW how to make a pretty nifty and tasty pot roast. The ribs were a slam-dunk.

Next? I don't know. But, I will look up a recipe because that will be better than my guessing.

Knowing what you don't know and doing something about it. May that mantra never be silenced.

A visit to Shattered Hope, the novel pulsing along

Posted on March 24, 2011 by Mark H Miller

Prologue:

To say he was unhappy with me is an understatement. Actually I weighted the humor more than the truth. It didn't work. I shared the following, "Walter, I'm writing a new book."

He was pleased, he the author of about twenty dozen books on the Old Testament [somewhat more than actual] and certainly the top OT scholar in the country. We sat at lunch in Webster Groves, Missouri. Was there for graduate studies in ministry.

Smiling his approval, "Mark, that's great. What's it about?"

"'Bout all the things in ministry I needed that seminary didn't provide."

He didn't laugh.

That was more than twenty years ago.

The new novel unfolds: Tricia Gleason spends her summer in Frisco, Colorado, her seminary obligation as a summer ministry intern. She planned, using basketball terms, to have it be a slam-dunk. Really, how hard can it be to read Sunday scripture, be a youth group leader, visit the elderly and teach a fly-fishing seminar?

That plan, something about the best laid plans of men and women, crashed her first night when the pastor of the Frisco church informed her that he and his wife were heading out of Dodge for eight weeks so his wife could recover from major back surgery. The erratic pulsing of ministry would be too much for her. She majored in worry.

In a heart-beat life changed for Tricia. NOW she was IT...far more than reading scripture.

424

Great evidence of what seminary hadn't taught Tricia. But, truth reigning, she'd only had one year of seminary classes. What she regretted is she hadn't taken an introductory preaching course, because her first preaching moment was less than a week away...and she knew she wasn't good enough to simply read the phone book for her sermon. She knew that.

But, what she didn't know is that Blake Trimball, a 20 year-old, battling the verbal taunting of his college classmates, plunged into depression. The taunting was triggered because Blake had been arrested for an armed robbery that he hadn't done. No one believed him, except maybe his mother, who winced at the possibility she may be wrong. His father was in Africa helping his clients shoot rhinos, his world being a big-game hunting guide.

More than a slight problem arose: Blake disappeared. Thoughts of suicide were muted but about to be blurted by friends of Blake.

As if that wasn't enough, a couple in the church was found, a murder-suicide according to Sheriff Wilson.

Ohmygoodness, what seminary hadn't taught Tricia. She preached her first sermon—resulted in an applauding congregation. You'd think she just won the Pulitzer Prize of first sermons.

Still, Tricia, pleased at that effort, especially that the phone book was left untouched, isn't sure the Cartwright's went the murder-suicide route. But, that's to be explored in the next chapters. I think.

I'm enjoying the first blush of my new novel, "Shattered Hope," the world of Tricia Gleason. Have even worked in some fly-fishing on a private ranch, a creek that has trout which exceed *the imagination of large trout.*

It may be the novel was triggered by my slap-in-my-face comment to Walter Brueggemann more than twenty years ago: what we need to engage life with that comes from anything but what we were trained for. Tricia's exploding world as summer minister intern is a prime example.

You know?

That's okay. Because life is not a world of cookie-cutting. Especially not for me.

So, here I go…into Tricia's world.

Oh, I forgot an important element. Blake didn't commit suicide. Good for him. And the armed robbery culprit—the guy who really did it—was caught doing it again. Sheriff Wilson, enjoying his second-donut-too-many, notified Tricia of this. For her, it was a burst of joy, what she called Blake's moment of Easter. The challenge, among many, was to get him out of the Good Friday cave…not sure that's possible.

Let me see…*Tricia, be good with your moment. Make carpe diem your experience.*

Been to hell lately?

Posted on March 25, 2011 by Mark H Miller

This was copied from yesterday's Yahoo.com:

By TOM BREEN, Associated Press Tom Breen, Associated Press – March 24, 2011

DURHAM, N.C. – When Chad Holtz lost his old belief in hell, he also lost his job.

The pastor of a rural United Methodist church in North Carolina wrote a note on his Facebook page supporting a new book by Rob Bell, a prominent young evangelical pastor and critic of the traditional view of hell as a place of eternal torment for billions of damned souls.

Two days later, Holtz was told complaints from church members prompted his dismissal from Marrow's Chapel in Henderson.

"I think justice comes and judgment will happen, but I don't think that means an eternity of torment," Holtz said. "But I can understand why people in my church aren't ready to leave that behind. It's something I'm still grappling with myself."

The debate over Bell's new book "Love Wins" has quickly spread across the evangelical precincts of the Internet, in part because of an eye-catching promotional video posted on YouTube.

Bell, the pastor of the 10,000-member Mars Hill Bible Church in Grand Rapids, Mich., lays out the premise of his book while the video cuts away to an artist's hand mixing oil paints and pastels and applying them to a blank canvas.

He describes going to a Christian art show where one of the pieces featured a quote by Mohandas Gandhi. Someone attached a note saying: "Reality check: He's in hell."

"Gandhi's in hell? He is? And someone knows this for sure?" Bell asks in the video.

In the book, Bell criticizes the belief that a select number of Christians will spend eternity in the bliss of heaven while everyone else is tormented forever in hell.

I cannot remember any time in my life—and if it happened, I have buried it for sure, when I haven't had real trouble with people *convinced* they know what happens to us when we die physically. Oh, there are deaths in the weekly journey, at times known as a weakly journey, but what happens when, as a jaundiced friend of mine once intoned, "Time for me to have my toes pointing up and six feet under."

The minister, Chad Holtz, it turns out was sent packing from his North Carolina church because of "other matters, this was the breaking one." Something about a position supporting gay marriage. That doesn't fly in the Methodist Church. Hey, more than with them...with lots of others.

I find it pointless and useless to query *who's going to hell and who isn't?*

Two arguments:

First, I find it ridiculous, actually offensive and profane, to say, "Only if you accept Jesus Christ as your Lord and Savior will you be saved and will you enter heaven." I've written on this before—probably excessively so—contending I refuse to believe in a God who is that myopic in accepting people. To believe that Jesus Christ is the only way to know God is what I call the arrogance of Christianity. Yes, for me, tagging along with the great theologian, Reinhold Niebuhr, *Jesus Christ is the Supreme Revelation of God's Love*, but not the only revelation. Nuf said there.

Second, who gets into heaven? I get biblical on this one, at least how the question might be answered. It's found in I Corinthians 15, when antagonists to the Apostle Paul push him with the question, "Paul, you talk about the resurrection of the body when we die. Tell us, BY WHAT FORM will our body be resurrected?"

I suppose they want to know if they will look better in the heavenly posturing.

Paul is better than good with this. In so many words he responds, "You are asking the wrong question. The question is not, 'By what form will our bodies be resurrected?'; the question is, 'Do you have faith in God that God will cover that base'"?

That works for me. The world today is my focus. What happens to me when I die? Honestly, it's not that I couldn't care less. It's just that the question leads only to a wrinkled brow and in NO WAY helps me with doing what I can for today to be worth more than hell or a damn.

I believe in God. I believe in God's purpose for my life: to live with affirmation and value and generosity. And I believe in making a good dinner for tonight.

And, when my *day is done and the ashes to ashes happens*, I'm not even going to fuss if there's no fly-fishing ahead.

Two Incidents…the good, the bad

Posted on <u>March 26, 2011</u> by <u>Mark H Miller</u>

Two incidents. Within an hour of each other. Not sure if they mean anything, but they've marinated in my mind the balance of the day, so that has to mean something.

The first: a stop at Target. Took a while, but with some help, I got the items needed. Each check-out line was backed up. I got to one…ahead of me was an elderly lady [that means her hair was white like mine] in a wheel-chair provided by Target—the automated chair and the shopping basket. She grimaced and I felt badly for her, but the cashier was more than helpful. Their conversation I could hear—it was perhaps the case the shopper had not purchased the right-sized-shirts for her grandchildren. She commented, "Oh, I'll take these; it's not worth it for me to motor back there."

I continued to feel sorry for her, *Ma'am, it must be tough to be handicapped like that…and then not to get what you really need.* My thoughts were muted, as they should have been.

I only had two items, in bottles, so I didn't worry about shirt-size. I walked out and *look at this*: the elderly lady [still with white hair], drove her handicapped-wheelchair to a corner by the front door, got up and walked briskly [not overstated] to her car. *What?*

I then went to the Fitness Center, and as an aside, my memory lapses are lessening. Today was the 6th straight day for pumping the bicycle and EACH TIME when I left I remembered where my car was. Won't tell you about the 7th time ago.

I walked in and was welcomed by Stephanie at the check-in counter. She seemed to be happy, a beaming face. That most often is her countenance, an "up" person. I am grateful to her because she asked once about the recent book and took some to sell to the 24-Fitness staff. I asked, "You look happy today. That's good."

430

She responded, "Oh, I don't know if you know. But, I've been promoted to Service Manager." I was so pleased for her, "Stephanie, that's wonderful news. Good for you. Your management has shown good judgment. Yes, they have."

Two incidents…each impacted me.

Of course I don't know the detailing of the first situation…maybe the lady REALLY needed the wheel-chair-thingy. It just seemed odd to me how well she walked to her car.

Well, it won't make that big a difference, will it, in the coursing of my life or yours. But, it does seem to me that ALL of life is really incidental… some good and some bad…so the challenge becomes to be who I am and who you are and then some…for better and for much better.

Learning from a grandson

Posted on March 27, 2011 by Mark H Miller

I couldn't help it…pride as a grandfather was in overdrive. I had some time with my grandson, Dylan Miller, Andrew and Jennifer's son. He's between his second and third birthdays. We were walking through the HUGE Bass Pro Outdoor World store west of San Antonio.

The first moment was walking along one of their fishing rod aisles. The reminding note here is I am the self-appointed fly-casting coach for each of my five grandchildren, to become six in August. Dylan looked with that, *Can I hold one?* Now he didn't SAY that, but it's what I read in his eyes. Biased? Okay, but stay with me on this.

I pulled a rod down, handed it to him, and without ANY instruction, sportsfans, he held the rod correctly! Now, I didn't take it and hand it back to see how his memory was working. Once is good enough as you head toward your third birthday.

We started up high-tilting steps. I asked if he wanted help as he reached for the rail, barely grabbing it. He smiled, "Let me try, Grampa Mark." Goodness, how could I ever say let alone think, *no*!

We then saw the stuffed animals, lots and lots of them. He wasn't sure if they were real or not, so he held my hand as if I was the rail by the stairs. He pointed, "Look, Grampa, they aminals."

Inside I couldn't help myself: *Like son like father. For when his father began his first steps in the English language his favorite food, in his version, was either hangibers or bahsketti. Gotta love it.*

Then a moment I probably read waaaaay toooo much in it. We went to Chic-Filet [not sure if I got that spelling right]. Honestly? I'd never been there before, but Dylan's grandparents [they help Andrew and Jennifer in care for Dylan and his sister, Taylor] told me that *chicken nuggets, fries and apple juice* would be all it would take.

I couldn't believe the line to the ordering counter. It appeared that maybe only six or seven kids in San Antonio WEREN'T there…skads of kids.

We made it…they even served food to our booth…talk about service at a walk-up-to-the-counter place.

I had also been told Dylan loved the play room, so following my cue, "Dylan, would you like to play?"

Even before I finished the question he looked over my shoulder in that direction. Nodding his head was his chosen vocabulary.

He took off, went in. I came a tad tardy and he was already sitting on a bench removing his shoes—*the drill.*

He climbed and slid, climbed and slid. Squealed his delight, beaming after every slide.

Then an event.

A little girl fell on her own and started to cry. Dylan stopped. I could see it clearly—this time no grandparenting bias in overdrive—the father picked up his daughter and was effective in helping her.

But, I looked at Dylan.

He then watched…and watched…then went to a window to see the father and the little girl leave the restaurant. I saw in that considerable empathy. A faint smile.

Okay, maybe it was simply curiosity. But in that moment I *sensed* something deeper.

Who knows?

Maybe at 3 it will all change. Maybe at 3 he wouldn't even glance in the injured girl's direction. One never knows…but the difference between what will be…up for grabs…is different than what I hope…that Mr. Dylan will continue to be a caring spirit, now with his eyes, but for all the "then's" in each new day and year, it will be very much his DNA.

Got "fire in the belly?"

Posted on March 28, 2011 by Mark H Miller

Covering a few bases, which is metaphorically apt since the 2011 Major League Baseball season launches this week.

As many of my family and most of my former parishioners know, my support of the Chicago Cubs is never understated. That allegiance birthed when I began ministry in Chicago in 1966. Before that, especially as a child—which means days when the only professional baseball on the west coast was AAA. The Portland Beavers was "it"—for reasons I'm unsure of, I liked the New York Giants. Thought some of their players were beyond cool. Hey, as a 7 year old that word worked. I think.

But now. It's the Chicago Cubs all the way. Even though they haven't won a World Series in more than a century, they're still my team. I even looked up their schedule when I visit my son, Matthew, Sheila and Laura in May. Am disappointed the Cubs are out of town that weekend. Would have been fun to take the family and cheer for the perpetual losing Cubs.

Which takes me to *perpetual losers*. What does that mean? Actually, I think it's more a state of mind. It's how you consider yourself. Yes, people most generally, especially those who are not well balanced in dealing with the wins and losses in life, are overly tilted toward too much self-confidence or self-doubt.

For instance, on a personal level, I've only been on one team that "won." At least in terms of defeating other teams. It was 1962—I've narrated this before—when the Archer Blower and Pipe semi-professional team from Portland, Oregon, won the Semi-Pro World Series in Battle Creek, Michigan. What I remember most about that series is that it was the last time I pitched in a game. A good memory.

But, in the overall scheme of things, being a *perpetual loser* is a mind game. It's how we give to the daily rigors and benefits of life. Certainly in a public manner, all those #1 NCAA men's basketball team seeds who will watch next weekend's Final Four from their living room might be

434

considered losers. In winning the game they are. But, down deep, if I were their coach, I'd want to make sure they knew about their effort, their working together and the way in which they grew. Gosh, that almost sounds preachy.

One other NCAA comment. I think it's great...really great...that a team that was ridiculed for even being selected, Virginia Commonwealth University from Richman, is in the Final Four. And their coach, 34 years young, Coach Smart [a good one-liner would be, *He's not misnamed.*], is now being touted as the most attractive coach to be offered a head coach position at "major" universities.

Am wondering—pretty deep so I'm unprepared to put in print, but I'll glance for a word or two—in talking about my "last pitch," which was in 1962 just before I began seminary, I'm wondering this morning if I've pitched my last sermon. I've always believed that preaching—goodness, ministry in any form [I consider my son, Andrew, a minister in his coaching—helping players to grow and become more aware of their individual gifts.] requires a *fire in the belly*. Right now I think that fire is almost out.

That's not to be lamented or grieved or championed. It's just a "feel" I have right now.

That doesn't make this day...or any past or anticipated...either joyful or grim. It just makes it a day.

And who knows?

Maybe preaching will happen. In large part, "whatever" is the apt response.

But, what isn't "whatever," is to make sure today is more than just another day. And, so, to that end, now that our Silky Terrier, Gracie, has been fed, Diane's sandwich has been made, I get back to my novel, "Shattered Hope."

This will be a trying day for my protagonist, Tricia Gleason. She has her first funeral—a murder/suicide of a popular couple—and dealing with a grieving young woman whose partner was killed yesterday as she was bicycling.

The Sheriff will want to talk with Tricia about the murder/suicide, but she contends her detective hat is in the closet. Tricia will learn that's not all that's in the closet.

But, maybe I won't get that far today.

So, on to the day—another chapter, going to the Fitness Center, and making sure there's quiet time—time for gratitude, for lots of gratitude for the ways in which life happens…and might happen.

For, as I learned from my favorite early morning talk show when a child in Portland, Oregon, *Today well lived makes every yesterday a dream of happiness and every tomorrow a vision of hope. Live well, therefore, in this day.*

Gonna give it a try. Hope you do, too.

A contention: in any day theology's more important than politics

Posted on March 29, 2011 by Mark H Miller

The premise: theology is more important than politics.

The argument's factoring.

Last night President Obama gave us information on his decision to enter the harsh realities of Libya, contending our action, partnered in a modest manner by NATO countries, the prime two are Great Britain and French, kept the slaughter of Libyan people from happening. He went on to indicate we will not send our American boots to that land.

He didn't say, however, how long we intend to be there, how to do an end-run on current Libyan leadership and who the rebels are, their leadership, their goals...and the like.

Before hearing those specifics, in listening on XM to the Catholic Channel, the question was raised, "Do you believe God is in control?"

All of that inroading into my morning thought and it occurred to me that most of us—myself not excluded—thinks primarily in political terms. Generally as a Democrat—in my case—or as a Republican, which includes most of my non-clergy friends. Or, more specifically as a liberal or a conservative.

That impacts not only the war arena, against which I stand in virtually every current account, be it Iraq or Afghanistan—or in the economic minefield, that includes what needs to happen to Social Security amongst other crucial issues, to name medical care as one.

Then it struck me...does it matter who I am politically? Certainly from an ego/hubris level, it does. I am not going to deny that.

But. And this is where I reasoned and faithed this morning, from the deeper perspective of who I am and how am I to order my life, politics is rather the surface, what most of us engage in.

I sense a deeper reality is theology—that is, what is the place of God in how I live and how I regard others.

For, I want and need God to be in control of my life...not to push my arm or unclench my fist with force. No, a thousand times no. For I am not a puppet and God's not a puppeteer. Rather, I want God to be in control of my life as Influence, as Guide, as Presence and as Empowerment.

Let me put this another way, contending that who we are religiously matters the most. You and I have seen, years ago now, the bracelet that had the initials WWJD. *What would Jesus do?*

That's a good start. But, for so many [this is my judgment, please understand that] it was never adequate. It falls far short.

Rather, if I were to wear a bracelet, as a reminder and encourager, it would have these initials: WWJHMD?

Many of you probably already have that figured out...but to help, here goes: *What would Jesus have me do?*

I can only answer that God, if I make it happen, is in control of my life—as I have mentioned, to empower me to live in a responsible and caring and empathetic manner. Because that's how I behold the manner of Jesus.

As far as the rest of the world, that's not for me to say or even comment. Why?

Because I can only impact initially my own manner of living.

How that might affect others is really not for me to say. THAT becomes God's Spirit in action...if it helps others, so be it. If not, at least I tried. At least I did that.

Oh God, please be with me...to guide, to forgive and to partner...so that today is a day well lived...and tomorrow a promise to be realized. Amen.

Getting Jack Nicholson's Autograph
Posted on March 30, 2011 by Mark H Miller

The Yahoo.com article this morning, March 30, 2011, brought back memories—good and funny, although the latter to some is anything but.

Here's the opening paragraph:

Lorraine Nicholson is just 20, but she's already following in the acting footsteps of her famous father, Jack Nicholson. "I think it opens up a lot of doors, but it's up to me to go through them," Lorraine told Access Hollywood Live's Kit Hoover and guest co-host Dean McDermott on Monday of having the Nicholson name in Hollywood.

Actually two reflections. No, make that three.

The first is humorous, at least my take. One of my Chicago friends, back in the 1991-97 second ministry stint in Chicago, offered me two "mid-court up-front tickets" to a Chicago Bulls playoff game; think it was against the Lakers, but that wasn't the prevailing memory. I got to the game early, which personally is my DNA. I'm not one of these *socially tardy* guys.

Most of the box seats on either side were empty. The players hadn't shown up yet for their warm-up drills.

Then a flurry. Something was happening.

I looked over about two rows and saw why: Jack Nicholson walked in. Didn't know it at the time, but he was the most famous if not most earnest Lakers fan. Thoughts didn't trickle, *Wow, Jack Nicholson. My favorite all-time actor. What timing! I'm going to show his film, 'One Flew Over the Cuckoo's Nest' tomorrow night at church, part of our 'Theology of the Movies' seminar. I have always thought—then and now—his portrayal of Randel Patrick McMurphy is classic.*

Thoughts continued, *Why don't I ask him for an autograph?* Couldn't think of any argument against my question.

I walked over and stood right in front of him, almost bumping his knees. Close but not pushy was my sense of it.

He looked at me...well, truth reigning he *stared* at me, eyes not focused, even glazed.

No mind to that.

Realized I had a pen but no paper. Didn't think it right to just give the pen and hope for the best. Reached in my coat inside pocket and found my date book, looked in it and found a deposit slip, not filled out. That was all, literally, in hand.

I handed him the pen and the deposit slip—my version of being creative if not classy, "Mr. Nicholson, my name is Mark and I'm a big fan of yours. In fact, I'm a minister and will be showing 'Cuckoo's Nest' tomorrow night. May I have your autograph?"

He looked at me, eyes still glazed, obviously feeling no pain.

"Mack?"

"No, Mark...M a r k. That's k as in kiss."

He scratched something, took the pen and signed deposit slip, turned around and handed them to the autograph seeker standing behind him.

Ah, a moment of infamy.

The second reflection is, of all the movies I've seen, if I were to take one scene as my all-time favorite, it would be from "Cuckoo's Nest," the marble water table scene when McMurphy [played by Nicholson] tried to move it. Some mental whackos in the Salem, Oregon mental hospital bet he could, others he couldn't. The latter won. The prized moment is when McMurphy left the water table room, looked back over his shoulder and said, with more truth than cynicism, "I tried. Dammit, at least I did that."

Wow.

The third reflection comes from his daughter's comment, *I think it opens a lot of doors, but it's up to me to go through them.*

I like that. In fact, it's an honest declaration...for life is before her. Sure, opportunities abound. Of course directors will give her a second look. Of course. Of course. Many of them follow.

But, what matters, down deep, at least to her...and I hope to each of us: no matter how we get to the new moment in our new day, what matters more than fame and family and academic credentials is our effort, our giving, our walking through that door called *future and opportunity.*

Whether or not we have a deposit slip in our pocket for our next autograph.

Are you happy? Consider this...

Posted on March 31, 2011 by Mark H Miller

In yesterday's Forbes.com an article entitled, "The Happiest Careers in America" made some helpful comments. [March 30, 2011] Meghan Casserly offered this:

A new study reveals employees value coworkers and personal control over compensation.

If you think administrative assistants hate their jobs, think again. A recent survey of the top 10 happiest professions in America, from job site CareerBliss. com, shows that they actually value their work, their colleagues — even their boss — more than dozens of other professions.

To evaluate the data, CareerBliss conducted 200,000 independent employee reviews from 70,000 jobs all over the country to collect 1,600,000 data points on nine factors of workplace happiness. These included the employee's relationship with their boss and co-workers, their work environment, job resources, compensation, growth opportunities, company culture, company reputation, daily tasks and job control over the work that they do on a daily basis.

What the results make clear is that employee happiness doesn't come from high paychecks alone. Instead, the three components of a job that employees overwhelmingly responded were the most important factors in keeping them happy were:

• The specific tasks a job entails on a day-to-day basis

• How much control the employee has over his or her daily tasks

• Relationships with co-workers and customers, including supervisors and colleagues

In fact, according to Heidi Golledge, CEO of CareerBliss, while "Salary is always an important component of every job ... the research shows that money is not enough to keep good employees happy. From the employer's perspective, realizing salary is not one of the key drivers of workplace happiness. Employers focus on the areas which will drive job satisfaction to create a happier environment for all."

It's my guess many would agree. As I consider the "jobs" I've enjoyed the most, the best ones came out on target with having specific achievable tasks and some control over when and how accomplished. The biggest factor, though, in happiness, was in the working relationships. In a specific way, truth emboldened, I could have worked all my life with Fred Trost, Herb Davis, Harriett Martin, Nate Miller and Hollis Bredeweg. Great sharing and supporting and understanding. Great.

To the opposite of that, the very most unpleasant employment experiences came from staff relationships that made getting ahead more important than working together. Or, in one stark time, the minister I worked with was more arrogant than intelligent. His ego dwarfed his heart and all that mattered was for him to be applauded. No need for details, but it's hard for me to imagine a more unworkable staffing. I courted misery. Was funless and joyless.

It occurs to me, the happiness indices—and you may find others more significant—are not only for the workplace. They MUST be in other settings, especially in the family or marriage contexts.

I consider them separately. In family the best time has been, especially of late, with family members who make it their agenda to be helpful and appreciative. When that's absent, when a family member presumes you can be counted on—and you are—and then you never hear again until you are needed. That's a *no thanks* situation.

In marriage, my reflection centers upon how Diane and I grow in our covenant. I've shared before…and I share now…we have a beautiful, powerful relationship, in a significant manner because we understand covenant: *each of us gives our fullest for the good of the relationship.*

That doesn't mean our roles are always the same. That doesn't mean we're without faults. I'm still trying to figure out the difference in a recipe between a pinch and a dash. But, it does mean when we have decisions to make, we are able to make them only after we assess all the options, and more importantly, answer the question, "How does this decision impact EACH of us?"

More can be said…but hopefully this blog will invite others to look at their lives, their place in the work environment, in the home and in other places and occasions and understand why they are happy… and if that lessens, what can be done to stop the drop of goodness and enjoyment?

It has been my experience, looking over the fullness, the best relationship is one that is inter-dependent. Not dependent—one upon the other; not independent, each doing their own thing and if synergy happens it is infrequent and unintended. And certainly not co-dependent. That's the worst, when one person in the relationship needs to make all the decisions, control all the next steps and will not regard others as having value and goodness.

I appreciate the comments from Forbes.com—hopefully they will be catalytic for others.

Now, how about some help on this pinch/dash business?

Winning the Lottery–what next?

Posted on April 1, 2011 by Mark H Miller

You may have read this—or heard about it. Before the narrative, some disquieting caveats:

First, I have never won the lottery, and perhaps have purchased no more tickets than one hand can count.

Second, it is the case—have seen it sufficiently to know that winning the lottery tends to ruin lives, fracture relationships and leave the winners worse off—with regard to emotionality, vitality and a genuine will to live.

Third…my wife, Diane, my day-brightener and beautiful spirit of encouragement now works for GTECH, which means specifically she is in their Austin office on a team managing the Texas Lottery—small print but large meaning: we cannot play the lottery even if we wished. Which we don't.

Now a point in truth. It was just announced that a team of seven Information Technology employees—as they have done again and again, purchased a lottery ticket. The guy who bought the ticket was about to do so, someone barged ahead of him, about which he offered no complaint, purchased a Snickers candy bar then a ticket. That was the winning ticket. EACH of "the team," after taxes, gets $19.1 million.

Happiness.

But, wait.

One of the team, one who only this time decided to not participate, is left without.

Seven get $19.1 million; one gets nothing.

Your take?

This is easy for me…and that may be transparent to the reality that I'm NOT one of the seven winners.

And yet, it's not academic, for I've been in situations when there's been a blessing of additional funds.

The question is: should the 8th be gifted some of the winning monies?

I make the case that he should.

No, he didn't earn it.

Yes, he made a decision not to participate—needs to take his lumps just like the millions and millions who purchased lottery tickets and had no winnings.

I understand.

But, in thinking about it today, I think the seven would end up feeling BETTER if they agreed to EACH gift to their 8th friend/team/member a portion. It wouldn't need to be big. The amount would be less important than the effort. Besides, out of $19.1 million, would an equal portion gifted to Mister Eight be a great sacrifice?

Hardly.

Generosity, at least for me, is a moment of growth…you grow when you give. Never, at least in my experience and theology is generosity a moment of loss.

At least something to think about.

I have to share a postscript: I received a church newsletter today saying the congregation would vote on the pews being removed in order to put in metal card-table chairs, chairs unyielding. In addition the pope was resigning with open nominations from the congregation. Of course. It's April 1, 2011 today. For the members it was a hoaxing newsletter. I appreciated the humor.

For me, even though posted on a Foolish Day, April 1 itself, I don't share my encouragement for seven gifting eight as folly or being disingenuous. In fact, every word is the voice of my heart and pulse of my soul. When writing my nose grew not at all, but hopefully the understanding of the positive correlation of giving and growth will be seen and embodied as verity.

The Cubs and my father…April 2

Posted on <u>April 2, 2011</u> by <u>Mark H Miller</u>

Most of the time…not all, but most…the value of effort is greater than the experience of winning. Certainly winning is essential, lest the sense of self shifts to unapparent. But I've always held that knowing a full effort was given…that measures just fine.

This somewhat lofty paragraph is my way this year to share my strong allegiance and support of the Chicago Cubs. I watched yesterday, April 1, their opening game in Wrigley Field against the Pittsburgh Pirates, a team that for over twenty years has yet to finish above .500. That's unimpressive.

Until the reality of the Cubs is mentioned: last World Series won was in 1908. Friends, that's more than 100 years ago—102 full seasons to be exact.

I watched today—appreciated Robert Redford threw a first pitch. Liked his left-handedness. Liked that Kerry Wood's returned—he received the most enthusiastic applause when introduced.

I appreciated the honoring moment for Ron Santo—he played 3rd base when I became a converted Cubs fan in 1966.

That brought back memories when Fred Trost and I would have a special "study seminar," a nice afternoon at Wrigley rooting on the Cubs. We dined at Franksville—have you eaten where 20 different hamburgers were listed?—our favorite was "#7, heavy on the mayo."

Back to yesterday, opening of the new season. The honoring of Santo—probably the most endorsing Cubs fan and former announcer, he died this past year—was touching. Even though I thought his baseball playing was so much better than his radio announcing, still he was special. A nice touch—and his daughter and son—now adults—sang at the 7th inning stretch, "Take me out to the ball game."

And wadda ya know...the Cubs were ahead and apparently cruising, 2-0.

It didn't last when some guy from the Pirates—I refuse to name him—hit a grand slam homerun, followed by a 2-run homer.

Final score: 6-3 Pirates.

Okay, there are 161 more games. But, honestly? The Cubs might be eliminated from any possibility of wearing championship rings by Memorial Day.

Another season. Down the drain. Hey, I'm not a pessimist as much as a realist.

I won't give up, though. I won't. The theme of *effort important and victory nice* will continue.

Maybe next year?

A little early for that, but having played baseball, knowing a tad or more about it, and watching Soriano strike out again on a ball one foot outside [his pattern last year], and seeing the Cubs drop their first game to Pittsburgh, what can be said?

Wincing was my only response.

Until I noted today is April 2, 2011. As mentioned, 1908 was the last time the Cubs won the World Series.

That's a long time ago.

But, I now realize there's something so much more important about April 2. Because 103 years ago my father was born, April 2, 1908...

He died in 1994 and never ever gave up on the Cubs.

So, why should his son?

Broken Rims

Posted on April 3, 2011 by Mark H Miller

I've got a never-been-proved-theory.

Here goes the launch: *You ask someone to tell you about their life, their origins, their pulsing through each year and their answer will be triggered mostly by how they are feeling in that moment the question's asked. In other words, consideration of the self in the moment says the most about what we choose to recall. If a person's feeling rotten, fractured, dismal, you can be sure the metaphor Good Friday will champion. Or, if a person's feeling on top of the world, Easter will be seen in every vignette.*

I'm feeling the latter this morning.

Watching NCAA's Final Four triggered a memory that could have been bad. But, I'm not feeling that way, so here's the positive twist. I played basketball in high school—and sometimes reached, at least in my mind, the lofty height of mediocrity. I was, maybe if I tiptoed, six feet tall, weighed about 175 [lost forever the last 50 years] and played guard on our Jefferson High School basketball team, Portland, Oregon. Was a starter for two years.

The peak, goal, *greatest achievement* to reach in our world in those days was to make the State Tournament, held at the University of Oregon in Eugene. The moment came back to me last night as Virginia Commonwealth and Kentucky lost, which means Connecticut and Butler will play in the NCAA championship game tomorrow night, Monday, April 4, 2011.

Our basketball team wasn't very "big," the term to indicate very tall centers and forwards. And, it probably could be said, okay in a humorous but truthful way, *we weren't very big, but boy were we slow.*

I remember it rather clearly. We had a play-off game against Franklin High School. Win and go to Eugene. Lose and go home. My last opportunity to look back at mediocrity.

450

The game was played at their gym, but our fans showed up. Loud, even raucous. My primary job was not to score. My primary job was to be, what is termed the *point guard*, to pass well. We had a pretty good scorer—more on him in a moment. Franklin didn't dumb-down on us. They smothered our scorer, which left me alone at the top of the key. No three-pointers in those days, unless you were fouled when making a shot.

They left me alone, so I shot. Why not? It was a play-off game, so expect the unexpected. I don't think surprises ever frightened me. Well, maybe they have, but for another day.

It was beyond me that I made three straight lonnnnnnnnnnnng shots. Well, they were from the top of the key, but in my *not big but slow* world they seemed to have been launched from mid-court.

Franklin didn't get it. They continued to smother our scorer. The fourth shot. Thought recently it would make a good novel title, "Fourth Shot," but didn't think then. The ball arched just fine and I thought, *Wow, eight points the first quarter...on to Eugene.*

But, it wasn't to be. The ball didn't just *clank* off the basket rim; it *broke* it. Never happened before...and as you can assume, never again.

Game stopped. Probably resumed about 30 minutes later, because it took time to find the janitor. But, the only thing that resumed was the game. Not my scoring.

We ended up losing in overtime. I ended up with eight points. Our scorer got 30.

No Eugene. No state tournament.

Now, on this Sunday morning, if I were feeling really crappy, I would focus upon not making it. The story would feature *the broken* rim and how many times I experienced that over the decades. I would focus upon our rival high school, Grant, making the State Tournament most of the time. I would focus upon being a loser.

451

But, not today.

What I'm proud about is that I was Terry Baker's teammate, and probably led our *not big but slow* team in assists as Terry won the state scoring championship. He went on to be, maybe the last, a two-sport All-American at Oregon State University—in football and basketball. He also played baseball. He was unique—threw a football left-handed and a baseball right-handed. Won the Heisman Trophy Award his senior year at OSU. Was drafted by the, then, Los Angeles Rams, but didn't make it. His passes did more ballooning than zooming.

I think of Terry this morning. And I think of Mel Renfro, who was a sophomore at Jeff when I broke the basketball rim, went on to become All-American as a halfback at the University of Oregon, then to All-Pro status for the Dallas Cowboys as a defensive safety. I think of Jim Lonborg, a fellow starting pitcher at Stanford, who went on to pitch for the Boston Red Sox in a World Series, in the 1960's.

So, in telling about *days gone by*, I think of the benefits of where and when of my younger days.

Sure, there's the broken rim. But now, I look at it far differently than I did that night. Just *one of those things*, but not something that changed my life. I won't let it.

How about you? How do you deal with your broken rims?

Value in Losing
Posted on April 4, 2011 by Mark H Miller

I've never seen it, except with Avis, long-ago promotions. I've never seen a college hoop fan [pick any sport for it is apt] look at the camera, see the red light on top go on, and flash two fingers, chortling away, "We're Number Two! We're number two!"

And who would have thought, that with much dismay, shattered visions and slumped shoulders, the players, coaches, families and fans of Connecticut and Stanford women basketball teams now have to pack their bags and return home, not playing tomorrow night in the NCAA Women's Basketball Championship Game.

My guess: NO ONE, except maybe a few parents of Notre Dame and Texas A&M players, had them in the Championship Game.

A truth: of the millions and millions of "bracket-fillers" for the men's NCAA basketball, only one lady got the men's full bracket correct, with Connecticut and Butler the final two. [On that I will root for Butler since one of my fine associates graduated from there. Although I don't fancy their bull dog.]

Back to the theme: not wanting number two. Even more, not winning. Worse but on target yet: losing.

The only worse thing to say than *he's a loser* is to be indifferent. It really is. Some think *hate* is the opposite of *love*. Not so. *Indifference.*

I wrote about "broken rims," how that happens. Today I write about the same with an additional twist: ***Can there be any benefit in losing?***

It's more than a spin to say to those who didn't make the final two but played in the tournament, *After all, you did make the tournament.*

But I'd like something additional, when losing.

The less than modest memory is my first summer of high school American Legion baseball, Portland, Oregon, 1955, when our team declared itself undistinguished with a 1-13 record. I remember being down, I remember reaching up to touch bottom. I remember one parent telling us, "People look at you…and see you as less than meets the eye."

Well, it was rather vivid…preached a few years later.

Still not the major point when losing…actually two points..hopefully pertinent and connectible, because I know of no one who is exempt from losing.

First:

WHAT CAN BE LEARNED? INDIVIDUALLY AND IN A GROUP—MEANING ANY GROUP, LIKE FAMILY, BUSINESS, CHURCH, BOWLING LEAGUE, ANY ATHLETIC TEAM. **How might I have done better?** What are the instances that if I had done B and not A, we would have benefitted? All of life should be teacher.

Second: THERE NOW SHOULD BE NO TEAM IN ANY COLLEGE SPORT, NO MATTER IF THEIR RECORD IS BOTTOM-FEEDER, WHO DOESN'T HAVE MORE HOPE THIS MORNING THAT MAYBE **THEY CAN MAKE IT.**

Think of this: tonight when Butler and Connecticut face off, neither of them was ranked #1 or #2 in the brackets.

Last night the Texas A&M coach—I like his humor when interviewed during the game told the interviewer, Rebecca Lobo, a great college basketball player herself, that Texas A&M "could use you tonight—we'd be better." I also like when he said how GOOD it is for women's basketball that the perennial favorites [Stanford has been to the last four Final Four] aren't playing for the championship. On target. He really is.

All this on a Monday morning…

454

To learn, no matter the situation. And to have hope.

Finally, to never lose a sense of humor. I conclude with an e-mail this morning from one of my favorite clergy colleagues, naming him "Jimmy," which know he will love…hopefully. In reading about breaking rims, in reading about managing when you don't do well, he wrote, in reference to our seminary days in New Haven, when one of the alternatives to study and class was to play in our four-on-four basketball league:

Mark-O,

I have almost no basketball stories, but I did play on the Bellamy Hall "B" team with Gary Hartpence. We had an unblemished record that year: not one single win. One game I hit two whole baskets, breaking no rims.
Jimmy

Sense of humor—final reminder this morning—the Stanford alumni listened to Jack Curtis, the new football coach. The alumni expected Stanford to win, win, win. This was in the 1950's. Curtis made a short but never forgotten statement in answer to the question, "How's the team, Coach?" He twisted his mustache, waited and then offered, "Well, we won't be very big; but we sure are slow."

Love it…why? Because not everybody in every instance can be Number One. But, no matter, everybody can give their fullest, everybody can learn, and if you are slow, there's walking, and that has its value. Just ask any doctor.

Truth of life: Time to go fly-fishing

Posted on <u>April 5, 2011</u> by <u>Mark H Miller</u>

I don't remember the source, but the substance took. *Your teachers don't always need to be those who hold chalk and write on blackboards.*

That just happened this morning, Tuesday, April 05, 2011. My first action [yes, overstated] is to feed Gracie, our Silky Terrier, make Diane's sandwich for lunch and heat up a cup of coffee. Then it's on to thoughts about yesterday. Paramount is my regret that Butler didn't win—but even more they set a record for the lowest field goal shooting percentage in the history of NCAA Men's Basketball Division I Championship games. I also thought of the ache—deep and going deeper that each Butler player, coach, family and fan must feel this morning. Have been there and experienced that. Terrible anguish.

Thought of writing about that, but wasn't sure words would work. Went to e-mail and to my surprise, not to my expectation, I read the following and it preached to me...on two levels. It comes from a fishing webpage. Of the many I get, it often is the best written and most thoughtful. Read on...

Finally, Dry Fly Fishing

The weather may be sunny or snotty — you never know what you're going to get when April finally rolls around. But even the nastiest April is still the start of trout season in much of the country, and that's a good thing no matter what the conditions.

By the end of the month, many of us can expect to finally start having some reliable dry-fly fishing. This is the kind of fishing that many anglers long for most keenly during the short, cold days of January and February. For the dry-fly diehard, no other form of angling is as exquisite or exciting as action at the surface, the one-on-one showdown between angler and trout.

You squint at the stream to identify the insects drifting perilously downstream atop trout-infested water. Maybe you know at a glance what they are, or maybe you don't and need to run down a checklist to pick the right imitation: How big is it? Mayfly (upright wings) or caddis (down wings and no tail)? What color? You check your box and search out the fly closest in appearance to the natural.

But you also know that presentation is just as important as pattern, maybe more important. Your fly has to float downstream as naturally as a fallen leaf. So you stalk into position, in a spot where there are no fast currents between you and your target that will drag your fly off course.

Three ways it touched me.

First, I ALWAYS [emphasis real] value good writing, try to learn from it. Even though pretty early this Tuesday morning, eyes blinking open although more gradually than normal, the *Finally, Dry Fly Fishing*, commentary flowed well and, in my own experience, was accurate. The writer knows well.

Second, it went to the center of my heart, making clear how much I LOVE to fish, especially with Diane. And, of the fishing options before us, truth fully stated, our favorite fly-fishing for trout is in Colorado and with a close second, Montana. It is also the case close friends are making it clear: we should add a third venue, Wyoming. And along with the encouragement is an invitation to stay at their B&B. I mean, really, there are some invitations that should never be refused.

The second point, though, strikes at one of my passions: to fish. I don't lack biblical reference in that the disciples were fishing when Jesus called them as partners in the world of recognizing the pain of others and doing what you can to reduce that pain. It also strikes me [like the verb?] they went *back to their nets* when Jesus was crucified, spent the entire night fishing, ended up with empty nets, met Jesus [they didn't know it was he] and followed his directive to go back out, throw the nets to the other side of the boat. Ah, full nets happened.

That's how Diane and I feel when we wade or drift a river, casting that dry fly, watching it float. When we are successful in the casting, it's as if the fly is unattached, bobbing and dancing with the current….. then BAM, FISH ON. The river turns from placid to exploding when the trout attacks the dry fly. And the battle is on. Pretty flat-out real and inspirational and….well, I think you get it.

And then the third [hey, most sermons have 3 points—is in my DNA when writing also] lesson this morning comes from the script itself: *But you also know that presentation is just as important as pattern, maybe more important.*

How true, how true. The presentation is how you cast. Okay, that's obvious, but push that reality to "the way you live." For in your living, there is presentation, there is gesture, there is statement.

But, life is more than presentation. The *pattern* is the fly used—whether dry or nymph [surface or down deep]. And for me, hopefully in your own life no less, the pattern is the substance, the centering of your life, the values in your heart, the pulse of your soul. It is the centering of who we are…that in my understanding, is understood by whose we are.

Pattern. My identity, my faith, my centering personhood, my very being.

More than fancy words. It's the full reality of the day, the living, the manner.

And. To move from metaphor to reality, it's April…and when followed by May and then summer and fall…wow, FISH ON! LIFE ON!

A way of being better: keep less.

Posted on April 6, 2011 by Mark H Miller

We have a neighbor, Stephanie, who helps in many ways. She gives us contacts for housecleaning and landscaping. [Admission: for house-husbanding, my ineffectiveness is in trimming trees and bushes and dusting all the corners.] She shows interest in how we are. She always wants to know, especially when Diane was hospitalized these past 12 months, what she and her family could do for us. Caring. Genuine. Valued.

This all came together last night when Stephanie sent each of us in the cul-de-sac an invitation to donate clothes, pictures [old fishing rods, maybe?] for a garage sale with proceeds being donated to the local elementary school student activity fund.

We wrote her with our appreciation for her invitation [and ALL her help the two years of our residency in Austin] and our willingness to contribute.

Not sure why, but this idea of gifting, of working with others to bring benefit took me back to a new venture during my last pastorate.

It was circa 1991-97, Elmhurst, Illinois. Some in the church—read that part of my staff and some of the Church Council—thought the idea would "result in no interest." That was the polite version.

But, since I come out of the school of "why not" rather than "how?" we went for it. I figure the *how* will happen. And, honestly, it usually does.

The invitation went like this: Would our church provide a meal, one night a month, for up to 250 people at a Soup Kitchen, sponsored by one of our denomination's churches? The deal was we'd purchase and prepare the food in our church kitchen, transport it [about 40 minutes drive] to the soup kitchen, then serve the food. Many of those being served counted on this evening meal. It was their only meal of the day.

We made the announcement one Sunday morning before each service, asking people to work one night, to see how it would go for them. There would be six people to prepare, deliver and serve the meal.

Following the coffee hour after the second service I was amazed...really. Forty-eight people signed up.

The abundance of volunteers led to a new twist of complaining...some people not happy because they needed to wait six months before they could help. Love it.

Then a couple came forward, "Mark, we want to gift our church portable food warmers, so no re-heating is necessary at the soup kitchen."

What does this mean?

Personally, it means when I go through what we want to contribute, I will enjoy doing it, because it will be of benefit to others.

But. Even more importantly, that experience of having so many sign up [and NO ONE dropped out during my ministry in coordinating the program of serving] indicated to me that people NEED to have something to do for others. They really do. All it took was a game-plan and an invitation. The incredible sign-up made it clear: helping others is important to experiencing value in living.

Put another way, I believe what this means is the best way to care for your self, for my self, for our own individual self, is to care for someone else, for others, for those we may never see.

It doesn't matter who ends up wanting my shirts at the garage sale. What matters is the gifting will bring value to the person who wants my shirt and added resources for the children in our elementary school.

Talk about a good deal...yes, indeed.

Game on.

Dealing with hate and evil
Posted on April 7, 2011 by Mark H Miller

Maybe it's just *preacher-speak* and maybe it means nothing, but I offered it anyway, the only quote I know from St. Augustine. Goes like this, his manner of facing the enemy, the one for whom forgiveness, at best, is a bad idea: **More than not, it's our enmity and not our enemies that does us in.**

I have no quarrel with that…hating someone is self-eroding, is self-contaminating, to coin a word, is self-unelevating.

I thought of Augustine but didn't quote him recently, when……………

A friend called, one of the kindest, most understanding, tolerating persons I know. In fact, to quote someone else, Bill Coffin, and I know more than lots of quotes from him [they work every time], she is a person who, if she told you HER sins—well, it would be like being pelted to death by popcorn.

The concern, that very evidently was guilt revisited and revisited ad infinitum was clear, "Mark, this man was as bad and gross and….yes, even evil, more than anyone I know. He was a neighbor…and a cousin to boot.

"He died. But, it was outrageous and I boiled inside because so many people stood up at his funeral and extolled his virtues. There were none. Did I say I boiled inside? Now, he's dead. And, I've got this anger toward him and guilt toward myself. It's terrible. What do I do?"

Thoughts raced like a car ahead of the pack at NASCAR, *Whoa, what do I do? This friend "boils" inside? Goodness, I never thought she'd get riled up beyond a twitch, or a flutter of her stomach. I recalled the Augustine quote…she was his best illustration…and Coffin…another illustration of understanding…and I knew, because there are legions of us in echo, "Sometimes easier to love the neighbor than some family members." And, I had no doubt that evil lurks in the hearts and actions of…dare I think*

461

it…EACH of us. The real trouble is when the lurking becomes the actual lunging. She related this man was so evil he bragged that he drove off the road to hit a dog and let it writhe to its death. Now, that's evil. I recalled the Railroad Killer, the one who took a sixteen-pound sledge hammer and pummeled to death one of my clergy and his spouse while they were sleeping. And, it jumped at me, I remembered the closest I came to evil as a child—when a neighbor boy, about my age, tied two cats together by their tails, hung them over a clothes line, dowsed them with gas and lit a match. Now, THAT'S evil. All of that tsunamied in my mind. It's obvious, though, my preacher-speak, especially…well, nothing came to me. Ever felt helpless, literally, when someone needs you?

"Mark, I never confronted him. And now. He's dead. I cannot say that's a good thing. Who am I to say things like that? I know. We will all die. But, my concern now is I didn't care enough to talk with him about my dislike of him. And now, I don't know what to do, because he wasn't all bad…and some of what was said at his funeral was probably true—at least somewhat. I just never experienced it. But, now, I'm filled with guilt and yes, still anger, and yes…."

Then it struck me. *Dump it. Jettison. Get rid of it. Don't let it be self-consuming.*

So I finally offered to my friend, "Have a suggestion. Think about it. Go off by yourself somewhere…or in a room. But, be by yourself. So it's just you and God. Offer your thoughts, your wrath, your fury and your guilt to God. And ask God to take it from you. Tell God your regrets, your wish you had done it differently. Give God your *should list*, and ask God to take over all that. God has big shoulders and a heart that has no limits—but is always with you. Let God take it from you.

"Why do I say this? Because, quite honestly valued friend, I believe guilt is self-judgment and grace is God's judgment. Let God's grace take your guilt…and that hopefully will be of benefit."

She was very grateful, had not thought in those terms before.

Was I right? Hey, I may not be sleepless this morning, Thursday, April 7, 2011, but I am clueless.

Except.

What I shared I believe in my heart...about guilt and grace.

And, what I also know in my heart...the soul experiences well-being when grace pushes guilt away.

Yep, I believe that.

God's judgment of me is MUCH more important and vital and vitalizing than looking in a mirror.

You choose: crazy, inane, stupid...or necessary?

Posted on April 8, 2011 by Mark H Miller

No common vocabulary will mention it. Most of us, until consulting with a dictionary, don't know what it means. And yet, the word, both definitively and functionally makes for a stronger self.

In fact, it is a word that keeps most relationships unfractured. Most marriages reside in the place called civility when this action is experienced.

Any ideas?

Before the definition comes, an example....in a recent Yahoo.blog by Chris Chase...perhaps you read it, or heard it on a news or human interest program.

It's about a 10-year-old boy, Cliff Forest, Jr., who took $8,500 from his college fund reserve, to buy William "The Refrigerator" Perry's Super Bowl XX ring. Cliff saw the ring at Mickey Mantle's Restaurant in New York. Cliff Forest, Sr., father, said he wouldn't have approved his son's spending, "but his mother is a little more soft-hearted," he said.

Perry, a former Chicago Bears defensive lineman, had put his ring up for auction in 2007 for reasons unknown.

Here's the twist: Soon after buying the ring the younger Cliff heard about Perry's battle with Guillain-Barre syndrome, an autoimmune disease that can cause paralysis. Figuring the former football star would be happier with the ring, Cliff set out to return it.

"He only played in one Super Bowl," Cliff, Jr. said. "I thought he would want it more than I did"

The Chase article continued, *Cliff was unsuccessful in his attempt to get in touch with Perry. It wasn't until his mother started working the phones and set up a meeting before an autograph session in Chicago that Cliff was able to complete his good deed. He took a flight to Chicago, met Perry and handed him the ring. Cliff got two signed jerseys with the note, "The Fridge, Thanks!" and five signed football cards. "He was very appreciative and he said, 'thank you,'" Cliff said.*

What struck me in this...within the maize of protest that his spending $8,500 from his college reserve fund was an inane, foolish thing...is the importance of his heart's voice over possession of the ring itself.

For sure—and is there anyone within reading distance who cannot name some "inane, foolish thing" that is still in our possession—for *whatever reason* having the Fridge's ring was tremendously important to Cliff. To him it was worth it.

Throw away his age. He knew what he wanted.

But.

He read of Perry's illness [And, personally, having known someone, a close friend, who was comatose for months with this disease I can offer it's unrelenting, and at times, fatal.], came to the conclusion he should gift the ring back to Perry. He probably didn't know why Perry sold it. One could guess financial need.

Still, chiding and protest from others aside, here's what secures me to this story, the important word that makes for wholeness. Down deep I believe this word is operative in what Cliff Forest, Jr., did:

It is this: ***unrequited.***

Defined as

1. not returned or reciprocated: *unrequited <u>love</u>.*
2. not avenged or retaliated: *an unrequited wrong.*
3. not repaid or satisfied.

I don't know William Perry, or any of the players. And I surely wouldn't have interest in purchasing his Super Bowl XX ring.

But, that's not the point.

I believe in the centering of my heart that Cliff bought the ring for himself and would treasure it. Then, he read of Perry's medical struggles and thought it would be better to gift the ring. I don't call it *soft-hearted*. I call it *truth-hearted*. And I don't believe for a minute that this 10-year-old figured his gifting would be his 15-minutes-of-fame. I don't believe he gifted the ring so he could get something back from Perry. I believe he gifted the ring without the need to be reciprocated. He gifted the ring because of Perry's need.

That, it seems to me, is the quintessence of love, gifting something, sharing something, telling someone something, putting time, sweat and energy into something for someone else, not expecting something back.

Oh, we do expect something back, that's the human thing.

But, I believe, when we give unrequitedly, there's a shift in our life, in our world, in our very being. I believe that shift is when the human becomes holy.

Unrequited.

It works. Go ahead and try it. You will be more than surprised. You will be amazed at how selfless gifting is the way someone might receive it and sense, *Whoa, could this be an angel impersonating a human being?*

Recently some from the blog readership have asked if the blogging will be put into a book and if there are books previous to my blogging that have similar themes and writing style? In short form the answer to both questions is *yes*.

I am grateful for the inquiries, because it gives me a chance to list previous books. Because I do not know who specifically reads the blog [yesterday it reached 300], I use this day, Saturday, April 9, 2011 as posting of that information. Tomorrow will resume the regular blogging.

Also, one other comment, albeit personal, but stay with me on this. As I've mentioned in at least one previous blog, I'm no longer preaching, having concluded, at least for now, interim ministries. Diane pointed it out—and hopefully she's spot on with this—"Mark, the blogging has become your pulpit." Yikes, that's not how I looked at it...but hey, maybe/hopefully she's correct. Honestly? In whatever way the blogging helps in the journey, I am grateful. At the very least.

Now, if anyone wishes to track down the earlier books, those that precede last October when my daily blog began, here's the information:

Books on Epistles:

Road Signs On the Way To Fishing No longer available through the United Church of Christ printer. I have some copies, so if interested, please let me know, markhmiller@att.net

Cast Your Nets Available from www.amazon.com; www.authorhouse. com; and my personal web page, www.drmarkhmiller.com

Hooked On Life Available through the publisher, www.whitefishpress. com; www.amazon.com and my personal web page.

I do have some copies [modest amount] of each of these at home. If interested, can autograph and mail to you for cost/book of $20, including postage. Please let me know.

Murder/mystery novels:

Murder On Tillamook Bay, a Tricia Gleason Novel Publisher indicates will be printed and available early this summer from www. whitefishpress.com; www.amazon.com and my personal web page.

Although *nothing's in writing*, my publisher, Dr. Todd Larson, and I are exploring the possibility of publishing novels completed, **Mask of Sanity, Second Tricia Gleason Novel; No One Is Innocent; and Joshua's Secret**. I'm closing in on identifying the murderer in my new novel, **Shattered Hope, Third Tricia Gleason Novel** very soon and will add that to the publishing options.

Enough for now, but did want to share what's available. Thanks in advance for interest you may have.

Go, Tricia!

Peace,

Mark.

A Kind Face of Humanity

Posted on April 10, 2011 by Mark H Miller

I received the following from my life-long friend, Doug White, who in turn received it from his son, John. The humanity of people can be evidence of a greater good. A better value. A consideration that we each have our strength and vulnerability. Not to deny the latter but to champion the former. And, who knows, perhaps each of us, in the manner we have responded to the more critical community and/or personal moments of crisis, have echoed what we now read. I hope.

10 things to learn from Japan

1. THE CALM

Not a single visual of chest-beating or wild grief. Sorrow itself has been elevated.

2. THE DIGNITY

Disciplined queues for water and groceries. Not a rough word or a crude gesture.

3. THE ABILITY

The incredible architects, for instance. Buildings swayed but didn't fall.

4. THE GRACE

People bought only what they needed for the present, so everybody could get something.

5. THE ORDER

No looting in shops. No honking and no overtaking on the roads. Just understanding.

6. THE SACRIFICE

Fifty workers stayed back to pump sea water in the N-reactors. How will they ever be repaid?

7. THE TENDERNESS

Restaurants cut prices. An unguarded ATM is left alone. The strong cared for the weak.

8. THE TRAINING

The old and the children, everyone knew exactly what to do. And they did just that.

9. THE MEDIA

They showed magnificent restraint in the bulletins. No silly reporters. Only calm reportage.

10. THE CONSCIENCE

When the power went off in a store, people put things back on the shelves and left quietly

Measuring Success

Posted on April 11, 2011 by Mark H Miller

"The measure of success is what you've recently accomplished," said Phil Jackson, following the Los Angeles Lakers' 5th straight defeat.

This quote from Phil Jackson triggered some thoughts. Not sure why, but what's working inside the heart and soul, in addition to figuring out if Tricia will stay in ministry [my current novel], is my battle with politicians. Frankly [is there any other way?], I found it worse than negative how EACH person, no matter their party, including President Obama, played, again and again the *blame card* as the possibility of a government shut-down appeared likely.

I guess it was the cynical side of me that always thought—that's the truth—a shut-down wouldn't happen. Which made, at least for me, the preceding blames and disclaimers nothing less than folly.

Rather than seek a vote that served, what James Baker said yesterday on CNN, "the national interest," it was, in the face of anticipated defeat, posturing on how it wouldn't be YOUR fault—it's THEIR fault.

That disgust, in an unexpected way partnered with Phil Jackson, who, along with a few others, excels in victories.

So, I ask…and perhaps you do also: **What, on this Monday, April 11, 2011, does it mean to be successful?**

Phil Jackson offers the first answer: success and victories are synonymous. Most believe that is the primary measuring stick. You don't believe me? Just ask any alumni about his/her football team. Talk to the women basketball head coaches at U Conn and Stanford and Notre Dame.

The dictionary gives us some options:

First, the favorable or prosperous termination of attempts or endeavors.

Second, the attainment of wealth, position, honors, or <u>the</u> like.

I get caught up in that.

I.E. If you have more money than I, does that make you more successful? If you are the President of my denomination and I'm not, does that make you more successful? If I never made "Most Likely to Succeed" [which is true] in high school, does that make me less successful?

Example: I continue to get newsletters from churches I served, and from clergy colleagues I admire. Honestly, the latter is more helpful than the former. In the latter—and two for sure are Joanne Carlson Brown in West Seattle and Ed Middleton in Dallas—there is an emphasis upon living a good life that reflects caring, compassion and generosity.

In the former the newsletters, in an almost droning manner, let their congregations know about church meetings that need to do something about budget atrophy, all the while offering numbers on worship attendance [as you can imagine dwindling rules the day] that are less today than yesteryear.

So, does that mean I was unsuccessful in my term of ministry in those churches? Does that mean their current leadership is less than meets the eye?

My first, gut reaction is affirmative to each.

I realize, however, I'm wrong on this…and it takes the dictionary as my instructor.

…to the last dictionary definition of *success*:

Obsolete . <u>outcome.</u>

That helps. Considerably. For success is not about results; it's about effort. Success is not about more in attendance; it's about more in faithful ministry.

To put it more directly. The best answer to, *Are you a successful person?*—is not anything less than how you live in matters of integrity and fidelity and effort.

It's nice to know the dictionary preaches…claiming that a definition of success no longer has to do with outcome.

The question is, do we believe that?

Because, and I'm not preaching to the choir on this, I'm preaching to myself. Can I care less about the outcome and more about the fullness of effort?

Maybe.

Maybe not.

At least it's something to work on, because even at 70 who wants to be obsolete?

Do people change? Probably not.

Posted on April 12, 2011 by Mark H Miller

For one who has trundled along the path labeled *ordained ministry* for more than a few weeks, for one who's been privileged and cursed to field the questions, loving affirmations and scathing tirades of church members and clergy, what I'm going to say now may be anathema for at least any good-seeking, other-considering readers.

Believe me, this is not a tease.

Oh yes, I'd rather tell you about my back-bouncing-eggs for Spring Chinook Salmon trip, fishing with Zorba in late April, losing to the current in his 22-foot sled boat in hopes the nibble from the salmon will turn to slashing and then water exploding as a 28 pound chrome-bright salmon enters the fray. Or about ten days in Colorado late July or three days on the Olympic Peninsula in November, or about the mantra, illusion *yes*, but oh so favorable even more *yes*, that the days of fishing are not counted toward the days you will live—in fact, it's a credit system. That is the more you fish the longer you'll live. Don't believe me? That's fine.

I'd rather muse on all that, and, down deep, even more about next Sunday, when our granddaughter, Taylor Miller will be baptized in San Antonio. But, I won't. Tell you about fishing, or about whether Tricia solves what has turned from a homicide/suicide to a murder/murder or about Taylor, although to say she's a happy child, greeting all of life with waving hands and a melting smile, is an understatement.

This morning, after getting some e-mails that had negative slants and a call or two that leaned toward disfavor, here is my unproven theory: **Down deep people don't change.**

My theory, experienced by experience, is probably like Swiss cheese, holes but not holy. And, if my theory has any veracity, then why ministry? If people are who they are and they don't change, why bother?

What prompts my thought is thinking about the road traveled. I do that a lot in these early days of retirement, re-thinking how I reacted to situations that were on either edge of the good or evil occasions, of church members whose ability to complain never changed. Of people…

Here's my concern: people, to the core, have basic manners of living that are "set," and tend to not really vary. Oh, there may be glimpses of change, like a flash of lightning, but the resulting thunder tends to be patterning of earlier times.

For instance, I am not in a good position—geographically—to attend many family functions. But, when I do, I have yet to visit with any relative who is different, in terms of temperament, attitude, opinion and fashion. It's as if the conversation last year echoes, almost to the same topics as the conversations fifty years ago.

Of course this needs to be anonymous, lest someone reads this and knows I'm talking about him or her.

People are who people are and essentially they don't change.

Other words: Nurse Ratchet is Nurse Ratchet. Lucy McCorkle is Lucy McCorkle. I can mention the former because she personifies the entrenched person whose will must prevail, who believes viability comes from controlling others. Lucy? I've mentioned her before, as she journeys in life toward her 100th birthday, living in Denver, who ALWAYS sees the good and value. She's never met a glass that was half-empty.

And yet. Make that, and double-yet.

What I must say, is that even though I can illustrate my *others don't change theory* ad infinitum, down deep I've never been swayed to not give my best to help someone, to try to understand the bemoaning tirade on what a terrible minister I have been or to visit them in prison… after their promise to do better in life was shattered. And to hold out hope, their lives are not stuck in cement.

Yes, there are times, when life's frustrations are almost a guarantee. Or someone can be depended upon to be understanding and tolerant and caring and helpful. [I know who those are in case the shadows are too ominous.]

But, it's a battle within for me. And I'm sharing it this morning...

So far, it's only been a theory unproven. Thought but not acted upon.

Why?

Because I learned from my mother...and now from the most wonderful wife in the world...what matters the most is not whether or not people change. What matters the most is if my life, my words, my actions, my very living is neither factored nor influenced by the likelihood people don't change. Why? Because I'm very focused that change is not my agenda. Caring is. Being kind is. Being generous is.

Because the day I don't care...well, hopefully that won't ever be.

For goodness and hope, may it be the same for you.

Care.

Because in the final analysis it's really a God-matter on changeability.

Not mine. Or yours.

Pitching in a field of anger

Posted on April 13, 2011 by Mark H Miller

Saw most of the Chicago Cubs-Houston Astros on television last night. My Cubs [it's okay to be possessive about this.] looked, quite honestly and accurately, no better than an AA league team [two levels below major league skills]. Dreadful. Not a good game. 11-2 is a pasting.

That then took me to an incident in my life—a real downer—I don't believe I've ever shared. It went like this:

I was a sophomore at Stanford and had been penciled in as the starting pitcher in our first league game—was in Los Angeles against the Bruins of UCLA. It was an honor.

Now, please understand Stanford was a better school than a baseball team. To say we underwhelmed held truth. Once in a game or two we actually whelmed. But. You understand, I'm pretty sure.

My pre-game ritual was the same...to be by myself, jog to loosen up, stop and pray—never for victory but for my best effort—and then warm-up. Took about 15 minutes.

I then went to the dug-out to focus on the first UCLA hitters.

Then it happened. The sunlight left, a shadow covered me. Caused by a fellow pitcher, also a left-hander, who had transferred to Stanford for his last two years—was a junior and thought HE should have started our first league game.

I thought he was to wish me a good game, a full effort, teamwork and all that.

I was wrong.

"You aren't worth spit. [Not what he said, but this is a G-rated blog] You won't last. You don't deserve to be starting pitcher. You're an embarrassment. You're a failure."

477

He turned and walked away, spit for emphasis—missed my shoes.

Then I recalled how this person was hostile toward everyone—I just happened to be the target that day. He used his spit on the ball for advantage, never was caught. And when no one was looking [except a few of us], when he pitched, he would kick dirt over the pitcher's mound—started white with chalk but by the 2nd inning it was a flat dirt pitching plate. He then stood to pitch…about 2 feet closer to the plate. Never was caught.

Back to the game—by this time in my less than famous career, I had learned to pitch a slider…somewhere in velocity between a curve and fastball with a slight dip at the last moment—a reliable *get a grounder for a double play* pitch.

The game went well, until the 6th inning—think it was. UCLA figured me out, the slider didn't slide and the curve ball was flat and the fastball…well, you get the idea.

Coach Fehring walked to the pitcher's mound which meant I would leave the game. But, it was proper I wait until the relief pitcher arrived. It was my antagonist. He didn't smile; he sneered. Coach Fehring didn't hear him, "See, you don't have it…never did."

I looked him in the eye as Coach Fehring handed him the ball. I saw hate and contempt and arrogance.

Don't remember what I said, but I know…and it was all I could muster, it wasn't a returned sneering statement. Was something like, "Go get 'em."

I thought of that last night as I watched the Cubs—Russell their pitcher, for his first start, was really not "on," but the team together was even less "on." They were miserable. They lost.

Back in 1960 we lost that game to UCLA.

And then I realized...*I have this season and two more years to pitch. Cannot let the other guy get my goat. Have to play within myself...have to finish.*

What happened to Mr. Spit? He never made it, was always sneering and hostile and dropped out of school. He did sign a professional baseball contract but didn't last one season.

I never signed a baseball contract—not because I believed what my antagonist said. No, it was simply my judgment that I wasn't that good.

My point, though, for every one of us...there will be people who chide, who sneer, who spit. They can be engaged, they can be confronted.

But.

I chose to work on the slider, the fast ball, the curve...and then work on pitching from the pulpit.

And I can say...I wasn't the best...and I wasn't necessarily the winner... but, thanks be to God, I've been able to finish...and that is what counts.

Thoughts about Faith from Diane

Posted on April 14, 2011 by Mark H Miller

Dear Blog Readers: Diane shared a reflection. Wanted to send it your way… thoughts about dealing with life's challenges. Enjoy! Mark.

What is the heading of one's life…do all the subtitles add up to one's banner? Is one's life deemed unsuccessful without that banner in large caps? Have you lived a life of capital letters or one of small print? Or perhaps, to see one's life one needs to read between the lines. Does it matter….does it matter to you?

Today coming into work, listening as usual to the Catholic Channel, Greg and Jennifer were sharing a real life moment in their lives. Jennifer was on a roller coaster for too many minutes of the day with home schooling for 4 boys and as co-host of a weekly radio show. She was overwhelmed with the workload, the chaos, the challenges of a working mother and wife. Should she quit the homeschooling of her boys, should she leave her job at the radio show and have her husband move that forward?

There was much crying and the associated tears, there was anger and eventually through reading, journaling and prayer there comes peace and happiness.

What was the turning point? Who was the turning point? As always there comes an answer if we are willing to turn over our problems to God.

It can be so easy to love God and yet so difficult to serve Him and to trust our everyday lives to Him.

"Yeah, I'll let you know when I need you, but I think I've got it covered for the most part." Isn't that what many of us think and how we live? Is it a function of trust, a function of faith or lack of it or is it a bigger issue…perhaps arrogance?

Jennifer decided to turn her problem over to God believing that He would guide her through. It's very human to get to a point in our lives when we can't handle the situation we find ourselves looking to something, someone bigger than ourselves, bigger than our universe. The more difficult problem can even become how do we listen to God? Do you hear God talking to you, guiding you, loving you? Are you listening?

The roar around us stops us from hearing our God…the intentional and unintentional. Could it be you are afraid of the answer from God?

Diane D. Miller

April 14, 2011

Words Ahead of Thoughts

Posted on April 15, 2011 by Mark H Miller

Ever said something before thinking…or calculating the possible consequences? Most of the time, footnoted throughout most sputtering, the result is less than desired, a massive *oh no!*

However. Once in a while the word before the thought ends up closer to the graded A than F.

Carly Gilstrap [what a name, right—fit for a novel someday] was our "Civics/Local Government" teacher our senior year in high school.

Her favorite mantra, offered toward the end of one of her "clean up the city and get legal efforts" was, *I don't tell everything I know.*

Somewhere toward the end of my senior year—maybe this very month, April, circa 1958, Miss Gilstrap [decades before the Ms. Moniker became apt] took on private garbage dumps in Portland, Oregon.

It would be extra credit for some of our students—those teetering on not making it—if they went on a "special field trip" with Miss Gilstrap to check out a local, and in her judgment [which turned out to be true] unlicensed neighborhood garbage dump. The pictures of two of our classmates and Miss Gilstrap holding up what was much more than a mouse [think you can imagine] from the illegal dump made the local paper.

She shared the adventure with our class.

Well, my father was a garbage man and knew about the illegal dump. He never used it, but still, he was aware.

So, words blocks ahead of thought, I raised my hand, "Miss Gilstrap, my dad's a…."

She smiled in appreciation…I could sense her mind ticking, *This can be good additional information, so I'll get it from Mark.*

She asked me some pertinent questions, and finally, she asked, "Can you tell me the names of the dump owners?"

I looked blank.

"Mark, did you hear my question?"

I nodded.

"Good. Please share that information."

I shook my head…side to side, not up and down.

"Why not?"

"Miss Gilstrap, I don't share everything I know."

I then thought, *Oh no, I'm sunk…glad my college application has already been accepted.*

She locked in her stare.

Then, she started to clap and pointed to the class: "Class, that's EXACTLY what I'm talking about."

The only sound, at least that I remember, was the HUGE sigh of relief I exhaled.

Two months later the final grades came out. Miss Gilstrap didn't give me an F.

Words before thoughts. It doesn't always work out…but once in a while.. well, actually once…it did.

I loved Miss Gilstrap…feisty, never held-back in seeking justice. And, good for her and phew for me, she told me later, privately, "You get it."

I figured that was better than not getting it, or muting all words until the thoughts get caught up.

"Can you hear me now?" ...no longer heard

Posted on <u>April 16, 2011</u> by <u>Mark H Miller</u>

A smattering of news items:

The Verizon, "Can you hear me now?" guy, Paul Maricelli, is out of a job. He was the *main guy* for nine years, is now released from the contract. That happens. What struck me, though, is his sharing that people would drive up and down his Connecticut street and yell homophobic slurs at him—he's gay and affirms his sexual orientation. The really hurtful moment came recently at his grandmother's funeral—at the graveside as they lowered his grandmother's casket into the ground, someone leaned over and whispered to him, "Can you hear me now?" That's cruel.

Still on homophobic slurs, you probably heard of or read about Kobe Bryant's rant from the bench in a recent Lakers NBA game...it was the slurring "F" word. He's been fined $100,000 and from top to bottom in the league—office to players, there's no regard for Bryant's slur. Except some say, "This happens in the heat of battle." Bryant himself shared with a LA sports radio program that he's not negative toward gays... it just came out in the heat of battle. Maintains it's just "the way it is" with the drama and emotion of professional sports.

I disagree. To have said what he said makes it clear—at least to me: no regard for, respect of or acknowledgement that sexual orientation is not a decision; it's a discovery. Have held that forever, but with one blast from Bryant, the demeaning of others results in fierce protest.

I thought, *Gosh, Kobe, what if you did something overly aggressive, blatantly uncalled for in fouling an opponent—what if someone stood and shouted the N word at you. Just emotional? Not real judgment? Give me a break.*

Then I read this, about support for a San Francisco Giants baseball fan rooting for his team against the Dodgers in LA. The fan was pummeled, smashed and almost killed, has evidently suffered irreparable brain damage—all because Dodger fans took their anger out on him...a fan of the enemy. Evidently the Dodger organization has announced two important adjustments: increase in game security and significant modification of beer availability.

To that I read this about support for the brutalized fan, *Giants pitching ace Tim Lincecum is giving $25,000 to assist the longtime San Francisco fan who was attacked outside Dodger Stadium last month.*

Now, that's a class act.

The world in which we live, correct?

Tomorrow is Palm Sunday, a day of a parade…as Jesus rode into Jerusalem on a donkey, people shouted, "Alleluia!" That word means, "Praise to God"…and…"Help/save me."

In our day we need to be helped and saved…from slurs, from rage and from indecency of word and deed, whether it's a ball game or the work place or the home.

Then comes Holy Week. Too many people want to shift from Palm Sunday to Easter. But, life itself says, NO. For in every life there is Good Friday…when the shadows prevail and death raises its head. When we acknowledge the pain and struggle, the harsh realities that are not stranger to us—when we're really honest about them—then it will be that the dawn of Easter will be the emerging and prevailing truth. Death doesn't win. Nor do the "F" or "N" words.

What prevails is the "L" word…from God, "I am with you, I will always be with you. Whether you live or whether you die, I am with you. In a word, I LOVE you."

May Easter win…with each of us.

Impact less important than Effort

Posted on <u>April 17, 2011</u> by <u>Mark H Miller</u>

The devastating story goes like this:

Handsome and friendly, Clay Hunt so epitomized a vibrant Iraq veteran that he was chosen for a public service announcement reminding veterans that they aren't alone.

The 28-year-old former Marine corporal earned a Purple Heart after taking a sniper's bullet in his left wrist. He returned to combat in Afghanistan. Upon his return home, he lobbied for veterans on Capitol Hill, road-biked with wounded veterans and performed humanitarian work in Haiti and Chile.

Then, on March 31, Hunt bolted himself in his Houston apartment and shot himself.

Friends and family say he was wracked with survivor's guilt, depression and other emotional struggles after combat. [Yahoo.com, April 15, 2011, Kimberly Hefling]

Shared often, perhaps into the realm of tedium, I've never clapped and cheered for war. Perhaps, sadly offered, the single most consistent benefit of the war is the economy—tends to be stronger.

Have a couple of reactive comments:

First, this IS a tragedy of epic proportions. Yes, during ministry the most throat-clenching time, a gulp when words mute themselves, is when parents must bury their son or daughter…no matter the age. There are few exceptions—cannot name one right now—when a parent hasn't wished *trading places* had been optional.

Second, I am unconvinced our being a military presence with boots on in Iraq and Afghanistan has justification.

But third, and this dilemma is real and has evidence in almost every breathing face: NONE OF US knows the layered truth in another.

For each of us there is the public face and the inside persona. Often they are not less or more than strangers to each other.

Personally, and of course this is the risky part but I will offer it, there are instances when I'm surprised of myself at the *inside rage* I experience over certain events. But, I keep them muted. Not that I'm afraid of offering protest—it's just that I'm not sure of its benefit—even deeper, does it matter?

That doesn't mean my face—now bearded—and my words and actions are guilty of the charge, *phony*. It simply means there are layers of who we are.

I don't, not in the blink of a moment, think one person anywhere or anytime can read and understand all the layers. And, probably, in most instances, we ourselves are not aware of them within the self.

All I feel in writing this is a foreboding sense that people can be spontaneous—and others very calculating—in making life/death decisions.

I believe that is beyond our control—with regard to others.

What is NOT beyond our control are two dynamics: be good at self-management and MAKE SURE we not cause someone else's purpose for goodness and value to become lost, sinking them into a crater of despair.

Be agents for the good is what one of my seminary professors said, again and again. We may never know how we've done that...but you know what? **The impact is less important than the effort**...why? Because what we do is our life. What results is not ours...and will never be.

I'm okay with that...focus upon doing good...and doing it well.

And then, as my college baseball coach use to say in his pre-game chalk talk, "Fellas, give your best...and let the chips fall where they may."

Joy from Unexpected Places

Posted on <u>April 18, 2011</u> by <u>Mark H Miller</u>

I'd like to take five minutes of your day…well, accuracy: 4 minutes 57 seconds. Below is a link…it was sent to me by a clergy colleague, Dale Staggemeier, pastor at St. John's UCC in Rosenberg, Texas. He sent it last Friday—as a reminder of life's essence.

I played it, remembered it when he sent it during Advent.

I was overcome by emotion, as I think of this week…a week of passion, betrayal, denial, bread and wine, crucifixion, shadows, dawning light of a new truth proclaimed on Easter Sunday.

Friends, as I think about this week…and quite honestly, am swirled by the events of this past year—personally, family-wise, national and international, it dawned on me…how MUCH I need to never lose this link…for its proclamation.

It is profoundly emotional for me…a declaration not an apology. I need to know that Good Friday doesn't win. I need to know that shadows are only evidence there is light somewhere. I need to know that's God's promise to never abandon me…or any of us…is never broken or lost. It is always kept.

So it is, Monday, April 18, 2011, Monday of Holy Week. And also, not without coincidence, my mother's—Esther Miller—101st birthday. *Mother, happy birthday…I know in my heart of hearts and the voice of my living, that you are well, that heaven and you are just fine. And knowing that for you and Dad, it is well in my soul. And I know…more than anything…had you and Dad been in that food courtyard, you would have stood and sang like never before. Oh, yes.*

Alleluia!

[Give yourself a gift—tap into the joy of this event:]

<u>http://www.youtube.com/user/AlphabetPhotography</u>

Writing–more than words on a page–so much more

Posted on April 19, 2011 by Mark H Miller

The learning curve is less steep when the teachers are sharp. I have learned from many—make sure commas are few and exclamation points next to non-existent; avoid participles at all costs; fiction needs to be believable; don't write about what you don't know; sending group e-mails requires etiquette, which is realized when the blind-copy address line is used; avoid conjunctive *ands and buts* as much as possible. No sentence should start with either *There is...*or...*There are.*

And on it goes.

To add to this, as I enter the last lap of the current novel, "Shattered Hope"—a hint or two: Tricia has solved the murders but is broken into pieces in an unexpected way, causing her to wonder about career futuring—I discovered some gems...not in order but each in value. Found on Huffington Post's web page, the alert to same from Diane. Ah, what a blessing to have such a great research colleague. [I'd put an exclamation point there, but my professor, James Thayer, would wince.]

Consider these about writing:

The writer, when s/he is also an artist, is someone who admits what others don't dare reveal—Elia Kazan

To me, the greatest pleasure of writing is not what it's about, but the inner music the words make—Truman Capote

Ever tried. Ever failed. No matter. Try again. Fail again. Fail better—Samuel Beckett

What is written without effort is in generally read without pleasure—Samuel Johnson

It's never too late to be what you might have been—George Eliot

Words are sacred. They deserve respect. If you get the right ones, in the right order, you can nudge the world a little—Tom Stoppard

Good writing is supposed to evoke sensation in the read—not the fact that it is raining, but the feeling of being rained upon—E.L. Doctorow

There is nothing to writing. All you do is sit down at a typewriter and bleed—Ernest Hemingway

If people cannot write well, they cannot think well, and if they cannot think well, others will do their thinking for them—George Orwell

River of Dreams

Posted on April 20, 2011 by Mark H Miller

Can you want something too much? Is a schedule too-star-marked for, to be personal, a fishing trip?

The answer to each is affirmative.

Of all the fishing options—second to fly-fishing with Diane on any Colorado or Montana river—is back-bouncing eggs for Spring Chinook salmon.

Have done that for thirty years, even more.

It goes like this: In a boat, loaded up with cluster-egg-baited hook, a small sinker, modest leader of perhaps three feet. The guide slows the motor down at the top of the hole.

Line is let out, bounce, bounce. Then the rod's raised to let out more line, until the bouncing eggs are downstream, maybe twenty feet.

The guide "loses" to the current as the bouncing continues, a personal replication of a metronome.

It's a fascinating way to fish—none of this putting the rod in a holder and waiting it to bend out of control and the reel to sing away, line yielding to a surging salmon.

None of this using heavy equipment, so heavy you can hardly tell a fish is on.

No, a thousand times no.

Rather, this is personal. You, the eggs and …and…and…

Maybe the bounce will stop. Maybe the tap-tap will interrupt the metronome.

You wait, holding the rod still, watching the rod-tip chatter away.

"RIP CITY" is the usual Northwest war cry...at least it is for me... when the hook is set.

Then. Oh yes, then. The solid pull of the salmon, the rod suddenly gyrating and the reel singing away. The river erupts.

FISH ON.

Oh, baby, yes, indeed.

I've played that tape for over five months—focused on next Tuesday and Wednesday, when I'm all set to back-bounce eggs with Zorba, my Oregon guide, to fish in the Willamette River just south of Portland.

Two days of anticipation, delight, and maybe...just maybe a salmon or two for canning and gifting. They make much better gifts than candy or flowers or wine when invited to dinner somewhere.

Yesterday, more out of curiosity. No, that's not true. To feed my excitement and enthusiasm is more apt. I went on line to gather in the latest fishing reports of Springer fishing on the Willamette.

I looked twice, then thrice.

Nothing. Nichts. Nada. Zeeeeeerrrrrrrrooooo.

Only the dreaded comments, *River is chocolate milk spilling over the banks. Won't be fishable for...*

Okay, today is Wednesday...that provides six days for the rain to lessen if not stop altogether. That allows the chocolate milk to flow to the Columbia River and to the Pacific Ocean. That allows for back-bouncing.

Yes? No? Maybe?

Hey, I live with hope…and anticipation…and the pulsing metronome…

Which means today is Wednesday and has its own agenda…helping Tricia along in the novel, meeting a landscape guy and trying to remember where the new flowers should be planted, doing my bicycle-thing at the Fitness Center and walking Gracie to the mail box. That's all important, not even to say tonight's dinner and then hoping the beloved San Antonio Spurs don't go down two games to the Memphis Grizzlies.

And yet. The deep pulsing includes a flowing river, a river that flows through Portland, Oregon. Will it happen? Have I hoped too much?

So it is. Quiet reflection this Wednesday, April 20, 2011. On a clear day in Austin with temperature at 85 degrees.

Wonder if there are Spring Chinook Salmon in Lady Bird Lake, mid-town Austin?

How do you back-bounce on a lake?

A Warring World...now...tomorrow, too?

Posted on April 21, 2011 by Mark H Miller

Many of you are aware that the *real learnings* in my ministry began a week after my ordination, circa 1966, when I walked into Fred Trost's office at St. Pauls Church, Fullerton and Geneva Terrace, Lincoln Park, north side of Chicago. I should have known it would be swirled, impacted and graced by two incredibly gifted ministers, Fred...and Herb Davis.

I should have known that when they interviewed me for the third staff position, Assistant Pastor in charge of youth ministry and a summer day camp. We sat in Fred's living room...and for over two hours the *conversation* focused upon theology, biblical understandings and how faith functioned. I used italics for *conversation*. More aptly a *grilling*—with tolerating tones. They are so very competent.

That was in 1966. I left that ministry in December of 1969, a month after Matthew was baptized, to begin a new position in Eugene, Oregon.

But I didn't leave the relationship with Fred. In fact, I can say, with more truth than humor, that when I did things well in ministry it was *Fred's impact/guidance/ beliefs/ wisdom and experience*. When I didn't do well I hadn't listened to him well enough.

This is prologue to verify that my friendship with Fred is inviolate. He's now retired, living in the summer climes of Wisconsin and the winter climes of Arizona. To be retired from his Wisconsin conference ministry, though, doesn't mean he's muted in his reflections upon life and the ways in which life wins and loses.

I received an e-mail yesterday from Fred that focuses upon a common malady, one with which I agree. It has to do with war and our military involvement. He's given permission to share:

It has been a good winter for us; mostly quiet, calm and refreshing,... though I confess that I get down in "the dumps" when I think of what is taking place in the world in our name,... i.e. the Obama

494

wars and the death and crucifixion being visited upon so many innocent people, including little children. I am weary of reading General Petraeus' "apologies" for the "mistakes" we make with our missile attacks and the flights of unmanned drones. Cowardly. And I see no end to it, and this drags me down. One feels helpless. And the president's rhetoric doesn't "cut any ice" any more. We are a brutal country with a vicious foreign policy ready to crush any people that stand in our way,… crush them like bugs. We have never learned the meaning of repentance, and our "exceptionalism" is the source of so many cruelties. I have little sense that "the Church" is able or willing to resist the madness in any way, shape or form, and this is what devastates/attacks the hope that is in me.

Footnoting—well, no, paragraphing Fred's beliefs—it is my firm belief, were I given benefit to offer input to key decisions on our military involvement, I'd appreciate first learning the deeper causes, read that justifications, for our military forces to be in Western Europe, Japan, Afghanistan and Iraq. On the latter two it has always been my conviction our being there does not strengthen their national posturing—rather it more than anything strengthens the force, manpower and resolve of the terrorists. We actually fuel them rather than lessen their numbers and destructive deeds. I believe the real problem is Pakistan, a place where Special Forces would be more effective.

That doesn't mean I don't value our military. Contrary to that, particularly because General Officers in the Broadmoor Church invited me to attend two War Colleges—Army in Carlisle, Pennsylvania and Air Force in Montgomery, Alabama. Those two seminars—for American citizens, 50 of us chosen from many professions—gave valued insight into the deeper truths of the needs to have good preparation and information militarily.

I do not believe for a minute war leads to peace. I believe war leads to war. I join Fred in his lamentation—and believe such sharing is timely, given the ominous shadows being cast by current day realities in Libya, congressional considerations of a time table to remain in the Middle East militarily. Timely because tonight Diane and I will attend a Maundy Thursday service, tomorrow is Good Friday and Sunday is Easter.

Might it be—as I echo Fred's words and offer some personally—may it be our future will know and experience more about Easter than Good Friday? For now, I find, especially as Texas is being consumed by fires, that in a metaphorical way many of my friends experience the burning of their spirit and dashing of hopes—verities of Good Friday.

May our prayers transform our own lives...to be people of peace, to be people who...

[the conclusion of this blog is now handed to you...]

We All Stammer

Posted on April 25, 2011 by Mark H Miller

Saturday, known for almost 45 years in my clergy world as Holy Saturday, was generally spent making sure the Easter Sunday sermon was both brief and deep, like the ever-flowing stream.

But, no more for this retired preacher.

Not in a preaching mode and feeling no nervousness or regret about it, I sat down to peruse the news—my step is with yahoo.com

So much to weigh down the spirits.

Such does not need narration, since no one can avoid the trigger point. Simply drive by a gas station.

Didn't feel like much, and thought, *Time to see where and how Tricia is.*

Through the night I was bothered because a new circumstance popped up in the novel, one which I was certain would take at least another few chapters to unravel.

Looked at the word meter on the Word Document—had already reached 105,000. Remembered one of my most helpful professors had said that "generally good fiction is between 90,000-110,000 words."

Well, who wants to write bad fiction?

I then had *one of those moments*, realized why I had been bothered by the new wrinkle. It didn't belong, had some unbelievability to it. Not wanting to offend anyone, especially Sue Grafton who counseled against such *writer cramping*, I deleted and re-wrote.

Honestly? I wasn't sure how it all happened, couldn't even tell you if the phone had rung, even though my hearing aid was in place.

And there. Right there. In that moment, Holy Saturday morning. Tricia found all the pieces of shattered and scattered hope and there it was, the last sentence, the right and good and fitting closing sentence.

A deep breath.

And yes, a tear or two [that's understating] to have "Shattered Hope," at least the first draft completed.

Copied it to my laptop computer and then two DVD's.

Then two things happened.

First, I was able to surprise Diane by sharing the DVD—she has been the best support in the world—such great support. Only right and good for her to have the first completed draft.

Then, an afternoon experience.

Given our life-rhythm in recent years, watching films has become less prioritized. Diane suggested we watch "King's Speech," which was so heralded and won, I think it was, four Academy Awards.

Friends, if you see only one film and no more, give yourself a gift and see "King's Speech."

Brilliant—more than the acting.

Brilliant in terms of how King George VI, but known to his speech therapist/teacher/friend/advocate/corrector as "Bertie," coped with his stammering.

So moving, and then I thought, on Holy Saturday, how fitting. A film about stammering—and knowing after the first breath a baby doesn't stammer. Yet, it happens.

And in a real way, I know of no one who doesn't stammer—that is, who doesn't find life to be awkward, difficult, fractured and at times, personal experiences when hope shatters.

Diane and I were so moved by "King's Speech," for the ways in which it shared how the human struggle—the stammering in life—can be recognized and reduced.

It was perhaps the most memorable Holy Saturday—simply wanted to share.

No matter how much we stammer, no matter how hard it is to put shattered pieces of hope back together...I do believe it can happen. It did for Tricia and those she helped in the novel. But, ever so more vital, it CAN happen for you and me.

Why?

Primarily because life didn't halt with Good Friday or Holy Saturday, but continued in a new way when the tomb was empty on Easter morning.

THAT is the greater emphasis...that it is the power of the empty tomb that Good Friday doesn't win—and in faith and trust and belief, it never will.

A Day of Juxtaposition

Posted on <u>April 29, 2011</u> by <u>Mark H Miller</u>

There can be, without doubt in any breath, no day that more reflects life's juxtaposition than today.

Tears of joy…from Westminster Cathedral for the Royal Wedding. I happen to be one who appreciates high liturgy, the prayers, the responses and the choir that was as close to the voice of angels one could wish. Touching would be understatement. A celebratory moment. The future waits.

Tears when looking at flat land, houses crumbled to no identity, as neighbors shared, "I have no future." The news accounts brought clearly how horrific—more than 300 dead—homes brought to pieces by unforgiving tornadoes reaching 200 miles per hour—keepsake pictures, plaques, everything personal lifting the value of decades, generations, lives who passed before lost forever.

Somewhere in there—all future and no future—you and I live and move and have our being.

Times when we cannot imagine how life can be more joyful—and then, the opposite.

The question raised—at least in my heart and soul and mind—how do we cope?

By the blessings of family and friends…

By the opportunities afforded through employment and retired projects that keep us from the edge labeled, *boredom*.

But most of all, my faith, knowing that whether we live or whether we die…and for so many of us, myself never excluded…we do both, sometimes in the same day…at least emotionally fractured and put back together…whether we live or we die…no matter what or when or how…I believe fully, even when shadows darken the day…that God is not only with us…but is for us…and can be known through us.

And, as I've counseled, primarily to myself, shadows are only evidence there is light somewhere.

May that light shine and through our prayers, beckon God's Spirit to be of presence and of comfort and peace, for the newlyweds and those newly homeless.

So may it be.

Dealing with Distractions

Posted on May 14, 2011 by Mark H Miller

The sentence was both clear and compelling...and, to continue the alliteration...confounding.

It goes like this, in description of bin Laden, as his world of plotting and encouraging his supporters to destroy the will and maim the confidence of his enemies, directives by most accounts reached into many lands:

For a man working from home, there seemed to be many distractions.

My reflection this morning, Saturday, May 14, 2011, a day in which I will attend the funeral service of Jim Breeding, one of the finest laity I have known—Jim died this past week, a member of the Round Rock Christian Church and valued friend—will not focus upon bin Laden or his maniacal [was it really, as some contend, insightful and clever? Not.] game plans.

Although I was somewhat disconcerted at the woo-hoo-ness hoorayed by so many with bin Laden's assassination. Sure, point out the evil—I know I can and have. And yet, my sentiment is this: *God creates all life and all life has value to God. Yes, some act in manners that shred the value and dissipate the humanity. Yet, let us not cheer death as much as we give our fullest through love to life.*

But, not to ponder the "distractions" to bin Laden. I don't roam. I zoom the lens upon my own journey...and maybe through this blog, the window can become a mirror...

To wit, **consider distractions**.

I start by acknowledgement I am a focused person. I have goals and hopefully those goals have purpose. I am an organized person...on the Myers-Briggs, on the scale of "organized" [J] or "I'll get to it tomorrow or sometime" [P] the personality test indicated I am a capital J. In fact, some call me "Dr. J" and that has nothing to do with basketball.

As organized—probably compulsively so—each day has its purpose, its place, its game-plan. Admittedly in the world of retirement it isn't complicated. I mean, really, how crunching can it be to feed the dog, make a sandwich for Diane's lunch, peddle the fitness center bicycle, get to San Marcos upon occasion for mediating conflicts at the Hays County Reconciliation Center, go to H.E.B for groceries and many times, prepare dinner?

The new hope is to become a mediator for a retirement center in Austin. But, that's for next Fall—and I do consider "Fall" to be a time of year and not a theological condition.

Back to *distraction*. Yet, when the "game-plan" gets knocked off course, when the doctor makes it clear a dreaded disease is no longer awaiting arrival, when the phone call messes everything in the family networking, when a publisher pushes a "not-now" button, when a new novel refuses to come to the mind let alone the computer, when anticipated change in employment is muted, those can be considered distractions.

To all this, at least from this heart and soul, the first question is never silenced: WHY? *Why is this happening? Did I do something wrong? Are there forces working contrarily to my purposes? WHY…WHY…WHY?*

It is my contention—short of theory, resident with hypothesis—the "why" question is pointless, almost always. For two reasons: first, it's always evident…when you hit someone from behind driving on the highway you were distracted, happens to any of us behind the wheel… or the second reason: there is no answer. So pursuit of the unanswerable for some ends up with collapse into a frustrated heap.

For me the key question goes like this: **What does each distraction mean?** Not *why did it happen*, but WHAT *does it mean?*

Because, in full candor I believe ALL of life is messaging something. I don't believe there is anything that happens to us that cannot bring some value to my life.

To a point, **I don't think life has distractions…I think life has life.**

None of life is to be denied or ignored. All of life is to be breathed...as long as breath happens.

Every apparent obstacle [i.e. distraction] can become an evident moment of growth...and who knows...a step into a new future never thought of or reasoned before.

Death is not always an enemy
Posted on May 15, 2011 by Mark H Miller

This happened to be made public because of the earned reputation of the person—Harmon Killebrew who's a Hall of Fame baseball slugger, formerly of the Minnesota Twins. Here is his statement:

"It is with profound sadness that I share with you that my continued battle with esophageal cancer is coming to an end. With the continued love and support of my wife, Nita, I have exhausted all options with respect to controlling this awful disease. My illness has progressed beyond my doctors' expectation of cure. I have spent the past decade of my life promoting hospice care and educating people on its benefits. I am very comfortable taking this next step and experiencing the compassionate care that hospice provides. I am comforted by the fact that I am surrounded by my family and friends. I thank you for the outpouring of concern, prayers and encouragement that you have shown me. I look forward to spending my final days in comfort and peace with Nita by my side."

It is not my purpose to comment upon how Killebrew reached this decision…to let life take its course, likely to mean death sooner than later.

What I respect, though, is his decision. I consider it more than courage. I honor it as a way in which Killebrew centered love in his circumstance. That's what occurs to me. And, from what I have gleaned over the years—make that decades of following professional baseball closely—he is a class act, reflecting self-respect, integrity and courage.

Certainly a case can be made to never give up with medicine and prayer. And certainly there are situations in which "incurability" is inaccurate.

And yet. Isn't there always an *and yet?* I have had experiences with former parishioners when their circumstance eroded, both physically and emotionally, when vegetated state would be an exaggeration. I've commented before how there's no illness more severe to human life than Lou Gehrig Disease [ALS], which is the atrophy of the muscles to the point that death comes when the muscles no longer can keep the lungs functioning. To put this directly, there are conditions worse than death.

Personally being in such a situation is both perilous and onerous. And yet, it's part of life.

I can remember my mother once commenting, well before her last year that she NEVER [her emphasis] wanted to be a problem to any of her family, in terms of caring, supporting, providing aide. Honestly, I heard her but never paid attention.

And yet. [There it is again.] Because of my full love for her, should she have been in the same situation as Harmon Killebrew and believed in the same decision as he, I would love her no less, and make sure that pain was absent—as much as possible—and comfort was abundant.

No less I would hope my family would honor me in a similar circumstance with whatever decision that needed to be made.

Fishing without a pole–no thanks.

Posted on May 17, 2011 by Mark H Miller

My friends are always thinking in my direction. This morning— probably the 5th reception of same—I got this note: *Mark, As soon as I saw this I thought, "Here is a spot where Miller might be able to catch a fish."*

I clicked the link, www.indianaoutdooradventures.com and there it was...two guys zooming along in their boat, maybe the speed limit, maybe not, and without any effort, fish leap into their boat...one, then two, then...

Entitled, "Fishing without a pole!", they limit out...and have no pole.

You get the imaging.

And, it is hilarious. And very much, I am feeling good that my friends, when fishing's the topic, at least glance in my direction, and at times, send me a good option: go to Indiana, track down photo-shop and go for it.

But, with respect for Nike aside, and maybe it's the new day, but going deeper, it occurs to me: *That's not my kind of fishing.*

Brings to mind a fishing day with a guide—very enjoyable and knowledgeable guide, in fishing a section of the Frying Pan River in Colorado, not far from Aspen. We waded the river. He pulled on my arm, touched a finger to his lips, then pointed. His version of *don't move or make any noise.*

I'm good at following directions—especially from a fishing guide. He squinted and then his eyes opened wide as he pointed again and whispered, "Cast in that direction and hold on."

Before I cast I looked, and sure enough—think it's called "sight-fishing," there was a very large trout idled next to the bottom.

More than anything it was frustrating—not that my efforts went in vain, which they did—but simply this, *I didn't want to see the fish before it struck.*

I'd rather be surprised. I'd rather give the fish a chance.

Recall another fishing guide friend who "got his limit—the last fish—when it literally jumped in the damn boat. How special is that."

Well, okay, the limit was reached.

But.

Not that I'm honorable, but I would probably throw the fish back and keep fishing, want to limit-out the best way.

What does this mean?

Not sure.

Other than the joy of fishing is when you cast, your dry fly floats as if unattached to the tippet [leader] and suddenly disappears. You set the hook and the river explodes.

THAT is what fishing's all about…

Not sure what to call it, but maybe these two words apply: *mystery* and *surprise.*

To me those two components make fishing what it is…never predictable.

Always expecting.

Ever hoping.

And then, and at times when you're thinking in lots of elsewheres, the fish strikes. Life then engages in a great event…a thrashing fish, a deft-management of the rod, reel and line…

Back to the Roaring Fork.

We left the sight-fishing and stood on the bank...about 1 5 yards out was a huge boulder. The guide advised, "Mark, cast above that boulder...might be Mr. Big Trout on the other side...let's see."

I couldn't see a thing...the anticipation pumped adrenalin.

I can still feel the excitement, the anticipation, the wonder.

Made the cast...a better effort that missed the tree limbs on the shore behind me...the fly floated *right where it was supposed to!*

Everything in my body and mind and heart was focused...the fly kept floating...*no one at home.*

I tried again...and again.

The guide looked at his watch, "Okay, last cast; time to go."

With no lessened anticipation...actually probably more, the cast was my best of the day...and half-way in the drift...

WOW.

Yep, don't take the mystery and surprise...and exploding river...for granted...and always known.

Great way to stay more than arm's length from boredom.

Yes, indeed.

Voice of the Leaning Tree

Posted on <u>May 18, 2011</u> by <u>Mark H. Miller</u>

A guide buddy, Ball Ball in Forks, Washington, shared this picture recently on his Facebook page. Even if you haven't fished, even if it will never be a glint in your eye, the guess is it's hard to not "get a feel" for the moment.

Bob's customer is playing a winter steelhead on the Sol Duc River, his favorite in the Olympic Peninsula in Northwest Washington, just north of his Forks home.

Obviously it's morning...the air is chilled, quivering the body...also foggy, the sun working to get seen. The fisherman is holding his pole up, never dropping it to the fish—pointed poles end up with snapped line and escaped fish. He is waiting to see what the steelhead will do, left hand poised to reel...

Am sure he knows the mantra in bringing a fish to the boat, *lift up and reel down*. Never the reverse.

Everything's focused…no bleating cell phone, no computer keyboard clicking away, no bills to pay or money to earn, no doctor visits…just the moment.

Then.

Look at the background…see the tree? The huge tree? It's leaning, almost tilting. Rooted close to the river, its source of life.

Focus on the tree…how it leans to its source…not to topple because it is rooted deeply in the earth.

It then occurred to me…in this picture the tree is not background. It is foreground. Its own metaphor-message on how life itself happens.

Winds blow as we grow. Rivers sometimes go over their banks. And at times, yes even in a land where the average rainfall is 120 inches annually, the earth gets dry, *draught* cannot be denied.

And yet the roots secure the tree.

Might even be preached someday…you think? Starting to marinate a little: *The tree and faith…one and the same.*

Could be. Could be.

Fist Pump at a Ballet Recital

Posted on May 23, 2011 by Mark H Miller

Fist pump at a ballet recital?

Explanation forthcoming.

Yesterday, Sunday, May 22, I had the unbridled joy to attend my granddaughter's ballet recital. Laura, age 7, danced yesterday, along with 22 other dance classes, at the Winnetka Community Center auditorium.

The opening announcement, an apology, said the air conditioning had worked "yesterday," but not so today. My thought was "yesterday" was probably the first day it was needed, given Chicago's "windy world," which honestly is more a political than climatologically reference. There were no groans or *why not's?*

Let the recital begin.

It was the full spectrum of skills—from two high school girls somehow smooth and well-choreographed dancing on those toe shoes [obviously my descriptive accuracy and correct vocabulary lacks considerably here] was beyond impressive. There were the 9 in a group, dancing as "pre-ballet," with maybe three different steps.

And to each there was great music—at least for me, be it jazz, concert, hip-hop, boogie-woogie, stage musical. At one point, because it is one of my most favorite songs, I was touched deeply to see the beautiful ballet dancing to "Somewhere Over The Rainbow." I love the possibilities when *troubles melt like lemon drops.*

And then, 22nd in order but first in our eyes and hearts, Laura and her class danced. Goodness, *grandfather pride* reached a new height.

During the afternoon, as you would never doubt, each ballet presentation resulted in applause. I noticed, though, it went beyond the *socially polite pitter-patter.* Rather, it was applause, a few declarations of "YES!".

512

Which was fine...this was a community auditorium, folks, not a Chicago Metropolitan Theatre.

Then I noticed it...actually hard to miss...when during a couple of the times...a father...had to be...across the aisle and down a couple of rows...was showing his multi-tasking. He held the video phone camera [I still can't tell the difference between an I-phone and I-Pad.] in his right hand to capture the dance of his daughter. All the while, pumping his fist with his left arm. Animation fully evident.

It was a wonderful moment, the enthusiasm and affirmation of a father... his daughter, stretching the point, perhaps six years old.

After the final act—when each of the 23 groups was introduced and we were told to meet the children and youth in the gymnasium, I went over to the fist-pumping father, tapped him on the shoulder and shared how much gladness I experienced with his fist-pumping, "Sir, we see fist-pumping when our children hit a home run or score a 3-pointer, but goodness, how special, to fist-pump your daughter dancing in ballet."

Loved it.

And, when we met Laura in the gymnasium and thanked her teacher, not once, not even a thought or murmur, did anyone say a word about the lack of air-conditioning.

Here's a picture of Laura...as we left so she could dance...and bring her grandfather joy and gladness and gratitude. Wonderful.

Laura in ballet costume

Life–much more than, "How are you?" "Fine, thanks." "Bye."

Posted on May 27, 2011 by Mark H Miller

A comment came…unexpected but welcomed. With friends, the discussion, a topic somewhere 180 degrees to my interest, was something like this, "What do you talk with your caddy about?"

Guess it was triggered when someone wondered if Tiger Woods might ever recover his victory status in professional golf.

I listened, then someone pointed in my direction, offered by that someone who hardly knows me…at least that was my guess…saying that he NEVER talks with his caddy about himself or the caddy, other than asking if the distance to the green can be reached with ??? club. On the other hand, the person offered, still looking at me, "I bet by the end of 18 holes you could start a biography on the caddy."

I took that as a compliment, but that was easy, because I've never had a caddy.

And yet, I thought about that yesterday when I went to the post office, one I frequent about weekly. I know most of their names. Yesterday it was listening to the clerk from near where my son, Andrew, and his family live, a rather lengthy commentary on how his father's having more than trouble adjusting to a nursing home and a catheter. I like Guy—a whole lot—and since he's from Boerne [where Andrew and family live], we have something in common. He needed to talk…and for those moments no one waited.

Then as I left, Mark, another post office clerk, waved at me…we make it "a deal" we share the same first name. He had asked about Diane [at the time when she was scheduled for the lumpectomy] and said he would pray for her. I know two things: he meant it…and his word was good as gold. Yesterday as I left, "Mark, how's your wife?"

Now, where does all this go?

Not sure…

515

Certainly not to be self-exclaiming or self-demurring. Simply to say we each are who we are...and it caused me to think, whether or not I ever get to the golf course, let alone afford a caddy, how does each of us relate to others...self-serving, other-caring...or we really don't give a damn as long as we get what we are wanting?

It's more than a curiosity...and as we enter Memorial Day weekend, and the Best Buy clerk just shared with me about my lame laptop computer. I told him I would see him soon and he shook his head. "Nope, I'm gone soon and will be back in a year."

"Oh?"

"Yes, I'm being deployed to either Iraq or Afghanistan, my second tour."

The silence was real. I didn't know what to say...because I SO RESPECT Blaine...he's helped me before. But, I also have such "fussings" about why American military boots are there in the first place.

The conversation was engaging and affirming...then it was time to go.

"Mark, thanks for offering your prayers...I'll take them with me."

All in the course of each day...meeting, greeting and when it can happen, move waaaaay beyond the short social, "How are you?" to get to the substance.

That, however. is for each of us to decide.

At least something to ponder...because I so believe life is what happens when you and I move past the social amenity to the spiritual necessity— what REALLY matters in our lives and in those at the post office or the golf course or the fitness center or the computer store.

Cry a river...build a bridge...and walk across it.

Posted on May 29, 2011 by Mark H Miller

Cry a river.....build a bridge...and walk across it.

Short, direct and so instructive, even inspirational.

If only. If only we each could function in that manner.

For it is the case...especially these days when I'm able to reflect upon the life of yesterday, yesteryear and yesterdecade...there is no one I know, even if with a glance, who's not had the occasion[s] to cry a river, to experience the wasteland of pain, stress, brokenness.

That, for no moment, means we all are experiencing the clouds and storms relentlessly. Although I'm sure for some—victims of tsunamis, residents of Alabama and Missouri—it appears the struggle will never end.

Still.

What do we do when, as a friend said to me once when I began ministry, "Mark, you'll have days when you have to reach up to touch bottom, when you will never think Good Friday will ever end, when you find that you are only as good as your next phone call."

I respected him...and found his feet were well grounded in reality, a reality that at times as he stepped in life, would become boggy.

So, who among us...can you name at least one person...best personifies the opening declaration of cry, bridge, walk?

For me, and I offer this with profound humility realizing both are God's greatest gifts to me, are my mother and my wife, Diane.

I've written often before, but for mother, Esther Schnell Miller, she lived in this manner, "Mark, everyone should die young, as late as possible." Oh, did she ever. The picture below is the final picture of mother...

fulfilling her last wish, to see her first great-grandchild. The picture is of my nephew, Brian Grey and new daughter, Zeli, just a week after she was born. Mother smiled and two days later, as a friend said, got her new wings. Mother died with no unfinished business. How special. Yes.

Meeting Diane in the Denver Airport in August of 2000 was a gift of God. Yes, two pilots boycotted the flight from Denver to Austin, and yes I was able to get the "last flight out of Dodge," and yes, I *happened* to stand in line waiting to board immediately ahead of a lovely lady whose cell phone battery was dead, who borrowed my phone to call United to see if she could get on the flight. I've shared this before.

Little did I know this lady, a lady from the south, and I would exchange wedding vows a year later…and with God's blessings, will celebrate our 10th wedding anniversary this August.

In these years, it has been the case, as Diane has faced the multiple surgeries, the unrelenting pain, the tough world of medical setbacks, she never complains, she is literally unwilling to spell the word wine with an 'h,' and says, time and again, "Why remember all the bad…that has no value, it only pushes me down. I will not keep a record of wrongs for anyone, especially for myself. Rather…."

And the affirmations following the "rather's" are always, without exception, good and perceptive and valued and encouraging.

In all my days…as I now await the month for my 71st birthday and 45th ordination anniversary, I give thanks for the two key bridge-builders in my life…and with some luck…maybe once in a while, I can construct a bridge over that crying river. And, maybe the same for you.

Wanted to share a picture of each of them…with thanks to God for how life is good, how relationships matter, and as Diane shows, fish can still be caught…and released! Yes, in deed; yes, in faith; and yes, in love.

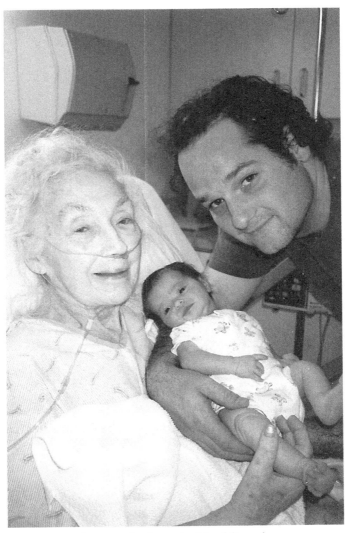

My mother in the hospital holding her great-grandchild, Zeli, and her grandson Brian

Diane holding a trout and a net on the Colorado River

Life...holding on to the stump

Posted on May 30, 2011 by Mark H Miller

Knew nothing about it.

But, recently on HBO's "Real Sports with Bryant Gumbel", a compelling story was shared. The pitching coach of the Boston Red Sox, Ron Johnson, lives on a farm in Tennessee. His daughter, Bridget Johnson, age 12, loves to ride horses. Last summer she and her sister were riding to a friend's to go swimming.

At one point they crossed the county highway, just below a hill. A car, proven to be driving above the speed limit, hit the 12 year old Bridget.

The result was worse than horrific, whatever that word might be. *Disastrous?*

Her leg was severed as she was thrown to the pavement. She went one way, the leg the other.

Another driver came upon this terrible scene and could see the young girl was bleeding to death.

He leapt out of his car, ran to Bridget and gave his strongest grip, squeezing the end of her severed stump. He didn't let go until emergency help arrived.

He didn't give his full name, didn't want any recognition. But did allow his first name was Bernie.

Nothing more...and he left.

Quite a story.

Bridget has had the necessary surgeries and has returned to her life, as it now is.

And then something more happened, as if this wasn't enough. One of the Yankee coaches went to his players, explained the situation. Ron Johnson and he were best friends, had spent many years together in the minor leagues. In response, the Yankee players donated money to help with medical expenses. In addition, one of the Red Sox players gifted a new horse.

The opening day this year, in April, the Yankees played at Fenway Park against the Red Sox. This is one of the most storied rivalries in all of sports.

The scene was powerful...Bridget, we might call her a wounded healer, went to the pitching mound and threw the first pitch. Kevin Youkilis, the Red Sox third baseman, who gifted the horse, was the catcher.

In that moment, every player—Yankees and Red Sox alike—stood and applauded.

Yes, sports are important. Yes, it's part of the value of life.

But.

Life itself transcends victories and losses. Helping someone. Just "being there."

Bernie. I'll never meet him. Nor will you.

Still, the image of him holding for life on the stump of Bridget.

THAT'S life...holding on...because it's the right thing to do.

Not only for others.

But also for ourselves.

Easy to judge, but really, who doesn't limp?

Posted on June 1, 2011 by Mark H Miller

Not sure the year let alone the Sunday. Doesn't matter. The substance does. Was during a Bill Coffin sermon at Yale when he talked about "each of us is human; none of us is innocent."

He shared the story of a Yalie coming to his office complaining about anyone belonging to a church, "Dr. Coffin, I want nothing to do with church…everyone who comes there plods along with a crutch. It's ridiculous. Why don't you name it accurately…you're a peddler of Crutch Christianity."

To which Coffin responded, "Friend, who isn't limping?"

I thought of that…and one more thing…when I learned that Jim Tressel resigned as head football coach at Ohio State, a resignation prompted by his not reporting his players when they sold their rings and other memorabilia, a clear violation of NCAA rules.

Now sportscasters and other pundits are having a field day, citing the Ohio State quarterback who was one of the transgressors, who's been suspended for the first five games next fall, who on the day Tressel resigned was driving a snazzy Nissan, 300-something-or-other, a car that was his third since entering Ohio State.

Second part of this was how the Tressel resignation triggered many scenarios I experienced with clergy during my watch as Conference Minister…and on a more personal note the time I left parish when it wasn't all my call [at the time I thought my world was really a perish-world]. Yes, Coffin heralds the truth: no one is innocent. But, I thought…both with other clergy and myself, *there are others who are guiltier*.

Oh yes, a sin is a sin is a sin.

But, I protest. Not necessarily. Now, this is not stating the groundwork for permissible sinning. I've always considered "sin" best defined by a

German theologian, Paul Tillich, who defined sin as "separation." That is, anything I do or say or don't do or don't say that causes separation between me and at least one other person.

Okay, we are human. Okay, no one is perfect. Okay, there are those actions or words we wished we could retract and do over. But, it doesn't work that way.

I have no thought let alone hunch that the Ohio State quarterback will play another football snap at Ohio State.

But, you know? It's simply too easy to point fingers, to say, "He's really a jerk."

And, when you consider Tressel, his button-downed world publicly championed the good, honest effort. A position he left considerably when he muted what he knew, never reported the infractions.

I wonder? What if the violators were 3rd string on the football team?

And yet, it goes deeper.

Most of my time is not smiling at the indiscretions, thinking, *how hypocritical.*

Not a moment.

For the lesson here is what we find most important.

Where we haven't messed up?

When we've done the right thing?

When we know we've done the right thing?

Nope.

I think the far greater moment is when we have been wrong, when we've caused separation, to repent. Whoa. What is this? Well, read on, for I consider no unrepentable sin exists.

Yep, you heard it from me. For I consider repentance not the language from the 19th century or from a television preacher.

Rather, I consider repentance, in it purest occurrence, to be a "turning around."

In other measurements, it's a willingness to talk about shifting 180 degrees from errancy.

And then it is the greatest when our talk is walked…and wadda ya know…we walk in a new direction.

Whether or not the *usual suspects* will do that is really of no matter to me.

Nor is it how you order your life. For me?

I need to take care of myself…and hope, when I make the error, I learn and the next time…well, you got it….right?

More Thoughts On Sin

Posted on June 2, 2011 by Mark H Miller

Wanted to say a little more about sin. Some rambling, yes. But, somehow connected. I hope.

Over the years, whether serving a church as a called [read that, permanent] minister or interim, I recommended the worship service included a Confession of Sin and Assurance of Pardon. There was the unison Confession, then, and this was most important for me, the "time of silence," then followed by the Assurance of Pardon. It was not my business what the sins of others were. I simply figured the silence allowed, maybe for the only time that week, for each person to get in touch with their soul and conscience—since I consider them inextricable.

Seemed to me if a person could be honest with themselves and the ways they faltered, they would be both receptive and grateful to know that God forgives.

Cannot prove my theology, but **I do believe that God's forgiveness and love [again, inextricable] are greater than any sin.**

What's important is not to know we are forgiven, no matter what. What's important, as I alluded in yesterday's blog, is this: what do we do about it?

I can remember one pastor, really a good guy, who *seemed* to never take sin too seriously. His sense of humor even went to the name for his horse: Calls. Worked well for him when the church was called, his secretary simply said, "The pastor's out on Calls." The caller didn't realize, *calls*, was not a noun but a proper noun. Once I told this pastor-buddy, "I bet you only confess sins that are either trivial or humorous."

He nodded, "Got me."

Then there are those who, in my words, "don't take sin seriously enough and take grace too seriously." They are the aloof ones, the indifferent ones, the ones who figure God will forgive them no matter what.

In a theological sense, that may be...**God does forgive. What's of matter, though, is what we do with God's love and willingness to be gracious.**

I have never, at least of what I'm aware, taken advantage of God's abundant love and forgiveness.

On the other hand, I've never believed in a *fire and brimstone* God who keeps a list of what we've done wrong and will make sure we will suffer for it.

That God is to be rejected. A wrathful referee who brings the tsunamis of suffering upon us. No, thank you.

Yes, I know people who are good because they then think nothing untoward will happen.

A personal example. When I began ministry in 1966 my monthly salary, plus housing, was $400/month. One of the St. Pauls Church parishioners would take me out for lunch monthly. When we returned to my church office he would hand me $50, "You need this for food." He later allowed the reason he did this was not because he thought it was the right thing to do. Rather, he said if he helped me financially, it was a good security policy warding off anything bad that might happen to him.

I never offered my opinion. Probably should have, but didn't. Guess that made me lean more toward greed than gratitude. Not sure.

But. What I am sure about, is this, in the world of being imperfect: I do not believe in a God who punishes. And I'm not ever trying to be good as a shield against something bad happening. Rather, I try to be the best person I can because I believe that's the best way in which life is most valued.

God will love me—and you!—no matter what.

And, whether or not when I die an earthly death I will have a spiritual future...that's not for me to decide.

What is for me to decide is how I order each day. Not to be favored by God...that's God's business. But to be living a life that has greater meaning.

Does this make sense?

I know. Rambled a bit...maybe a few bits. But hopefully you will consider your own life, who your God is and whether or not that God has a lanyard, whistle and is wearing a referee's shirt.

Mine doesn't.

And, neither should I.

For, as I've shared with clergy and parishioners over the years, my fervent hope is this: *our willingness to listen and understand is greater than our need to judge.*

First fishing trip with Mr. Dylan, my grandson

Posted on June 3, 2011 by Mark H Miller

Another memory…had to be more than sixty years ago…and will be linked to tomorrow.

My father gave me my initial interest in fishing. The adventure was clear: "Mark, we're driving to Cannon Beach, to stay at Mr. Grimshaw's house. Then tomorrow Mr. Grimshaw and two of his sons and your father and you will go fishing in the Columbia River…we'll fish for salmon. I hope you enjoy it."

What?! *Enjoy it?* How could I not?

The year was 1947, "Mr. Grimshaw" owned a tire company [Michelin Tires, which was no generic tire] and was the sponsor of my father's fast-pitch softball team. Dad was the coach. They were best friends.

The Grimshaw house sat on the bluff just south of Haystack Rock… probably where I'd take my last breath, if I had that choice. [Sorry, that just slipped in.]

I remember going to bed early—a 4 a.m. wake-up call was not my routine. I remember even more being awakened by my father, probably midnight, "Mark, I'm sorry, but I have bad news. We just learned the weather's going to be bad tomorrow, so you'll need to stay here. Mrs. Grimshaw can show you how to make a sheet into a balloon."

What? Who in the world wants to turn sheets into balloons? I wanted to turn my expectation into catching my first fall Chinook salmon.

Fast forward to tomorrow.

I am ready. I don't know if Dylan is.

Here's the deal. Andrew and Jennifer asked if Diane and I could visit them this weekend, the prime purpose of which is for me to take Dylan [and the others coming along to clap and cheer] to the Boerne City

529

Lake for a fishing time—the occasion a "license-less" fishing day with a parent and child.

This is it. The first time I can show my grandson how to cast. Am I ready or what? [understated, of course]

I purchased Dylan's first rod [he is 3 years old], stretching all of 2 feet and six inches, with a Zebco reel, which means it's the easiest to cast.

I checked with a bass-fishing friend who advised I get "perch hooks and earthworms and bobbers." Now, admittedly I'm not a "bait-guy." Strictly flies, nymphs and streamers. So, to not compromise totally on my fly-fishing ethic, I'm tucking a couple of artificial worms in my pocket—called San Juan Worms. Real imitators, for sure.

Of course there will be a "pre-fishing-casting-class," their backyard our "lake." And then. Tomorrow morning, Saturday, June 4, 2011, Mr. Dylan and his grandfather will have their first fishing adventure.

I'm confident the weather will cooperate, so we won't have to wake him up early and say the trip won't happen. And who knows, maybe grandfather and grandson will catch a fish or two. But, fishing and not catching isn't all bad. I'd hate to spoil him with lots of fish—then the pressure would really be on the next time[s].

Although I must admit...no concession here...that day back in 1947 learning how to transform a bed sheet into a balloon and ride the surf just south of Cannon Beach wasn't so bad. Just didn't match my anticipated world of fishing.

We Did It!

Posted on June 4, 2011 by Mark H Miller

We did it! Dylan's first fishing experience went beyond dreams.

He didn't hesitate when we arrived yesterday, jumped up and down, "Grampa Mark, we going fishing!"

Undeniable in his anticipation…and even more, expectation.

We checked in at the tournament registration booth at Boerne City Lake, the "captain" handed us two tickets for a raffle…we were number #37.

One of the staff took our picture—

**Mark holding Dylan's hand going fishing
for the first time—Boerne Lake**

531

Not a complicated technique required…casting rod, Zebco reel, bobber, perch hook…we had practiced the night before…no sweat, Dylan had it figured out.

Important for the worms to wiggle—they cooperated just fine.

Both holding the rod/reel/bobber, the first cast left impression out of the picture—went about 3 feet, just off the rocky shore. The "team" reeled in and cast again. Better.

"Dylan, watch the bobber…if it sinks, that's a fish biting."

He nodded as if the world's greatest truth was just offered. Hey, at 2 and a half, it made sense to him.

The gentle wind pushed the bobber.

Time to reel in and cast again. Better.

Enthusiasm got up higher on the meter…pushing a ten.

Hey, fishy, grab that worm. Now, truth is it was only a thought.

But, I opened my eyes big-time, when the bobber twitched, then sank!

"Grampa, where's the bobber"?

The team effort continued, as we held the pole and reeled.

And. There. It. Was.

DYLAN'S FIRST FISH: A PERCH.

Hey, we're not into measurement—length and weight. A first fish is a first fish.

A while later, another sinking bobber…second fish.

Andrew and Taylor joined us [Taylor's 8 months of age] as her brother and Grampa cast away.

Time to go. Everyone was pleased. Dylan the fisherman. He didn't protest the new identifier.

Here's a portrait of Grampa and Dylan ready to cast again….and then a picture…maybe even a portrait of Andrew, Taylor and Dylan, holding Mr. Fishy.

Please don't pay that much attention that Taylor's one shoe got lost. But, on the way back to the car, we found it. So, nothing was lost. But, deeper with great verity, EVERYTHING was gained…was it ever.

Mark and Dylan

**Andrew holding daughter Taylor and
Dylan holding pole and first fish**

A Child Speaks…More Than a Voice

Posted on June 5, 2011 by Mark H Miller

Some footnotes in sharing a weekend with a grandson, about whom I could describe as perceptive and logical not precocious and cunning [scenario one]. As being practical and not judgmental [scenario two]. As looking for an improved future not an exaggeration [scenario three].

Examples in order of the previous commentary:

Scenario One: Leaving the first fishing adventure, walking over some gravel and stones, he said, "Dad, I hurt my toe." Sure enough a rock had lodged in the front of his sandal. The problem was erased…well, not exactly. More apt, the rock was removed. The pain lingered.

Andrew picked Dylan up and carried both him and Taylor. Dylan is 2 and a half and Dylan is 8 months.

As we approached the car we could all see beyond the car was a playground..slides and swing and the like. No one said anything.

Well, not exactly true.

Dylan saw the slide and swing and said, actually rather matter-of-factly, pointing to the slide, "Dad, if I get on the slide my toe will get better."

He did…and it did.

Scenario Two: At breakfast this morning, Dylan was Andrew's souse chef, cracking the eggs in a rather blunt but effective way [like in *smash*], making the pancake batter [smooth and not lumpy] and pouring the batter in the pan for the world's biggest pancake. Problems arose: only 30% [at most] of the pancake batter made the pan and then in trying to bring water to the dog's water dish, Dylan dropped the glass container, leaving chunks and splintered glass on most of the kitchen tile floor.

No loss, though, as we all cleaned up and Dylan was apologetic rather than oblivious or pouty. All was well.

535

Sitting at the table, Dylan had picked up his own fork and knife and began on his meal...scrambled eggs on one plate and less than "together" pancakes on the other. Andrew sat next to him and a couple of times reached for a piece of pancake.

Without saying a word, Dylan got himself down from the chair, walked away, opened a drawer, then came back. Looked at his father, handed him a fork, "Dad, here."

Scenario Three: We took time in Boerne to feed the ducks bread, even three little chicks and lots and lots of turtles. Dylan was encouraged to throw first with his left hand, then his right. Of course he doesn't know the word *ambidextrous*, but might be a seed planted, who knows?

As I put him in his car seat, to say good-bye with a great good-bye hug, I asked, "Dylan? How many fish did you catch?"

Smiling beyond measurement, he raised two fingers, "Two!"

Then he paused, smiled, "Grampa...next time let's catch five."

Learning from Mistakes

Posted on June 7, 2011 by Mark H Miller

I've never been this good…and truth pushing through…am not really considering it.

My wonderful friend, Jim White, also a retired minister, flyfishes with the best of them. He's one of those guys who is fishing guide, author, counselor and articulate. Great combination.

The only time he and I fished when we had an imbalance [my way, of course] was a year ago when we fished for steelhead on the Sol Duc River in Washington's Olympic Peninsula. I caught 8 steelhead and Jim, quite admirably and willingly was photographer and clap and cheer guy. But, really, who's counting, right?

Jim is the kind of fisherperson [he likes the inclusive language] who literally can reach a river, turn over a couple of rocks to see what bugs abound, and then tie that particular bug into a killer fly.

Now, I realize for the cynics, it might go like this, "Hey, he's been to that river before and KNOWS what is there before he gets there."

Well, maybe, but to a guy who only buys flies on line [I have tracked down the best prices.] Jim's tying by the river impresses me considerably.

In recent correspondence [am now getting to my point today] Jim has mentioned previous times we have shared. He reminded me when Diane and I lived in Issaquah, Washington, and Jim visited us to share some fishing adventures, when Gracie, our Silky Terrier, chewed his shoelaces to pieces. Not a Hallmark moment.

At any rate, when Jim wrote about how the rivers in Colorado are unfishable today—he has a special lake to be an alternative to sitting at home tying flies—so he spends time at this lake. That reminded me of a great mistake [the point is about to arrive] I made fishing.

Yes, fishing is not all casting and catching. Sometimes the bushes and branches and mean rocks intervene. Add to that what happened to me.

It was our first time together…back in the 80's, fishing in northern Colorado on the Hohnholz Ranch. Jim had organized some of his church guys to take a few days for a "theological seminar by the river". [I never asked him if he considered the trip's expenses IRS deductable.] I went along…to fish and not to seminar.

Here's the first truth. I was less than not good at fly-casting. Since—I paid attention to casting techniques of his seminar members—the others were terrific at fly-casting, I spent most of my time finding unpopulated water.

One afternoon I came upon a beautiful drift and saw some rather large German Brown trout sipping away. *Ah, this is Miller time* I reasoned.

Got out a pretty large dry fly, called a Royal Coachman, and even though my novice-rating would not change, actually made some good casts…and on one cast, you couldn't tell the leader and the dry fly were attached. They were.

At a spot I actually thought it would happen, *SMASH*, the large trout hammered the Royal Coachman. I set the hook, the fish splashed and was gone.

That happened three more times.

What is this all about? I'm making good casts, the fly is aimlessly floating and the fish agree, worth striking.

Being clueless, before the sixth cast I retrieved the fly.

I looked at the fly. Looked around to see if anyone was looking. Shook my head.

Truth was the fly had lost its hook.

Not a trivial detail.

I should have checked after missing the first strike.

But, no. I refused to see that I needed to change my way.

Brought to mind the definition of insanity, *Doing the same thing over and over expecting different results.*

Just a reminder.

To me.

One of the benefits of a mistake is to use it as a lesson. To not make it again.

And truth holding since 1982, whenever a fish hits and is gone: I look at the fly…or the nymph…and make sure the hook has not broken off.

Ergo, a mistake is really only a mistake if the lesson is lost.

Ever Ride a Horse?

Posted on June 9, 2011 by Mark H Miller

[Note: this blog came to mind when I learned that one of my previous associate ministers, Nate Miller, has been called to be Senior Pastor at the First Congregational Church in Greeley, Colorado. In his note he mentioned that his wife, Eileen, keeps her horse near their new residence.]

Someone asked me if I've ever ridden a horse…a REAL horse, not one of those pokey, slumped-back kind that walk in slow speed on the beach. Well, no one *really* asked, but in case they do, here's my response.

I HAVE. Yep, happened during Spring Break my second year in seminary. Seminary was in New Haven, Connecticut and the horse-riding took place north of Houston…at the ranch/farm of a seminary classmate, George Heyer. George's family owned the ranch.

It had a small lake stocked with bass.

As I grabbed a pole and walked to the boat on the lake's shore, George beckoned me elsewhere, "Ace, let's go for a ride."

Well, since he was the host and very gracious, generous and inviting, I agreed. Not sure why he called me "Ace," but it stuck. [He is now retired as a professor of ethics and doctrine at Austin Presbyterian Seminary—our friendship continues in spite of what follows.]

He insisted on putting on the saddles [*whew, because I didn't even know how to get on this snorting animal]*, which was a good thing, since it was all I could fathom as to which side to mount.

Forget the horse's name, but, you'll see, probably was something like, *Belligerent, One-Mind, Deaf.*

I knew we were in for a forgettable ride, because George mounted his horse, and before he could grab the reins, the saddle slipped and both he and the saddle fell to the ground.

Other than pride dented, nothing else amiss.

Finally.

We were both on the horses and off we went. Walking. Just fine.

Till we reached the open field beyond the fence. The horse then picked up the pace. I didn't know if it was a gait or trot. I knew it wasn't a gallop.

Then I was wrong. The horse, whatever its name, took off. I left George behind. I held on for dear life. [I wasn't wearing a mask, nor did I have a silver bullet and *Belligerent* was not white.]

Suddenly I looked up: nothing but trees ahead, a TALL wooden fence with barbed wire on top—just like a prison I thought. But, my thoughts didn't stay there.

How in God's name can I get Belligerent to stop???!!! Well, let me be honest. It was not in God's name; it was in my name, my well being, my sanity, my....

I gave my best version of primal scream, *WHOA!* [All right, what do YOU say to a horse in this rather critical moment?] The fence seemed to have its own legs, rushing at us.

And then. Yes, right. And. Then. *Belligerent* changed identity to, *Stop Now.*

And he [maybe a she, I don't remember] stopped.

But I didn't.

I held the reins and suddenly catapulted out of the saddle and grabbed *Stop Now*'s neck like a wrestler from WWF.

And then, boys and girls, it was eye-to-eye, as I looked straight into the stopped creature's eyes.

I'm sure his eye-language was offering, "Well, I stopped, what are you looking at?"

He then flipped his head back [maybe up?] and I crashed back on the saddle.

Except.

I didn't land on the saddle. I landed on the saddle horn.

Well, in that moment I figured two realities might jump in: either I was a permanent tenor or I would be fatherless.

Anyway. Should someone ever ask me about horse-riding, I'll simply say, "Call George Heyer."

And, hopefully he will have forgotten, which then might be the best answer. Yes?

Oh, there is a post-script. The next day I barely got out of bed and had only one purpose in life—for that day—as I limped to the lake, got in the boat, made a cast just short of a lily, reeled twice and BAM!

Hey, I'd much rather tell you about how big the fish was.

When Faith Decides

Posted on June 11, 2011 by Mark H Miller

The headline got my attention:

Valedictorian Chooses Faith Over Speech

Laura Cole is Valedictorian at Vacaville High School in Vacaville, California. On Thursday her Jewish faith indicates no electricity can be used until dark. That means, because her faith trumps everything, she cannot use the microphone to give her speech. It also means she cannot use a car to come to graduation. Or use her camera. Power and electricity can be used after darkness arrives.

She shared her situation with a teacher. They came up with a compromise. Laura will pre-record her speech. It will be played during graduation ceremonies at the proper time. Laura will stand at the podium.

This may seem to some as irrelevant. I don't. Couldn't help but recall that Sandy Koufax, as good a left-hander as there was in professional baseball, didn't pitch a World Series game because that particular day was a Jewish holiday.

In watching the newscast and listening to Laura Cole, I am impressed that what she believes and how she lives are redundant.

How many of us can say that? I know I cannot.

But, deeper, it poses an important question: What is the place of faith in our daily world, in the decisions we make, the ways in which denial is more than a river in Egypt?

When in parish ministry many parishioners made a big deal of giving something up for Lent. Most of the time it had little impact. I tried to switch that emphasis by asking people to "take on something new that helped others" during Lent.

Did it matter?

Am clueless.

But, the question does not beg to examine the manner of life we live. Laura said, "In life there are easy choices and hard choices. Most of the time the harder choice is the right choice."

Could be.

On another dynamic. I am certain EVERY person attending the graduation ceremonies will be aware of the faith-witness of Laura Cole. For a few moments they will look through a window at her and ponder the decision she made...because of her faith. And then, I hope it happens, that window will transform into a mirror and the question will be asked, "What about me...what if I were valedictorian and had to decide?"

Because in life...for each of us...we all carry both a window and mirror. They both can be helpful.

So I ask...how about you? Your faith? Your life?

I guess it might go like this: maturing in life is increasing the occasions when our faith is the most important factor in what happens.

Agree?

Today Brings Back Yesterday

Posted on June 13, 2011 by Mark H Miller

Not sure how this goes…here and there…or with you. Do you do this? When you see a name…person or place…ever happen that it triggers an experience and your thought goes to the rear-view mirror?

That happened to me recently. I read that over 70 Air Force Cadets were taken for medical treatment because of a lightning strike at their base near Hattiesburg, Mississippi.

Yes, I thought about the Air Force Academy [have you ever seen or worshipped in their sanctuary? It's a marvelous place.] But it was toward *Hattiesburg* my thoughts focused.

Was the Spring of 1965. That academic year I was a campus minister intern for the Student Christian Foundation at Southern Illinois University in Carbondale, Illinois. The Director of the Foundation was Malcolm Gillespie—an United Church of Christ minister. Great guy. His genius was in his prophetic gifts, seeing what needed to be done as Christians to encourage racial fairness. Our Foundation had contact with ministers and a neighborhood organization in Hattiesburg.

One thing led to another. And before I knew it I was driving south from Carbondale to Hattiesburg, my car having trouble holding the front tires to the pavement. Why? I was loaded with elementary education books… trunk, top and back seat…to be delivered to a Voter's Registration Office and then distributed to local churches.

I was also there to help register voters—yes, they were African-Americans [Negroes was the identification in the 60's] and yes, they lived in hovels/tents/make-shift shanties in muddy, muddy fields.

Honestly? I never took into account it might be dangerous. Never. That doesn't mean I had a fear-by-pass. No. It simply meant that because of Mac's inspiration and my own sense of "the time is now for voter registration," I went. Talking the talk was not enough.

Yes, I was confronted at the border by some "local citizens," each of whom stood by their parked motorcycle and bandanas covering their hair, t-shirts tie-died and cigarette packs folded into their sleeves. They wanted to know what I was doing…had to stop for gas…believe me it wasn't a Shell or Chevron. Nope, mom and pop place. But, the gas gauge was to the left of empty.

The conversation was actually civil. They asked. I answered, "I'm headed to Hattiesburg to meet with some city leaders and to bring books to help in the children's education." They didn't ask about voter registration and I didn't think it was an obligation [nor at all smart] to say anything about that.

I remember coming back about a week later. Tired, really tired. But, grateful that I could at least help "the cause."

I was scheduled to preach the next Sunday, Easter Sunday, at a Presbyterian Church in Marion, Illinois. The minister—forget Joe's last name and he's probably forgotten mine for a reason I will now reveal—was President of our Foundation Board of Directors. His youth group was leading the Sunrise Service and they asked me to preach. As I think about it, was to be my second sermon ever…the first was as a 16 year old in my home church in Portland, Oregon.

Marion was probably an hour away and the service was set for 6:30 a.m.

I set my alarm for 5 a.m. No problem I figured. Being a fisherman, sleeping in was never an option.

With this exception.

It was about 2 a.m. and then 3 a.m. and then 3:30 a.m. my phone rang. Because I was concerned maybe the call came from one of our students, I answered each time.

And, each time there was no greeting, only a charge, "You nigger lover. Damn, will you ever learn? You should go back to Africa with them."

Not exactly a warm greeting. The local newspaper had made the trip public. That was the result.

But, there was another result. I woke up Easter Sunday morning, 1965.

Looked at my clock…said 7:30 a.m. Whether or not the alarm rang, I was clueless, but not blameless.

I called the minister, "Joe, I hope you got Jesus up, because I certainly didn't get up."

He laughed, "Well, we missed you, but I understand."

I think he did. Because at the Board meeting the next week, my last as campus minister intern, he never said a word.

Gosh, all that in seeing "Hattiesburg" in today's news. More than that, though, I do hope and trust those 70+ Air Force Cadets are okay.

How Do You Measure Time?

Posted on June 15, 2011 by Mark H Miller

An important weekend…for both Diane and me. It is a birthday weekend, a time to measure time in terms of months and years. Although entering my 72nd year this Friday [the 70th birthday was by far the most difficult] I'd rather measure my life in terms of what I value and in what manner I can help others value their lives more.

Diane [and her sister, Cheryl] celebrate their birthday on Sunday, June 19. Again, measured in terms of years and months. I'll celebrate her birthday, however, in terms of being healthier.

As many know, this past year has been one medical challenge after another. However, it is encouraging that Diane's feeling better, even thinking about whipping me big-time fly-fishing. I'd love that. It is also encouraging she enjoys her work at GTECH, especially now a new project has been sent her way as a Senior Project Manager.

The third moment to celebrate will be Father's Day. Honestly? I've never seen that as something extraordinary. Although, I was able to spend high quality time with each son recently, Matthew in Winnetka and Andrew in Boerne. Both visits were wonderful—as in full of wonder. The experiences included soccer matches, ballet concerts and fishing tournaments, with ample time spent diagnosing the problems and offering the solutions to the dilemmas facing the Denver Broncos [our rooting for them will neither be compromised nor qualified]. Those visits make this Father's Day a day of gratitude—profound and full— for each of them.

Certainly I am always father and they are sons. And yet, the bonding gets stronger in terms of mutuality and covenant. Love the word, *covenant*, which essentially means each person gives their fullest for the good and strengthening of the relationship.

Many of you—and I am heartened by this, my pulse quickens in appreciation for your interest—have asked about when "Murder On Tillamook Bay" will be published? The publisher hopes to get my first novel available soon. His reader/editor is almost completed with his review. We anticipate receiving the "wrapped" editing, giving us the "go for it" wave yet this month. I'll keep you posted when it's a done deal.

So, my "time" is measured, as is Diane's, by a date on the calendar. However, I'd much rather not pick out a day, but consider moments upon moments for the ways in which the joy of the heart and peace of the soul come together in celebration.

Older I become....

Posted on June 16, 2011 by Mark H Miller

I've offered this before, but memory has fled, at least on this. Oh, memory isn't forsaking me all day today...I actually remembered without a second thought where I parked my car at the Fitness Center... that was before I left it. And at the HEB grocery store, after I left it.

Yeah for memory.

Memory, though, can bring benefit, which is the point here, a comment by a former parishioner. His comment went like this, "Mark, the older I become the better I used to be."

I like that. It's the salmon that "weighed more than I could lift," the high school batting average, "in the .400's" [*Really?*], the time I pitched against University of Southern California the year they won the national college world series. [Well, yes, but I only pitched to one batter in the top of the 9th, we were behind by two runs and in the bottom of the 9th, with two outs and the bases loaded, our pinch hitter slammed a home run.]

Hey, why do we have to qualify it? A win is a win is a win.

And, where this now heads, so is a loss.

Okay, most of us learn more from our losses. And some of us [read this, fans in Cleveland] moved beyond ecstasy when Miami lost and LeBron James couldn't hit the ocean if he shot from a battleship. I wasn't one of those who bashed James.

But, to linger...to go over and over and over. Does anyone ever learn what ad naseum means?

Life is life and we make what we can of it.

And we do remember our past. **But, all is nothing if we don't value who we are most ultimately.**

For, who we are is whose we are. Yes, this gets preachy.

But, I've found, when Good Friday Moments scream at me, "You idiot, you are a hopeless slob!" and as a consequence depression controls every breath and step…or when something really cool happens and all's right with the world—the fate then is our arrogance is greater than our intelligence. I've found my most basic identity has nothing to do with me. Nothing. Zilch. Nichts. Or what happens to my day. Or what my day happens to me.

I've always admired even-keeled people. I'm not one of those. But, my own challenge…be it today or yesterday or a trip this weekend…no matter what, can I hopefully remember who I am and whose I am?

More than a husband. More than a father. More than a Grampa. More than a friend. More than a blogger or novelist. More than the CFO of our family and chief duster of our furniture. More than a previous pastor or conference minister. More than a wily fly-casting angler, I am a child of God and God don't make junk.

I'd write more…but just remembered. Have a haircut. In fact, will get 'em all cut..what's left of 'em. So, it's off to my haircut lady, Marie C., the owner of…get this…has-to-be Texas, right?: "Cut-N-Shoot Hair Salon."

When a Parent Buries a Child

Posted on July 10, 2011 by Mark H Miller

Someone asked me, not recently but it's returned to thought this Saturday morning when reading about the death of the Texas Ranger fan at the ball park two nights ago, "What's the worst time for a minister?"

Goodness, how many different "worsts" can there be? Try the label, *innumerable*.

Personally, aside from all the rants and tirades of parishioners [not all sermons are endearing…and if you've forgotten *Aunt Shellie's surgery*, the unforgiving attitude is relentless…or if you ask 18 year-olds voting for the first time to vote for a *peace candidate who vows to end the Vietnam War now with no bombs attached…be ready for an irate—read that, furious—parent to stand in protest and break out with "God Bless America!"]* the single most difficult situation is when being with families who have to bury their child.

Never considered this before, but somehow a series of the "worst of times" surfaced…not with details, but the first infant I baptized was dead, an early funeral was for a 4-year old who died of cancer. I stood with the mother of a 2-year old. His lifeless body was pulled by scuba divers from a swollen creek. On that one, my son, Matthew was 2 years old…I came home, ran into the family room where he was playing and hugged him like there was no tomorrow.

It goes on and on…the 16 year old comatose and brain dead…the support system was withdrawn as the family and I held hands. The mother put her hand on her son's forehead and the father on his son's heart. Then the horrific death of one of our clergy and his spouse bludgeoned to death by the Railroad Killer in Weimar, Texas. Their parents sat in the pews the next Sunday, Mother's Day. That was perhaps the most difficult sermon I've ever had to preach.

And in my last interim pastorate we experienced the devastation when three died…two sons and a daughter…in unexpected and tragic ways… one in a car accident, one in a homicide and one when the only son of our organist, a graduate of West Point and as fine a person anyone could meet, stepped on a land mine in Afghanistan.

It's the worst, the hardest, the most challenging...to EVERYONE, not just the convening clergy person...when a parent buries a child. And what I've learned, not as a surprise: AGE DOESN'T MATTER. It doesn't. The "child" can be 50 and the parent 80. Somehow it messes up the natural, expected passage of life to death...when a parent buries a child. Supposed to be the other way around.

Of course I am utterly clueless...and nothing can change that...how each person deals with the tragic inside himself or herself. All I could do..and it's not exceptional for a moment or heartbeat...is to be a caring presence.

It's like this: *just be there and care and listen. Just be there and be empathetic not sympathetic. There's a big difference. The former is to be one in spirit... at their level. The latter is to look down as if you are unaffected. Never let the latter win. The listening is the most important...because people want their thoughts, their fright, their plunge into hopelessness recognized.*

It goes on...*never deny the tragedy, never say "it will be all right." Why? Because it never may be all right. It may never be. Somehow let people grieve. Grieving is not an enemy; it can be therapeutic. And realize it may take months, even years, for a grieving person to recognize the devastation caused by the death. On that I remember one of my sons, six months after a dear friend died, started to cry at the dinner table. "What's wrong?" He looked at me, "Dad, he died. He's not here anymore." Sometimes "later" happens. Not sooner.*

Never lose touch with the devastated family...check on them...inquire, connect, affirm them.

And, in most cases...thank God for this...people realize life goes on...and because of the tragedy, they begin to not presume life and anything that happens. They celebrate life more...and give greater and deeper thanks for the dawn of a new day...a new day that provides a chance for more life, more goodness...and, in the best of instances...never to deny the ache and the emptiness…but to gulp, take a deep breath and offer, "Day, here I come…big-time here I come."

Life is worth living…because we don't know how long…but, we can have lots and lots to say about how well. Yes we can.

Father and Son—More than a Baseball Game
Posted on July 13, 2011 by Mark H Miller

A beautiful embrace. Beyond words but echoed in my heart. Robinson Cano from the New York Yankees had just won the home run hitting contest Monday night in Phoenix—part of the All-Star extravaganza. The pitcher tossed a couple of balls in the air, beamed like a floodlight and embraced Cano.

The pitcher?

His father, Jose Cano, formerly a pitcher with the Houston Astros.

What a special embracing moment. Father and son. One helping the other "make good and make it well" before a national audience. Special.

My lessons in parenting as a father to my sons, Matthew and Andrew, came primarily from my father, Hank Miller.

His hard work. He was a garbage man, an independent operator with his own truck. Got up 4 a.m. every morning, rain or shine [and in Portland where you rust and not tan it was more of the former], came home late each afternoon and never complained. Never.

Presence. Presence was his present to me.

At my baptism I was told that morning before leaving the house, my father put on his best shirt and tie [not a vast selection, for sure]. My mother was surprised because my father was not a church-goer, although he knew attending for his first-born's baptism was expected. As they left the house my father said, "Es, I'm taking Mark up for his baptism."

"Oh, Hank, you know that's for the godparents to do; that's our German heritage." Evidently he didn't hesitate, "Nope. I'm taking him. He's my son."

Then my first glove. He put it on my right hand. I was right-handed, I believe. "Dad, how come?" "You need to pitch left-handed. That will be better."

Goodness, how that worked out.

Presence. Presence [and the glove] was his present to me. When I pitched my first game as a high school freshman, before the first pitch I looked behind the screen along the first base line...there was my father, still in his work overalls, the truck parked nearby, stood next to a very tall Douglas fir tree. He was taller.

My high school senior year, the first few games I was miserable at hitting. Gave *weak/paltry* their best definition. It was Sunday night, my father asked if I would be interested in some "hitting suggestions." Always a question, never a demand. I needed all the help I could get. "Mark, you're not swinging down. Swing down and pop-ups become line drives." We worked for an hour on swinging down...at the Miller Field, our driveway with the garage door the backstop.

What a lesson it was...no more pop ups. And, even at 71 I remember ending up with a .429 batting average, 21-49. Lots of 7's there. Because of my father.

I thought about all that Monday night when Jose Cano and his son, Robinson Cano embraced. Father and son.

And also thought about it this week as Andrew and Dylan and Taylor and I fished together for the 2nd time...at Boerne City Lake. At two and a half years of age Dylan's getting the hang of it...yes, indeed. "Grampa, the bobber's gone...fish!" Andrew and I beamed...father, son, grandson.

May that be only the beginning...the fish are already trembling.

Thoughts About Capital Punishment

Posted on July 22, 2011 by Mark H Miller

Times to forget the human…but who can do it?

Times to deal with the divine…but who can do it?

The pulse-point is execution…one is to happen soon in Texas…guilt is not the question. Mercy is.

One of those shot, one eye less because of the heinous crime that killed others, has said in so many words, "Executing him will not benefit anyone."

What about it?

I'm pretty sure—make that positive—if someone murdered those closest to me—in an act of deliberation and intention, I would soften my opposition to lethal injection. That's the anticipated human factor considered.

But, truth?

Never have been for capital punishment.

For one theological reason, "To take the life of someone is to usurp God's prerogative." Not that God kills. I don't believe that. But, because taking life is not purposive. Oh, there are reasons…but not any that merit the ultimate decision—to kill someone.

It's no honor to live in the state that wins the legal injection number every year. But I do. Ah, Texas, *bigger and better*.

Now, this is not to turn the other cheek. I remember my favorite notion-resource, William Coffin, who once said, "How many turn the other cheek so as not to see the evil?" That's good.

And, I remember another Coffin-quote when preaching about the Good Samaritan, when he said, "What should be done beyond helping the wounded man by the side of the road? The other thing is to high-tail it to the officials and demand they clean-up that horrible road."

That's good.

But. To take a life of someone who's taken a life? One time I had this theory: *Okay, go with lethal injection if it will return the life of the victim.*

Silly?

But, go deeper with me. The human/divine consideration.

Let me take a biblical step for a moment to make my case. In Genesis, the creation story in Genesis One, it says that you and I are "made in God's image, after God's likeness." My doctoral professor at Eden Seminary in the 80's, M. Douglas Meeks, brought new insight to that phrase. He explained, *To be made in the image of God is the authorization to represent God.*

That has never left me.

And, from this corner of the world, thinking through my fingers tapping on the computer, I am against capital punishment. Because it is not an Act of God as I consider it. And, if I [read that, *all of us*] are to represent God, how can the injection to stop breathing and living be an act of God?

Death can come in its own time. But a needle changes that. Of course, the guilty have already done that to someone endeared. But, somehow that is the human response to get the eye for an eye...can it slow down...and at least let the divine in us catch up? And, maybe even take the lead?

Something to consider.

A timely postscript: I write this PS Thursday night, July 21, 2011. The Texas execution took place as scheduled last night. Then I read about an execution just an hour ago in Georgia, a man accused in 1993 of murdering his parents and sister.

What I read next in the best terms puzzled...but perhaps more honest, angered. Another Georgia inmate on death row, however he did this is still unclear, saw to it tonight's execution was videotaped...so he could verify that capital punishment is cruel and unusual punishment. The news bulletin then described the two minutes after the injection... actual calm, at which point the execution was successful—eyes closed, the body was still.

Gracious, that's not even poetic.

And then a final thought...no better, a last thought tonight...not to say this is apt in these two executions, but we've all read about the execution of someone who later was declared innocent. That happens also. Another cause to keep in mind.

Enough for now. I'm still opposed to capital punishment. Needed to share.

You?

God is not a computer

Posted on July 23, 2011 by Mark H Miller

It looked good. My computer said "This is important." It was a new program from Windows Vista or something like that. [As you can tell, my computerized vocabulary is limited…and that is a gross overstatement.]

So, I clicked, "install."

I then asked Diane, "I'm going ahead with this. What do you think?"

A question asked tardily I readily admit.

She cautioned, "I'd like to see that Internet 9 be given more time…to iron out the wrinkles."

Oops. That's the kind version of my "Oh no!"

I clicked "STOP!"

But it was too late.

After the computer was restarted, I remember what introduced the option to install: *This is important.* So, I reasoned with more trust than wisdom, *Oh, if they say it's important, it must be. What can go wrong? I have Windows.*

How utterly incorrect were my thoughts.

I clicked on the internet—no go. I clicked on again and hit the *find out what is wrong* button. Answer: *All is connected correctly.*

Stumped. Flustered. Frustrated. That's the polite version.

But. I'm the one who went ahead and now am in a pickle.

560

So, I thought, *Why not go back to the moment before I hit the 'install' button? Why not see if I can uninstall and get back to where I started this morning?*

So, I did. Found the listings of installations, found this current one, hit the *uninstall* button…and waited as was advised and restarted the computer as advised…and, bingo. All was well. Internet Windows 9… or something like that…was history.

It occurred to me this is a parable of life that doesn't happen. Don't I wish, though, I was wrong. But I am not. And you know it as well as I. We cannot live life with one finger on the "uninstall" button.

Doesn't work that way. Life is lived. Good things happen. Screw-ups happen. And many times…more than we admit…we are at fault.

There is no uninstall button in life.

But there is a Holy One…the God of all Creation…who when life is abysmal, even tragic and deadly…is the first heart to break. And when we need the uninstall button to correct a wrong that has caused damage to others, to relationships that matter, there is no uninstall button. But there is God, whose willingness to listen, understand and forgive is MUCH GREATER than God's need to judge and punish.

That's how I look at it. God is more than a computer.

It's not called *uninstall*. It's called *grace, mercy and forgiveness.*

Thank God.

Sharing New Blessings...beautiful gifts indeed

Posted on <u>August 3, 2011</u> by <u>Mark H Miller</u>

The blessings of life came this week. Our grandson Noah Herman was born—by c-section—Diane relates that all are well—Teela and Jason and Noah's 4-year old twin brothers. Our prayer is that his health continues well and starts to gain weight [born at 6 pounds 2 ounces]. A joy—God's gift.

Another blessing had not been planned. I believe I have mentioned that Hugh and Jane Smith are two of the most wonderful former parishioners— members of the last church I served. They retired to Tucson. Each summer they spend at least a month at the YMCA Camp in Estes Park.

In August of 2000 they asked if I would visit them and all their family in Estes Park and officiate at their 50th wedding anniversary re-commitment vows. I was delighted.

A heart attack had other plans for me, which meant a stent was necessary and plane tickets were cancelled. They understood.

Last week Monday I visited them at their cabin in Estes Park—one of their daughters was there for Monday evening—a great time of visiting. Tuesday morning Hugh and Jane and I had breakfast before I departed for fly-fishing and visiting friends in Carbondale and Frisco, Colorado.

As I sat with them at their breakfast table—it struck me: *I owe them re-covenanting/wedding vows.* So I asked them if they would like to exchange wedding vows. They were more than pleased.

In that moment we considered the kitchen our sanctuary...one of the most beautiful moments I've ever experienced in ministry. Perhaps the greatest "make-up" effort in all my life. Beyond beautiful.

A third blessed event—totally unplanned, a good definition of a serendipitous moment.

A wonderful friend, Bryan Austill [lives in Dillon, Colorado—is a Methodist minister and therapist, his wife, Kari, a Lutheran minister] and I shared a day of fishing and reflecting. Bryan is a great fly-casting coach—helping me improve my technique so my grandchildren are not mislead when they try-out their fly rods.

We sat down by the Arkansas River for lunch—beautiful blue sky, the 14,000 foot mountains across the valley still with 20-foot-deep snow patches, the river gurgling its value.

Another fisherman came up to visit—we had met him briefly when we parked. As we visited David shared he was going fishing with a guide in a couple of days and somehow that led to talking about the various guides we each knew. One of them David mentioned, "Is a great guide—the best woman guide I know."

Bryan smiled, looked at me, then at David, "David you should ask Mark to tell you about a special woman guide he knows."

What a great lead in to Tricia Gleason and the new novel, "Murder On Tillamook Bay."

David was gracious to ask, "Tell me how it starts."

Was more than pleased to.

He then said, "Mark, that sounds more than interesting. However, I need to say it...but since you both are ministers I am compelled to tell the truth...you are now causing me to break a vow I made 16 years ago."

I thought *What? We're here to fly-fish, not to break vows.*

He didn't wait for my inquiry, "The vow? I promised myself 16 years ago I would never read another fiction book. Yours sounds worth breaking a vow for. And, I have a couple of fishing buddies—I'm gonna gift your book to them."

Goodness. Who would have ever thought a fly-fishing day would turn into a marketing moment?

One final blessing.

My Rabbi Guide, whom I've mentioned often takes me to our very own private stream, Muddy Creek. It's on ranch land and only Matt Krane [my guide] can fish there. He needs permission, though, from a resident of the ranch. Which we got.

I fished and fished and fished and had moderate luck. But, all the while I was in complete denial that I had little breath left—it happens when you go from sea-level to 10,000 feet and wade streams and plough through thick bushes and weeds to get to the "honey bucket" spot in Muddy.

About 2 p.m. I was exhausted. We ate lunch in the ranch cabin. Matthew looked at his watch, "Hey, preacher, we've got more time for more fishing."

I couldn't believe my response, as I looked down the slope at the flowing creek, a creek teeming with very sizable trout, "I'm sorry, but why don't you go ahead? I need to sit and get back my normal breathing."

About 15 minutes later it struck me, *This is the dumbest thing in the world...to sit and only LOOK at Muddy Creek and not fish? Go away, Mark.*

So I put my waders back on and walked with Matthew to Muddy. He went downstream and sent me upstream. He put on a new grasshopper dry fly and another dry fly for me—"Grasshoppers everywhere...that should work."

I caught some nice trout—14-17". It's all catch and release although the trout don't know that.

Then it happened.

It really did. And I want to say, when I looked at the water flow—not too fast...about 3-4 feet deep, I thought, *I have a feeling Mr. Trout lives here.*

A glossary moment: *Mr. Trout* is a fantastic trout that is at least 20" in length. I've caught 19" trout but never into the League of Twenty-Inchers.

The cast was the best I could make...and about 10 feet from the end of the drift MR TROUT [the caps are to indicate we are talking gigantic] introduced himself [maybe herself]. Never in all my life have I seen a trout that big—at least 24" and had to weigh 4 pounds. It didn't strike—it attacked the grasshopper, I set the hook and the battle was on. Upstream...across the stream toward some underwater bushes, turned and came right at me—I had to reel like there was no tomorrow—and then it just plumb stopped and didn't move. I pulled as slightly as I could to encourage movement—toward me and my net, of course. Although I looked again at the fish and then at my net—a mismatch and MR TROUT had the edge—by a few inches.

Then it happened...the line went slack. MR TROUT had had enough and returned to his world.

Nope. No picture. No evidence.

But I can say...what an incredible blessing...to play MR TROUT [it was a German Brown—brilliant spots—a body that looked like a football].

Yep, he won. But, so did I! It was such a blessing—to make the perfect cast...no tug on the flies so they appeared to be unattached...then BAM.

I'll never forget it...and as you can appreciate, have replayed the adventurous moment again and again.

And will continue to.

Yes.

From Worst to First

Posted on August 7, 2011 by Mark H Miller

Diane and I watched the National Football League Hall of Fame inductees speak last night. I found it a compelling experience…especially in listening to Deion Sanders and Shannon Sharpe. To be elected to the HOF is the highest honor for a football player. Such designation, so evident last night, means the world to the athletes and their families.

What impacted me is how in almost every case, but especially for Deion and Shannon, there was every possibility they would be quick-sanded to their first years' environment and expectations. Poverty, reaching up to touch bottom, others expecting them to establish mediocrity as a moral principle and *level of achievement* were the touchstones of how they began life.

In each presentation there was cause for celebration…for they each made it clear: this was an effort by themselves, to recognize—make that seize—the strength of their gifts and make something of it. But, necessary, even more, to realize that no one makes it alone. And no one makes it without a dream. As stated, so very profoundly, by Sanders, "If your dream ain't bigger than you, there's a problem with your dream."

I was touched, especially by Shannon Sharpe, who went to college with two brown grocery bags holding his belongings and heard, "You'll never make it." Then in a pre-season game with the Denver Broncos, was told by an assistant coach, "Shannon, your name is on the cut-list. How you do tonight will determine if you stick with the Broncos."

He was a tight end and as he drove to the game, it rained…big-time. He thought *all we're going to do is run the ball*. Which happened. But. He was on the special team for kick-offs and punt returns. He performed with great effectiveness…when he returned to the locker room his name had been erased from the cut list.

Then, in perhaps the most riveting moments, he shared two perceptions… one, acknowledging his brother Sterling who played for the Green Bay Packers. Shannon said, "I am the only player who has been inducted into the Pro Football Hall of Fame and am the second-best player in my family." The standing ovation touched me deeply. Even more when the camera focused upon Sterling, who had introduced his brother, tears dropped from his chin.

Then the deepest and most powerful moment: Shannon asked his grandmother, when money was no longer absent [players make more than chump change], "Grandma, I want to build you a big house. How big do you want it?"

Her response was, size wasn't important, she just wanted to sleep in a house…that when she woke up, she wouldn't be wet from the night's rain. Giving evidence of two things, in my mind. One, she's a very humble woman. Two, for decades where they lived in a rural country home…the roof never stopped leaking.

Powerful.

What hit me…I was mesmerized…was the common ground: each believed in himself, each was told they'd never make it…and each never made it alone. Through the entire evening, each honoree used the negative to make more of himself, to make sure, although the support of others was crucial and necessary, they ended up never being someone else's opinion.

Then this morning—Sunday, August 7, 2011—it hit me. No, I've never been into any Hall of Fame, no, I never played professional baseball, no, no, no to any particular national honor.

Yet, this morning it struck me. When I was a freshman in high school, October of 1954 to be exact, I was cornered in the high school locker room and told I was the most worthless athlete in our freshman class. Turns out that horrifying moment ended up being, more than anything I can remember, the greatest motivator in my world. For I wanted to make sure I never proved them right. It wasn't worst to first. No, not at all. But, it did fuel me to never miss a class, to make sure the fast ball hit the outside corner and to make sure that ministry was more than a good idea.

About the Author

Dr. Mark Henry Miller and his wife, Diane, live in Austin, Texas. Mark is a retired United Church of Christ minister, having served churches as a pastor and conferences as a Conference Minister since 1966. "Voice of My Heart" is a collection of his blogs written since October, 2010. But they are more than blogs. In their own way this book is a step or two as autobiography, a step or two of reflections upon the daily ruts and routines and a step or two on how life can be more than a good idea about hope and growth. Mark has had his first novel, "Murder On Tillamook Bay," and three previous books of pastoral epistles published. All of which can be tracked down on his web page, www.drmarkhmiller. com His educational background includes some time in libraries and classrooms at Stanford University, Yale University Divinity School and Eden Theological Seminary. His real classroom, though, continues to be the pulse of life itself.